MW00569286

Parenting

A Life Span Perspective

Parenting

A LIFE SPAN PERSPECTIVE

Carole A. Martin
Rutgers—The State University of New Jersey

Karen K. Colbert
Iowa State University

THE McGRAW-HILL COMPANIES, INC.

New York   St. Louis   San Francisco   Auckland   Bogotá   Caracas   Lisbon
London   Madrid   Mexico City   Milan   Montreal   New Delhi
San Juan   Singapore   Sydney   Tokyo   Toronto

McGraw-Hill

A Division of The **McGraw·Hill** *Companies*

This book was set in Palatino by The Clarinda Company.
The editors were Beth Kaufman and LG;
the production supervisor was Paula Keller;
the photo editor was Inge King.
The cover was designed by Carla Bauer.
Project supervision was done by Tage Publishing Service, Inc.
Quebecor Printing/Fairfield was printer and binder.

Cover photo: Jim Corwin/Stock, Boston.

PARENTING

A Life Span Perspective

Copyright © 1997 by The McGraw-Hill Companies, Inc. All rights reserved.
Printed in the United States of America. Except as permitted under the United
States Copyright Act of 1976, no part of this publication may be reproduced or
distributed in any form or by any means, or stored in a data base or retrieval
system, without the prior written permission of the publisher.

This book is printed on acid-free paper.

8 9 10   QPF/QPF   0 5 4

ISBN 0-07-040768-1

Library of Congress Cataloging–in–Publication Data

Martin, Carole A.
    Parenting: a life span perspective / Carole A. Martin, Karen K.
Colbert.

      p.   cm.
    Includes bibliographical references and index.
    ISBN 0-07-040768-1
    1. Parenting.   2. Parent and child.   I. Colbert, Karen Karal
II. Title
HQ755.8.M35 1997
649'.1—dc20   96-22890

PHOTO CREDITS FOR CHAPTER OPENERS

Chapter 1: Erika Stone. Chapter 2: Susan Lapides/Design Conceptions. Chapter 3: Joel Gordon.
Chapter 4: Mimi Forsyth/Monkmeyer. Chapter 5: Jill Fineberg/Photo Researchers. Chapter 6:
James Carroll/Stock, Boston. Chapter 7: David M. Grossman/Photo Researchers. Chapter 8:
Tony Arruza/The Image Works. Chapter 9: Erika Stone. Chapter 10: Bob Daemmrich/The Image
Works. Chapter 11: Erika Stone/Photo Researchers. Chapter 12: Frank Siteman/The Picture
Cube. Chapter 13: Michael Grecco/Stock, Boston.

About the Authors

CAROLE A. MARTIN has taught undergraduate and graduate courses at Rutgers University, Trenton State College, and the University of Wisconsin-Madison in the departments of psychology, human development, and education. She directed a university laboratory preschool and developed an interdisciplinary graduate training program for personnel serving young children and their families. Her primary research interests include parent beliefs, assessment issues, and early childhood curriculum. Outside the university, she has worked as a parent educator and has served as a consultant to schools, hospitals, and foundations. Dr. Martin graduated from Bates College with a degree in psychology and went on to earn an M.A. from the University of Connecticut in child development and family relations. She received an M.S. in educational administration and a Ph.D. in child and family studies from the University of Wisconsin-Madison.

KAREN K. COLBERT has taught a variety of undergraduate- and graduate-level courses at Iowa State University, Colorado State University, and the University of Wisconsin-Madison. She is currently at Iowa State University and is the Project Coordinator for a research study examining the transition of Head Start children into the public school system. Her past research interests have included the transition to parenthood, infant temperament, and intellectual functioning across the life span. Her experiences as coordinator for the Mother's Center in Fort Collins, Colorado influenced her dedication to the social and educational support of parents in all stages of parenting. She received her bachelor's degree in child development from Iowa State University, and both her master's degree and Ph.D. in child and family studies from the University of Wisconsin-Madison.

To Jack, Molly, and Patrick
C.A.M.

To Jim, Jamie, and Mikki
K.K.C.

Contents in Brief

Contents

List of Boxes

xix

Preface

This book began, as many do, with an unmet personal need. After several years of teaching courses on child rearing and parent-child relations at different universities, we both arrived at the same conclusion—there was a gap between existing scholarship on the topic of parenting and the content of undergraduate textbooks. When we began to talk about closing that gap, there were specific themes and principles that gave form to our vision.

First, we saw the need for a book that balanced current theory and research with childrearing applications. Accordingly, the organization of this text and the coverage of topics is shaped by the empirical studies and theoretical discussions of contemporary scholars. Although we rely heavily on the field of psychology, we recognize that an authentic understanding of the topic requires a multidisciplinary framework and, therefore, contributions from family sociology, pediatrics, education, and anthropology are evident.

Second, our approach is developmental and contextual. This means that ecological systems theory is an important cornerstone of our discussion, because it captures the interdependent and dynamic nature of parenting. We are interested in child rearing as a phenomenon that affects and is affected by personal development, the devlopment of others, and society as a whole. This translates into a life-span perspective on parenting.

The text is organized into three parts. Part One introduces the reader to the parenting process and sets the stage for analyzing issues that will be developed in later chapters. Here we include a historical overview of parents' roles, an outline of the major variables that influence parent-child relations, and a discussion of parent education. With this information as a backdrop, the next chapter reviews the developmental and family theories upon which the study of parenting is based. The way in which these theories are linked to various parenting strategies is also presented. In an effort to adequately represent the growing research on cultural and structural variables, an entire chapter is devoted to the topic of diversity.

Part Two explores parenting issues across the lifespan, beginning with the transition to parenthood and continuing through parenting adult children. Each chapter focuses on the parenting role during a particular developmental period, reviewing pertinent theory, research, and practical issues. The interplay among cognitive, social-emotional, and physical development of the child, various parenting stages, and the changing social context is emphasized.

In Part Three chapters are organized topically in order to give special attention to important contemporary issues. We begin with a chapter on single parenting, divorce, and stepparenting that includes a comprehensive review of changing demographics, pertinent developmental literature, clinical needs, and policy questions. Our chapter on parenting children with special needs highlights the influence of child characteristics on the parenting process and the family system. In contrast, the chapter on parenting in high-risk situations emphasizes adult characteristics and contextual variables—teen parenting, parents with substance abuse problems, parents with disabilities, and child maltreatment. Finally, the last chapter focuses on working parents and child care. We believe that Part Three will give readers a better understanding of topics that have received much attention from researchers, parents, practitioners, and policy makers.

Our goal is to provide students with a scholarly overview of parenting without neglecting practical applications. Although this is not a "how-to" book, we are interested in the "real world" implications of current theory and research for parents and their children. Our discussion of research issues will give students a better understanding of design problems, conflicting results, and measurement dilemmas. This knowledge will make them critical consumers of empirical parenting studies and of childrearing information in the popular press.

For us, parenting is one of the most exciting topics that applied developmental psychology has to offer. Through this textbook, we hope that we have succeeded in communicating our enthusiasm for the issues to professors and students alike.

ACKNOWLEDGMENTS

Finishing this project took longer than anticipated, as we had to balance writing with typical life events (illnesses and family moves) and unexpected life events (the flood of 1993). We would like to thank the many people who have been helpful in the process of preparing this book.

First, we would like to let the people at McGraw-Hill who participated in this project know that we are grateful for their suggestions and guidance. Jane Vaicunas originally helped to get this project going, and her initial faith in the book was instrumental to us. Renee Shively Leonard and Beth Kaufman continued to encourage us along the way. Inge King was a pleasure to work with as photo editor, and Tony Caruso did a great job preparing the manuscript for production. Our thanks to everyone.

Second, we would like to thank all of our colleagues who assisted us in many different ways. We would particularly like to thank Julie Elmen, who was extremely helpful in establishing a vision for the book, and Susan Silverberg, who facilitated the writing of a difficult chapter. And many thanks to the reviewers who contributed to making this a better book: Nancy Ahlander, Ricks College; Sandy Bucknell, Modesto Junior College; Linda S. Budd, University of Minnesota; David W. Catron, Wake Forest University; Sarah S.

Catron, Wake Forest University; Stewart Cohen, University of Rhode Island; David S. Duerden, Ricks College; Juanita V. Field, Plymouth State College; J. Eileen Gallagher Haugh, St. Mary's College of Minnesota; Michael F. Kalinowski, University of New Hampshire; Melissa Kaplan-Estrin, Wayne State University; Duwayne Keller, University of Connecticut; Judy B. Lindamood, Bunker Hill Community College; David MacPhee, Colorado State University; Gary L. Schilmoeller, University of Maine; and Ellen L. Wray, Hutchinson Community College.

Third, we would like to thank our families and friends for their interest, encouragement, and patience during the completion of the book. We are especially grateful to our parents, since they are responsible for giving us many opportunities to become the people we are today.

Finally, we are deeply indebted to our coparents, Jack Creeden and Jim Colbert. Without their support and long-suffering forebearance, this project would not have been possible. And we are grateful to our children, Molly and Patrick Creeden and Jamie and Mikki Colbert, for the intensive hands-on parenting experiences they have given that keep us humble and continually learning about the parenting process.

Carole A. Martin

Karen K. Colbert

Parenting

A Life Span Perspective

PART ONE

Introduction to Parenting

The Parenting Process

All around us the process of parenting is taking place. By definition, this process usually involves adults giving birth, protecting, nurturing, and guiding children. The study of parent-child relations has grown tremendously in recent years; parenting is recognized as an important human experience that changes people emotionally, socially, and intellectually. This complex process affects participants and bystanders—adults, children, and society.

The lives of parents and children are connected over the life span. Unlike other mammals, human babies are relatively undeveloped at birth and have longer periods of dependency on adults, yet they usually enter the world with characteristics and abilities, such as smiling and crying, that attract attention from others. During this period, most parents are drawn to the infant on an emotional level and use their greater physical strength, knowledge of the world, and social skills to ensure the child's survival.

Over time, children become more autonomous, but parents still have a strong influence. For example, some parents actively teach language, athletic skills, or moral codes. Others model behaviors ranging from politeness to gender roles. Parents also affect children's development by selecting settings for them—neighborhoods, play groups, day care centers, and church affiliations. As an "audience," parents are continually providing feedback to children regarding their growth and development.

Through the parenting process, children influence adult development. They enrich and intrude upon marriages; they redefine parents' daily schedules and social circles; and their presence increases the work that must be done to keep the household running smoothly. Raising a child brings adults into the world of children's ideas, schools, and fads and fashions of the youth culture. At every age, children's behavior evokes strong positive and negative emotions. In the past, social scientists were interested only in how parents affected their children's development. This limited perspective has been revised, and more attention is being directed at the way in which the parenting experience changes how adults think, feel, act, and are viewed by others.

This book takes a developmental, life-span approach to the study of parenting. We are interested not only in how parents interact with infants and young children but also in how the relationship evolves when children become teenagers and young adults. As we explore parent-child interaction across the life span, themes of stability and change are evident. Does the quality of the relationship in infancy tell us anything about how either the parent or child will develop in later years? We are interested in common parenting patterns as well as individual differences. For example, what factors might make the child-rearing experience different for a married suburban couple than it is for a single parent living in rural poverty? We are aware that parent-child relations occur within a social and cultural context, and understand the need to explore the effects of social support and public policy on the parenting process. How do societal attitudes toward mothers, fathers, and substitute child care providers enhance or undermine parenting efforts?

In this chapter, we begin with a historical look at parenting. Next, the particular contributions of parents, children, and contexts to the parenting process are described. Finally, child-rearing goals and various approaches to parent education are reviewed.

There are two ways to look at parenting in the past. First, it is important to consider how society defined parental roles at various points in history. Those definitions were built on philosophies about the nature of children, religious influences, society's economic needs, and children's chances for survival. Second, the way in which parenting was conceptualized by social scientists reveals the influence of various theoretical perspectives at different points in time. People studying child development were influenced by societal attitudes and public policy, but they also generated new ideas that led to revised parenting beliefs and practices. Thus, the universal process of child rearing changes in response to various historical contexts. Highlighted below are some examples of these changes.

Ancient Greek philosophers wrote about the importance of child rearing for the future of their society. These writings, although biased by an elite male perspective, offer the first systematic theorizing on the topic of parenting (French, 1977, 1995). Plato suggested that it might be best to remove children from their parents at an early age and devote state resources to educating children to fulfill various roles. In contrast, Aristotle believed that most children would benefit from the personal and social stability offered by families. Both philosophers agreed that parents influenced child outcomes and that differences in parental practices would result in individual differences in children.

Some historians have argued that prior to the seventeenth century in Europe, childhood was not considered a unique part of the life span. Using artwork, diaries, and artifacts as evidence, they conclude that children were treated like uncivilized, miniature adults during this period (Aries, 1962). For example, children dressed in adultlike clothing and were expected to participate in adult work. This perspective has been tempered by later historians who point to numerous examples of ways in which children occupied a special status (French, 1977). For example, records that refer to toys, children's games, and schools suggest adult consideration for this unique developmental period.

From the twelfth to the seventeenth century, the influence of religion, specifically Christianity, on child rearing becomes more evident (Bell, 1979). Children were sometimes described as symbols of purity, with fragile souls that needed to be nurtured. On the other hand, the doctrine of original sin portrayed children as innately wicked, needing strict parental control. Viewing children as inherently evil, parents used harsh punishments to force obedience and mold their offspring into morally acceptable adults.

During the seventeenth and eighteenth centuries, European philosophers advanced ideas suggesting that childhood was a time of innocence (Bell, 1977). John Locke viewed children as "blank slates," neither innately good nor innately evil. He believed that children's personalities were shaped through the child-rearing efforts of parents and other aspects of the environment. Since lifelong habits were formed in the early years, parents were advised to patiently nurture children's curiosity, model appropriate behaviors, and gently control children's impulses with rewards and punishments. A later philosopher, Jean-Jacques Rousseau, emphasized the natural goodness of children and cautioned against harmful adult training. Because he conceptualized childhood as a unique part of the life span, Rousseau advised parents to be "child-centered." By this he meant that parenting practices must be based on the child's evolving abilities and needs at each stage of development.

The feelings of attachment that characterize parent-child relationships today were noticeably lacking in earlier descriptions of parenting. It is possible that high child mortality rates and a limited understanding of child development contributed to this unemotional tone. Parents may have avoided attachment when disease, unsanitary homes, and limited medical care gave the child limited chances of surviving birth and the first few years of life. Under these conditions, parents focused on the child's physical needs. The lack of affection may also have been linked to parents' failure to appreciate competencies in their young children. For example, if parents did not understand that crawling, crying, and mouthing objects are an infant's way to explore and communicate with the world, they might ignore the child or punish these immature behaviors.

The industrial revolution in the late nineteenth century changed family life by altering the roles of adults and children, as well as the setting in which they developed. Fathers, who previously had been responsible for educating children and instilling morals, became "breadwinners" outside the home. Mothers, whose primary roles had been giving birth and feeding children, became "household managers," with almost exclusive responsibility for nurturing children. Several societal changes—a prosperous economy, lower infant mortality rates, the isolation of mothers and children in the home—may have fostered more sentimental ideas about parenting and led to an idealized notion of mothering. In the late twentieth century, conceptions of mothering and fathering have changed in response to the women's movement, fathers' interest in taking on more nurturing roles, increasing diversity within American society, and more formal research in child development (McCartney & Phillips, 1988; Lamb, 1986).

The historical trends briefly summarized in the preceding paragraphs are based primarily on changing political, religious, and philosophical beliefs about child rearing. Attention must also be focused on the way in which social science research has influenced and reflected the parenting process. This includes the child study movement among academics and the child welfare movement among social policy makers, both of which took hold in the late nineteenth century (Smuts, 1986).

Charitable foundations were interested in preventing social problems, and believed that intervention with children and their families was crucial. Psychologists formulated various theories about child development, all of which had implications for parenting. Behaviorists such as John Watson based their advice on the "blank slate" theory, believing that parents could mold proper habits in their children by carefully controlling their schedules, rewards, and punishments. In contrast, Sigmund Freud and other psychoanalysts advocated a more lenient parental style that would support the child's emotional growth. Inspired by pediatrician and scholar Arnold Gesell, the maturationists carefully documented natural patterns of development and suggested that parents be responsive to the child's cues. The relationship between these theories and parenting strategies will be explored more fully in Chapter 2.

Because formal research on children came into its own at the beginning of the twentieth century when middle-class mothers were taking primary responsibility for child rearing, many of the early studies focused on maternal influences on development. Father's role was often viewed as indirect; that is, he provided income, emotional support for the mother, and an appropriate sex-role model. Although Rousseau had mentioned the role of fathers in his seventeenth century treatise on child rearing, it was not until the late twentieth century that psychologists began to acknowledge the nurturing potential of men (Lamb, 1986). Similarly, the child's contributions to the child-rearing process were ignored at first, but more recent studies have highlighted the ways in which children influence parents. Finally, the effects of culture and community on parenting are now receiving attention.

This more scientific approach to the study of parent-child relations has influenced public policy and the parent education movement in the United States. In 1914, the Children's Bureau began publishing *Infant Care,* a free pamphlet designed to carry expert advice regarding children's development to the general public. Today, information about development and child rearing is being passed on to parents through classes, books, newspaper reports, and videotapes. Efforts on the part of professionals and policy makers to support families are signs that our society understands the importance of the parenting process for adults and children in today's world.

This historical overview highlights some political, economic, religious, and philosophical influences on parent-child relationships, as well as the way in which social scientists have studied this phenomenon over time. It should be apparent that, although parenting is a universal process, it is by no means static or absolute (Garcia Coll, Meyer, & Brillon, 1995). There are variations on child-rearing themes that are often tied to a particular historical context.

INFLUENCES ON PARENTING

Parenting is a more complex process than it appears on the surface. The unique characteristics of parents and children, as well as the settings in which they interact, determine how they will influence each other over the life span (Figure 1-1). Sometimes the influence is direct, such as when a parent is attracted to a child's smile. In other instances, the process is more indirect. For example, parents who are satisfied with their jobs may have more emotional energy to invest in their children. Before beginning to look at parenting over the life span, it is helpful to identify the determinants of parenting.

Parent Contributions

The foundation for parenting begins long before individuals assume this role. When people become parents, they bring with them a unique combination of personal traits and experiences. Adults vary in their levels of maturity, energy, patience, intelligence, and attitudes. These characteristics will affect their sensitivity to children's needs, their expectations for themselves and their children, and their ability to cope with the demands of the parenting role (Dix, 1991).

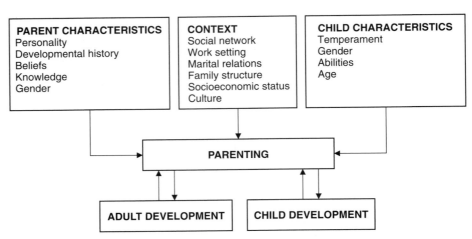

FIGURE 1-1. Influences on parenting.

A parent's developmental history, including his or her own childhood, influences child-rearing behavior. Intergenerational transmission of parenting styles may occur either as a result of direct learning, or because early relationships affect the prospective parent's social and emotional development. When parents experience harsh discipline as children, they are more likely to repeat this pattern with their own children (Simons, Beaman, Conger & Chao, 1993). Women who remember early interactions with their mothers as supportive are more likely to have positive relationships with their own children (Main & Goldwyn, 1984). Some parents, however, may recognize that they received less than optimal parenting and seek other models. In a sense, their personal experience serves as a negative model of what they would like to avoid with their own children.

Parents bring their own ideas about how children develop, learn, and feel to the parenting process. These beliefs are cognitive foundations for caregiving. They may include developmental timetables, ideas about the relative importance of heredity and the environment, expectations regarding the parent-child relationship, and thoughts about what constitutes good or bad parenting. Where do these ideas come from? Beliefs about the nature of children and the role of parents begin forming in childhood, but their form and content may evolve over the life span. Some beliefs are passed down as part of a prevailing culture or they are constructed by parents as a result of their experience with children (Goodnow & Collins, 1990; McGillicuddy-DeLisi & Sigel, 1995).

Parental beliefs are important because they influence child-rearing values and behaviors. For example, parents who believe that children benefit from exploring their environments tend to value self-direction and allow infants more floor freedom (Luster, Rhoades & Haas, 1989). Abusive and nonabusive parents think about children in qualitatively different ways, a topic explored more fully in Chapter 12 (Newberger & White, 1989).

Parents acquire knowledge of child development through classes, books, other adults, and experiences with children. Mothers with greater than average knowledge about infant development have babies who score better on developmental assessments (Dichtelmiller, Meisels, Plunkett, Bozynski, Claflin & Mangelsdorf, 1992). Studies have shown that adults with more experience are better at recognizing and interpreting infant cues, and acting appropriately in problem-solving situations (Cooke, 1991). Experience may be a factor in explaining the different child-rearing behaviors of parents with firstborns and laterborns.

Mothers and Fathers

Most of the research on parenting has really been a study of mothering. At one time, it was believed that only mothers were biologically predisposed to care for children, because they gave birth and breastfed babies. The myth of "maternal instinct" was based on these biological facts and the historical events that isolated mothers in the home. Unfortunately, when studies describing optimal child-rearing practices exclude fathers, people erroneously conclude that constant maternal care is required for children to become good adults. The belief that full-time devotion to children is necessary for maternal happiness is also based on such faulty logic (Sternglanz & Nash, 1988).

Parents who believe that children benefit from exploration will understand toddlers' curiosity about how things work.
(*Susan Lapides/Design Conceptions*)

Because the study of parenting has focused on mothers, they are often blamed when children have problems and may feel guilty when children are not perfect (Caplan & Hall-McCorquodale, 1985). Although mothers and fathers make unique contributions to the parenting process (Lamb, 1986), these differences may be based more on societal expectations and training than on biological programming.

Most of the research on fathering has taken place during the last two decades. Initially, studies of "father absence" dominated the field, because people were interested in what happened to the sex-role development of boys in families headed by single mothers (Biller, 1970). Later, fathers were cast as having an indirect effect on child rearing because they provided emotional support to mothers (Bronfenbrenner, 1979). Current investigators also study the direct effects of fathering and reciprocal interactions between father and child. Such studies have revealed, for example, that fathers spend more time with sons and are more playful than mothers in their interactions (Lamb, 1986).

What determines the extent of father involvement in today's families? First, fathers differ in their desire to be involved. Many men are content to watch from the sidelines, while others want to be involved in caretaking from the beginning. Second, a certain level of skill, self-confidence, and sensitivity toward children is important. Because the fathering role is rapidly changing, today's fathers have few models of active fathering and may not have had the same type of experience with children that mothers have had. Third, maternal attitudes are an important factor. Some mothers expect fathers to be active coparents, while others view child rearing as their area of expertise and authority. They serve as "gatekeepers," preventing or encouraging fathers. Finally, one of the main stumbling blocks to increased paternal involvement has been the commitment to paid work by men and the inflexible practices of employers (Lamb, 1986; Palm & Palkovitz, 1988).

It is essential that we recognize the diversity among men and women in terms of their parenting skills and attitudes. Supportive services for parents may not have kept pace with new ideas about parenting (Russell & Radojevic, 1992). Box 1-1 discusses some strategies for involving fathers in parenting programs.

Child Contributions

Children come into the world with different physical traits and a unique style of interacting. *Temperament*, or behavioral style, is an important child variable influencing the parenting process. A child who is charming and adaptable will present different parenting opportunities than will one who is fussy and rigid. Given the variability in parent characteristics, certain parents are bound to be more accepting of a difficult child than others. This topic is explored more fully in Chapter 5.

A child's *gender* will affect the parenting process, because parents and society have different expectations for girls and boys. These stereotypes vary across subcultures and influence the way parents structure the child's world, the feedback they give the child, and the goals they have for the child. As Box 1-2 points out, even parents who try to be nonsexist in their child-rearing practices may struggle. The match or mismatch between parent gender and child gender is also important. Sons seem to draw fathers into more active parenting roles, and this higher level of involvement benefits children of both genders. When there are boys and girls in a family, a daughter may not get as much attention as a son, but she is more likely than her friends in all-girl families to have a father who is actively involved in parenting (Harris & Morgan, 1991).

Children's *abilities* can make a difference in how the parent interacts with the child. When children are exceptionally talented or have developmental problems, parents may treat them differently. If children do well, parents attribute some of that achievement to their own child-rearing efforts. When children are not successful, parents are more likely to use biological explanations for their level of abilities (Himelstein, Graham, & Weiner, 1991). These beliefs about abilities may lead to different approaches to discipline and varying levels of parental involvement. More detail on this child variable is presented in Chapter 11, which focuses on the parenting of children with special needs.

Box 1-1 Parenting Programs for Fathers

The special contributions of fathers as parents, as well as the problems inherent in modern fathering, must be acknowledged (Palm & Palkovitz, 1988). Although many parenting programs are designed to serve both mothers and fathers, the special needs of fathers may warrant unique approaches to parent education and support. Consider the needs of fathers at various points in time. During pregnancy, the father lacks the physiological changes that signal the transition to parenthood, but childbirth classes can provide an opportunity for involvement. Hospital-based interventions during the postpartum period have been successful in encouraging early father involvement and interest in caretaking (Parke & Beitel, 1986). Fathers of preschool children have responded well to parent education programs that include group discussion and parent-child play time (McBride, 1990).

There are several strategies that may increase father involvement in parenting programs (Palm & Palkovitz, 1988) and thereby meet the needs of a large constituency:

1. *Begin early.* Involving the father during the pregnancy and early postpartum stages acknowledges the importance of his role and may encourage father participation in parenting.
2. *Provide male role models.* Whether it is a group leader, fathers modeling techniques on a videotape, or fathering examples in child-rearing literature—all of these methods are vehicles for demonstrating competent fathering roles.
3. *Recruit fathers for programs through mothers.* Mothers are more likely to be tied into the parenting network and are often "gatekeepers," influencing fathers' involvement with their children.
4. *Consider a program that includes a father-child activity period.* This format capitalizes on fathers' playful nature and gives them an opportunity to observe male models. Also, since most fathers have limited time with their children, this approach does not take them away from their children. It also provides practice in interaction skills and real examples for discussion.
5. *Consider offering parenting programs at fathers' places of work.* This approach acknowledges the dual role of worker and parent and increases access for career-oriented men.
6. *Accept the fact that levels of paternal involvement vary.* The parent educator must support the father and his family on the level that they have chosen, whether that is an egalitarian or a traditional approach to parenting.

Box 1-2 Nonsexist Child Rearing

Boys and girls are treated differently by their parents and other adults in accordance with cultural beliefs and societal expectations. With the women's movement calling attention to the way in which unequal treatment can result in unequal opportunities for females in the Western world, some parents have attempted to raise their children in a less sexist fashion. Several practical ideas have emerged from research on parents who are committed to this approach (Statham, 1986). Mothers and fathers who wish to engage in nonsexist child rearing might consider the following suggestions:

1. *Attempt to foster a child's potential in all developmental domains rather than restricting that child to what is considered "appropriate" for boys or for girls.* The goal of parents who actively embrace nonsexist child rearing is not to reverse traditional sex roles; rather, it is to encourage children to develop valued characteristics that may have been traditionally viewed as either "masculine" or "feminine." For example, parents might encourage nurturance in sons and achievement in daughters.
2. *Censoring sexist books, toys, and television may be a less effective strategy than using these as opportunities to discuss unequal treatment.* If a parent wants to encourage the child to think critically about sex role stereotypes, children must be viewed as active participants in the sex-role learning process.
3. *Modeling nonsexist roles in terms of household tasks, child care responsibilities, and decision making exposes children to a wider spectrum of male and female behaviors.* This practice is sometimes difficult to achieve because the structure of society maintains traditional sex roles. Inequities in the salaries of mothers and fathers, inadequate child care, and pressures on men to devote more time to job than family make it difficult for parents to share tasks equally.
4. *As with all aspects of parenting, the emotional relationship between parent and child is critical in determining how effective nonsexist parenting approaches are.* Encouraging active discussion about sex-role attitudes and responsibilities will have better results than imposing parental values in an authoritarian manner.

Parents committed to nonsexist child rearing may encourage nurturance in their sons, even when this is not consistent with traditional views of masculinity.
(*Robert V. Eckert, Jr./Stock, Boston*)

Even among families committed to nonsexist child rearing, there is more ambivalence about the outcomes for boys than for girls. Girls gain tangible things, such as power and opportunities, while boys gain nontangibles, such as sensitivity and emotional openness. This fear of "holding back" sons leads many parents to take a noninterventionist stance; that is, they will allow a son to have a doll or take ballet if that is what he wants, but they are not likely to initiate a nontraditional approach.

The child's *age* is an important factor to consider in the parenting process because it influences child-rearing tasks and parent expectations. The physical, intellectual, and social development of the child determines her or his level of independence and ability to communicate, and the degree to which the child is influenced by people outside the family. Parents treat infants differently from the way they treat adolescents. Behavior that is unacceptable for a school-age child may be more tolerable when coming from a preschooler. Parenting techniques that are effective at one age will not work with children later on. Parents' feelings and behaviors may be based on their age-related expectations for the child. For example, parents get more upset by older children's misbehavior because they are more likely to see problems as a stable part of the child's personality (Dix, Ruble, Grusec, & Nixon, 1986).

If parents have more than one child, they may be called upon to be different kinds of parents with each one because of their unique characteristics. The "fit" between parents and children with respect to personality, gender, and abilities will contribute to the conflict and harmony in their relationship. As they progress through the life cycle, parents and children continue to adapt and readapt to one another.

The Context of Parenting

It is likely that the parenting experience of a young, single mother and her four children living in urban poverty will be very different from that of an older, professional woman living comfortably in the suburbs with one child and her husband. Why? Because the development of parents and children is affected by a context that includes other relationships, multiple settings, and cultural values.

When most research on parent-child relations was taking place in psychology laboratories, the context of development was being ignored. Urie Bronfenbrenner (1979, 1989) advocates an *ecological* approach to the study of parenting that takes into account multiple contexts. Ecological systems theory assumes that relationships among parents, their children, and other individuals are interdependent. Interactions between any two members of the system will affect and be affected by other system participants. Furthermore, the contexts in which development occurs are constantly changing.

People in the immediate environment of the child and the parents—relatives, neighbors, babysitters, schoolmates—are part of the *microsystem,* and have the most direct influence on child rearing. These separate dyadic relationships between children and significant others are bidirectional, such that interactions affect both participants. Also important is the *mesosystem,* Bronfenbrenner's term for the connections among people in the child's multiple microsystem. An ecological perspective suggests that the development of parents and children is enhanced when these connections exist. For example, if parents and teachers both interact with a child, they will all have a better understanding of that child if they share information.

The *exosystem* is a setting that affects parenting even though it does not include both parents and children. For example, the parents' social network may offer child-rearing advice that will eventually affect the quality of life for the child, or a child who enjoys a smooth routine at a day care center, may be in a better mood to interact with parents later on.

Finally, the *macrosystem* refers to cultural values and customs that influence parenting. Cross-cultural studies highlight the ways in which variations in belief systems and social environments affect child-rearing goals and practices. People in the United States are affected by different beliefs and laws than are parents in other countries. Similarly, contemporary American society includes diverse subcultures, with a variety of ethnic roots and religious affiliations—all of which influence microsystem and mesosystem interactions. Although research on parent-child relations has often been limited by the use of white middle-class samples, there is an increasing recognition that the studies must be broadened to include other groups representing different cultural contexts. The way in which cultural diversity influences parenting is explored more fully in Chapter 3.

Directly and indirectly, social institutions such as schools and the media give subtle messages about the "shoulds" of child rearing. For example, when a parent sees a movie about a seemingly ideal family, he may decide to adopt the parenting style projected or he may feel inadequate because his family does not meet this ideal standard. The priority given to the needs of parents and children is often reflected in a country's public policies. Throughout this text, examples of contemporary American policies that influence child rearing are highlighted.

Socioeconomic Status

A family's *socioeconomic status* (SES) is indexed by parents' education, income, and occupation. The parenting process is influenced by SES because of varying financial resources and child-rearing attitudes. For example, poverty creates a high-risk context for parenting when low-income families are crowded in inadequate living quarters, have few resources for meeting emergencies, and experience high levels of daily stress. Because of this, there is growing concern about the increasing numbers of American families, especially ethnic minorities, living in poverty (Huston, McLoyd, & Garcia Coll, 1994). In Chapter 10 our discussion of parenting in high-risk situations highlights the complex relationship between SES and child-rearing processes. Finally, SES is related to the positions mothers and fathers hold in the work place. Employment-related status, benefits, and stresses have direct and indirect effects on parenting practices, an issue discussed in detail in Chapter 13.

Family Structure

Family size, the age spacing of children within the family, the number of parents in the home, and the birth order of children describe what is known as *family structure.* None of these factors directly "causes" differences in children. Rather, family structure causes changes in the parenting process because people interact differently and resources vary when the group size and composition vary. For example, firstborns get more individualized adult attention, but parents also have higher expectations for them. In contrast, the youngest child may be babied for a longer period of time. In large families, the opportunities for individual parent-child interaction are limited, but there may be more opportunities for sibling interaction, which is also stimulating.

Diversity in family structure, most notably the increase in the number of single parents and stepparents, is an important variable to consider when describing the parenting process. There are ethnic variations in family structure that are related to cultural goals and practices. For example, the availability of extended family members within the same household may provide children with multiple caregivers and parents with a sense of shared responsibility.

Social Support

To a certain extent, parenting is a "public performance" (Goodnow & Collins, 1990). Children, spouses, friends, and relatives comment about or judge the actions of parents. When a stranger in a supermarket makes negative remarks about a child sucking her pacifier, the parent may become worried or embarrassed. On the other hand, when a neighbor praises a mother for breast-feeding her baby, she might feel reinforced.

There are three general ways in which *social support* influence parenting. First, parents receive emotional support from others. When mothers and fathers can share thoughts and feelings about parenting and other life issues with others, they feel good about themselves. Second, social networks offer instrumental support such as child care assistance and advice. Finally, friends and family serve as parenting models. The social network offers information about expectations for child development and models of techniques for dealing with particular issues (Belsky, 1984; Cochran & Brassard, 1979; Cochran, 1990).

In the same way that financial resources can buffer parenting stresses, social support has been identified as an important part of the parenting context. The sources of social support include the marital relationship, social networks such as neighbors and friends, and the institutions such as schools and employers. Ethnicity, family structure, and socioeconomic status can influence the size, composition, and usefulness of a parent's social network (Cross, 1990).

The parenting partner is often the primary and most intense source of social support. *Coparenting* refers to the way parents work together as a couple, negotiating child-rearing issues and supporting each other. Coparenting may be conceptualized as how similar parenting styles are, or how supportive mothers and fathers are in the course of daily interactions involving caretaking. A parent may reinforce the efforts of the other parent, or contradict and undermine those efforts (Gable, Crnic, & Belsky, 1994). The notion of coparenting may be applied to intact families or to divorced, separated, and remarried families.

The quality of the marital relationship will affect a parent's emotional well-being. Conversely, the energy devoted to the caregiving role has the potential to strain spousal relationships (Lerner, 1994). Either spouse may provide his or her partner with child-rearing advice, share caregiving tasks, and meet adult needs for intimacy. For example, a warm, supportive wife who has a high degree of satisfaction with her children can positively influence her husband's parenting style (Simons et al., 1993). Although they are related issues, marital satisfaction and coparenting exert independent effects on the parenting process, such that effective coparenting can occur within the context of marital dissatisfaction (Gable et al., 1994).

Social support from significant others is also important for parents in single-parent families. One study of low-income, single mothers demonstrated that when these women were in stable partnerships, their parenting skills and their children's behavior improved (Egeland & Farber, 1984). This theme is explored more fully in Chapters 10 and 12.

Social isolation is one of the factors associated with high-risk parenting. The most frequent resource used when coping with child-rearing concerns is the parent's personal social network (Koepke & Williams, 1989). Relatives, neighbors, coworkers, and friends share their knowledge of children and their experience with various parenting problems. Sometimes parents actively seek information, but often the process is more subtle, with attitudes, values, and beliefs about parenting being acquired through ongoing interaction with others. When parents lack a personal social network for support, they are less effective parents. Mothers who have mutually rewarding contact with friends are the most effective in their interactions with their infants (Crnic, Greenberg, Ragozin, Robinson, & Basham, 1983).

Despite the potential benefits of social support, not all parents rely on social networks to the same extent. For example, in a study of the way in which fathers use other people to gain information about parenting, 27 percent of the men who had access to relationships that they might have used for advice, chose not to do so. Fathers who were most likely to use the network were those who perceived their parenting role as particularly important and positive (Riley & Cochran, 1985).

The positive effects of supportive networks are evident, but not all social contacts enhance parenting. If family members interfere with parenting decisions or friends criticize child-rearing techniques, the parent's confidence may be undermined. Also, not all advice is good advice. Some members of a social network may be offering suggestions that are based on "old wives' tales" rather than on proven practices. For example, grandmothers may insist that it is important to begin feeding infants solid foods in the first month of life so that they will sleep through the night. In contrast, pediatricians recommend that parents wait until the baby is at least four months old, because they believe that this feeding pattern is inappropriate for the child's immature oral-motor skills, unnecessary to meet the child's nutritional needs, and unrelated to infant sleep schedules. Parents may feel guilty about ignoring their own mothers' advice or frustrated by their attempts to force-feed an infant who is not ready to swallow solid foods.

PARENTING AS SOCIALIZATION

Parenting is an important part of socialization, a process by which children learn to behave according to social expectations and standards. In the context of the family, children develop competencies that will enable them to live in the world. This same context offers parents an opportunity to grow and develop over time. What are the goals that parents have for themselves and their children?

Parenting Goals

Why do people have children and what do parents want *from* their children? A cross-national study of parenting goals revealed that some of the more common reasons for having children include fulfilling parental needs for economic help, affection, stimulation, fun, adult status, and a social identity (Hoffman, 1988). In some cultures, the child will contribute to the family economically by becoming involved in the family business and supporting parents as they age. In our society, children are more of an economic liability, so parents look to them for affection, enjoyment, and a sense of immortality. Chapter 4 provides an in-depth look at the decision to parent or remain childless.

What do parents want *for* their children? Despite cross-cultural differences, there are common parenting goals. First, parents want children to survive and to be physically healthy. Second, they hope that their children will develop abilities that allow them to become economically self-sufficient. Finally, parents want children to acquire culture-specific goals related to achievement, religious beliefs, and personal satisfaction (Levine, 1988). Depending on the culture, parents may teach their children to continue societal traditions, or they may encourage uniqueness and individuality to be ready for a changing future.

Parents are hopeful that children will become competent human beings at each phase of their life. In our culture that might mean that children will develop healthy self-esteem, independence, and social responsibility. In other cultures, goals of obedience and group dependency may be more important. Solutions to child-rearing issues will be based on culture-bound goals, social environments, and belief systems.

Given the number of factors influencing the parenting process, what is the probability that child outcomes will be positive? According to Jay Belsky and his colleagues (Belsky, Robins & Gamble, 1984), three conditions influence child outcomes—parental resources, social supports, and child characteristics. When all three of these factors are positive, the child's chances for success are high. For example, competent children are more likely to develop when a psychologically stable parent has adequate income, neighbors and relatives who listen to parental concerns and provide help with child care, and an easygoing child without medical problems. However, when the parent is plagued by a stressful job, has few friends, and is attempting to deal with a difficult child, the chances of child competency evolving are lower.

Parenting Stages

Raising children changes parents. Although the parenting role is often considered a sign of adulthood, it can be a humbling experience. Parents may be surprised when so many aspects of their lives are being influenced by a child weighing less than ten pounds! Not only do parents gain insight into children's behavior but their own strengths and weaknesses surface. When parents experience the world through the developing child, they are called upon to answer questions that they have not thought about for a long time. As they help children with homework, they are exposed to new ideas. When a child becomes involved in an activity such as music or sport, life is enriched. Finally, the child brings new people into a parent's social network, including other children, teachers, and other parents.

According to Erikson's theory of personality development, the psychosocial stage that people face in middle adulthood is "generativity." The task at hand is to make a contribution to the next generation, and child rearing is one way to meet this need in a meaningful way. A recent longitudinal study grounded in this theoretical framework investigated how participation in child rearing influences middle adulthood outcomes for men and their children (Snarey, 1993). Parenthood cannot be considered a simple developmental stage for adults, however, because the nature of the role responsibilities and the focus of the parent-child relationship change over time.

Ellen Galinsky (1987) has outlined six developmental stages of parenthood that roughly follow developmental stages of the child's life. Child-rearing tasks change with the child's age; therefore, the experience of parenting changes over time. The process begins during pregnancy with the *image-making* stage. During this period, parents prepare for their new role and become more aware of parent-child relationships that surround them. For example, advertisements for children's products, news stories on the quality of schools, and parents loaded down with diaper bags and stuffed animals may suddenly catch the prospective parent's eye. The emotions of expectant parents range from excitement to concern about the responsibilities that lie ahead.

The *nurturing* stage begins at birth and continues throughout infancy. As the label suggests, parents and children become emotionally attached during this period of intensive caregiving. The child is dependent on the parent for survival; therefore, parents must learn to nurture the child physically and emotionally, while balancing their own adult needs.

The *authoritative* stage occurs during the child's preschool years, ages two through five. Because children are beginning to assert themselves, parents are called upon to set limits and enforce rules. The transition from exclusive nurturing to a more controlling and sometimes adversarial role may catch parents by surprise.

During the *interpretive* stage, parents tend to the needs of school-aged children. During middle childhood, children move out into the community and parents are called upon to help the child interpret that outside world. The task of teaching values and morals to children requires parents to clarify their own views. The *interdependent* stage describes the parent-child relationship during adolescence. This is a time when children's developing competencies enable them to share more control with the parents.

The *departure* stage is a reflective period for parents. After children leave home, parents evaluate their successes and failures in the child-rearing process. While accepting the child's separate life, many attempt to maintain connections with their adult children.

Although some people might argue that parents are in the business of working themselves out of a job, it may be more accurate to view parent-child relationships as life-span issues that change form over time. Parenting behavior evolves in part because children's needs change, but also because parents' expectations change. In Chapters 4 through 9 we present a life-span perspective on parenting and a more detailed understanding of these stages.

In families with more than one child, parents are in different stages of parenting simultaneously.
(*Elizabeth Crews/The Image Works*)

EDUCATION FOR PARENTHOOD

Although the parenting process is complex and the potential outcomes for adults, children, and society are important, preparation for the parenting role is not systematic. It is often assumed that children will survive and thrive if parents are well intentioned and follow their natural instincts. An opposing viewpoint suggests that knowledge of parenting and child development should be shared with all parents and potential parents in a more systematic fashion.

Parent education through literature, professional consultation, or discussion groups has been a part of American culture for more than a century (Young, 1990). An increased interest in this field may be related to social changes. Today's parents are concerned about raising children in a changing world, a world in which community consensus about child-rearing practices is lacking. They may reach out informally to their naturally occurring support networks for answers to parenting problems, or they may take advantage of more formalized educational opportunities. Parent education programs have a variety of goals and may be preventive or remedial, individualized or group oriented.

Goals of Parent Education

Various programs target different aspects of parenting—including knowledge, skills, attitudes, and social support. For example, some professionals believe that it is important to influence parents on a cognitive level. An example of this approach would be one that presents parents with child development *knowledge,* assuming that well-informed parents will be more effective in dealing with their children. If parents have realistic expectations of child behavior, they may be less frustrated by temper tantrums in toddlers or by moodiness in teenagers.

A slightly different approach is to teach parenting *skills.* For example, some programs teach behavior management skills, such as how to use praise and punishment effectively, how to condition a child to sleep through the night, or how to ignore some irritating behaviors. Others focus on communication, teaching listening skills and ways to express feelings that will help parents get their messages across to children. A more detailed explanation of these approaches is presented in Chapter 2. Those who advocate skills training believe that it is not enough to broaden the knowledge base of parents; rather, it may be more important to give them specific tools for interaction that can be used in common parenting situations. This approach to parent education seeks to change parent behavior.

Another strategy is to focus on parenting *attitudes* in an effort to bring parents to a better understanding of the emotional side of child rearing. Parental feelings about discipline, achievement, or self-esteem are examples of attitudes that might be explored in child-rearing literature or parenting classes. The focus for this approach is on affective change, with the hope that new attitudes will result in more positive parent-child interactions.

Parent education programs can serve a *social support* function. In urban and suburban neighborhoods alike, parents often feel isolated. Parenting centers offer a variety of educational programs, a chance to mingle informally with other parents, and an opportunity to explore the joys and frustrations of child rearing with mothers and fathers having similar experiences.

A relatively recent trend in parent education and support has had the goal of *empowering* parents to determine what they need to be better parents. This approach acknowledges the contextual determinants of parenting and helps parents deal with sources of stress that impact on parenting, such as inadequate housing, unemployment, or marital stress. The empowerment process focuses on supporting parents as they work on meeting the needs they have defined for themselves (Powell, 1988).

Approaches to Parent Education

Formal parent education occurs through written publications, classes, discussion groups, consultations with professionals. The amount and type of written materials devoted to the topic of parenting has rapidly increased in recent years. Books, pamphlets, newsletters, and magazines on parenting are plentiful and modern American parents consult these types of materials more frequently than did earlier generations of parents (Clarke-Stewart, 1978; Geboy, 1981). There are advantages to this format. First, printed information can be widely distributed and used by parents at their convenience. Second, a parent can refer back to written material when a need arises. Finally, parents can be selective and read only those articles or sections of a book that relate to their own concerns. Obviously, literature-based parent education has some shortcomings. This is primarily suited to middle-class and upper-class parents. Illiterate parents or those who do not enjoy reading are unlikely to seek parenting information from written materials. It is also probable that some written resources, such as magazine articles, will not be available when the parent needs them. A quick look at the parent education section of your local bookstore may be overwhelming, with various titles, topics and approaches presented. Box 1-3 suggests some criteria to use when judging parenting books.

Developmentally paced newsletters are an interesting concept. These publications are sent to parents with information that coincides with the age of the child. For example, parents of six-month-olds might be reading about teething and child-proofing, while parents of toddlers are reading about tantrums and toilet training. The newsletters may include suggestions for activities that enhance parent-child interaction. A parent can subscribe to these newsletters for a small fee or, in some states, university extension services or public health departments distribute them free of charge. The advantages of this format include low cost, convenience for the parent, the right information at the right time, and accessibility for parents living in isolated areas. In a national study, parents who received newsletters reported increased parent-child interaction and increased confidence. The greatest improvements were noted in parents

Box 1-3 Guidelines for Evaluating Child-Rearing Books

1. *Does the book present a set of rigid rules or simple formulas that promise parents success?* A good text provides options that acknowledge the complexity of the parent-child relationship in various contexts. Avoid books that guarantee positive child outcomes if a certain parenting prescription is followed.
2. *Does the author's background make him or her an expert on the subject at hand?* Appropriate author-content matches might include a pediatrician writing about health-related issues, a teacher discussing school-related issues, and a psychologist exploring early emotional development. Be cautious when authors assume the role of experts on topics outside their areas of expertise.
3. *Is the information in the book based on theory, research, or clinical experience?* All three sources of information have merit, but the specific source may determine how applicable the advice is for your situation. For example, parenting methods that have been found to be effective in low-income, single-parent homes

   might not work for other types of families. A good child-rearing book is based on more than opinion.
4. *Does the book assume a traditional family structure and middle-class values?* Beware of books that are gender biased—parenting is not just mothering! Similarly, understand the limitations of a text that does not appreciate cultural differences in parenting goals and methods.
5. *Does the author address only the child's needs or are adult needs also considered?* Some books give endless advice about how to raise children to be healthy, socially competent, high achieving, and emotionally stable, but neglect parental needs to feel appreciated and competent.
6. *Are the child and the parent portrayed in a positive manner?* Some books induce guilt in parents by blaming them for all of the child's problems. Others portray children as demons who torment parents and must be endured. These extreme views neglect the dynamic nature of parent-child relationships and the potential joy that both partners in the dyad can experience.

who would normally be considered at risk for inadequate parenting—teenage mothers, low-income mothers, single parents, and poorly educated mothers (Riley, Meinhardt, Nelson, Salisbury, & Winnett, 1991). Some disadvantages include the inability to ask questions and share information with other parents. Also, in giving parents age-paced information there is a risk of causing anxiety in the parent whose child does not seem to be behaving like the child in the newsletter.

Parent education also takes place in discussion groups and child-rearing classes. This approach can be more cost-effective than individual consultations with a professional, but it also requires more time and effort from a parent. Although some parents may benefit from the social support of a group, others will lack the social skills needed to talk and listen (Powell, 1986). Groups tend to function better when participants share something in common, for example, same-age children, similar religious beliefs, or similar socioeconomic status (Fine & Henry, 1989).

Technology offers innovative approaches to parent education. Television specials, videotapes, and audiotapes can be used to transmit child-rearing information to parents. Community "hotlines" and "warmlines" provide individualized information and anonymous support to parents who telephone with questions.

Timing

Although parent education occurs informally throughout the life span, formal programs can be designed for people at various stages of life. The needs, motivation, and accessibility of the target population will influence participation and outcomes.

Preparenthood

It can be argued that parent training should occur before adulthood, so that individuals have some understanding of the parenting role before they take on the responsibilities. Parent education for teenagers is offered in health and family living courses at high schools. One advantage of this approach is that the information reaches a large audience with diverse backgrounds. However, since many teenagers perceive parenting as a distant future event, they have little motivation to learn the information. Participation by young adults in college parent-child development courses is less universal. Although students generally enroll because they are interested in the topic, the impact on future parenting is unknown. Without opportunities to apply what they learn, information may be forgotten long before it is put into practice.

One time when many people seek out parenting information is during pregnancy. The motivation is high and the opportunity to put what is learned into practice is imminent. However, programs targeted at prospective parents tend to focus on childbirth and ignore the needs of parents after the baby has arrived. This topic is explored more fully in Chapter 4.

Parenthood

Many people engaged in the tasks of parenting have high motivation for gaining information, skills, and support. Limitations in time and energy, however, can compromise good intentions. The typical person using parent educa-

*CATHY © 1995 Cathy Guisewite. Reprinted with permission of UNIVERSAL PRESS SYN-
DICATE. All rights reserved.*

tion resources is likely to be female, middle-class, and the parent of a firstborn
child under the age of five (Clarke-Stewart, 1978). Fathers who are most likely
to seek out parenting information are those who are highly invested and
involved with the role. Older, college-educated fathers whose wives are
employed outside the home are likely candidates for parenting classes (Palm
& Palkovitz, 1988). Interventions may also be targeted at high-need groups
who would not normally seek parenting information on their own. For example, parenting programs designed to meet the needs of teen mothers or those
with substance abuse problems are described in Chapter 12.

T. Berry Brazelton (1990) has introduced the concept of "touchpoints" for
intervention. He suggests that prior to a child's developmental spurt is the perfect time to intervene with information about development. He maintains that
when parents are in the throes of toddler tantrums or teenage rebellion, the parent-child system is out balance and it is difficult to reach parents because of their
anxieties. *Before* a developmental change, parent educators can convey to the
parent what is likely to happen and why, so that parents are prepared and do
not have to learn new information at a time when they are exhausted by the
energy being put into the child's efforts to achieve the next milestone.

Although there is probably a relation between the timing, type, and effectiveness of parenting education, it is doubtful that a single time span represents a critical period for intervention. If interventions are matched to changing needs, a "multitime intervention strategy" is likely to be most effective in
dealing with various groups of parents (Parke & Beitel, 1986).

Parent education and support networks cannot solve all situations; some
require more attention than a book or a class can provide. Parent educators
must also understand the limitations of their programs and make appropriate
referrals to therapists and physicians.

Effectiveness of Parent Education

If the goal of parent education and support is to improve the well-being of parents and children, it would be useful to understand the effectiveness of various
approaches. Researchers disagree on what changes they should expect, when

and how to evaluate outcomes (Kaplan, 1980; Medway, 1989), and the adequacy of existing assessment techniques (Sabatelli & Waldron, 1995). Various studies have measured parent outcomes such as verbal responsiveness, teaching skills, child-centered attitudes, satisfaction with the parenting role, child development knowledge, and self-esteem. Effects on children have focused on cognitive skills for the target child or younger siblings (Powell, 1986).

Should we expect immediate results from parent education or will the effects of intervention take shape over time as the parent interacts with the child? Positive outcomes reported immediately after a program may fade over time. On the other hand, the most significant effects may not be evident until many years after intervention. For example, a family support program that served low-income families during the child's first two years was still demonstrating positive results ten years after the intervention. Participating parents were more likely to have become financially self-supporting, they had more nurturing relationships with their children and their children enjoyed greater school success (Seitz, Rosenbaum, & Apfel, 1985). Unfortunately, such longitudinal studies are uncommon in this field.

Although many studies report high levels of parent satisfaction with parent education programs, some psychologists have suggested that this type of information may cause some parents to feel inadequate, by making them overly dependent on professionals (Hess, 1980). Research needs to determine the conditions under which a parenting program is unproductive or undesirable.

SUMMARY

- Child rearing is a complex process affecting parents, children, and society. The unique characteristics of the participants, as well as the historical and cultural context, will influence the process and its outcomes. Because parent-child relationships evolve over the life span, a developmental perspective is needed.
- There is no single best way to bring up children, no single route to being a "good" parent. Research findings reviewed in this text will highlight issues related to various practices and beliefs. The role of public policy and parent education must also be considered. As we take a scholarly look at the parenting process, let us not lose sight of the fact that it is an essential task that can be both enjoyable and challenging.

Theories, Strategies, and Styles of Parenting

One job parents have is to make decisions about what kinds of experiences and opportunities should be provided to help maximize a child's individual development. Some parents approach this task with care and planning, while others are more haphazard in their efforts. Even parents with the best intentions can find it confusing to sort through the available information regarding parenting. Models of parenting surround us. Each person possesses a developmental history containing information about the way he or she was parented as a child. Some parents are still in the process of being parented themselves, bringing a generational or life span perspective to the process. In addition, books, films, and classes are accessible as sources of information. Upon examining the information available to them, parents quickly perceive that much of it is contradictory, unappealing, or simply doesn't work with a particular child. Even if it does work when a child is one age, it may not be appropriate at another age.

This chapter will examine theories, strategies, and styles of parenting, emphasizing practical implications for parenting when possible. In addition, there will be a specific discussion of discipline-related issues. The theme of the chapter centers on understanding the parent-child relationship as it develops across time and within various ecological systems. Families vary in age, race, cultural background, socioeconomic status, religion, values, and contextual settings. How could there be one "right" way to to parent when there are so many diverse needs and circumstances?

THEORIES

We all have our own theories of parenting. If you have doubts about that particular statement, imagine the following scenario. You are out dining at a nice restaurant with a treasured companion. Right as the waitress brings your first course, a child at the table next to yours starts to whine loudly. The parents seem to be having difficulty persuading the child to behave properly. The child escalates into a full-blown tantrum, complete with kicking and biting. In the meantime, you can't even converse with your companion because of the commotion and unpleasantness going on. You have the urge to say something to the parent. Your advice would indicate your theory of parenting. Does your gut-level response tell you to spank the child, physically remove the child, distract the child, or reprimand the parents for bringing a child to a place that is inappropriate for him or her to be? Now think about whether your advice would differ depending upon whether the child was two, six, or thirteen years of age.

Theories are influenced by general developmental beliefs about children of various ages and stages, as well as individual interpretations or beliefs. Parenting strategies—those that have been experienced personally as well as those that have been observed—influence the development of an individual's theory of parenting. Of course, commonalities exist among various people and groups, but each individual theory has its own evolution and premises. People evaluate and change strategies and techniques to meet their own individual needs.

One common goal of parents is to explain or understand the development of children so that they can predict or anticipate future events. A *theory* (a set of concepts whose purpose is to explain and predict some phenomenon), can be used to shed light on different aspects of development. Throughout this book, we will be examining ideas from five global classes of theories; family systems theory, biological theories, cognitive theories, learning theories, and psychoanalytic theories. A basic understanding of these theories is necessary to understand concepts and concerns as they are presented in our chronological examination of parenting in the chapters ahead. As you read this chapter, two questions should be kept in mind: Do these theories describe and reflect the diverse contexts for parents' and children's behavior? How do they help parents in their day-to-day parenting? The usefulness of the general theories presented will depend upon each person's individual "theory" of parenting.

Family Systems Theory

One way in which to view how one should parent is through the lens of the familial experience—the context of the family. Family Systems Theory suggests that the family is a system, or a complex whole, in which no person can be seen independently. Each family member can be observed only in his or her relationships with other people within the system (Becvar & Becvar, 1982). Parenting is not a linear process, where parents influence children. Instead, it is a multidimensional process, where parents influence children, children influence parents, parents influence each other, and children influence each other. For example, a parent may nurture each child within the family, but must also nurture the relationships the children have with one another because they are all part of the system as a whole. Changes in the relationship between a parent and one child may affect the other children within the family. Systems operate on a continuum, ranging from *open* (where the individual family system has lots of interactions with the environments around it) to *closed* (where there is no interchange or very little interchange with other environments). Parenting may differ drastically, depending upon whether the family system is actively engaged in various social contexts (for example, neighborhoods, social institutions, or cultures) suggested by Bronfenbrenner's ecological systems approach in Chapter 1, or is relatively isolated.

There are many characteristics of the family system. There are two characteristics, however, that are particularly applicable to parenting. First, family systems exhibit *mutual influence.* It is difficult to determine the causes of behavior within a system when each person's behavior is a stimulus for another person's behavior. Conflict often results when causality is attributed to a person within a system, especially in parent-child relationships. Since there are many factors at work in different situations, family interactions are very complex and multidimensional. The parent who simplistically perceives that his teenage son's shoplifting is the reason his family is having problems may be missing other possible scenarios, such as the child's shoplifting to get attention from parents, or to draw parental attention away from marital problems.

Family systems also exhibit *adaptability.* Family systems are capable of the change and reorganization required to deal with developmental stress points such as the birth of a child, an adolescent's quest for independence, or the death of a family member. Adaptability, however, can be relative to the situation, and some family systems have more capacity to change than others.

Adaptability does not imply that change is smooth; families often experience difficulty when undergoing transitions. Divorce is an example of a transition that many families encounter in which the adaptation process is not easy. But reorganization processes aimed at dealing with new sets of circumstances that arise in families are essential to the system.

Family Systems Theory does not provide practical parenting information, but rather a framework for understanding the complexity of the relationships within families. This perspective may help parents view the inner workings of their family in a broader context.

Biological Theories

Biological theories contend that children have inherited a number of attributes and behavioral predispositions that will have a profound effect on their development. Two approaches are emphasized: *ethology* (the study of the biological basis of behavior including its evolution, causation, and development) and *behavior genetics* (the study of the particular combination of genes that an indi-

Adaptability within a family system is exemplified by
the changes everyone makes when a new member is
added to the family.
(*Frank Siteman/Monkmeyer*)

vidual inherits, especially in relation to specific abilities, traits, patterns of behavior, and experiences).

Ethology

Ethology emphasizes biological factors and focuses on the broad picture of inherited attributes that we have in common and that make us alike (Thomas, 1985). A well-known ethological concept is *attachment,* an evolutionary system of signals between infant and caregiver that encourage a social relationship thought to be necessary for survival. Attachment, which is explained in greater depth in Chapter 5, helps to exemplify the main point of ethology—to understand how certain behaviors are adaptive or helpful for a species. Researchers using an ethological approach are concerned with *critical periods* in development, limited periods of time during which it is biologically advantageous to learn specific behaviors, but during which environmental stimulation is also necessary. Understanding how humans interact with specific environments, whether they are harsh or nurturing, is another goal of ethology.

The practical implications of ethology for parenting are limited, and may not be immediately helpful in suggesting child rearing practices. According to this perspective, relationships are evolutionary in nature. Therefore, it is difficult to predict how certain environmental factors will affect the behavior of parents and children over time. However, this perspective is very helpful as an overview for parents regarding the importance of environmental contexts in understanding biological behavior. Social, cultural, and physical environments contribute greatly to developmental outcomes, and must be considered carefully during the parenting process.

Behavior Genetics

Behavior genetics looks at unique combinations of genes that help to make individuals different from one another. Examples of this approach include research on concepts such as intelligence and shyness. Many studies in this area focus on twins or siblings, trying to sort out genetic and environmental contributions to individual differences. This approach may be helpful to parents in recognizing and accepting children's individual differences, but is unlikely to help parents make decisions regarding what to do when faced with various child-rearing dilemmas.

Cognitive Theories

Cognitive theories study the processes of intellectual development, which also have implications for personal and social development. Two theorists, Jean Piaget and Lev Semanovich Vygotsky, have contributed greatly to our knowledge of how children acquire knowledge. The research generated from these theories has helped us to better understand how children learn within different environments.

Piaget's Cognitive Developmental Theory

Jean Piaget based his cognitive developmental theory on the belief that thinking is an active process that people use to organize their perceptions of the world. He believed that children are curious, active explorers who respond to the environment according to their understanding of its essential features. This cognitive developmental theory is important to parenting because parents need to know how the child perceives events and will respond to these events in any given situation.

Adaptation is an important concept in Piaget's theory because it draws attention to the fact that people must constantly adjust to the changing demands of the environment. This is achieved through the process of *assimilation*, where the person interprets new experiences in terms of existing information and just adds the new information to what is already there, and *accommodation*, where people must change or modify their cognitive organization to be compatible with the new information or idea. The parenting role itself can be viewed in terms of adaptation. Parents must assimilate and accommodate to the changing demands of the growing child.

A working example of Piaget's theory might be as follows. A toddler who has a yellow Labrador retriever as a pet may have organized the concept of "doggie" as an animal with four legs and fur. If this toddler sees a poodle for the first time, he might say "doggie," and get the parental feedback that yes, the poodle is indeed a dog. This is the process of assimilation—fitting the new experience into existing informational structures. If this same toddler sees a cow for the first time and says "doggie," the parent would be quick to point out that this animal is not a dog, but is something called a cow. The toddler must then accommodate the concept of "doggie" by adding some other characteristic or criterion, such as barking, so that doggies and cows can be distinguishable. This simplistic process is used at all levels of development.

Piaget's theory has had many implications for educating children. His description of the stages of cognitive skills has been instrumental in sequencing curriculum in schools according to various learning tasks (Thomas, 1985). In addition, his ideas are responsible for the effort to find a healthy balance between letting children explore by themselves, and guiding or directing children's thinking. Throughout this book, we will be using Piaget's stage theory to help us understand the individual child and his or her changing cognitive needs at each stage of development. Cognitive developmental theory definitely offers ideas and guidance for cognitive areas of child rearing, but is not as helpful with other areas of development, such as socioemotional or physical development.

Vygotsky's Dialectical Theory

To add to this knowledge about cognitive development, Soviet psychologist Lev Semanovich Vygotsky proposed that cognitive development is a socially mediated process that includes discussion and reasoning. In other words, cognitive advances occur for children when there is cooperative communication between the child and a knowledgeable member of society, such as a parent. Vygotsky was instrumental in examining differences in children's behavior in relation to culturally specific practices. His theory was particularly focused on the relationship between thought and language (Thomas, 1985).

A key concept in Vygotsky's approach is the *zone of proximal development*, the distance between a child's actual developmental level and what the child might be able to do if she or he had guidance from a capable adult or peer

Learning is facilitated by parents who engage in sensitive communication that is uniquely tailored to the abilities of the individual child.
(*Erika Stone*)

(Bruner, 1985). Parents certainly fit in the role of the capable adult who has a serious interest in passing on cultural values and knowledge. Guidance usually occurs in the form of a verbal prompt or demonstration that is sensitively tailored to the individual child's current abilities. The transition from being helped by others to self-regulation in problem solving is a gradual one (Wertsch, 1979). Recent research suggests that children as young as six months of age are able to actively participate, facilitate, and contribute to the management of these joint learning activities (Mosier & Rogoff, 1994).

As was the case with Piaget's theory, Vygotsky also offers ideas and guidance for narrowly defined cognitive areas pertaining to child rearing. The idea of sensitive communication, individually attuned to a child's unique needs is a powerful one, but it is not clear how to implement and transfer what is currently known to the context of the individual parent-child relationship. Future research may provide parents with more definite guidelines on effectively applying the zone of proximal development to child rearing.

Learning Theories

Theorists who are very interested in behaviors subscribe to learning theories. Learning theorists (or behaviorists) try to figure out the immediate causes and consequences of behavior. This is not a stage theory, but a stimulus response situation (as first postulated by John Watson). Behaviorists consider life a continual learning process, where new responses appear and old responses fade away.

How Learning Occurs

It is suggested that learning occurs in three ways. The first is learning by *association,* or routines. We tend to develop favorable attitudes toward objects, activities, and persons that we encounter on a regular basis. Classical conditioning (or respondent conditioning) is a way in which learning can take place by association. A person learns to associate a neutral stimulus with a meaningful one over time, and then begins to respond to the neutral stimulus as if it were meaningful. Parents of one-year-olds often use classical conditioning. Concerned parents often say "That's yucky" or "That's icky" (the neutral stimulus) before proceeding to the toddler to remove whatever dangerous, poisonous object he or she has in the mouth (the meaningful stimulus). Eventually, the child begins to spit out the contents of his or her mouth when the parent says "That's yucky" or "That's icky" even if the parent does not make a move toward the toddler to remove the substance. The child has learned to associate those words with the appropriate action.

The second way in which learning occurs is through *consequences.* Operant conditioning (or instrumental conditioning) as proposed by B.F. Skinner deals with the modification of behavior through the use of consequences. A person evokes a response with an action, then associates this action with the consequences it produces. A person is more likely to perform a certain act if it has been reinforced or rewarded in some way. People are unlikely to repeat acts for which they have been punished. If parents want to increase the frequency of a behavior, anything that the child views positively and wants, needs, or desires can be used as a reward. Examples might be food, attention, or money. Praise is a positive reinforcer, and can be quite effective when it is specific and sincere. For example, an eleven-year-old who does some unrequired house cleaning is more likely to do it again if the parental response is one of surprise, delight, or praise (positive consequences) than if the efforts are met with parental criticism or are not noticed (negative consequences).

The last way learning occurs is *modeling,* or imitation. This is the acquisition of new feelings, attitudes, and behaviors by watching and listening. This is the heart of Social Learning Theory as proposed by Bandura and others. People learn from watching other people, even if they have not experienced the same reinforcers they have witnessed in others. When teaching new behaviors, parents can use modeling as a powerful technique. The parent simply does what he or she wants the child to do in the presence of the child. Most children want to do what adults do, and will try to imitate the behavior. Parents find out quickly that children love to mimic adults, and sometimes do so when parents are not exhibiting the best behavior themselves. For example, parents who spend hours in front of the television every night may have difficulty convincing their children that it would be more fun to read or play games than watch TV. Once the child performs the desired behavior, positive reinforcement can be used as a reward to increase the likelihood of the behavior's occurring again.

Learning Theory has provided parents with many helpful strategies to use in child rearing. Operant conditioning entices a person to behave in a specified way by applying consequences immediately following the behavior. Many parenting strategies apply this principle, and emphasize changing children's behavior by using a contingency system of rewards and punishments that can increase the likelihood of a behavior, decrease the likelihood of a behavior, or teach new behaviors. Many behaviorists have followed Skinner's lead and have developed techniques for parents to use with their children. The techniques to be discussed will be based on work summarized by Krumboltz and Krumboltz (1972) and Crary (1979).

If parents want to decrease inappropriate, unwanted behavior, *extinction* (or ignoring) is a technique that can reduce or eliminate undesirable behaviors. Extinction involves paying no attention to the behavior, and is best used when the behavior is annoying (such as nose picking) rather than dangerous or destructive. Another technique, *substitution,* involves redirection of an activity by replacing the inappropriate activity with another form of the same activity—one that is acceptable. The parent simply decides what is wrong or objectionable about the activity and substitutes a new tool or different location so that the activity is acceptable. Explanation of why the substitution is being made can help the child begin to use a problem-solving approach. Substitution

Most children want to model or imitate parental behavior.
(*Claire Rydell/The Picture Cube*)

is more than simply distraction, since it indicates the changes that will make the activity acceptable.

Shaping is a behavioral technique aimed at teaching a new behavior. If an activity is too difficult or complicated to be learned at one time, shaping breaks the larger task into more manageable pieces. It requires the parent to plan in advance by assessing the situation, to develop a plan for breaking down the task and explain it to the child, to implement the plan, and to evaluate and revise the plan as needed to assure that progress is being made. Parents use shaping strategies every time they first teach a child new skills, whether it is to put on a coat, bat a ball, or drive a car.

Psychoanalytic Theories

Freud's Psychosexual Stages of Development

Many parents have heard of Sigmund Freud, and may even make jokes about some of his speculations that have become outdated. Freud strongly believed, however, that early experiences had long-term effects on social and personality development. This belief certainly has implications for parenting. Psychoanalytic theories, which originated with Freud, were based on observations of emotionally disturbed adults looking retrospectively at their childhood years. Freud's theory centered on psychosexual gratification, and he proposed stages of conflict or crisis, focused on particular areas of the body, that needed to be resolved. According to Freud, personality centered on three components; the *id* (our unconscious irrational impulses for gratification), the *ego* (the cognitive, reality-based logical part of the personality), and the *superego* (the relentless conscience).

Freud's theory has practical applications for parents (Thomas, 1985). First, psychoanalytic suggestions have influenced child rearing in the area of children's emotional needs. In particular, Freudian theory emphasized the importance of the infancy period for emotional development, and addressed topics parents were often reluctant to think about, such as sexuality and aggression. For example, many of his beliefs about the timing and emotional climate of the toilet training period are still used today. Schools and therapy settings have communicated Freudian ideas to parents, including the symbolic meaning of children's play, their need for physical contact, and a better understanding of their inner motivations. Psychoanalysis was the original basis for many of the clinical intervention models present today. Limitations of Freud's theory for parents include its narrow focus, its questionable scientific research practices, and its sometimes demeaning attitudes toward the development of females.

Erikson's Stages of Psychosocial Development

Erikson's Stages of Psychosocial Development are based on the ideas of Sigmund Freud. Erikson, however, modifies Freud's theory in several crucial ways. First, Erikson stresses that children are active, adaptive creatures who are not passively molded by parents. Second, he extends Freud's concept of ego and maintains that humans are rational, as opposed to the irrational, conflicted beings that Freud observed. Last, Erikson's stages are not centered on a body part like Freud's, but on the person's relationship to the social environment.

This theory will be referred to in various chapters of this text because it provides a framework that has implications for parenting. Erikson outlines eight developmental stages that depend on the successful resolution of a psychosocial crisis, which can be found in Figure 2-1. His stages parallel human development from birth through old age. One of Erikson's stages deals specifically with the adult desire to be responsible for looking after the needs of young people. In the crisis of generativity versus stagnation, Erikson touches upon themes that relate to the process of parenting itself, the desire to give of oneself and contribute to the next generation. Overall, however, the usefulness of Erikson's theory for parents lies mostly in its descriptive value. Erikson's insights into the psychosocial tasks of development at each stage seem to be valid and representative (Thomas, 1985). Because of their face validity, these ideas may inspire thought, discussion, and understanding on the part of parents. The theory is limited, however, in its ability to help parents figure out what they should do to be helpful to children at each point in development.

Clinical Applications for Parenting

Parents are interested in trying to find effective, practical strategies for child rearing. Parenting shelves in book stores are full of materials that promise to help parents with the problems that inevitably occur in raising children. Many approaches, most of which are loosely based on a clinical model of some sort, are available to parents in the form of a program or class for parents taught by instructors who have been trained in the approach. A recent popular example is *How to Talk So Kids Will Listen and Listen So Kids Will Talk* (Faber & Mazlish, 1980). Some have their basis in psychoanalytic theory, while others (such as the more humanistic approaches) developed out of a backlash against Freudian concepts. It is not possible to describe and evaluate all of these parenting strategies within the confines of this chapter. In an effort to provide parents with tools and points of view that could be most helpful in develop-

Basic Trust versus Mistrust

Autonomy versus Shame and Doubt

Initiative versus Guilt

Industry versus Inferiority

Identity versus Identity Diffusion

Intimacy versus Isolation

Generativity versus Stagnation

Ego Integrity versus Despair

FIGURE 2-1 Erikson's psychosocial stages.

ing individual theories of parenting, the ideas of Dr. Rudolph Dreikurs, Dr. Thomas Gordon, and Dr. Thomas Harris, and their approaches to parenthood are presented in Boxes 2-1, 2-2, and 2-3 respectively. These approaches reflect some strategies that have been used for a longer period of time, and whose basic tenets can be found in more contemporary approaches.

These contemporary strategies of parenting have several similarities (Hamner & Turner, 1990). First, the strategies stress the importance of a democratic relationship between parents and children. They emphasize respect for the feelings and needs of both parents and children. Second, communication skills play a major part in establishing healthy parent-child relationships.

Box 2-1 Strategies for Parenting: Dreikurs's Approach

Dr. Rudolph Dreikurs, student of famous psychiatrist Alfred Adler, was convinced that parenting should take place within a democratic atmosphere. He advocates family meetings, where problems are discussed and solutions are suggested by various family members (Dreikurs, 1964). Adler's influence led him to believe that humans are active social beings, capable of evaluative thinking. The focus of his approach is mutual respect and joint decision making on the part of both parents and children. Dreikurs's views are based on two assumptions. First, he assumes equality between children and parents in terms of the value and worth of each person. Parents and children are very different, but must have equal status so that there are no "superior/inferior" positions. Second, he looks at behavior in terms of dynamics. He believes that behavior is purposeful, so the goal for parents must be to understand, encourage, and motivate behavior that is appropriate.

Dreikurs proposes that misbehavior occurs because children lack knowledge, information, or experience. Based on his belief that behavior is purposeful, Dreikurs talks about what he calls the *goals of misbehavior*. The first goal is *attention*; children like to be noticed, even when the attention is negative in nature. The next goal is *power or defiance*; children mistakenly believe that being the boss or doing what they want is what makes people important. Revenge or retaliation occurs when children believe that they can feel significant only if they can hurt others or get even with someone who hurts them. The final goal of misbehavior is

inadequacy or deficiency, where children are discouraged and give up or withdraw because they feel that is their place. Understanding the goals of misbehavior helps parents consistently respond to the needs of the child.

Perhaps the most well-known technique that Dreikurs (1964; Dreikurs & Grey, 1968) proposed is that of *natural and logical consequences*. The natural consequences technique allows the child to experience the natural results of his actions. For example, if a child forgets his baseball hat at home, the natural consequence is for him to have to play the game without it. If the natural consequences are dangerous or inappropriate, logical consequences can be used. Logical consequences involve behavioral outcomes that are imposed upon the child, but are logically related to the behavior in question. For example, a child may not be following bicycle safety rules when she or he is riding on busy streets. The natural consequence, being hurt or killed due to carelessness, is not an acceptable consequence to the parents. Therefore, the parents impose restrictions on the use of the bike for a certain time period until the child shows the parent that he or she can ride safely. This consequence provides a real learning situation for the child that is logically linked to his or her misbehavior. Natural and logical consequences cannot be disguised punishments, but must be aimed at helping children learn to make responsible decisions. The parent's goal is to mold a child who is socially responsible.

Improving the clarity of both verbal and nonverbal communication is recommended. Third, the goal of most approaches is to raise a responsible child who can eventually learn to make informed choices. Therefore, strategies emphasizing decision making and choice are often employed.

The last similarity addressed (Hamner & Turner, 1990) deals with the many limitations of these approaches. There is very little research to attest to the actual effectiveness of various approaches. Most strategies do not differentiate their approaches based on the sex or age of the child even though there are many differences in behavior based on sex and age. In addition, there is an assumption that the strategies apply equally to all cultures, socioeconomic classes, and individuals, even though they appear to be aimed at the white middle class. No one strategy can be used to produce successful parenting

---

 ## Box 2-2 Strategies for Parenting: Gordon's Approach

Dr. Thomas Gordon advocates a democratic approach to parenting (and all relationships) that is based on effective communication strategies. Gordon emphasizes that everyone has difficulties or problems in relationships at times, including parents and children. What most people lack are the skills for settling these problems and coming up with a workable solution. He organized classes around his ideas in 1962, and his book, *Parent Effectiveness Training,* or *P.E.T.* came out eight years later (Gordon, 1970). Since then he has published several other books pertaining to these ideas, and his parenting courses have been taught all over the United States.

Gordon talks about the *problem ownership principle,* which has become a popular frame of reference for parenting problems. Whose problem is it? It is important to identify the ownership of the problem because different techniques or skills are needed depending upon whose problem it is. There are three possibilities; the parent owns the problem, the child owns the problem, or there is no problem. Problem ownership is decided by looking at whose needs are not being met. If the parent's rights are being interfered with, the parent owns the problem and must confront the child. Gordon suggests that parents confront children by using *"I-messages,"* where a parent tells a child how some unacceptable behavior on the part of the child is making the parent feel. It is an effective means of communication because there is no

blaming involved, and the child feels less resistance. If the child is frustrated or unhappy, the child owns the problem and the parent must be prepared to use helping skills. An important communication skill Gordon describes is *active listening.* This involves having the receiver of the message listen and try to understand what the sender is saying or feeling. As soon as the receiver thinks he or she has the message, that person puts it in his or her own words and says it back to the sender to verify whether what the sender was saying was heard accurately. If this is to work in parent-child situations, the parent must be willing to listen and help the child, as well as accept the child's feelings.

Finally, Gordon proposes a *"no-lose" method of resolving conflicts.* Usually conflict resolution results in someone's winning and someone's losing, which often provokes power struggles, persuasion, and coercion. The "no-lose" method encourages people to find a solution that is acceptable to both parties. Participation in this process develops thinking and problem-solving skills, as well as improved communication skills. The steps involved in the "no-lose" method are as follows: (1) identify and define the conflict, (2) generate possible alternative solutions, (3) evaluate the alternative solutions, (4) decide upon the best acceptable solution, (5) work out ways of implementing the solution, and (6) follow up to evaluate how it worked (Gordon, 1970, p. 237).

Box 2-3 Strategies for Parenting: Harris's Approach

Dr. Thomas Harris, author of the book *I'm OK-You're OK* (1969), is a proponent of *transactional analysis,* or TA. This method was developed by Dr. Eric Berne, with whom Harris studied for a number of years. Transactional analysis is an interpersonal theory that defines social relationships between people, and addresses how personality develops within the context of the social environment. Harris believes that these interchanges determine people's overall pattern of life. He also believes that all people can learn to analyze their transactions and become more effective at understanding social relationships. The first step in learning to do this is to understand the terminology.

The basic unit of recognition between people is called a *stroke.* Strokes can be either physical or verbal. If a stroke feels good to a person and helps that person feel okay about herself or himself, it is a positive stroke. If the recognition is painful and leaves the person feeling bad, it is a negative stroke. All strokes, whether positive or negative, can be either *conditional* (based on a person's actions and performance) or *unconditional* (based on simply being alive and existing). A *transaction,* then, is an exchange of strokes between two people. Another variable involved in stroking is the personality structure, which Harris refers to as *ego states* (organized ways of defining, processing, and reacting to information from the surrounding world). There are three observable ego states. The *child state* is present from birth on and contains the person's basic feelings and needs as a biological being. The child contains the creative, spontaneous experiences of existence. The *adult ego state* is the logical, thinking part of a person who gathers and logically processes data from the social world. The *parent ego state* contains all of the rules about what should and should not be done based on values and traditions. It is the part of a person that records the behavior of significant others, especially parents, in determining what is important and what the person actually does.

These three ego states determine the effectiveness of the person's communication. If the ego state addressed is the one that responds, for example, parent to parent or adult to adult, the transaction is *complementary.* Complementary communication can proceed indefinitely, since the communication is effective. If the ego state a person responds with is not the one the speaker intends to have answer, however, such as parent to child or adult to parent, then a *crossed transaction* occurs. This can cause a communication breakdown, and is not an effective means of successfully exchanging thoughts. In addition, ulterior transactions can occur where there is a hidden agenda. The covert message says one thing, while the tone of voice and gestures of the person say another. An example might be when a message is spoken from what appears to be the adult, but the body language definitely says its the parent speaking. This type of communication is ineffective because it is confusing. People have to choose whether to respond to the spoken message or the hidden message.

The accumulation of stroke transactions, based on personality structure and communication styles, helps to make up basic life positions regarding how a person feels about himself or herself and others. Harris proposes *four basic life positions.* The first and healthiest position is "I'm OK-You're OK." From this position, the person feels satisfied with herself or himself most of the time and is comfortable with other people. People who feel OK about themselves and others are able to undergo personal growth. The second position is "I'm Not OK-You're OK," where people feel inadequate and inferior when compared with others. People who feel that they are not OK often feel depressed. The third position, "I'm OK-You're Not OK," usually involves an insecure person who is angry, distrustful of others, and condescending—one who defines others as inadequate or unworthy. The final position is "I'm Not OK-You're Not OK," in which the person does not trust anyone, including himself or herself. People with this overall position feel as if they cannot win, and that life is not worthwhile.

relationships; multiple strategies must be evolved to meet the specific situational needs of individual parents. The diversity of families within differing cultural and ecological contexts suggests the need for parents to develop individual theories of parenting, picking and choosing strategies and techniques to meet the unique needs of each parent and child.

PARENTING STYLES

Much of the literature on strategies of parenting emphasizes that parenting behaviors should occur within the context of warm, nurturing, accepting interactions. Evidence suggests that parents evolve a style of interaction with their children based on two dimensions: *parental warmth or responsiveness* and *parental control or demandingness* (Erikson, 1963; Maccoby & Martin, 1983). Both of these concepts can be seen as continuous, overlapping variables. Parental warmth/responsiveness refers to how accepting, responsive or affectionate a parent is, as opposed to how rejecting, aloof, or hostile. Parents who are on the high end of the parental warmth continuum smile, encourage children, and try to see things from the child's perspective, while parents who are on the low end criticize, punish, and ignore children, often showing insensitivity to the child's emotional needs. Parental control/demandingness refers to the establishment of high standards and expectations for children within a supervised setting. Parents who exert much parental control make demands of children and strictly monitor their behavior to make sure that they are following the rules. Parents who are low in control, however, demand very little from children and are more lenient and less restrictive, giving children more freedom

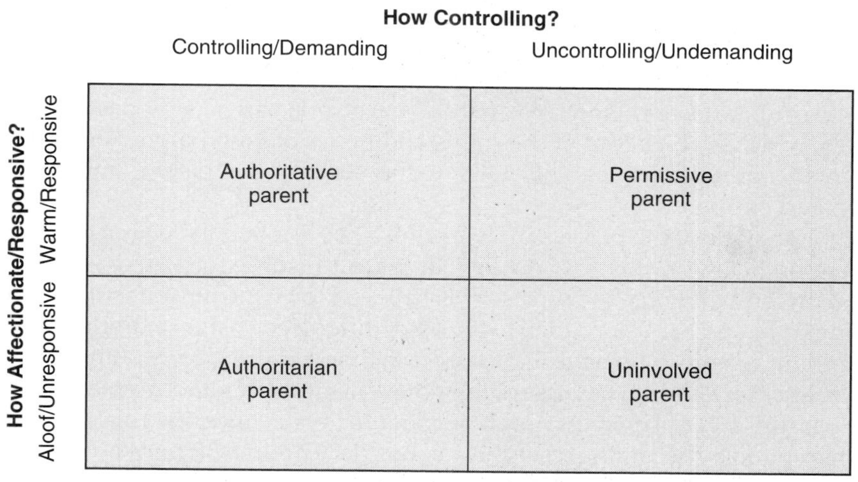

FIGURE 2-2 Dimensions of parenting. Taken from: Maccoby, E.E. & Martin, J.A. (1983). Socialization in the context of the family: Parent-child interaction. In E.M. Hetherington (Ed.) & P.H. Mussen, (General Ed.), *Handbook of Child Psychology. Vol. 4: Socialization, personality, and social development* (4th ed.). New York: John Wiley & Sons.

with little guidance. Since parental warmth/responsiveness and parental control/demandingness are different characteristics, it is possible to be high on both, low on both, or high on one and low on the other. The possible combinations are illustrated in Figure 2-2.

One of the leading researchers in the field of parenting styles is Diana Baumrind, who set out to discover relationships between different styles of child rearing and the social competence of children. Baumrind used lengthy interviews, home and school observations, standardized testing, and home studies of 134 preschool children and their parents. Based on these two major dimensions of responsiveness (warmth) and demandingness (control), she identified three main patterns or types of parenting: authoritarian, permissive, and authoritative (Baumrind, 1967, 1971, 1980). These patterns are important, since how children feel about themselves and how they relate to others is often strongly linked to the way their parents treat them at home.

The first pattern is called *authoritarian* parenting, and occurs when parents are high in control, but low in warmth. These parents have an absolute set of standards and expect obedience without any questions or comments. They often rely on force to get cooperation from their children, and are largely unresponsive to children's rights and needs. Children who are routinely treated in an authoritarian way tend to be moody, unhappy, fearful, withdrawn, unspontaneous, and irritable.

Parents who are high on warmth but low in control are called *permissive* parents. These parents are generally noncontrolling and nonthreatening, and therefore allow children to regulate their own behavior. They are nurturing, but avoid making demands (such as participating in household chores, or having a firm curfew) on the child. The problem is that too much freedom is developmentally inappropriate for young children, which in turn encourages behavior that is more impulsive and aggressive.

Finally, parents who are high in control and high in warmth are called *authoritative* parents. These nurturing, yet demanding, parents set clear standards that are developmentally reasonable, and then enforce them by setting limits. Warmth, affection, and explanation are also a part of this democratic approach, which is respectful of the rights and needs of both parent and child. Children of authoritative parents tend to be socially competent, energetic, friendly, and curious.

Although none of the parents in Baumrind's study exhibited characteristics that were both low in control and low in warmth, subsequent research has revealed this style. *Uninvolved parenting* is believed to be the most unsuccessful parenting style, and has been added to the other three. It consists of extremely lax, uncontrolling parents who have either rejected their children, or don't have the time or energy for children because of their own life problems and stresses (Maccoby & Martin, 1983). The message these parents give is uncaring neglect, and children respond by becoming resentful and hostile. Children of uninvolved parents tend to be lacking both socially and academically. Research suggests that children of uninvolved parents are more likely to engage in delinquent antisocial acts during adolescence (Patterson, DeBaryshe, & Ramsey, 1989).

Although we have identified four parenting styles, it is important to remember that these are not rigid prototypes. No parent is perfect all of the time. Parents are human beings who react differently in various situations, depending on their mood and the circumstances. Overall parenting style across a variety of situations can usually be identified, but total consistency is unrealistic. There are times when authoritarian parents are permissive and vice versa.

In addition to the differences within individuals, research findings suggest that there are cultural differences in parenting styles as well. Perhaps the values and parenting styles that work best for middle-class white families may not work for other ethnic groups (Julian, McKenry, & McKelvey, 1994). For example, African-American parents may be more strict because they are trying to prepare their children for coping with the realities of racism and discrimination (Taylor, Chatters, Tucker, & Lewis, 1990). Because they may be less able than white parents to rely on neighborhood support for their parenting, inner-city African-American parents may have a more difficult job, which may necessitate that they use more active management strategies to be effective, vigilant, proactive parents (Elder, Eccles, Ardelt, & Lord, 1995).

Parenting style is an important concept, because it may influence many aspects of a child's development. Differing styles may affect the number and nature of social interactions in the home, as well as the amount of verbal stimulation. This in turn may mediate the quality and quantity of information to which the child is exposed (Portes, Dunham, & Williams, 1986). It is crucial to remember, however, that parenting style does not account for all of the variability involved in the parent-child relationship. Individual personality variables, such as resiliency and empathy, must also be explored.

DISCIPLINE

Many parents and researchers alike struggle with the concept of discipline. What is discipline? What should parents do when children exhibit certain behaviors? In a recent study, discipline was the child-rearing concern parents of young children sought information about most often, with 69 percent of the sample indicating their desire for additional help (Koepke & Williams, 1989). Parents want their children to learn to avoid doing things that interfere with

CATHY © 1993 Cathy Guisewite. Reprinted with permission of UNIVERSAL PRESS SYNDICATE. All rights reserved.

their safety, health, or development. Parents are interested in *child compliance,* where the child obeys immediately, or shortly after a parental request is made. Parental actions influence compliance.

Disciplinary Strategies

The word *discipline* means "to teach," not "to punish," as some people might guess. Helping children see the possible consequences of their actions, helping them learn self-control, and helping them find alternatives to unacceptable behaviors all come under the category of discipline. There are very few studies that specifically deal with the effectiveness of various discipline strategies. Time-out, a brief period of social isolation given after a child exhibits problem behavior, has been recommended for younger children, while consequences such as removing privileges or brief work chores have been recommended for older children (Chamberlain & Patterson, 1995). Humiliating a child, trying to control behavior through fear, or imposing physical punishments are not recommended strategies for any age.

Crary (1979) synthesized a number of approaches to parenting and came up with a starting point for solving behavior problems in young children. Her six-step solution can be found in Box 2-4. The steps can be adapted to different strategies and points of view that are consistent with parents' individualized theories. Many of the frustrations that parents experience can be avoided through careful planning and forethought. For example, to counteract behavior problems, parents must reduce boredom, plan transitional activities such as at meal times and bed times, and foreshadow to prepare young children for new events. They can also make environmental modifications (Gordon, 1970)

 ## Box 2-4 Six Steps for Solving Behavior Problems

1. *Define the problem behaviorally.* Decide specifically what the child does or says that is bothersome. The definition should be clear enough that someone else could look at the child's behavior and count the number of times the behavior occurs. General words and personality traits should be avoided; instead behaviors should be described specifically.

2. *Gather data.* Find out the actual frequency of the problem (how often it occurs), the context of the problem (when and where the behavior occurs and who else is involved), and the developmental level for the behavior you want the child to perform.

3. *Determine who owns the problem.* Problem ownership divides behavior into three groups, depending upon whose needs are not being met.

Either the child owns the problem, the parent owns the problem, or there is no problem.

4. *Generate alternatives.* The goal of generating alternative solutions is to get as many alternatives as possible. Don't limit the process by evaluating and rejecting ideas at this time. Be creative.

5. *Evaluate alternatives and implement one.* This is the time to cross off the ideas that are too expensive, time consuming, damaging to the child's self-esteem, and so on.

6. *Evaluate the solution.* If it is successful, be happy. If not, then try again.

Adapted from:

Crary, E. (1979). *Without spanking or spoiling: A practical approach to toddler and preschool guidance.* Seattle, WA: Parenting Press.

that will help children control their negative behaviors and therefore reduce the occurrence of parent-child conflict. Enriching the environment and providing interesting things for a child to do may help a bored child with a high activity level stay out of trouble. Simplifying an environment by removing toys and options for play at selected times, such as getting ready for bed, may help a child settle down and make transitions more easily. Also, allowing a child to have more independence in self-care skills and putting toys away can reduce child-caregiver tension. Last, it is always helpful to prepare a child for changes in the environment by discussing important events ahead of time so that children can plan.

Punishment is not usually recommended as a disciplinary strategy. Although it is sometimes effective in stopping an unwanted behavior, there may be negative effects. Aggression, passive helplessness, or avoidance may result when harsh physical or verbal punishment occurs. This is especially true when the child perceives that parental behavior is unpredictable, as when parents who are out of control yell and hit when punishing children (Grusec & Goodnow, 1994). If parents do decide to use punishment as a disciplinary strategy, Parke (1977) suggests that timing and providing an explanation are important points to remember. Punishments are more effective when very little time passes between the misbehavior and the punishment. Punishment is especially effective if it occurs during the unwanted behavior, as opposed to afterward. A short explanation given along with the punishment increases effectiveness because it involves reasoning with the child.

Discipline requires clear communication and flexibility on the part of parents (Grusec & Goodnow, 1994). Disciplinary strategies should match the child's age, developmental level, needs, and individual personality. Parents must be able to use many different strategies in response to situations that arise in parenting.

Inadequate Discipline Practices

Gerald Patterson and his colleagues have been responsible for designing and carrying out many studies on topics related to discipline and child compliance. In a recent comprehensive review (Chamberlain & Patterson, 1995), they have suggested four inadequate discipline practices—practices that do not work well. They are inconsistent discipline, irritable explosive discipline, inflexible rigid discipline, and low supervision and involvement.

Inconsistent discipline can occur in an individual parent when she or he has a standard for child behavior but then gives in to child demands or doesn't follow through with consequences. A parent who is unpredictable in expectations and consequences—for example, when the child exhibits the same behavior and yields a parental laugh one time and a spanking the next—is inconsistent. Since mothers and fathers are different people with differing points of view, it is sometimes difficult for them to agree on specific child-rearing matters. This is another source of inconsistency, when parents disagree on basic rules, monitoring, and consequences.

Irritable explosive discipline is characterized by long harsh episodes of loud, high intensity strategies such as hitting and yelling, which are accompanied by escalating punishments. *Inflexible rigid discipline* occurs when parents rely on a single disciplinary strategy for all transgressions. No adjustments are made to take into account the severity of the infraction or extenuating circumstances surrounding the incident. Parents who use inflexible methods do not usually use any verbal reasoning in their discipline. In *low supervision and involvement*, parents are unaware of their child's activities and peers and rarely engage in joint activities with their children. Poor supervision has been linked with many problem behaviors, such as aggression, delinquency, and substance abuse.

Discipline is an important part of the parenting role. Identifying these four patterns of inadequate discipline can be helpful in planning and implementing more effective discipline methods for families. An important message for parents of older children is that it is never too late to try to deal with discipline problems more effectively. For example in an intervention study of aggressive and delinquent boys (Patterson & Capaldi, 1991), parents were successfully taught more effective ways of communicating and more constructive ways to handle negative behaviors (instead of using hostility and coercion). Parents' belief in their own effectiveness may enhance the quality and skill of their caregiving (Baumrind, 1993).

Discipline and Coparenting Relationships

As Chapter 1 stated, coparenting refers to the way parents work together as a couple, negotiating child-rearing issues and supporting each other. The quality of the relationship between marital partners may influence how well they can successfully work together in their parenting (Emery & Tuer, 1993). Emotionally sustaining parenting partnerships are characterized by mutual respect, where each partner values the parenting abilities of the other. Parenting can be a difficult job, and the support of another caring adult may increase parental confidence and enable parents to better deal with the stresses of parenting more successfully.

Some evidence suggests that parents who agree on basic child-rearing attitudes and practices have children with better developmental outcomes (Block & Block, 1980). Boys in particular may be adversely affected when parents disagree about child-rearing strategies, both with regard to inconsistent parenting and arguments about child-rearing practices (McHale, Freitag, Crouter, & Bartko, 1991). Parents' general approach to handling conflict and disagreement may contribute to children's well-being (Howes & Markman, 1989), with effective communication and constructive conflict management skills between spouses leading to more positive outcomes. Overt conflict between parents may interrupt effective parenting (Gable, Crnic, & Belsky, 1994). More research is needed to help resolve the many unanswered questions about the direct and indirect effects of conflict between coparents.

Taking a practical or clinical approach, the American Academy of Pediatrics (1995) has identified some typical problems encountered in coparenting relationships. Inconsistency between parents, noncommunication about significant issues, confusion and uncertainty about what the rules should be in a particular situation, and overt conflict between parents are all difficulties coparents may face. Recommendations for solving these problems require basic conflict resolution tools such as listening, clarifying different points of view, respecting the feelings of each person, jointly generating alternative solutions, and negotiating.

SUMMARY

- Theories are the basis for parents to understand and explain their child's development.
- Family Systems Theory suggests that families are a context for parenting. Families interact in complex ways, and exhibit adaptability as they change and reorganize across time.
- Biological theories look at what makes people alike and what makes them different from one another.
- Cognitive theories, such as those of Piaget and Vygotsky, help parents understand how children learn within different environments.
- Learning theories emphasize that learning occurs through association, consequences, and modeling. Many learning strategies and techniques exist for parents to use.
- Freud's psychoanalytic theory emphasized the emotional needs of children. Erikson's Stages of Psychosocial Development provide a framework that has implications for parenting.
- Many strategies available to parents are based on clinical applications.
- Parental warmth and parental control are dimensions that influence parenting styles. Authoritarian parents are high in control but low in warmth, permissive parents high on warmth and low on control, and authoritative parents are high in both warmth and control. Uninvolved parenting is believed to be the least successful parenting style.
- Discipline practices are a major source of concern to parents. Inadequate discipline strategies include inconsistent discipline, irritable explosive discipline, inflexible rigid discipline, and low supervision and involvement.
- Cooperative coparenting relationships may enhance children's development.

CHAPTER 3

Parenting Within Diverse Cultures and Contexts

The parenting process takes place in various contexts. Much of the early research on parent-child relationships investigated white middle-class families, neglecting the cultural and structural diversity that characterizes contemporary family life. It is now recognized that culture, ethnicity, and minority status shape beliefs and behaviors related to child rearing. Attention has also been directed toward nontraditional family structures, including those of homosexual couples, to determine how these contexts influence the parenting process.

Theoretical perspectives that highlight diversity need empirical support. Unfortunately, the research base in this area is still quite limited. Much of the research on parenting is not generalizable to diverse populations (MacPhee, Kreutzer, & Fritz, 1994). Some studies do not report information on family background, while others fail to separate the effects of socioeconomic status, ethnicity, and family structure. Also, many of the studies that do include diverse populations focus on social problems rather than normal development. Clinical psychologists and service providers, sometimes representative of various subcultures, offer another source of information about the connections between diversity and child rearing. However, the nonrandom nature of their samples and the potential biases inherent in being a participant observer are limiting factors of these reports.

While acknowledging the shortcomings of the research base, this chapter explores diversity in parenting. It begins by describing the relationship between culture and child rearing, and then examines research on parent-child relationships in African-American, Latino, Asian-American, and Native American families. The last section of the chapter focuses on one type of structural diversity—parenting among gay and lesbian couples. Family structure is a theme that receives attention again in Chapter 10 when the topics of single parenting and stepparenting are discussed.

CULTURAL CONTEXTS

Culture refers to the patterns for living that a group of people passes onto future generations through its language, customs, values, and activities. Culture shapes goals, behaviors, thoughts, and feelings. Family roles, rules, and celebrations may be related to ethnic roots. Ideas about work, play, and success are transmitted over generations and reinforced by those who share the same ethnic identification (McGoldrick, 1982). Child rearing is influenced by culture, but it is also a vehicle by which culture is transmitted from parent to child (Harkness & Super, 1995).

It is important to note that culture is not deterministic; that is, the influence of culture on the parenting process varies across people and situations. Not all members of a particular group will behave in the same way. There are individual differences among members of a group with respect to how strongly they identify with the culture (Hanson, 1992). This can be partially attributed to varying degrees of *acculturation*, the process of changing beliefs and behaviors as a result of being exposed to another culture.

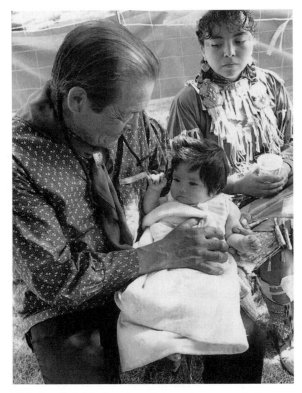

This family's Native American culture may influence
parental expectations, children's roles, and the
extent to which relatives and friends participate in
the childrearing process.
(*Joel Gordon*)

Ethnicity and Parenting

Research on parenting and ethnicity began by focusing on social problems and
comparing various groups to Caucasians. This approach can lead to interpreting differences as deficits. Furthermore, it neglects the variability within
groups. For example, a particular problem is that race is often confounded
with social class, because of the higher incidence of poverty among certain
groups. If the average income and educational level of an ethnic group are
lower than the national average, child-rearing differences that appear to be
associated with culture may, in fact, be caused by inadequate resources. When
studies control for socioeconomic status, more similarities than differences
across groups emerge, and the true role of culture in parenting is highlighted
(McLoyd, 1990; Julian, McKenry, & McKelvey, 1994).

Regardless of ethnic background, the child-rearing practices of most parents are guided by a desire to do what is best for children (Garcia Coll, et al.,
1995). It is often assumed, however, that the beliefs and behaviors associated
with Caucasian middle-class parenting in the United States are universal.

This approach oversimplifies the developmental process, neglecting the fact that optimal child-rearing patterns for one group may have different consequences for those who do not share the same sociocultural context (Ogbu, 1981). The result can be a mistaken notion that authoritative parenting is the norm, that competition and individualism are valued, and that an orientation toward the future guides the behavior of all parents, instead of the white middle-class populations polled (Spencer, 1990). A consideration of cultural variations in parenting suggests areas of overlap and divergence (Garcia Coll et al., 1995).

The major ethnic groups in the United States have notable differences that will be explored later in this chapter, but they also share common traits. For example, it has been noted that families who have an ethnic identity are more likely to be part of supportive extended family networks. There is also a tendency toward a collective, rather than an individualistic, orientation (Harrison, Wilson, Pine, Chan, & Buriel, 1990).

Many ethnic minority families function simultaneously in at least two contexts. The parenting process takes place within the subculture of the home and neighborhood, but it is also embedded within the larger society represented by school, work, and the media (Boykin & Toms, 1985). Individual parents and children experience different acculturation opportunities and demands (Garcia Coll et al., 1995). One result is varying degrees of *biculturalism.* Bicultural individuals understand and participate in two cultures at the same time. Parents and children who are able to retain their ethnic identities while adapting to the majority culture have been found to have higher self-esteem (Julian et al., 1994). Because they tend to be more flexible in their thinking about human development, bicultural parents may be more accepting of a variety of outcomes for their children and more supportive of diversity (Gutierrez & Sameroff, 1990).

For some subcultures, language differences will influence the parenting process. Language can be a barrier to accessing services meant to support parents and children (Chan, 1992). Within families, there may be intergenerational language differences that make it difficult for family members to communicate about parenting (McGoldrick, 1982). When children serve as translators because they understand English but their parents do not, the balance of power within the family is disrupted and parent-child relationships can be strained (Garcia-Preto, 1982). Conversely, bilingualism helps transmit culture, facilitates communication between generations, and enables use of supportive services (Hanson, 1992).

If a racial or ethnic identity is important, how is this nurtured in multiracial families? When people of different races marry and produce biracial children, parents and children do not share the exact same racial identity. Some biracial children may feel that they cannot identify completely with mother, father, or either cultural community (Miller & Miller, 1990). Multiracial families are also created through transracial adoptions. Although some policy makers have argued that transracial adoptions should not be encouraged because racial identity will suffer, others have suggested ways to nurture diversity within these families. See Box 3-1 for ideas about parenting issues related to parents and children who do not share a racial or ethnic background.

Minority Status and Discrimination

Racism influences child rearing. Families from minority groups often experience prejudice, discrimination, and social inequity based on their cultural uniqueness. Racism adds stress to the daily lives of minority adults, and it also introduces an added stressor into their parenting roles. Parents may feel torn between protecting their children from the outside world and giving them the tools they need to cope with racism. All children need to feel protected in their homes, but for minority children the message may be double-edged: They are given unconditional love within the family and taught that they cannot always be protected from the racist outside world (Peters, 1985).

Prejudicial attitudes can result in minority parents' being judged more harshly than majority parents. Sometimes this happens because of generalized negative attitudes about a particular racial group. Other times it is because the parents are being judged by standards that are inconsistent with their world view. "Different" parenting styles are not necessarily "bad" parenting styles.

 ## Box 3-1 When the Race of the Child and That of the Parent Are Different

In some families, parents and children have different racial and ethnic roots. For example, multiracial families are created through transracial and intercountry adoptions. Lois Melina (1986) offers the following child-rearing suggestions to adoptive parents in multiracial families:

1. *Parents must be aware of their own prejudices.* When adoptive parents see themselves as "rescuing" a child from a potentially disadvantaged life, they cast their children as victims. A child should not be made to feel that she owes her parents a debt that can never be repaid.

2. *When a couple chooses to become a minority family by adoption, they are changing the race of the family for generations to come.* Be aware that some extended family members may not be supportive of this choice. Parents themselves may not even recognize the magnitude of their decision until they become grandparents.

3. *Parents must be tolerant of all racial differences, not just of the child's group.* Allowing racial slurs of any type sends a message to the child that these differences are not valued.

4. *Be wary of basing expectations for the child on race or ethnicity.* If Caucasian parents expect their

Asian daughter to be outstanding in math or their tall African-American son to excel in basketball, they are perpetuating dangerous stereotypes.

5. *Parents may encounter unique sibling issues in multiracial families.* Some people suggest that having more than one adopted child from the same racial background allows for a special kind of support within the family. Parents should be aware that Caucasian siblings of minority children are often put in the position of having to educate their peers about adoption.

6. *When minority children enter school, it is more difficult for parents to protect them from prejudice outside the home.* The mismatch between the race of parent and child might be perceived negatively by school-age peers who strive for conformity. Parents may choose to live in a racially mixed school district, hoping that their children will fit in and that diversity will be valued.

Source: "When the Race of the Child & Parent are Different" from *Raising Adopted Children: A Manual for Adoptive Parents* by Lois Ruskai Melina. Copyright © 1986 by Lois Ruskai Melina. Reprinted by permission of HarperCollins Publishers, Inc.

Efforts to support the parenting process must take into account culture-specific child-rearing values, attitudes, and behaviors. Culture may predispose individuals or families to think about problems, intervention, and treatment in ways that are different from those of the majority culture (Hanson, 1992). What is viewed as problematic or possible will differ among families with different cultural backgrounds (McGoldrick, 1982).

Minority families are often misunderstood. Practitioners must be careful not to misinterpret the behaviors and goals that ethnic minorities have for their children. For example, an emphasis on obedience and self-control may be misinterpreted as an effort to make children passive or subordinate, when it is intended to be a mechanism for socializing children to cope with racism (Julian et al., 1994).

Acknowledging the diversity within subcultures, teachers, therapists, and other interventionists must resist stereotyping. It is important to determine each family's orientation to specific child-rearing issues and the extent to which the family operates biculturally (Hanson, 1992). Service agencies are sometimes viewed with suspicion by ethnic groups. A working relationship with the subculture may depend on establishing credibility with respected members of the community, who serve as community gatekeepers (Chan, 1992). Cultural sensitivity includes letting the family define who should be involved in decisions about the child, rather than assuming that only the mother and the father are relevant. See Box 3-2 describing cross-cultural competence for professionals.

In the past, mainstream American institutions such as schools and social service agencies encouraged minority groups to learn the ways of the majority culture and fit in. Through this forced acculturation process, languages and traditions were often lost. Today there is a more positive view of multiculturalism that encourages diversity and mutual understanding. Given the current demographic trends presented in Table 3-1, this positive orientation toward diversity is essential. Taken together, "minority" groups in the United States are fast becoming the new "majority."

AFRICAN-AMERICAN FAMILIES

African Americans are the largest minority group in the United States, making up approximately 12 percent of the population (U.S. Bureau of Census, 1992). Although this group is represented in most geographic areas and at every socioeconomic level, a disproportionate number live in poor urban environments. The fact that 50 percent of African-American children live in low-income families means that their child-rearing environments are significantly different from those of middle-class whites. It also means that researchers must be careful to distinguish between the effects of the subculture and social class on the parenting process.

Values and Beliefs

Researchers report a tendency among African Americans to place a high value on interpersonal relationships (Harrison et al., 1990; Wilson, 1989). Similarly, professionals working with African-American families have noted that daily life often centers on interactions with people, not objects, and that both males and females are taught to express emotions. A sense of belonging to and caring about the group develops in the context of family, friends, and church— relationships that support child-rearing efforts (Willis, 1992; Wilson, 1989).

It is not uncommon for African-American women to be socialized as caregivers, family decision makers, and wage earners (Washington, 1988). National statistics reveal that, in comparison with other women in the United States, African-American women are more likely to become mothers at younger ages, have more children, be single parents, and have higher rates of participation in the labor force (U.S. Bureau of Census, 1992). It has been argued that the romanticized image of a strong, nurturing black matriarch creates unrealistic expectations for those women who are trying to provide for their families under adverse conditions (Washington, 1988; Greene, 1990). There is concern that African-American mothers may devote so much of their energy to caring for others that they are at risk for neglecting their own needs and personal development.

 ## Box 3-2 Supporting Diversity in Families: Suggestions for Professionals Working with Parents

If cultural values and ethnic identity are important components in the parenting process, professionals working with families must be sensitive to these issues. Developing cross-cultural competence requires flexibility, a willingness to explore the unfamiliar, and a belief that there are alternate pathways to healthy developmental outcomes for parents and children. Parent educators, day care providers, teachers, counselors, health professionals, and personnel in social service agencies can become more effective in their work with parents if they are sensitive to diversity. Cross-cultural competence can be enhanced by:

Self-awareness Exploring one's own cultural heritage leads to a better understanding of personal values, behaviors, and beliefs. When professionals have this self-awareness, they are more likely to recognize how their own cultural identity can affect professional practice. This is the first step in developing sensitivity.

Culture-specific information Learning specific traditions and rituals characteristic of other cultures helps professionals understand parenting behaviors, appreciate family priorities, and offer appropriate support. There are many ways in which this

information can be acquired—reading about various cultures, interpersonal sharing with members of another culture, participating in cross-cultural activities and celebrations, or language learning.

Effective cross-cultural communication Verbal and nonverbal communication is inextricably embedded in culture. Groups differ in their use of words and gestures, in the pace and loudness of conversations, and in the meaning they attach to eye contact and body language. Interventionists working with parents can be more effective if they adapt their communication to a style that is comfortable for the family. Listening more than talking, and observing family communication patterns may be useful techniques.

These recommendations are based on the assumption that cultural differences should be acknowledged and respected, rather than ignored or minimized. Celebrating diversity supports parents and strengthens society, because it forges connections among people and dispels problematic stereotypes.

Source: Developing Cross-Cultural Competence: A Guide for Young Children and Their Families, pp. 36–40, 44–45. Brookes Publishing Co., P.O. Box 10624, Baltimore, MD 21285-0624.

TABLE 3-1. Total Number, Composition of Subgroups, and Geographic Location of Ethnic Minority Groups

Ethnic Group	Total Number	Composition of Subgroups	Geographic Concentration
African American	28.2 million	African-Caribbean, recent immigrants from Africa	South, Northeast
American Indian/ Alaskan Native	1.5 million/ 64,103	Largest tribes: Cherokee, Navajo, Sioux, Chippewa/ Aleuts, Eskimos	Northwest, West
Asian Pacific Americans	10.0 million	Chinese, Japanese, Korean, Vietnamese, Cambodian, Thai, Filipino, Laotian, Lao-Hmong, Burmese, Samoan, Guamanian	West, Northeast
Hispanic	18.8 million	Mexican, Puerto Rican, Cuban, Central and South Americans	Southwest, Midwest, Northeast, Florida, and California

Source: Harrison et al. (1990). © The Society for Research in Child Development.

The role of fathers in African-American families has also been examined. Unlike other subcultures, in which men are stereotypically portrayed as uninvolved in domestic issues, the division of labor in many African-American families is reported to be more egalitarian (Scanzoni, 1985). Young black males are more likely than their white counterparts to be taught to cook, clean, and care for babies. As a result, when they become fathers they may be more actively involved in child care and household tasks. However, economic factors also affect the experience of African-American fathers (Bowman, 1993). High unemployment and underemployment for this group can minimize their role as breadwinners in some families, and lead to withdrawal from the family—especially when their children can benefit from public assistance programs only if the father is absent from the home (McAdoo, 1981). Recent research efforts have attempted to identify the conditions under which economically marginal African-American fathers stay with their families. One hypothesis is that this type of role strain may have a less damaging effect on fatherhood when cultural resources such as kinship bonds and flexible family roles exist (Bowman, 1993).

Because of their history of being subject to prejudice and discrimination, many African Americans recognize the importance of a positive racial identity.

In some cultural and ethnic groups, young males are encouraged to care for younger siblings. These skills may serve them well when they assume parental responsibilities later in life.
(*Elizabeth Hamlin/Stock, Boston*)

One study found that older, educated mothers make special efforts to teach their children about race, especially when they live in a mixed-race neighborhood (Thornton, Chatters, Taylor, & Allen, 1990). Another study noted a tendency among African-American parents who had experienced racism to foster in their children the survival skills necessary for coping with such treatment (Peters, 1985). Unconditional love from family and friends is one way to build positive self-esteem that can protect children from the adverse effects of discrimination. African-American parents may struggle with the question of how to best prepare their children for life as minorities in America—wondering whether their children must imitate or accept white values in order to succeed (Greene, 1990; Comer & Poussaint, 1992).

Education is typically associated with achievement and success for both majority and minority cultures. Some scholars have suggested, however, that education takes on special significance in the African-American community because discrimination and family history may block other avenues of mobility (Scanzoni, 1985). When education is seen as a means to a better life, parents may be particularly invested in their children's school success.

Parenting Practices

A wide range of disciplinary practices is found in African-American families, but the tendency to be restrictive and expect immediate obedience has been noted by several researchers (Peters, 1985; Julian et al., 1994). Mothers who combine strictness with nurturing support tend to be older, more educated, and more religious (Kelley, Power, & Wimbush, 1992). In contrast, among families suffering economic hardship, there is more of a tendency to be power assertive and arbitrary (McLoyd, 1990). When comparative studies are done, African-American parents report more frequent use of physical punishment than other ethnic groups (Franklin & Boyd-Franklin, 1985). It has been hypothesized that this may be due to intergenerational transmission of disciplinary practices.

Some African-American parenting styles may be a response to racism and discrimination. Although parents do not want to overwhelm their children or be overly protective, they may feel the need to prepare the child to live in a society where African-American children are given less leeway for misbehavior (Peters, 1985). For the large numbers of African Americans living in poor urban environments, parents may be especially worried about their children's future. This concern may be translated into firm discipline, efforts to nurture self-esteem, and the encouragement of academic pursuits (Jayratne, 1993).

In their efforts to foster a positive African-American identity in children, parents must scrutinize the messages that are conveyed in everyday life. Parents are advised to expose their children to books, television shows, and movies that offer positive portrayals of African Americans. They also must be aware of the messages that are communicated about their culture through the school curriculum. When black families are living in all-white settings, parents may feel the need to arrange contacts with other black children and adult role models (Comer & Poussaint, 1992).

Parents and children may benefit from the informal support networks that exist within the African-American community. For example, church participation brings young and inexperienced parents into contact with community members who serve as role models and offer emotional support. Adults who are unrelated to the children may feel a sense of responsibility for supporting the child-rearing process, by correcting a child's behavior or intervening to protect the child (Willis, 1992). This network of caring sometimes results in informal adoptions, whereby a friend or relative takes over child-rearing responsibilities on a temporary or permanent basis when the parent cannot manage (Comer & Poussaint, 1992).

LATINO FAMILIES

Latino families in the United States include many groups with unique histories and cultures. Mexican Americans are the largest subgroup, but Puerto Ricans and Cubans are also heavily represented. Latinos make up 8 percent of the population and Spanish is the second most common language in the United States. Because approximately 25 percent of these people live in poverty, care must be taken not to confuse social class differences with cultural differences (U.S. Bureau of Census, 1992).

Values and Beliefs

In comparison with other racial groups, Latinos have larger families and lower divorce rates (Zuniga, 1992). In traditional Latino cultures, children symbolize fertility and security for the future (Garcia-Preto, 1982). In some families the parent-child relationship may be considered even more important than the marital relationship, and parents may be expected to sacrifice the fulfillment of personal needs for their children (Zuniga, 1992). It is not uncommon for parents to maintain an intense connectedness with their children from infancy

The strong affectional bonds in this Latino family may enhance the parent-adolescent relationship. Conflict may develop, however, if parents tend toward overprotection of females and severely restrict their teenage daughter's activities.
(*Bob Daemmrich/Stock, Boston*)

through adulthood and, as a result, they may never experience an empty nest stage (McGoldrick, 1982).

Familism, a strong identification with the family, is central in most Latino cultures. Family includes not only nuclear and extended family, but the larger network of friends and neighbors with whom an enduring bond is established. Family loyalty, respect for parents, and a sense of duty toward other family members are emphasized. This strong family orientation can be a source of social support, but it can also interfere with individual advancement. Practitioners who work with Latino families note that group cooperation, obedience, and getting along with others may be considered more important than success in the outside world (Zuniga, 1992).

Male dominance and female submissiveness describe traditional gender-typed roles in Latino families. However, this description has been challenged by social scientists who believe that it is based on biased research that reinforces inaccurate stereotypes. A revised model of Latino families, supported by empirical studies, suggests that a range of role patterns exists, including shared decision making and egalitarianism (Mirande, 1988). In traditional families, males are expected to make most of the important decisions for the family outside the home; however, women control the household. Women have primary responsibility for the daily care and nurturance of children; thus, their identity may be largely defined by their maternal and marital roles (Garcia-Preto, 1982; Bernal, 1982; Zuniga, 1992). Traditional roles have been altered by acculturation, current social conditions, and the economic context. For example, family financial needs have resulted in more women of all ethnic groups entering the work force. Contemporary Latina women are also more educated than their female predecessors were. Under these circumstances, gender roles within families may become less rigidly defined, a topic explored in more detail in Chapter 13.

Parenting Practices

Counselors and educators have noted a relaxed attitude among some Latino parents with regard to their children's attainment of developmental milestones (Zuniga, 1992). Parents may indulge and placate young children, rather than pushing for independence. As children get older, however, obedience, respect, and taking on household chores become more important. Mastering relationship skills may be emphasized more than academic achievement (McGoldrick, 1982). These practices support the family's interdependence.

Research on the parenting styles of Latinos suggests a variety of practices. Although parents may be permissive and indulgent with infants and younger children (Vega, 1990), emphasis on obedience as the child gets older may lead to a more authoritarian style. Strictness in the context of high nurturance is guided by a desire to protect children and instill respect for adults (Garcia-Preto, 1982).

Professionals working with traditional Latino families have noted that boys and girls may be subject to different parental treatment. For example, if the cultural ideal of male dominance persists, sons may be raised to repress feminine traits. Aggressive behaviors may be tolerated in boys, but considered unacceptable in girls (Leadbeater & Bishop, 1994). The belief that girls need to be protected and concerns about sexual purity lead to more parental restrictions for daughters (Zuniga, 1992; Bernal, 1982).

In traditional Latino families, children may remain emotionally dependent on their parents over the life span. The close connectedness between mothers and daughters is particularly noteworthy. The interdependence of the extended family means that families have many resources to call upon for help with child rearing (Zuniga, 1992).

ASIAN-AMERICAN FAMILIES

Only three percent of the American population is Asian, but that number is expected to triple during the next 50 years (U.S. Bureau of Census, 1992). Immigration patterns have resulted in a very diverse group of Asian Americans, including Chinese, Japanese, Koreans, and Southeast Asians. The earliest immigrants were primarily farmers and laborers, while more recent groups have tended to be highly educated professionals (Chan, 1992).

Values and Beliefs

The central values in many Asian cultures—family, harmony, education—are rooted in Confucian principles. Virtues such as patience, perseverance, self-sacrifice, restraint, and humility are held in high regard. Self-interest is subordinate to the good of the group. When parents readily sacrifice their personal needs and wants in the interest of their children, they are showing concern for the most important group in their culture—the family (Chan, 1992).

In traditional Asian families, roles are strongly influenced by the age, gender, and birth order of family members. Women have primary responsibility for child rearing, while men are financial providers and disciplinarians. Practitioners working with Asian Americans report strong emotional ties between family members. For example, a mother's strongest bond may be with her children, especially the oldest son. A father's primary attachment may be to his own mother, rather than his wife. Oldest sons are often expected to guide the development of younger siblings (Chan, 1992; Shon & Ja, 1982).

In most Asian-American subcultures, education is highly valued and children are taught to respect learning and knowledge (Chan, 1992). This priority supports biculturalism for Asian-American families living in the United States (Garcia Coll et al., 1995). The cultural tendency to attribute academic success to effort rather than innate ability (Stevenson & Lee, 1990) also influences the parenting process. Guided by this belief, parents and children may feel greater responsibility for children's school performance. By doing well in school, children honor their parents and also increase their chances of occupational success, thus enhancing the family's social status and economic well-being (Chan, 1992; Shon & Ja, 1982). Individual independence that allows children to achieve is encouraged, and is not viewed as a threat to family interdependence (Lin & Fu, 1990).

Individuals who identify with their Asian culture are more likely to emphasize connectedness and minimize individualism. In traditional Asian-

American families, when children misbehave or are unsuccessful, it reflects badly on the parent, especially the mother. Child-rearing practices may be based on an underlying assumption that children are inherently good, but that proper training during the early years is also important (Chan, 1992).

Parenting Practices

The care of Asian-American infants has been described by some professionals as indulgent and nurturant (Chan, 1992). Babies are perceived as relatively helpless. Observations of Asian-American families reveal that many mothers do gratify their needs immediately, rather than imposing rigid feeding and sleeping schedules. There is an emphasis on close physical contact between mother and infant, with infants being carried or held much of the time.

The relative permissiveness that characterizes the care of Asian-American infants and toddlers gives way to more demands from caregivers when the child reaches the preschool period. At this age, parents expect the child to be more independent and to take on greater personal responsibility. For example, children may now be expected to dress themselves and complete chores (Chan, 1992).

When they reach school age, Asian-American children share many adult rituals and routines. They attend weddings, funerals, and business functions and, in these settings, they learn socially acceptable behaviors through participation, observation, and imitation. In many families, older children are expected to set a good example for their younger siblings by modeling adult behaviors. It is not uncommon for parents to respond to sibling arguments by scolding the older child for not setting a good example and by scolding the younger child for failing to respect the older brother or sister (Chan, 1992).

The mainstream American cultural practice of giving children "choices" is less common among Asian-American parents, who are more likely to make decisions for their children. They may devote much energy to securing an appropriate education for their children and to controlling the child's interactions with the outside world. This can include restricting activities with peers until much later ages than local norms (Chan, 1992).

When Asian parents are evaluated in terms of the parenting styles described in Chapter 2, they are found to be more controlling and authoritarian than the population at large (Lin & Fu, 1990; Chao, 1994). A recent study found that Baumrind's typology does not take into account the Chinese notion of "training." This child-centered concept includes beginning training at the earliest possible age, exposing children to the adult world, and comparing children's behavior (Chao, 1994). This culture-specific style may account for the distinctly different relationship between parenting and academic achievement among Asian-American children. Despite authoritarian parenting, children have high levels of academic achievement.

Parent-child relationships in traditional Asian-American families have been described as "formal." Because achievement and good behavior are expected, rewards and recognition may not be given. In traditional Asian-American families, children may be taught to suppress negative emotions and aggressive behaviors in the interest of group harmony (Chan, 1992).

From an early age, children whose families maintain their Asian cultural identity may be exposed to multiple caregivers. Mothers, grandmothers, older siblings, and other extended family members respond to the child's needs. This network of relationships sets the stage for the development of very strong family attachments (Chan, 1992).

NATIVE AMERICAN FAMILIES

It is difficult to talk about Native Americans as a monolithic group, because they represent over 300 tribes with distinct traditions and cultural patterns. Although our image of Native Americans living on reservations in the Plains states is reinforced by the media, more of these people live in cities. Native Americans have the lowest income, shortest life expectancy, and highest rates of alcoholism of any racial group in the United States. The effects of this poverty status include poor medical care, inadequate nutrition, and substandard housing—all factors that have the potential to disrupt parenting (Joe & Malach, 1992; Harjo, 1993).

The history of Native Americans has had a profound influence on child rearing. Until the mid-twentieth century, government efforts to assist this group disrupted families and cultural traditions (Harjo, 1993). Children were often taken from their families and educated in boarding schools in which Native American languages and traditions were not respected. Most children in foster care were in non-Native American homes. When these practices were discontinued, parents who had grown up without their families had lost some of their cultural identity and had few models for how to raise their own children.

Values and Beliefs

Many Native American tribes value harmony with nature and being part of a group. The meaning attached to the surrounding land may make it difficult for an individual or a family to relocate. Individual goals and autonomy are respected as long as they do not threaten the needs of the group. The spiritual side of humankind is considered an integral part of the culture, rather than existing in a separate religious institution (Joe & Maluch, 1992; Attneave, 1982). Native Americans are grounded in the present, but carry with them a respect for the traditions of the past. The transmission of culture often occurs through storytelling and tribal rituals.

Among many Native Americans, generosity is valued more than the accumulation of wealth. The cultural belief that it is important to help those in greater need may conflict with mainstream societal values focusing on competition and individual gain. The importance of sharing material goods is reflected in ceremonies, family gatherings, and day-to-day interactions (Attneave, 1982).

Professionals working among Native Americans note that child rearing is at the center of family life. Children are an integral part of the community and most social activities include the whole family. It is not uncommon for Native Americans, especially those on reservations, to live in multigenerational households (Joe & Malach, 1992). Because their culture values both age and life experience, Native American parents may seek child-rearing advice from older members of the community and tribal healers may be held in high regard (Attneave, 1982).

Parenting Practices

Native Americans respect the natural unfolding of human potential. They tend to believe that children's individuality is innate and that adults must enable children to become what they are destined to be. In some families, this belief leads to a child-rearing style described as "noninterference" (Attneave, 1982). In contrast with other cultures, Native American parents may envision their role as supporting, rather than forcing, development. Their noninterfering approach might be considered permissive or undisciplined by mainstream professionals. For example, some parents may not be overly concerned about eating and sleeping schedules, and they may allow young children to make their own decisions about school attendance and other daily activities. In comparison with other cultural groups, there is more of a tendency to let children learn from the consequences of their actions, rather than parental nagging. Shaming that invokes group needs may be used as a form of discipline, but physical punishment is not common (Attneave, 1982).

Extended family and friends are often actively involved in raising Native American children. These relationships provide security, affection, and multiple role models. Adults take on the responsibility of teaching same-sex children daily living skills and self-discipline. Grandparents may be primary caregivers and provide spiritual guidance. In some tribes, uncles provide most of the discipline so that the biological parents are free to engage in a more pleasure-oriented relationship with their offspring (Attneave, 1982).

Developmental milestones within various Native American communities may differ from those valued in the mainstream culture. For example, Native American parents may seem unconcerned about a child's progress in learning to sit or walk. Similarly, in some tribes language is of little concern until a child

TABLE 3-2. Developmental Milestones Across Cultures

Skill	Age Accomplished (in years)		
	White	African American	American Indian
Dress self	3.7	4.0	2.8
Do regular chores	6.1	6.3	5.4
Go downtown alone	13.5	12.8	10.6
Left alone in evening	14.4	13.6	9.2
Take care of younger sibling	13.1	12.9	9.9
Go on dates	16.4	16.5	15.7

Source: J.R. Joe & R.S. Malach (1992). Families with Native American roots. In E.W. Lynch & M.J. Hanson (eds.), Developing Cross-Cultural Competence: A Guide for Young Children and Their Families, (pp. 89–119). Brooks Publishing Co., P.O. Box 10624, Baltimore MD 21285–0624.

is at least three years old. Because these milestones are considered unimportant by some Native American parents, delays may go unnoticed. Some parents, however, will focus a great deal of attention on other milestones, such as the day a child is named or when a child first laughed (Joe & Maluch, 1992).

In traditional Native American families, children are encouraged to imitate adult behaviors, such as performing household chores and offering opinions on family matters. This practice fosters self-reliance at an early age. As noted in Table 3-2, Native American children assume responsibility for themselves in a number of developmental areas sooner than either Caucasian or African-American children (Joe & Malach, 1992).

STRUCTURAL DIVERSITY—GAY AND LESBIAN FAMILIES

Homosexual parents have been called "a subculture within a subculture" (Bigner & Jacobsen, 1989). Because of the stigma some segments of society attach to this status, it is difficult to determine the number of gay and lesbian parents raising children, but estimates range from 2 million to 8 million. These families are formed in a variety of ways. Most often children are born in the context of a heterosexual marriage before homosexuality is disclosed publicly or privately. A growing number of lesbian women, however, are choosing parenthood through artificial insemination, and a smaller number of gay men are becoming adoptive parents (Patterson, 1992).

Although there has been a considerable change in attitude about homosexuality and more openness with regard to same-sex relationships in our society, acceptance of this lifestyle has not been universal. One of the most controversial and emotional issues is the status of homosexual parents and their children. The following section reviews the literature on gay and lesbian parenting in an attempt to assess the ways in which this lifestyle influences the child-rearing process. Again, the empirical research base is limited, but autobiographical and clinical reports offer additional descriptive data. For example, April Martin (1993), a clinical psychologist and lesbian mother, has written an informative parenting handbook for homosexual parents based on in-depth interviews with fifty-seven families, insights gained in her role as a psychotherapist, and her own personal experiences. Similarly, a group of teachers interested in home-school communication interviewed gay and lesbian parents, their children's teachers, and school administrators (Casper, Schultz & Wickens, 1992). Although neither of these reports can be viewed as unbiased, they represent important attempts to pull together qualitative data on this topic from a variety of sources.

Homosexuality and Parenting

There is no consensus among gay and lesbian parents regarding the importance of disclosing or concealing their sexual orientation (Casper et al., 1992). Because of homophobia and discrimination, some gay parents do not reveal their sexual identities. They may fear that societal prejudices could cause them to lose custody or visitation rights. Pretending to be heterosexual and being dishonest with friends and family can be stressful for these parents.

Children's questions and observations about their unique families cannot be ignored. Some parents believe that asking children to keep their family structure a secret gives the negative message that the parental relationship is wrong (Casper et al., 1992). One study found that gay fathers find disclosure to their children more difficult than do lesbian mothers (Bozett, 1989). Box 3-3 offers suggestions for telling children about a parent's homosexuality.

In contrast with those who hide their sexual orientation, some homosexuals report that their parenting role forces them to be more open. Explanations may be necessary in dealing with babysitters, school officials, health professionals, and children's friends. This need to be public is especially important if two parents of the same gender are raising a child together and wish to have their equal parenting status recognized outside the family (Martin, 1993).

 Box 3-3 Guidelines for Disclosing Homosexuality to Children

Although disclosure of homosexuality might be difficult, parents and children stand to benefit if this information is imparted in an honest and sensitive manner. Jerry Bigner and Frederick Bozett (1990) offer the following guidelines for gay fathers. These suggestions, however, also seem appropriate for lesbian mothers.

1. *Come to terms with your own homosexuality before disclosing to children.* Parents who feel negative about their homosexuality or are ashamed of it are much more likely to have children who also react negatively.
2. *Children are never too young to be told.* They will absorb only as much as they are capable of understanding. Use words appropriate to the age of the child.
3. *Discuss it with children before they know or suspect.* When children discover a parent's sexual orientation by accident or from someone other than the parent, they are often upset that their parent did not trust them sufficiently to share the information with them.
4. *Inform, don't confess.* The disclosure need not be heavy or maudlin but positive and sincere. Informing in a simple, natural, and matter-of-fact manner when the parent is ready is more likely to foster acceptance by the child.
5. *Inform the children that relationships with them will not change as a result of disclosure.* Children whose parents were previously in heterosexual marriages may need reassurance that the parent is the same person as he or she was before.

Younger children may need reassurance that the parent will still be their parent.

6. *Be prepared for questions.* Some questions and possible answers are:
Why are you telling me this? Because my personal life is important, and I want to share it with you. I am not ashamed of being homosexual, and you shouldn't be ashamed of me either.
What does being gay or lesbian mean? It means being attracted to other people of the same gender so much that you might fall in love and express your love physically and sexually.
What makes a person homosexual? No one knows, although there are a lot of theories.
Will I be homosexual, too? You won't be homosexual just because I am. You will be whatever you are going to be.
Don't you like women (men)? I do like women (men) but I'm not physically and romantically attracted to them.

These suggestions are especially applicable when the parenting role began in the context of a heterosexual relationship. When a gay or lesbian couple chooses parenthood by pregnancy or adoption, the child is more likely to have grown up with knowledge of the parent's sexual orientation (Martin, 1993).

Source: J. Bigner & F. Bozett (1990). Parenting by gay fathers. In F. Bozett & M. Sussman (eds.), *Homosexuality and Family Relations.* Reprinted by permission of The Haworth Press, Inc.

Contextual factors affect parental decisions regarding disclosure. For example, it may be easier to be a parent who is publicly homosexual in a heterogeneous neighborhood that values diversity, than it would be in a more traditional neighborhood that is less tolerant of such differences. For men and women of color, racial and ethnic values may create either a hostile or an accepting context. Financial resources give gay and lesbian families choices, making it easier to live, work, and educate their children in supportive environments (Casper et al., 1992). A prevailing theme in this text is that parenting changes adult relationships, beliefs, and activities. The transition to parenthood for gay and lesbian couples is just beginning to be studied. Research findings suggest some similarities between heterosexual and homosexual couples in this regard—the relationship suffers when a child arrives, communication between the couple changes, sexual activity decreases, and careers may be disrupted (Stiglitz, 1990). A recent study on the division of labor among lesbian couples revealed that those with children are less egalitarian than those without children (Patterson, 1995).

Parenthood may also change the way in which the gay or lesbian couple is viewed by the outside world. Marriage creates a separate family unit for heterosexual couples, but the commitment between homosexual partners can be ignored by society until the couple has a child. Sometimes the parenting role bridges the gap between the homosexual and heterosexual worlds. Gays and lesbians who become parents may suddenly find themselves with more heterosexual friends with whom they share parenting concerns (Martin, 1993). Others report that their parenting role reconnects them with their families of origin in a more meaningful way (Casper et al., 1992).

Being considered "an unfit parent" by segments of the heterosexual world can make child rearing difficult for a homosexual parent. Gay and lesbian parents cannot always protect their children from prejudicial comments. Another concern is that positive portrayals of these families are lacking in the media. Homosexual parents may find that they must be particularly vigilant about how families are being discussed in school lessons (Martin, 1993; Casper et al., 1992).

Some of the typical sources of social support may be lacking for these nontraditional families. For example, extended families sometimes reject gay and lesbian partners, as well as the grandchildren being raised in homosexual families. In urban areas, social and political activism can be a source of support for homosexuals, but the parenting role often separates mothers and fathers from this network. Although homosexuality is opposed by some religions, many churches welcome gay and lesbian parents into their communities, providing an important source of support (Martin, 1993).

Studies comparing the parenting practices of homosexuals and heterosexuals reveal few differences. One study found that gay fathers tend to be stricter and use reasoning more often than heterosexual fathers (Bigner & Jacobsen, 1989). A study of lesbian mothers found that they tend to endorse less traditional sex-role socialization and emphasize a need to be accepting of diversity (Green, Mandel, Hotvedt, Gray, & Smith, 1986). Another comparative study reported that lesbian couples were better able to verbalize effective parenting skills, but noted that these results might be related to gender differences rather than to sexual orientation (Flaks, Ficher, Masterpasqua, & Joseph, 1995).

All of these studies share a common limitation—they are based on nonrepresentative samples that are primarily white, educated, and middle class.

Children of Gay and Lesbian Parents

Although being a same-sex couple or a homosexual single parent affects child rearing, there is no evidence that children's development is compromised by this context (Gottman, 1990; Patterson, 1992). Research has focused on three areas of concern: gender identity, sexual orientation, and social adjustment.

Gender identity for children of homosexual parents has not been found to be problematic. Both boys and girls seem content with their gender, but are notably less sex-typed in their behavior (Patterson, 1992). Studies of sexual orientation indicate that these children are no more likely to be homosexual than other children (Bailey, Bobrow, Wolfe, & Mikach, 1995), but they are more likely to experiment with same-sex relationships (Golombok & Tasker, 1996). A climate of acceptance within the family may also reduce fears of negative parental reactions for homosexual children (Martin, 1993).

The fear that children raised by homosexual parents will be psychologically vulnerable and have difficulties in social relationships has not been validated by research. A child's self-concept, moral judgment, and intelligence appear to be unaffected by parents' sexual orientation (Patterson, 1992). The best studies in this area use children in divorced heterosexual families as a comparison group, in order to separate the effects of divorce from the influence of having a homosexual parent.

Another concern is that the child will be teased and stigmatized because she or he is part of a family unit that is not accepted by many segments of society. It is true that children may feel ambivalent about coming from a nontraditional family (Martin, 1993). Adolescents who live with heterosexual mothers tend to keep a father's gay stepfamily a secret (Crosbie-Burnett & Helmbrecht, 1993). Clinicians have suggested that support groups of children from families with gay or lesbian parents might help children feel less isolated, although there is no conclusive evidence that this is true (Lewis, 1980; Patterson, 1992).

The age at which children learn of parental homosexuality may be important. Research findings in this area indicate that young children and older adolescents are better equipped to cope with the knowledge that their parents are gay or lesbian. Studies reveal that early adolescence is a particularly difficult time for children to deal with this revelation and this timing may adversely affect self-esteem (Huggins, 1989).

Public Policy

Attitudes about homosexual parents are sometimes reflected in court decisions and public policy. For example, when grandparents or a former spouse disapprove of a parent's homosexuality, child custody cases can become quite emotional. The outcome of these cases may depend more on the judge's beliefs and attitudes about homosexuality than on specifics of parenting capabilities (Pollack, 1990). There have been cases in which judges have awarded lesbian mothers custody on the condition that they not live in openly homosexual relationships. This restriction is probably not in the best interest of the parent or the child, because it removes from the child-rearing context an important source of social support. Lesbian mothers in stable relationships who can be open about their sexual orientation have been found to be psychologically healthier than those who hide their lesbian identity (Rand, Graham, Rawlings, 1982).

The parenting status of a nonbiological parent is generally not recognized by the law. When the couple separates, there is little legal recourse for nonbiological parents who wish to continue relationships with their children. It will be noted in Chapter 10 that this is also a problem for stepparents in heterosexual relationships.

To summarize, the research on gay and lesbian parenting offers no evidence that would support efforts to deny parenting rights and responsibilities solely on the basis of sexual orientation. Existing research is based on small, nonrandom samples, however. Most of the research participants have been Caucasian, middle-class and upper-class people with high levels of education, living in urban areas (Patterson, 1992). If future studies address these limitations, there will be more substantive information on which to base policy decisions and decide how best to be supportive of this type of parenting situation.

SUMMARY

- Parent-child interaction takes place in a variety of contexts, including different cultures and family structures. The values, beliefs, and behaviors that characterize a particular group will influence the parenting process, as will the way in which the group is perceived by other members of society.
- Cultural groups differ in their definitions of family, parenting goals, ideas about who is responsible for child rearing, expected developmental timetables, and disciplinary practices. While each of the groups discussed in this chapter has some distinctive characteristics related to parenting, there is also common ground. For example, African Americans, Latinos, Asian Americans, and Native Americans value cooperation, group loyalty and interdependence among family members. They also share a reliance on extended family and friends as a primary component of social support.
- There is considerable variability between people of the same culture or subculture—often determined by socioeconomic status and varying levels of acculturation. It is not surprising, therefore, that there are individual differences in parenting among those who share the same cultural identity.
- For culturally diverse families within the United States, the parenting process and the developmental pathways of adults and children are influenced by mainstream American society, by the ethnic or racial subgroup, and by their minority status. Biculturalism has been found to be an adaptive pattern, enabling parents and children to benefit from and succeed in two contexts simultaneously.
- With regard to homosexual parenting, the ambivalence with which people regard gay and lesbian parents introduces some unique stressors into the child-rearing process; however, the limited research in this area has

revealed few significant differences in child outcomes. The sexual orientation of parents appears to be a less important predictor of child development than the quality and content of family interactions.

- There is a general acceptance among those who study parenting that family diversity is an important variable; however, there are few empirical studies to support the theoretical model. Throughout this text, data on diverse family structures and ethnic groups are included whenever possible. When the data are lacking, efforts are made not to generalize beyond the populations studied. It is hoped that future research efforts will include families representative of different groups and, in doing so, provide the data necessary to expand our understanding of parenting processes.

PART TWO

Parenting the Developing Child

Transition to Parenthood

Becoming a parent for the first time is an exciting, yet often scary, process that involves many changes. Being responsible for the care of another human being twenty-four hours a day usually alters people's priorities in life. New parents often need to modify certain aspects of their previous lifestyles in order to meet the responsibilities of parenting. It may be as simple as taking a few extra minutes to gather the baby gear before going somewhere, or as extreme as having to give up a long-established routine, such as sleeping through the night without interruption. While some people easily adapt to having a baby, many experience some difficulty when making the adjustments required of them.

There are many diverse paths to parenthood, and many unique situations that may affect this experience positively or negatively; however, this chapter will focus on issues that are typically involved when becoming a parent for the first time. Unfortunately, research information in this area tends to be limited to largely white, middle-class, two-parent families. Certainly, there is a need for more culturally sensitive research studies. Information regarding people experiencing less typical circumstances upon entering parenthood can be found in other chapters. Chapter 10 discusses the challenges single people may encounter upon choosing parenthood, and Chapter 12 provides in-depth information regarding the potential risks of unplanned pregnancy and parenthood for teenagers.

Although the child's conception marks the biological beginnings, expectations and events that happen prior to that also affect the passage into parenthood (Goldberg, 1988). People prepare for parenthood before a pregnancy happens by exploring their desires to have children, trying to imagine what it would be like and how it would fit into their lives. The adjustment period following the birth of the baby is also important in determining the beginnings of parenthood. Expectations need to merge with the reality of parenting. In its broadest sense, the *transition to parenthood* includes the decisions leading up to pregnancy; the anticipation and preparation during the pregnancy itself; the labor, delivery, and birth; and the weeks of adjustment after the birth where people learn and practice parenting behaviors. This chapter will address the diverse experiences, both joyous and difficult, of new parents. In addition, factors influencing the transition to parenthood will be explored. Is the timing of parenthood an important factor? How does the infant's arrival affect the transition? A special focus will be placed on preparing and supporting parents during this time. In addition, ordinary parenting experiences that may challenge individuals to redefine themselves and their marital relationships within the context of the parenting role will be explored.

THE DECISION TO PARENT

Back in my day, we didn't decide one way or the other. Children either came along or they didn't. I told my daughter that she thinks about these things too much. You just can't predict what your life will be like regardless of whether or not you have kids. I'm glad I had my children before all these choices were available.

A 65-year-old "wannabe" grandma

The low rates of childlessness across cultures suggest that we accept parenthood as a normal part of adulthood (Callan, 1986). Historically, parenthood has been viewed as a developmental stage that affirms that a person has reached adult status (Hoffman & Levant, 1985). In the past, it was expected that all couples who were physically capable would have children. Some couples continue to hold these beliefs and do not give much thought to making a decision about having children; they assume that children will be a part of their future. But the availability of reliable contraception has given couples more choices about having children than ever before. Voluntary childlessness is now considered a viable life choice as opposed to being thought of as deviant, abnormal, or selfish. Today, the act of deciding whether to have children is part of an individual's growing awareness of the aging process, and contributes to the transition from childhood to adulthood (Lancaster, Altmann, Rossi, & Sherrod, 1987). Each person must decide whether parenthood is the best choice for him or her, knowing that the choice is final and irrevocable.

The issues involved in making this decision are complex. There is still a tremendous amount of pressure in our society for adults to become parents (Rossi, 1968; Somers, 1993). It is difficult to determine whether the desire to procreate is biologically programmed, if people are socialized to accept parenthood as a normal part of adulthood, or if it is a mixture of both (Callan, 1986). For most people parenthood is a lifetime commitment, and nurturing offspring often continues in some form or another until the parent's death (Lancaster, Altmann, Rossi, & Sherrod, 1987). The enormous responsibility of parenthood, as well as time and energy commitments, are major factors to be considered. How do people make a decision that has such far-reaching implications?

There is no clear-cut set of rules to follow when making the parenthood decision. Most people have strong gut-level feelings and emotions about whether or not they want to have children. From a rational perspective, one can assume that there is a set of rewards (positive compensations) and costs (losses incurred in the course of gaining something) associated with the decision to have a child (Campbell, Townes, & Beach, 1982). Individuals tend to make choices that maximize their rewards and minimize their costs. People must weigh the values and satisfactions children provide against the toll these responsibilities will take from other life goals, such as career advancement and leisure-time activities. These value-based decisions can only be considered within the context of cultural messages and direct experience (Michaels, 1988). It is helpful to begin the decision-making process by individually identifying current needs and beliefs regarding the importance of having children. When each person has explored these issues honestly, they can then be discussed between partners. Discussing personal values and priorities provides an opportunity for couples to map out how having children fits into their overall life plan. Individually and as a couple, people should explore the impact that pregnancy and parenting will have on them physically, socially, professionally, and economically (Pearson, 1990). The National Alliance for Optional Parenthood has compiled a list of thought-provoking questions that draw attention to some of the consequences of parenthood. A few of the most compelling questions to be discussed are included in Box 4-1.

The primary motivations for childbearing in both men and women center on opportunities to establish a close relationship with another human being and to actively participate in a child's development and education (Campbell, Townes, & Beach, 1982). While in some developing countries children represent economic gains, in our society parents anticipate psychological benefits from having children (Fawcett, 1988). Children may detract from the family's material well-being, and may impede the parents' ability to attain educational and vocational goals. It is interesting to note that people who are *voluntarily childless* recognize the benefits and satisfactions of having children, but do not rate them as outweighing the costs (Callan, 1986). To these people, benefits of adult-centered living are more significant than those of a child-centered lifestyle. Issues such as the irreversible nature of parenthood, and the lack of choice regarding the characteristics of the child are of great concern (Veevers, 1980). People who are childless by choice must be distinguished from those who decide that they want to be parents, but end up childless because of infertility problems. A discussion of issues pertaining to couples who experience infertility can be found later in this chapter.

People who choose to remain childless tend to be well educated, live in urban areas, marry late, work outside the home, and they are not, as a group, actively religious (The dilemmas of childlessness, *Time*, 1988). They also perceive that friends and relatives have rather negative stereotypes (such as "selfish," "hedonistic," and "irresponsible") about them based on their decision not to parent (Somers, 1993). Approximately one-third of the couples who are childless by choice make a deliberate decision before marriage and make their intention to remain childless part of the marriage contract (Veevers, 1980). Two-thirds of the people who ultimately decide not to have children remain

---

 Box 4-1 Am I Parent Material?

1. Could I handle a child and a job at the same time? Would I have time and energy for both?
2. Would I be ready to give up the freedom to do what I want, when I want?
3. Can I afford to support a child? Do I know how much it takes to raise a child?
4. Would a child change my educational plans?
5. Do I like doing things with children? Do I enjoy activities children can do?
6. Am I patient enough to deal with the noise and the confusion and the 24-hour-a-day responsibility? What kind of time and space do I need for myself?
7. How do I get along with my parents? What will I do to avoid the mistakes my parents made?
8. Does my partner want to have a child? Have we talked about our reasons?
9. Could we give a child a good home? Is our relationship a happy and strong one?
10. Do my partner and I understand each other's feelings about religion, work, family, child raising, future goals? Do we feel pretty much the same way? Will children fit into these feelings, hopes, and plans?

These questions were selected from a paper prepared by Carole Goldman, Executive Director of the National Organization for Non-Parents (NON), 806 Reisterstown Road, Baltimore, MD, 21208.

childless through a series of decisions to postpone having children until a future time that never comes. At first, the postponement is planned for a definite period of time, and then becomes indefinite as couples continue to put off having a child until they can "afford it," or until they "feel more ready." Serious deliberation about the pros and cons of parenthood usually follows until an implicit decision to be permanently childless is reached. About half of these couples consider permanent sterilization (Veevers, 1980).

Perhaps some of the variability in the "transition to parenthood" experience can be explained by the degree of planning for the pregnancy, since there seem to be differences between couples who plan to have a child and those who experience unplanned pregnancies. For some couples, the transition to parenthood begins with the decision to have a baby. These couples may begin anticipating and adapting to lifestyle changes associated with having a baby months before a pregnancy is achieved (Mebert, 1991). This could certainly influence how prepared and ready these parents are for the consequences of their actions. Couples who experience unplanned pregnancies may have to first adjust to the idea of the pregnancy before being able to make necessary lifestyle changes in preparation for the baby. Some couples may take more time to adjust than others, and those have an unrealistic time constraint, as they are already at various stages of pregnancy when they begin the process. The decision to parent is a serious undertaking, even for those who freely choose it. If parenting is thrust upon someone without choice, the parent-child relationship may be at risk, and special help may be needed before successful adjustment can be achieved (see Chapter 12 for further discussion of this topic).

THE TIMING OF PARENTHOOD

> Some people tell me to have my children when I'm young, so I have enough energy to enjoy them and I'm not so set in my ways that the change is too hard. Others say that older parents are more patient, and that my husband and I should travel and have fun first. Add in money and career considerations, and deciding when it's the best time to have children is an impossible task.
>
> *A 23-year-old woman*

The trend since the early 1960s in the United States has been to delay parenthood (Wilkie, 1981). About one-third of first births occur in women twenty-five years of age and older. Changes in the status of women in our society seem to coincide with delaying parenthood, particularly for women with higher levels of educational attainment who participate in the work force. Education at the time of marriage is the most important predictor of maternal age at first birth (Rindfus & St. John, 1983). The timing of a woman's first child is important because it can set the stage for other roles and life events. Since motherhood involves a substantial commitment of time and resources, having children at a younger age may have a negative impact on the goals and attainments of the mother. Research suggests that women who delay childbearing have more education, higher incomes, more career commitments, and more stable marriages than their younger counterparts (Roosa, 1988). Despite these demographic differences, however, Roosa (1988) found no differences between the delayed and younger childbearers with regard to marital adjustment and self-esteem during the transition to parenthood.

The timing of fatherhood can make a significant difference in a man's life. If a man does not feel ready to be a father, his parenting abilities may be compromised. Several factors that contribute to emotional readiness for fatherhood in new fathers have been identified by May (1982). First, the man's feeling about the stability of the couple's relationship is important. Men desire a loving, committed, supportive, and stable relationship before introducing a child into the situation. Second, a feeling of relative financial security is a major consideration, which is easily understood given the man's historical responsibility as provider. Last, men reported that they must have a sense that they have completed the childless part of their lives. They need to feel that they have met some of their life goals before starting a family. It is also important for them to believe that a child will not be totally incompatible with or prohibit other life plans and expectations. Recent research on the timing of fatherhood (Cooney, Pedersen, Indelicato, & Palkovitz, 1993) suggests that men who delay parenthood are more likely to be highly involved with their children. Perhaps the competing demands of early career pressures interfere with fatherhood for younger men.

Demographic differences between younger parents and those who delay parenthood may influence parenting (Heuvel, 1988). Because they have had more time for educational and career pursuits, financial stresses are often less of a problem for those who delay parenthood. Parents who are older at the birth of their first child will have had more time to mature and develop emotionally, which may translate into more effective and consistent discipline and closer family relationships. The disadvantages of later parenthood may include lower energy levels (it is physically challenging to keep up with young children) and more difficulty in making lifestyle changes (such as getting less sleep and leisure time, and having an unpredictable schedule). It may be easier for younger people to make lifestyle adjustments, since most people find it difficult to change long-standing patterns of behavior (Kach & McGhee, 1982).

For some adults, the *biological time clock* (the fertility deadline of the female) is the factor that precipitates a reassessment of the parenthood decision (Soloway & Smith, 1987). The biological constraints of fertility force couples to reevaluate their careers, financial security, educational goals, and marital commitment with regard to having a child. Instead of feeling that they have plenty of time to do it all, couples begin to perceive that time is running out. They realize that they must choose one way or another, or lose the opportunity to choose.

PREGNANCY

Pregnancy begins when an egg is fertilized by a sperm. The average pregnancy lasts approximately 266 days from the date of conception, or 280 days

(40 weeks) from the first day of the woman's last menstrual period. Conception signals the beginning of a series of physical and emotional changes in the expectant woman. Pregnancy is also a time of social change, where relationships with other people must be redefined in light of the coming baby. The basic physical changes that occur during pregnancy, as well as what steps can be taken in planning for a healthy baby, are addressed. In addition, the important social and emotional changes that both women and men experience as they ready themselves for parenthood are explored.

Physical Changes in Pregnancy

Although some women realize they are pregnant from the moment of conception on, most women are unaware of the pregnancy during the early weeks. The first sign of pregnancy is usually a missed menstrual period, although some women report breast changes (such as tenderness, darkened nipples, or a size increase) before the pregnancy is confirmed (Kitzinger, 1985). During the first two weeks after conception, the egg and sperm unite and travel through the fallopian tube into the uterus and implant in the uterine lining. The *placenta* forms to provide food and oxygen, and to excrete wastes. The *umbilical cord* connects the placenta with the developing organism and enables the nutrient and waste exchanges to take place.

The third through the seventh week after conception is a particularly crucial stage of prenatal development during which all of the major organ systems and body parts are formed. As cells begin to differentiate or specialize, they take on specific roles and group together to form organs. Each organ has a critical period in which it develops, and a specific time frame for doing so. During this period of rapid growth, the organism is most susceptible to environmentally produced defects. Unfortunately, many women are not even aware that they are pregnant until this stage is over. Prenatal development from eight weeks until birth is a time of less dramatic structural change. The cells in each organ mature, grow, and begin to function. The "details" such as eyelids, fingernails, and hair develop, and the fetus grows and fills out in preparation for birth.

Most people think of pregnancy in terms of trimesters, or three-month intervals. During the *first trimester,* women experience early signs of pregnancy, which may include tiredness and nausea. Most women experience a decrease in their energy levels at this time, and feel the need for naps. Nausea, although rarely serious, can be very troublesome. It can be managed during pregnancy by eating a few crackers before rising in the morning, getting up slowly, consuming small frequent meals, drinking fluids between rather than with meals, eating lightly seasoned foods, avoiding greasy and fried foods, and allowing plenty of fresh air to circulate when sleeping (Worthington, 1979).

The *second trimester* is often the most pleasant time of pregnancy, since nausea and tiredness lessen and the discomforts of pregnancy associated with getting bigger have not yet arrived. Because they are not as tired or sick as they were in the first trimester, many women experience an increase in energy that allows them to do more tasks and feel more productive. It is also an exciting time because the woman begins to "show" and to feel the fetus move (Kitzinger, 1985).

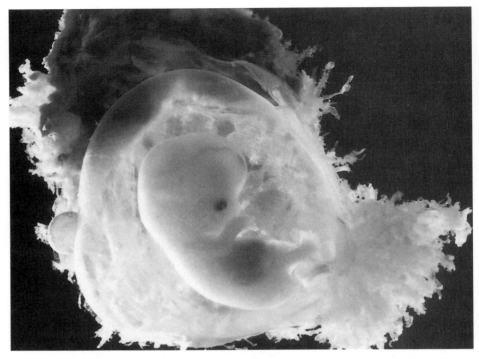

The third through seventh week after conception is a particularly crucial stage of
prenatal development when the the organism is highly susceptible.
(*Courtesy of Arthur Bowden/Henry Ford Hospital*)

During the *third trimester,* women begin to get heavier, which again robs
them of their energy. Many women experience physical changes, such as back-
aches, leg cramps, varicose veins, hemorrhoids, bladder infections, digestive
disturbances, and shortness of breath. Good posture, exercise, properly fitting
clothes and shoes, and adequate rest can reduce some of the discomforts of
pregnancy (Kitzinger, 1985).

Planning for a Healthy Baby

Parental behaviors that may affect a child's development begin long before the
birth process takes place. There are several things a couple can do prior to getting pregnant in order to plan for a healthy baby. First, they must acquaint
themselves with the health issues related to pregnancy, including both an
awareness of family genetic and medical history, and an examination of current lifestyle habits (Pearson, 1990). Second, they must become familiar with
prenatal tests and technologies so that they are well informed about their prenatal care and options. Last, they must increase their awareness of how to create a healthy prenatal environment.

Everyone wants to have a normal, healthy baby; however, parents have
varying degrees of control over many factors. Some birth defects happen
because they are beyond human prevention. Others are preventable, and can

be eliminated by educating pregnant women to avoid harmful substances (Kelley-Buchanan, 1988). A *teratogen* is any drug, chemical, pollutant, infection, physical agent, or material physical state (like diabetes) that can interfere with normal development during the prenatal period. The timing and amount of exposure to any of these potential risk factors is crucial. In the early weeks of pregnancy, for example, there seems to be an "all-or-none" phenomenon. Exposure to substances will either have no effect and the organism will not be harmed, or it will have a total effect, resulting in death and spontaneous abortion (also known as miscarriage). The organism is most vulnerable to defects during the formation of major organ systems and body parts, although a fetus can be harmed at any time during the prenatal period.

Genetic and Medical Issues

There are many genetic and medical factors to consider when planning for a healthy baby. Parental awareness of resources to address the complexity of potential genetic and medical problems is essential. Consultations with physicians or genetic counselors, as well as a knowledge of each family's medical history, are helpful steps toward planning for a healthy child. For example, some genetic diseases (such as Tay-Sachs disease) are hereditary, so a family's medical history is important. Similarly, knowledge regarding maternal intake of DES (a synthetic hormone believed to prevent miscarriages, which was widely prescribed in the late 1940s and early 1950s) in either family is important because DES has been linked with a higher incidence of cervical cancer and cervical problems in daughters and fertility problems in sons. The woman's personal history of disease is also essential, especially with regard to rubella (also known as German measles). The rubella virus is a mild childhood disease, but if a pregnant woman passes it to her fetus, it can cause hearing, heart, and skeletal problems and sometimes retardation. Recollections are often inaccurate, and a simple blood test can determine whether a person has had the disease. A vaccine is available and can be given safely up to several months before a pregnancy is planned.

Blood disease can be a potential problem when there is incompatibility between the mother and baby (Simkin, Whalley, & Keppler, 1984). People either have the Rh factor in their blood and are Rhesus positive (Rh+), or the Rh factor is not present and they are Rhesus negative (Rh–). If the mother is Rh– and the father is Rh+, the baby can be either. If the baby happens to be Rh+, he or she may develop a condition called *Rh disease.* There is a chance that the mother's body (after a first pregnancy) may produce antibodies that attack any leakage of red blood cells from the fetus into her circulation. In effect, the mother's antibodies attempt to destroy the fetus, which it rejects as a foreign substance. This may result in brain damage, heart failure, spontaneous abortion, or stillbirth. There are treatments available for this condition, including the intramuscular injection of a substance called RHOGAM to an Rh– mother, which avert problems with the antibodies. Babies who already have Rh disease can sometimes be treated with blood transfusions. But the best defense is awareness and preparation.

It is often difficult to obtain accurate information regarding the safety of prescription drugs for use with pregnant women. Thalidomide, a popular sedative used in the late 1950s and early 1960s, was taken by pregnant women to reduce nausea after research conducted on rats and human adults showed no ill effects. Unfortunately, the drug had a devastating impact on the human embryo (Vorhees & Mollnow, 1987). It has since been banned, but not before 8,000 babies were born with missing or deformed limbs, a direct effect of the drug. It is important to avoid many common antibiotics and painkillers during pregnancy because of their negative effects on the fetus. Therefore, when women get sick or hurt during pregnancy and an antibiotic or painkiller is essential to the mother's health, it is important to consult with a physician who is aware of the pregnancy to make sure the safest drugs available can be used.

Lifestyle Issues

Lifestyle habits may have a great impact on health and merit consideration prior to conception. Sexually transmitted diseases can be passed on to the fetus during pregnancy. The effects of many drugs are unknown, while others have been shown to be harmful to the developing fetus. In particular, alcohol and nicotine use during pregnancy will be discussed. Box 4-2 contains a partial list of risky substances that are best avoided during pregnancy. More information is becoming available as researchers work to discover the effects of certain drugs during pregnancy. For example, about 11 percent of babies born in the United States are born addicted to mood changing drugs such as heroin or cocaine. Researchers are currently studying the process of drug withdrawal, as well as other potentially negative long-term effects on the development of these children.

Sexually transmitted diseases (STDs) such as chlamydia, gonorrhea, syphilis, genital herpes, and AIDS can all be passed on to the fetus either by crossing the placenta or delivery through an infected birth canal. There is much variability in STDs and their detection, treatability, and possible negative effects on the developing fetus. Tests are available to determine the presence of some, but not all, of these diseases. Some STDs are treatable, some are not. Some have more serious effects at certain points in prenatal development than at other times. For example, a syphilis test is routinely done as a part of blood analysis during pregnancy. If the disease is diagnosed and treated before the fourth month of pregnancy, the fetus will not develop the disease (Hyde, 1990), preventing possible blindness and central nervous system damage. Even if there is no cure for an STD, there may be options available to prevent the disease from being transmitted to the fetus. For example, diseases that are passed on through the birth canal, such as genital herpes, can be avoided by performing a Cesarean section, where the baby is removed through the mother's abdomen.

The use of common drugs such as alcohol and nicotine during pregnancy is important to discuss because they are legal and accepted in our society. However, there is no safe minimal dosage for the intake of *alcohol* during pregnancy (Aaronson & MacNee, 1989), making abstinence the healthiest choice. Alcohol passes through the placenta almost immediately, entering the bloodstream of the fetus and potentially harming the fetal brain. Developmental outcomes are influenced by the frequency, timing, and quantity of alcohol involved. Even moderate social drinking may harm the fetus. If the fetus is

Box 4-2 Risky Substances During Pregnancy

alcohol a depressant drug. A number of alcohol-related birth defects have been identified. Heavy drinking can cause fetal alcohol syndrome (FAS), which is the third most commonly recognized cause of mental retardation. Lesser amounts of alcohol can also damage the fetus, depending upon the timing, frequency, and amount of alcohol used in conjunction with the individual metabolism of the person involved. There is no time during pregnancy when drinking is without some potential risk.

amphetamines stimulant and appetite-suppressant drugs. There is some evidence that amphetamine-addicted mothers have a higher incidence of pregnancy and obstetric complications, including bleeding after delivery and premature births. In addition to the complications already mentioned, women using the illegal drug methamphetamine had a higher incidence of infants with withdrawal symptoms, such as irritability, tremors, drowsiness, and poor feeding.

cigarette smoking refers to nicotine intake. The best-known consequence of smoking during pregnancy is the increased incidence of low birth weight, which makes an infant more likely to have medical complications. In addition, smoking is related to more premature deliveries, placental complications, bleeding disorders, miscarriages, and stillbirths.

cocaine a stimulant drug that produces an intense euphoric high. A common form of this drug is "crack." Risks include birth defects, growth retardation, sudden infant death syndrome, miscarriage, premature labor and delivery, and behavioral disturbances in the newborn period.

codeine a narcotic analgesic used to relieve moderate pain; a popular suppressive in cough syrups. It can become habit-forming with prolonged use, and evidence suggests that it can be addictive to the unborn baby as well.

heroin a narcotic that can relieve severe pain, but is used for its ability to elevate mood, induce euphoria, provide sedation, and permit sleep. Prolonged use results in physical and psychological dependence. Mothers addicted to heroin have increased rates of fetal distress, stillbirths, premature births, and illness and death in newborns. Newborns experience withdrawal symptoms characterized by a disturbed nervous system, including irritability, trembling, increased muscle tone, high-pitched crying, weak sucking, and frantic hand-to-mouth movements.

lithium an antipsychotic drug used to treat an illness called manic-depressive illness. Lithium use is associated with a higher risk of infant heart defects.

marijuana a recreational drug with THC as the psychoactive component. The evidence regarding marijuana use during pregnancy is inconclusive, largely because marijuana users often also smoke cigarettes and drink alcohol, making it difficult to sort out the effects of each substance. Hazardous labor (either prolonged and difficult or unexpectedly quick) occurs more frequently in women who smoke marijuana at least once a month during pregnancy. And smoking anything affects the functioning of the placenta, letting less oxygen and fewer nutritional substances reach the baby.

PCP a hallucinogenic drug usually smoked with tobacco or marijuana. The effect of PCP on the fetus is largely unknown at this time, although withdrawal-like symptoms have been reported in newborns of women who used PCP during pregnancy.

salicylates (aspirin) used to relieve moderate pain, reduce fever, and control inflammation. The risk of bleeding is the primary reason use of this drug is discouraged in the latter months of pregnancy. Salicylates interfere with the ability of the blood to clot, which prolongs bleeding time. Continuous high doses of aspirin are associated with prolonged labor and an increase in blood loss at delivery.

streptomycin used to treat tuberculosis. It can cause damage to hearing and balance, with hearing deficits ranging from minor high-frequency losses to total deafness.

sulfonamides anti-infective drugs commonly prescribed to treat urinary infections. This drug is discouraged in the latter weeks of pregnancy because it may raise the amount of bilirubin and contribute to newborn jaundice.

tetracyclines antibiotics used to treat a variety of bacterial infections. Exposure during pregnancy stains the developing teeth a yellow color, which can become brown or grayish brown when exposed to light. It is suspected, but not yet proven, that these teeth are then more susceptible to decay.

Adapted from: Kelley-Buchanan, C. (1988). *Peace of mind during pregnancy: An A-Z guide to the substances that could affect your unborn baby.* New York: Dell Publishing.

severely affected by the alcohol intake, permanent damage can occur and the baby may be born with FAS, Fetal Alcohol Syndrome. FAS consists of developmental abnormalities that may include small body and head size, heart and kidney problems, cognitive impairment, and motor retardation.

Nicotine from smoking passes to the fetus, speeding up the heart rate, interrupting respiratory movements, and interfering with the efficiency of the placenta. Smokers have twice as many premature deliveries, more miscarriages, and more stillborn babies as do nonsmokers (Kelley-Buchanan, 1988). Babies born to mothers who smoke are usually smaller and have more heart abnormalities. Smoking may contribute to structural abnormalities in the placenta (thereby reducing the flow of blood and nutrients), as well as raising the amount of carbon monoxide concentration (which may promote central nervous system damage and low birthweight) (Aaronson & MacNee, 1989). Although it has not yet been proven, some researchers are currently studying their belief that maternal smoking can lead to long-term difficulties in school performance. Results from research studies about the effects of secondhand smoke on the fetus are not yet available. However, children of smokers have higher rates of Sudden Infant Death Syndrome (SIDS), pneumonia, and bronchitis (Kelley-Buchanan, 1988).

Prenatal Technology

Couples have a variety of prenatal tests and technological advances available to aid in prenatal care. Even when both partners are healthy, there are still no guarantees that the baby will be healthy. It is not unusual for both men and women to worry about whether their baby is normal (Kitzinger, 1985). Many pregnant couples have fears that the baby will be deformed. Although many diseases and conditions are not detectable prenatally, two methods of prenatal diagnosis are commonly available to screen for some genetic and physical abnormalities. *Sonogram*, also known as ultrasound, uses high-frequency sound waves to outline the shape of the fetus. It can reveal anencephaly (an absence of part or all of the brain), hydrocephaly (fluid on the brain), body malformations, and kidney diseases. It is also used to detect multiple births and the position of the placenta. *Amniocentesis* is a procedure in which amniotic fluid is withdrawn through the abdominal wall by means of a syringe so that the fluid can be analyzed. Some chromosomal abnormalities and genetic conditions can be detected, such as spina bifida and Down's syndrome; however, there are no indications as to the severity of the condition. This technique also reveals the sex of the child. Because there is a small risk of miscarriage (1 in 200), this procedure is usually reserved for those who have an above-average chance of having an abnormal child. It is offered to all women over 35 years of age and those with a genetic history that suggests further examination. Sonograms can be performed throughout the pregnancy, but the timing of amniocentesis must be very close to the fifteenth week of pregnancy.

Prenatal Health

Some of the issues involved in planning for a healthy baby have been explored, most of which involve avoiding certain toxic substances or habits.

But there are also many positive steps people can take to create a healthy prenatal environment. The first step deals with *exercise.* The physical and mental
benefits of exercise in general also apply during pregnancy. However, women
who are sedentary, or have not done aerobic exercises before becoming pregnant are not advised to begin during pregnancy (Novak, 1990). Specific guidelines or restrictions can be determined by consulting with an obstetrician. Of
course, if any pain or discomfort should occur during exercise, the expectant
mother should stop immediately.

An important part of a healthy pregnancy involves *being well nourished.*
Eating moderate amounts from each of the major food groups and minimizing
fat intake are healthy steps for everyone to take. But pregnancy is a particularly important time to be concerned with nutrition, since poor eating habits in
the mother can result in premature delivery, stillbirths, mental retardation, and
a host of other long-term negative consequences. In addition, prenatal vitamin
supplements (especially for iron) are recommended. Making changes that
ensure better nutrition during pregnancy are also advantageous after the baby
is born, since parents are models for their children's eating habits.

Exercise is one way to help create a healthy prenatal
environment.
(*Hazel Hankin/Stock, Boston*)

Other tips for a healthy pregnancy include getting *plenty of rest* and sleep, *visiting the doctor* at regular intervals throughout the pregnancy, and taking care of *dental needs*. In times past, people believed a woman would lose one tooth for every child she bore. Although teeth are more prone to decay and gum infections are more frequent during pregnancy, dental problems can easily be prevented with regular dental hygiene and checkups.

Emotional Aspects of Pregnancy

> The first time I felt the baby move, I cried. It was just the slightest little flutter of movement, but I knew that there truly was a baby growing inside me. Somehow that meant more in terms of the reality of becoming a parent than anything else. Every time I feel movement, I'm reminded that a separate little being depends on me. Sometimes it makes me happy, other times I feel overwhelmed, but it always gets my attention.
>
> *A mother-to-be*

Mothers

Changing hormones within a woman's body during pregnancy tend to accentuate emotions. Women may cry more, from both happiness and sadness. Many women feel a deep sense of fulfillment when they are pregnant. Carrying a child makes them feel more alive and important than they ever have before. Men may also feel off balance emotionally when facing impending parenthood. Conflicting emotional highs and lows are common for parents-to-be during pregnancy. Finding out about a pregnancy can create a range of emotional reactions, from great joy to fear. Expecting a child can bring much happiness, but with the privilege come many responsibilities and changes that can lead to doubts and anxieties. It is completely normal for men and women to feel some ambivalence about a pregnancy, even if it is planned and wanted (Stemp, Turner, & Noh, 1986). Most couples experience some stress during pregnancy, and it is natural for them to express worries and concerns about a number of topics (Kitzinger, 1985).

Women face many changes related to the impending role of motherhood that may cause them concern emotionally. Many women experience moments of doubt about whether they will be good mothers. Some worry about their changing physical appearance, since this publicly represents the result of their most intimate relationship. Society's emphasis on thinness contributes to this problem; the discrepancy between pregnancy and the American ideal of how women should look can be upsetting. Often, women are concerned that their partners will not find them sexually attractive as the pregnancy progresses. It is also quite common for women to have apprehensions about the birthing process—fearing pain, medical procedures, the hospital environment, and the loss of control and autonomy.

Fathers

Men also face emotional challenges during pregnancy. They experience some of the same doubts and misgivings that women do about what kinds of parents they will be or whether they will be able to adjust to changes in their marriage. Many men wonder how they will balance their family life with their work life (Fein, 1976). Most have little exposure to role models of good fathers with successful careers, and very few opportunities to discuss these issues with other men. Typically, men report receiving little emotional support during pregnancy. In addition, men often feel neglected because of the attention given to the future mothers. It is also more difficult for a man to feel involved with the baby, since it is not growing inside him. As one father-to-be points out, "My wife has no chance to forget that she is going to have a baby. She feels it physically when it moves, and people notice and talk to her about how she's feeling and when she's due. Sometimes I go all day without thinking about it because there aren't those constant reminders."

The Marital Relationship

Couples must work together to make adjustments during pregnancy. Relationship changes can influence the emotional climate of the pregnancy itself. Communication, affection, and the distribution of power within the relationship (especially regarding decision making) are important markers of a woman's satisfaction with her pregnancy experience (Gladieux, 1978). Pregnancy can be a special time for couples to further develop their communication skills, sharing their worries and joys. Growing together during pregnancy and accepting the changes in each partner as they begin to assume their new roles as mother and father are important tasks in preparing for parenthood. The best predictor of postpartum marital adjustment for both wives and husbands is their level of marital adjustment during pregnancy (Wallace & Gotlib, 1990).

There are many exciting opportunities to share as a couple in preparation for parenthood. Being able to feel the baby move or hear the heartbeat are two joyous milestones. Choosing a name for the baby can spark many intimate discussions. Some couples enjoy keeping the name a shared secret, while others revel in telling close friends and relatives well in advance of the birth. Many tasks need to be finished before the baby's arrival. Expectant parents often find pleasure in preparing the baby's room together, and delight in shopping for clothes and other baby necessities. Most of all, they receive great emotional satisfaction in imagining what the baby will be like, and what they will be like as parents.

BIRTH

Birthing practices are influenced by social and cultural contexts, so they change throughout history (Haire, 1991). Forty years ago, arbitrary time limits were set for labor and delivery. Women about to give birth were moved from the labor room to the delivery room to make things easier for the medical staff. Mothers-to-be were automatically sedated and strapped flat on their backs. Many experienced overwhelming fear, and had no idea what was going to be happening to them. Fathers-to-be were expected to pace nervously in the waiting room and bide their time. Since then, the ideas of Dr. Grantly Dick-Read (in the 1950s) and Dr. Ferdinand Lamaze (in the 1960s) became progressively more developed and more popular in the United States. By the mid 1970s, there was a demand on the part of consumers to "humanize" birth because it was too medically oriented (DeVries, 1988). A movement began to eliminate the clinical isolation that used to accompany childbirth in the hospital. The focus shifted from the product of birth (the baby) to the experience of birth. Options such as birthing rooms, prepared childbirth classes, and the participation of fathers in the birth itself became acceptable parts of the process.

The foundation of all the changes in childbirth practices is "freedom of choice based on knowledge of alternatives" (Booth, 1989, p. 25). It is important to continue to focus on emphasizing the individual needs of women at this time, depending on their values and wishes. Not all women choose the option of taking childbirth classes or having their husbands present at the birth. In fact, there are indications that working-class and middle-class women may have different attitudes and needs during pregnancy and childbirth. One study (Nelson, 1983) suggested that working-class women had favorable attitudes toward interventions that made the birth process quicker and less painful, while their middle-class counterparts were more favorable toward birthing experiences that were free from medical and technological intervention. The important point is that women have options to choose from that are not based on a doctor's wishes, or one group of women's wishes. The choices should come from the women themselves.

Prepared Childbirth Classes

> The smartest thing we did during the pregnancy was to take childbirth classes. They helped my wife feel less afraid of the actual birth and got me more involved and informed. But best of all, we met some people with whom we became friends, who were trying to cope with all this just like we were. And now, when we're having a hard time with the baby, we can support each other. We can visit each other and it doesn't matter if we look awful and the house is a mess. They know exactly where we're coming from.
>
> *A new father*

Prepared (or natural) childbirth classes emphasize educated choice and forethought. The goals are to humanize the birth experience in a hospital setting, to educate the expectant mother and father about the birth process, and to provide group support through sharing with other pregnant women or couples. The rationale of these classes is that people who understand what is happening, can anticipate what is coming, and are psychologically and physiologically ready will have a more enjoyable childbirth experience. The classes usually meet once a week for six to eight weeks, beginning in the seventh month of pregnancy. The curriculum varies, but usually focuses on the physical facts of labor and childbirth, exercises to get the body ready to give birth, and the techniques of relaxation, controlled breathing, concentration, and visualization to manage labor.

It is wise to be selective when choosing a course so that it will best suit individual needs. There is an unfortunate perception in some classes that women should try to "achieve" a perfect birth, putting pressure on the woman to function in unrealistic ways. This often results in feelings of failure

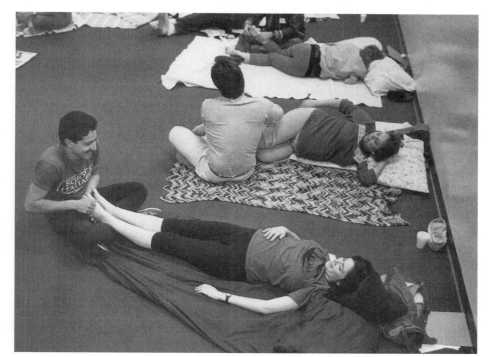

Prepared childbirth classes provide group support, as well as information about the
birthing process.
(*Elizabeth Crews/Stock, Boston*)

and unmet expectations after the labor and delivery. Childbirth is not an
Olympic event, where women are judged on their performance. Mothers
can't "fail." Each labor and birth is unique and experienced differently by different women. Sometimes medical needs must take precedence over plans
during the birthing situation. The goal is for both mother and baby to be
healthy.

There are two common misconceptions about natural childbirth. First,
being informed about birthing techniques does not mean childbirth will be
painless (it won't). Second, taking a course in natural childbirth does not prohibit the use of medication and drugs during the childbirth experience if the
woman desires it. Natural childbirth preparation simply gives her more tools
to use as an alternative to, or in conjunction with, medication. Since many
anesthetics also reduce the availability of oxygen to the fetus (Brackbill, 1979),
and may have adverse effects on the interactions between parents and infants
postpartum (Hollenbeck, Gewirtz, Sebris, & Scanlon, 1984), most preparation
classes give special attention to information about birthing drugs that have
fewer deleterious effects on the infant's health and interactions. Information
about various medications used in childbirth can be found in Box 4-3.

A woman usually chooses a partner to be her support person during the
pregnancy and birth. Most commonly, this is the father of the baby, but it can
also be a friend, relative, or paid professional. The support person attends

classes with the mother so that he or she will be prepared to deal with the changing needs and moods of the woman through labor and delivery. Women who have a supportive mate during pregnancy and delivery tend to view their birth experience more positively (Mercer, Hackley, & Bostrom, 1983).

 ## Box 4-3 Medications for Childbirth

Childbirth is pain with a purpose, and is qualitatively different from the pain of injury. Prepared childbirth classes give the woman tools, such as concentration, relaxation, breathing techniques, and visualization to use in controlling the pain. However, the amount of pain experienced by women in childbirth varies considerably, and endurance of extreme discomfort is not a virtue or a goal. All drugs for pain relief in labor pass through the mother's bloodstream to the baby, and some affect the baby more than others. It is important to understand how each type of medication works so that informed decisions can be made. There are basically three choices—tranquilizers, analgesics, and anesthetics.

1. *Tranquilizers*

Tranquilizers are used to make people relax and to lower their blood pressure. Tranquilizers tend to make the baby limp and floppy at birth, slow to suck, and may interfere with the newborn's temperature control. During labor, tranquilizers can change the pattern of the baby's heart rate. Mothers taking tranquilizers often suffer amnesia and cannot recall the labor and delivery. Common names of tranquilizers are diazepam and Valium. They are sometimes combined with analgesics, such as "twilight sleep."

2. *Analgesics*

Analgesics are drugs that provide pain relief without causing a total loss of feeling or consciousness. They lessen discomfort during particularly intense contractions, and may allow the woman to relax enough to sleep between contractions. The most widely used analgesic in labor is the narcotic Demerol. Some women like the slightly drunk, woozy effects of the drug, but others feel out of control. A common side effect is nausea. Other side effects of narcotic analgesics are emotional depression, lowered rates of respiration and heartbeat, and vomiting.

3. *Anesthetics*

Anesthetics are drugs that deaden sensation. *General anesthetics* may put a person completely to sleep. Others may numb one region of the body. The most common regional anesthetic used today is the *epidural.* The anesthesiologist places a needle holding a thin flexible tube into the woman's lower back. The needle is removed and the anesthetic is supplied through the tube as needed. Some women experience problems pushing the baby out, since muscle control is partially affected. There are very few problems with this procedure when it is administered by a trained anesthesiologist. Because it is difficult to administer, however, it may be inadvertently injected in the wrong location, causing the woman to have difficulty breathing and develop severe headaches after the birth. A second regional anesthetic is the *spinal.* This is usually given in one fast-acting dose right before delivery. It causes a loss of all muscle control in the lower body. Mothers often need to lie flat for eight hours after delivery to avoid a postspinal headache. There are also *local* anesthetics, which are specific to one area of the body. Local anesthetics during childbirth include the paracervical block, which deadens the area around the cervix, and the pudendal block, which numbs the nerves in the perineum right at full dilation before an episiotomy is given. Paracervical blocks are no longer as common, since the baby's heart rate is immediately affected and may slow to dangerous levels.

The information regarding medications during labor changes very quickly as new medications and innovations become available. Always check with a medical professional for updates.

Adapted from: Kitzinger, S. (1985). *The complete book of pregnancy and childbirth.* New York: Alfred A. Knopf.

Pollycove, R. & Corrigan, T. (1991). *The birth book.* San Bruno, CA: Krames Communications.

Prepared childbirth classes have the potential to improve parents' birthing experiences in a number of different ways. Not only do they prepare people for the physical and emotional aspects of birth, but they can also provide a group of people to interact and share with before and after the birth of the baby. This might be especially helpful for those who live far away from their extended families. Couples are often pleased with their training for childbirth, but they need information beyond what is typically offered in these classes (Wente & Crockenberg, 1976). Childbirth classes are not parenting classes, and very few give information about what to do after the baby comes. The need for parenting classes when the reality of parenthood begins is an issue that will be revisited later in this chapter.

Childbirth

Childbirth usually begins when the expectant mother goes into labor, experiencing contractions that follow a regular pattern of timing and intensity. Contractions usually feel like an elastic belt being drawn together tighter and tighter over the uterus and then being slowly released. As labor progresses, the length of the contractions increases and the interval between contractions decreases. During the first stage of the birthing process, the cervix thins and then stretches to a dilation of 10 centimeters (or about 4 inches). This stage lasts an average of twelve to twenty-four hours for a woman having her first child. Contractions are stronger and labor is shorter when women are in an upright position, walking and moving around in the early stages of labor.

The transition phase at the end of the first stage of labor is the most challenging part of the birth process for most women. Contractions follow each other very quickly and have sharp peaks. This phase may be very brief, or may last an hour or so. In any case, transition indicates that labor is nearly over. The second stage of labor is the actual *birth*. When dilation reaches 10 centimeters, the abdominal muscles push the baby through the birth canal, usually in a head-first presentation. This process can take an hour and a half for a first birth. The second stage ends with the birth of the baby. The third stage of labor, the *delivery of the placenta* or afterbirth, usually takes only a few minutes after the birth of the baby.

There have been many changes in birthing procedures in hospitals, but a woman who is giving birth today must still make many informed choices about her wants and needs. Some procedures that are commonly used in hospitals during labor have been at the center of a controversy among professionals in childbirth education who believe they are either unnecessary or harmful if used routinely, providing additional stress and discomfort for the mother (Goer, 1995). It is argued that these procedures may interfere in the natural process of birth and may cause as many problems as they alleviate. The controversial procedures include: (1) *amniotomy* (the artificial rupture of the membranes), (2) *intravenous drip* (a hollow tube is introduced into a vein in the arm or hand and fixed with adhesive tape so that fluids can be infused straight into the bloodstream to prevent dehydration), (3) *episiotomy* (a surgical cut made to enlarge the birth opening), (4) *induced labor* (a medical way of starting labor and keeping it going through the use of an oxytocin drip), and

(5) *electronic fetal monitoring* (a device that can be used externally or internally to record the fetal heartbeat and the pressure of the uterus during contractions). Although these procedures may be convenient for medical personnel to use, they are restrictive and may interfere with the woman's feeling of empowerment, comfort, and the natural progression of the birth (Raymond, 1988). More details regarding why these procedures are utilized and the pros and cons of their use should be discussed with individual doctors. It should be emphasized that the controversy centers around these procedures being used routinely on all patients; few would debate the merits of these interventions in the event of medical problems such as fetal distress, infection, or maternal emergency.

Complications

Unfortunately, the birthing process does not always go smoothly. Some complications can be safely addressed within the context of a vaginal birth. But sometimes situations arise that make it difficult, dangerous, or impossible to give birth vaginally. When this happens, the woman is anesthetized and the baby is delivered through a cut in the abdominal and uterine walls in a procedure called a *Cesarean section (C-section)*. This operation is considered abdominal surgery and carries a minimum six-to-eight-week recovery time. Sometimes the C-section is planned because the doctors know in advance that a problem will prevent a vaginal birth, but often emergency C-sections are done in response to problems that become obvious during labor. Regardless of when they are detected, conditions such as cephalopelvic disproportion (the baby's head is too large to pass through the pelvis), placenta previa (the placenta is lying at the bottom of the uterus and is blocking the baby's way out), a breech presentation (the baby is coming out bottom first rather than head first), and dystocia (nonprogressive labor) often indicate the need for a C-section. Other high-risk conditions, such as diabetes or chronic hypertension, multiple births, and very low birthweight babies, are also reasons for abdominal delivery. Most hospitals now allow fathers to be present for a C-section delivery, and more women are being given the option of epidural anesthesia (as opposed to general anesthesia) so they can be awake and aware during the birth.

Several debates surround the issues relating to Cesarean births in the United States. First, the rate has increased from 5 percent of all births twenty years ago to up to 24 percent currently (Cesarean Fact Sheet, 1991). This has caused some to question whether the C-section is being performed unnecessarily in many cases. At the same time, many doctors worry about malpractice suits and conservatively perform C-sections if there is any indication, no matter how slight, that there is fetal distress or prolonged labor. Another issue being addressed is that once a woman has a Cesarean, the procedure is usually repeated in subsequent births even if the conditions that resulted in the first C-section no longer exist (Campen, 1991). This is not always the case in other countries, and groups advocating VBAC (Vaginal Birth After Cesarean) are gaining support in the United States. Available estimates show that less than 10 percent of women who have had C-sections in this country are given a chance to try a VBAC, although the numbers are increasing. However, international studies show that between 50 percent and 80 percent of women who attempt VBAC are successful. Finally, C-sections require major recuperation on the part of the mother, which may lead to difficulties in caring for her infant. These psychological effects should not be overlooked; Cesareans should not be performed for doctors' convenience rather than need.

Postpartum Depression

Childbirth is a major stress, both biologically and psychosocially (Jones, 1990). Although postpartum emotional disorders have been documented since the 1850s, they have been given little official medical recognition. This has made research regarding the causes and outcomes of these disorders difficult to undertake. Since 1980, a growing number of studies, especially in Europe, have attempted to document the existence of postpartum emotional problems. Most women experience a wide range of emotional reactions during the postpartum period, many of which are depressive in nature (Berchtold, 1989). There are three kinds of postpartum emotional disorders—postpartum blues, postpartum depression, and postpartum psychosis.

The *postpartum blues,* also known as the "baby blues," consist of a mild, transient depression. Other characteristics may include mild episodes of anxiety, confusion, insomnia, restlessness, and feelings of exhaustion. It is believed to be a normal reaction caused by the shift in hormones immediately following childbirth. New mothers may experience frequent episodes of tearfulness and crying for a couple of days on a fairly predictable timetable. The blues usually begin on the third or fourth postpartum day and peak between the fifth and tenth day following childbirth (Jones, 1990). About 50 percent to 70 percent of all childbearing women experience the postpartum blues.

Postpartum depression describes a variety of mild to moderate depressive symptoms that arise within six months after childbirth. Up to 20 percent of mothers experience such symptoms as sadness, irritability, lethargy, loss of appetite, sleep disturbances, and lessened sexual interest. These episodes commonly last six to eight weeks, but may go on as long as one year (Hopkins, Marcus, & Campbell, 1984). Women experiencing such symptoms should seek professional help. The causes of postpartum depression are unknown, so there is no way to accurately predict who will experience a postpartum disorder. However, biochemical and psychosocial risk factors may include a previous episode of postpartum depression, being raised in an alcoholic or dysfunctional family, marital discord, isolation from family and friends, a difficult labor, and delivery of a premature or medically compromised baby (Berchtold, 1989).

In very rare cases, *postpartum psychosis,* a severe depression resulting in mental illness, occurs. It usually begins in the first month after delivery and includes symptoms of either euphoria and mania, or psychotic depression (Berchtold, 1989). Since the psychosis often starts with symptoms like sleep disturbances and fatigue, it is commonly misdiagnosed as postpartum blues until the symptoms get worse. Delusional thinking and hallucinations are common with postpartum psychosis (Jones, 1990). Infanticide and child abuse are definite risks, which makes early recognition and prompt treatment important.

Many questions regarding postpartum depression remain unanswered. How can family members best help depressed mothers through this experience? Do infant characteristics influence postpartum depression? What can professionals use as effective prevention and intervention strategies? How does postpartum depression affect the developing mother-infant relationship? More research is needed to clarify and supplement the sparse anecdotal and clinical information available (Hopkins, Marcus, & Campbell, 1984).

ADJUSTING TO PARENTHOOD

Becoming a parent for the first time is usually a joyous event that is celebrated with much excitement and happiness, but it can also be a difficult time for new parents. Perhaps becoming a parent is best characterized as an opportunity for adult development and growth that is both wonderful and stressful (Cowan, 1988). Early evidence suggested that the arrival of the first child is so disruptive it constitutes a family "crisis" (LeMasters, 1957; Dyer, 1963). Subsequent researchers (Hobbs & Wimbish, 1977) have found that there is great variability in the amount of stress and happiness experienced by different families. What are some of the factors that influence adjustment?

Difficulties in the Early Weeks

The biggest change that new parents must deal with is *lack of time* (LaRossa, 1983). Life can seem quite hectic after the birth of a child, and couples often report that they have less time for sleep, conversations, television, recreation, household chores, sex, friends, and personal grooming. In a sample of largely white, middle-class couples in their late twenties, 44 percent of the mothers indicated they were not prepared for the lack of sleep and energy that would result from having a baby, and 39 percent were not prepared for the time and responsibility involved in caretaking (Kach & McGhee, 1982). The physical demands of caring for a child and the emotional costs of being overwhelmed by the total responsibility of parenthood are common difficulties (Sollie & Miller, 1980). Parents' ability to negotiate with each other can greatly influence the amount of difficulty parents have in adjusting to their new circumstances. The division of family labor is a particularly touchy issue, especially if one spouse (usually the woman) quits a job outside the home to care for the infant (Kach & McGhee, 1982). Often, couples assume a more specialized division of labor, which sometimes includes the adaptation of more traditional roles.

There may also be a *lack of preparation* for the parenting role (Rossi, 1968). Aside from their own socialization experiences, couples may have no previous education about what it is like to be a parent. This may be especially true for men. Lack of knowledge about parenting may lead to difficulty in adjustment (Wente & Crockenberg, 1976). Fathers often lack even the minimal preparation and training that mothers may get because they are infrequent babysitters and are not encouraged to become involved with children. Also, the transition is an *abrupt change* instead of a gradual increase in responsibilities. There are few guidelines or rules that people can agree upon for raising competent, valued members of society.

The experience of husbands and wives during the transition to parenthood may be different. These *differing perceptions* may cause problems in understanding each other's perspective. One research study reported that wives were experiencing more problems related to their physical and emotional selves, such as feeling tired, upset, and worrying about their personal appearance (Russell, 1974). Husbands were bothered by problems that were largely external, such as in-laws, money, and the additional amount of work the baby required. These findings are consistent with the idea that men and women take on more traditional roles after the birth of a child.

The problems of *balancing the multiple role demands* of parenthood, marriage, and career can be stress producing (Miller & Sollie, 1980; Ventura, 1987). Role theory suggests that the birth of the first child marks the advent of a transition, where the role of "parent" is added to the other responsibilities of the couple. Although there are no hard-and-fast solutions to the problems involved in balancing the demands of parenthood with marriage and careers, adaptable coping strategies include patience, organization, and flexibility (Miller & Solie, 1980). It takes time and a willingness to make whatever changes are necessary before a new working system can evolve. One mother working outside the home expressed her theory of coping: "Develop a love for fast food and frozen pizza served on paper plates."

Joys in the Early Weeks

Mothers and fathers experience wondrous feelings of joy and happiness in the first few weeks of parenthood. Many are not prepared for the *love and attachment* they feel for the baby (Kach & McGhee, 1982). There are strong emotions and close, caring connections between parents and their newborns. Parents feel drawn to their infants and are extremely interested in and admiring of their abilities and activities. New parents often can't believe they feel so much love for their babies so quickly. Greenberg & Morris (1974) use the term *engrossment* to describe the preoccupation parents feel toward their infant. Parents derive many *emotional benefits* from their new child (Sollie & Miller, 1980). The baby is a source of affection, happiness, and fun. Many parents can't remember what they did for entertainment before they had a baby because of their excitement about each little sound and movement.

Parents also experience *self-enrichment* and development in the sense of becoming more mature and responsible, planning for the future, and becoming less selfish. New parents commonly reported that they never realized how self-indulgent they were before the baby was born and they experienced a change in priorities. A sense of *family cohesiveness* is another positive feeling for parents. The baby is an added bond between the parents that strengthens their relationship and gives their family a sense of completeness. Many new parents feel that they are "on their own" and separate from their family of origin for the first time. *Watching the baby develop* and grow, as well as anticipating future growth and accomplishments, is a pleasure for most mothers and fathers. Parents often fantasize about what their children will look like or be when they grow up. They enjoy contributing to the experiences and nurturing of their child.

The Impact of the Infant

I always thought that all babies were pretty much the same. We enjoyed Shannon so much in the early weeks after she was born. Sure, she cried a little, but mostly she ate and slept. But we almost went crazy after Sean was born. He hardly ever slept, and he cried for hours every day. We kept asking ourselves what we were doing wrong, but we were doing the same things we had done for Shannon. It was simply the difference in babies. Some babies are fussier and more demanding.

A second-time father

An important aspect of the variability in becoming a parent for the first time is the infant itself. All babies are not the same, and their behavior can have a significant impact on the ease or difficulty of the transition to parenthood (Roberts & Miller, 1978). Individual infant characteristics (also known as temperament, which will be discussed in greater detail in Chapter 5) influence how much time, energy, and stress child care activities will require. Fussy babies are more demanding and may make parents feel that they cannot meet all of the challenges they are experiencing. Both husbands and wives report being bothered when the baby interrupts their sleep and rest (Russell, 1974). Parents of babies who cry a lot, sleep very little, and are unpredictable with regard to eating and other bodily functions, experience many more disruptions in their lives and have to make many more modifications in their previous routines. Infant characteristics also influence parents' perceptions of their competence and self-esteem. Babies who are not easily soothed may make parents feel as if they are doing something wrong (Wandersman, 1980). Also, if parents had anticipated having a cuddly, sleepy infant and the baby is actually fussy and irritable, then expectations must gradually change to meet the reality of what they are experiencing. Violated expectations are often related to parental difficulties, especially in women (Levy-Shiff, Goldshmidt, & Har-Even, 1991).

Although the causes of postpartum depression are unknown, it has been suggested that the amount of time spent in infant caretaking and the extent to which the infant's behavior is viewed as problematic are important variables to be considered (Atkinson & Rickel, 1984). According to both the social stress and behavioral theoretical perspectives, the greater the disruption parents experience due to caretaking demands, the greater likelihood there is for postpartum depression. A calm baby with an easy disposition can make adapting to parenthood easier. Men and women who report having quiet babies also report experiencing less stress, while men who have crying babies who don't sleep much experience more stress (Russell, 1974). Infant crying and fussy behavior is reported to be a major stress for mothers and fathers (Ventura, 1987), and is related to feelings of depression for both parents (Wilkie & Ames, 1986). Guilt, helplessness, anger, and frustration were common reactions of these parents. It has been suggested that parents feel a loss of personal control when caring for a difficult infant, and experience a more positive adjustment if they perceive their infant as easier (Sirignano & Lachman, 1985).

The unique set of characteristics exhibited by each individual infant may also have an impact on marriages. The available information is far from conclusive, since some studies find no relationship between various infant characteristics and marital adjustment (Wallace & Gotlib, 1990), and others find that information on infant temperament improves the ability to predict which marriages will decline and which will improve in quality during the transition to parenthood (Belsky & Rovine, 1990). Further investigation of these relationships is warranted.

Parenthood and Marital Relationships

Many studies have suggested that marital satisfaction changes after the birth of the first child (Dyer, 1963; Meyerowitz & Feldman, 1966; Ryder, 1973; Waldron & Routh, 1981). Just how it changes, however, remains unclear. It has been assumed that adding a child disrupts the intimacy and communication of the couple, resulting in less quality and satisfaction in the marriage. However, some interesting marital patterns were found when couples who remained childless were studied along with first-time parents (McHale & Huston, 1985; MacDermid, Huston, & McHale, 1990). Husbands and wives in both groups experienced declines in their feelings of love and marital satisfaction, suggesting that these changes may be typical in all marriages. Over time, spouses start to spend less time doing things together and less time conversing with one another regardless of their parenthood status. However, the activities that the childless and parenting couples do together are different. Parenting couples share household tasks and child care responsibilities, while nonparenting couples share more leisure activities.

Even though most marriages experience some declines in marital satisfaction, the changes that occur for couples after the birth of their first child can be particularly challenging. Husbands and wives must renegotiate a new relationship that takes into account the addition of a new person. This process is complicated. Child care appears to be a crucial issue in marital reorganization. A recent study (Levy-Shiff, 1994) suggested that couples experienced less decline in their marital satisfaction when fathers were more involved in the infant's caregiving. Future research must continue to focus on factors that may either help marriages or make them worse during this transitional period.

Obviously, the impact of parenthood is not the same for all individuals and couples. Marriage is made up of three elements: romance, which emphasizes sexuality; friendship, which emphasizes mutual interests and supportiveness; and partnership, which emphasizes efficiency in working together (Belsky, 1981). A child may affect each area of marriage differently. Decreased sexual responsiveness on the part of the wife and not enough time to be alone together contribute to marital tensions regarding romance during the transition to parenthood (Wandersman, 1980). Partnership may, however, increase as the couple shares caregiving tasks. Although changes are common in marriages after the birth of a baby, there seems to be some overall stability in marital satisfaction from pregnancy through the postpartum months. In other words, good marriages stay that way, and troubled marriages don't get better (see Box 4-4) (Belsky & Rovine, 1990).

Research suggests that men may have a particularly difficult time adjusting to marital changes after the birth of a child (Wente & Crockenberg, 1976). It is easy to see how issues such as resuming sexual relations and responding supportively to postpartum blues can influence the adjustment for men (Peterson & Walls, 1991). It is a challenge to adapt when so many things have changed so drastically. The quality of the marital relationship seems to influence all aspects of fathering (Feldman, Nash, & Aschenbrenner, 1983). Sometimes mothers and fathers have problems finding a balance between being a spouse and being a parent. Marital and parenting factors must both have the

---

Box 4-4 Is There Sex After Parenthood?

Parenting Magazine conducted a survey on sex and parenthood (November, 1987). Six thousand people responded. The sample was self-selected, and tended to be older, more educated, and have a higher income than parents nationwide. Over three-quarters of the respondents had children under the age of two. Here are some of the findings.

Since I became a parent, I feel:	Mothers (%)	Fathers (%)
More in love with partner	44	55
Same	32	34
Less in love with partner	15	5
No time to even think about love	8	6

Since I became a parent, sex is:	Mothers (%)	Fathers (%)
Not as much fun as it used to be	34	20
About the same	30	41
More fun	16	19
Something from my former life	20	20

How often do you and your partner have sexual relations?	
Once a month or less	22%
Between once a week and twice a month	36%
Between once and three times a week	33%
More than three times a week	9%

The main reason I have sex less often than I'd like is:	Mothers (%)	Fathers (%)
I am too tired	43	21
My lack of desire	26	5
Lack of privacy	5	5
Partner is too tired	6	21
Partner's lack of desire	7	34
Marital problems	4	3

attention they deserve. Box 4-5 gives some suggestions for helping couples nurture intimacy after parenthood.

Preparing Parents for Parenthood

The motto "Be prepared" applies to many situations in life. Although it is not possible to prepare for every scenario, it can be very helpful to think ahead and gather needed information. Trying to prepare in advance for anticipated life changes during the transition to parenthood is an important part of the coping process. Seeking information increases self-confidence and competency (Hamburg & Adams, 1967). There is some consensus that participation in a parenting class can be a worthwhile experience for parents. As was discussed in Chapter 1, the sex of the parent, the timing of the class, and the class con-

---

 ## Box 4-5 Nurturing Marital Intimacy After Parenthood

The demands of children, at any stage, will place tremendous obstacles in the way of parents' trying to keep their own relationship alive. Yet the rewards of intimacy, including self-acceptance, open communication, sexual fulfillment, and mutual support, are well worth the trouble. It takes determination to overcome the challenges of combining marital intimacy with parenthood. Here are some suggestions to help establish or restore intimacy to a relationship.

Spend time alone as a couple regularly. Spending time alone when children are young is especially difficult, but patterns of behavior are being formed during the early parenting years that may persist. Taking a walk around the block or sharing a cup of coffee in the living room can provide the necessary time for staying in touch with each other. Hiring babysitters for brief periods of time can be helpful, as well as exchanging child care with other parents who are also in need of a few minutes alone. The goal is to make private time a priority, and eventually teach children to respect that private time.

Maintain personal friendships. Many people neglect their friends after marriage or parenthood, but that puts an unfair burden on spouses. Expecting one person to meet all of another person's needs is unrealistic. Actively maintaining other relationships through phone conversations and an occasional evening out is healthy for the whole family.

Share life maintenance activities. Parents must be interested in and participate in their lives together. By itemizing all household chores, child care responsibilities, financial dealings, and miscellaneous errands that need to be handled, you can share responsibilities. Sharing obligations increases the opportunity for joint decision making and mutual support.

Make dates. Couples must get in the habit of setting aside time with each other for activities like going out to dinner, making love, or discussing concerns that have come up. Initially, making these appointments may seem awkward and unspontaneous. But free time is rare when children are involved, so setting aside time ensures that opportunities to be together will really happen.

Appreciate each other. Give frequent compliments about things normally taken for granted, such as appearance, meal preparations, job performance, home repairs, and dealings with children. Be as specific as possible in giving spouses the praise, affirmation, and essential support they need.

Balance the children's needs with your own. Begin to make plans with a recognition that both the parents' needs and the children's needs deserve consideration. Often parents focus on what would be good for the children. Parents must also learn to nurture themselves.

Adapted from: *Growing parent: A sourcebook for families.* © 1983. Used with permission of Contemporary Books, Inc., Chicago.

CLOSE TO HOME   JOHN McPHERSON

© 1994 John McPherson/Dist. by Universal Press Syndicate

PARENTHOOD SIMULATOR

● ON   ■ TURBO
○ OFF
SETTING
● 2 A.M. FEEDING
● LOST PACIFIER
● CHICKEN POX
● WET BED
● TERRIBLE TWOS
● COLICKY BABY
● COLICKY TRIPLETS
● PROJECTILE VOMITING
● UNSOLICITED ADVICE

9-12   McPHERSON

**In an effort to prepare expectant parents for the
challenges that lie ahead, many obstetricians'
offices have installed parenthood simulators.**

*CLOSE TO HOME © 1994 John McPherson. Reprinted with
permission of UNIVERSAL PRESS SYNDICATE.
All rights reserved.*

tent represent crucial variables to be considered. Although contradictory
research exists regarding the benefits of formal education, many professionals
agree that an appropriate parenting class at the right time can help to reduce
the amount of difficulty parents might experience.

It is particularly important to involve men in some sort of preparation for
parenthood. Current demographics show that increasing numbers of new
fathers will become more involved with parenting than in previous generations due to economic factors (Presser, 1988); young couples who need two
incomes to make ends meet often also need to limit the number of hours of
child care they must pay for. Our society today seems to value greater involvement of men in the lives of their children, but if they are not prepared for the
experience, they may become discouraged (Hawkins & Belsky, 1989). Since
many men have little or no child care experience previous to their wives' pregnancies, they have little basis for developing realistic expectations about parenthood (Wente & Crockenberg, 1976). Some men are reluctant to ask for help

or admit that they don't have basic parenting skills, thus denying themselves the tools they need to be successful (Peterson & Walls, 1991). For these men, the hassles, frustrations, and responsibilities of parenthood may far outnumber the rewards. Research suggests that men who report being more prepared for parenthood also experience more gratifications from parenting (Russell 1974). Men who prepare for parenthood before the birth of their child by observing children, learning to physically care for children, and reading extensively about child development and parenting, are more likely to be interested in and involved with the care of their own babies after the birth (Fein, 1976). In addition, they have lower levels of anxiety about their parenting skills. Fathers who are unprepared for parenthood may be ambivalent about their performance as fathers, which could affect their self-esteem (Hawkins & Belsky, 1989). If they persist and, over time, develop the skills and attitudes necessary for effective parenting, their self-esteem and confidence about fatherhood may be enhanced.

When a baby is born, a man takes on the identity of "father." But the label does not ensure that he knows how to *be* a father. The term *fatherhood click* has been used to describe a parenting style in which fathers learn to actively nurture their children with hands-on fathering and attention (Daniels & Weingarten, 1988). When certain basic skills are learned, fatherhood becomes a fully realized developmental experience and "clicks" into place. Active father involvement happens at different times for different men. Some have a preference for one developmental stage over another. For example, some fathers are not very interested in infants, but become very active in parenting their children when they become preschoolers. As one father put it, "I started doing more with my kids once they could walk, talk, and go to the bathroom by themselves." Men who are over thirty when their first child is born usually click earlier in their children's lives, perhaps because they are more ready for fatherhood financially and emotionally. Other factors, such as work patterns and the ways couples negotiate their parenting may also affect the extent and timing of the fatherhood click.

Parenting classes may be very helpful to new parents during those first weeks after the birth when adjustment is at its peak (Stranik & Hogberg, 1979; Gage & Christensen, 1991). Given the anxiety, fatigue and helplessness these parents might be experiencing, topic priorities must be set (Ventura, 1987). In a study of 184 families with firstborn infants, new parents were asked to list the problems they had in the first year (McKim, 1987). The top four concerns were infant illness, infant nutrition, infant crying, and information on appropriate infant development and activities. These topics are certainly a starting place for planning programs for new parents. Parenting programs cannot erase all of the fatigue, conflict, and uncertainty involved in caring for and adjusting to a new baby. They may, however, help facilitate the adjustment by providing realistic expectations about infants and the changes taking place in the marital relationship (Wandersman, 1980).

Parenting classes are just one way to prepare parents for their job. Numerous books, cassette tapes, and videotapes are available on countless issues of importance to parents at every age and stage of the child's development. Talking with other parents, friends, relatives, or professionals is another way to gain information. It is important to be open to new ideas and be willing to learn and improve skills. Researchers continue to investigate interventions that may help ease the transition to parenthood experience (Cowan & Cowan, 1995).

Supporting New Parents

Supportive behavior on the part of others may benefit new parents physically and psychologically. As mentioned in Chapter 1, *social support systems* (or social support networks) are defined as relatives, friends, neighbors, coworkers and other acquaintances who interact with a person. These systems can be "close" or "loose," depending on how acquainted people are within the system (Gladieux, 1978). There are two major dimensions of social support—*instrumental* (tangible) support and *expressive* (emotional and psychological) support (Liese, Snowden, & Ford, 1989). In relation to the transition to parenthood, instrumental support could consist of a relative coming to help out after the baby is born, friends bringing meals, or financial help. Expressive support could be daily phone calls from a good friend or offers to babysit so the new parents can have some time alone. The potential problem with the social support system after the birth of a baby is that it undergoes certain changes in size, composition, and function (Gottlieb & Pancer, 1988). Perhaps the couple's preparenthood network was largely made up of people from the wife's work place, and she doesn't go back to work right away after the baby comes. Maybe relatives become more involved in the postbirth network. Sometimes friendships change because of changing interests and priorities. The experiences of couples with varying degrees of social support may be very different, and may be an important aspect of the transition to parenthood.

Limited information is available regarding social supports in the context of the transition to parenthood (Gottlieb & Pancer, 1988). What kinds of social supports are needed? How can we measure their effectiveness? More answers are needed. Available evidence, however, suggests that social support systems may serve as buffers or mediators of stress. Mothers reporting high stress one month after the birth of their babies were less sensitive and responsive when their infants were four months old (Crnic, Greenberg, Ragozin, Robinson, & Basham, 1983), suggesting that stress may interfere with optimal parenting. Another study, however, found a relationship between the types of support available to parents when infants were two months old and how well adjusted parents and marriages were when the babies were nine months old (Wandersman, Wandersman, & Kahn, 1980). These findings suggest that the amount and quality of social supports available to the mother may have a significant impact on the mother-infant relationship and maternal attitudes. It seems that the extent of the social support system itself does not have as much of an impact as the cognitive perception of support does (Stemp, Turner, & Noh, 1986). In other words, it's not how many people you know, but how you feel about the levels of intimacy and trust you have established in the relationships available to you. The emphasis is on quality, not quantity (Liese, Snowden, & Ford, 1989).

Grandparents and other intergenerational relatives have a very important role to play in providing social support to new parents. They can be very helpful in socializing first-time parents into their new roles by softening the responsibility of parenting and facilitating parent-child bonding (Fischer, 1988). Letting new parents know that they are not alone, and that others are available to help with the responsibility and work of parenting eases some of the overwhelming aspects of the transition. Having relatives, particularly the baby's grandparents, around in the postpartum period may be emotionally beneficial to all concerned.

SPECIAL TRANSITIONS

Sometimes special circumstances arise after the decision to parent is made. Some people experience difficulties as they try to conceive a child that change their hopes and dreams of parenthood. Others decide for many different reasons, including infertility, to adopt rather than have children biologically. This section deals with transitions to parenthood in two atypical circumstances. The first is the inability to conceive a child, and the second is adoption.

Transition to Nonparenthood

> The whole process is so frustrating. In addition to the humiliation of being probed and prodded by doctors who tell you when you can have sex and when you can't, you have to deal with friends and family asking all kinds of questions and telling you to relax and it will just happen. The uncertainty from month to month is maddening. Should I get excited and feel hopeful and positive, or should I try not to care so the disappointment doesn't hurt so much? I try not to, but I feel jealous of every pregnant woman I see. It makes me furious to hear about people who get pregnant by accident. I'm working so hard at something that's supposed to be natural, and I'm failing."

A woman experiencing infertility

The "transition to nonparenthood" is the term suggested by Mathews and Mathews (1986) to describe the experience of couples who want to have biological children, but are unable to because of infertility. *Involuntary childlessness* is defined as "the inability to conceive in spite of repeated efforts over a period of one year or more, resulting in unanticipated and undesired childlessness" (Sabatelli, Meth, & Gavazzi, 1988, p. 338). Approximately 95 percent of newly married couples want to have biological children at some point (Glick, 1977), but an estimated 14 percent of all married couples in the United States experience infertility problems (U.S. National Center for Health Statistics, 1985).

In trying to find a medical solution, infertile couples must go through a costly process that may involve an enormous loss of control and privacy in their lives. Their self-concept, identity, and sense of reality can be significantly affected, leading them to question the purposes and goals of their marriage (Mathews & Mathews, 1986). The stress of dealing with infertility can affect other aspects of marital relationships. Both males and females report that the experience of infertility had a negative effect on their sexual relationship (Sabatelli, Meth, & Gavazzi, 1988). Individuals with high self-esteem and high levels of marital commitment seem to be able to cope more effectively.

Because infertile couples commonly feel grief, anger, guilt, and depression while dealing with their problems, attempts are being made to understand the interrelated effects of infertility on marital relationships (Higgins, 1990). Exactly how infertile couples ultimately cope with their disappointment at being unable to conceive a child is unknown. Intervention strategies aimed at assessing and supporting infertile couples should be implemented in clinical settings, especially since the infertility treatments themselves can take several years to complete. Depending on the likelihood of the interventions working in each particular case, couples begin to prepare for the future. Many get ready for parenthood through alternative means, such as adoption or foster placements. Others begin the journey toward accepting their childlessness.

Transition to Adoptive Parenthood

Although research is available on many topics related to adoption, very little is known about the transition to parenthood experience in adoptive couples. Couples who adopt children face many of the same transition difficulties as biological parents. There are also additional stresses, however, that must be addressed as a part of the adoption process itself.

David Brodzinsky and Loreen Huffman (1988) have outlined six hurdles many adoptive parents encounter:

1. *Infertility.* The most common reason couples adopt a child is because they have an infertility problem that leaves them biologically unable to produce a child. These couples are at risk for psychological problems such as anxiety and depression, as well as marital difficulties in the areas of communication and sexual relations. Adoptive parents must cope together with the loss of the biological child they have wished for and fantasized about before they can create a healthy adoptive family.
2. *Uncertain timing.* The length of time the process of adoption can take is quite variable. It can mean several months or many years of waiting. Because there isn't a known timetable (as there is for pregnancy), it is difficult for adoptive couples to plan effectively. Physical cues and reminders are not present, and it could happen in a short or long period of time. This means that the couple themselves, their families, and their friends don't have a specified amount of time to change their perceptions and expectations and make adjustments as parenthood approaches.
3. *Social stigma.* There is a stigma associated with adoption in our culture, a feeling that it's somehow not as good as having children biologically. Some people are not supportive of an adoptive couple, especially when a child of different racial or ethnic background is involved. Adoptive parents are often put in the stressful situation of explaining or justifying their decision to friends and relatives. In addition to this anxiety, adoptive parents must undergo an extensive evaluation to prove their worthiness as

parents to social service agencies. These pressures can be upsetting and cause resentment in the prospective parents.

4. *Lack of role models.* Since there aren't that many people who become parents through adoption, finding a role model who can give information and advice on adoption-related issues can be difficult. Organizations of adoptive families have been formed in part to help with support issues.

5. *Placement.* The actual age at which an adoptive child is placed can complicate developmental issues related to parenting. Adopting an older infant or child who has experienced many caregivers may have implications for attachment and the development of trust. This is in direct contrast to a child who is adopted in the first few months of life.

6. *Biological risk.* Adopted children are more likely to have biological problems than nonadopted children. Prenatal problems, birth complications, and genetic vulnerabilities may have an effect on development, temperament, and the parent-child relationship.

Despite this impressive list of possible downfalls for adoptive parents, the few available research studies in this area suggest that, at least in the first few years of the family life cycle, these additional stressors do not have an adverse impact on family interaction and parent-child adjustment (Humphrey, 1975; Hoopes, 1982; Plomin & DeFries, 1985). In fact, adoptive parents report more positive expectations and satisfying experiences during the transition to parenthood than biological parents (Levy-Shiff, Goldshmidt, & Har-Even, 1991). It is possible that adoptive parents have learned better coping strategies because they are, on the whole, older and more mature. They also have greater financial security and resources. But it is equally plausible that the sense of loss and deprivation that many adoptive couples feel prior to placement makes them more appreciative of the positive aspects of parenthood and more willing to accept the major changes involved in the transition to parenthood.

Issues become even more complex when we go beyond the traditionally preferred adoption of a young infant. Societal changes, such as the availability of abortion and contraception, and the increased numbers of teenage mothers who keep their babies, have led to a decline in the number of healthy infants available for adoption. Because the demand for infants is large and the supply is small, many people have become increasingly willing to adopt children who are loosely described (for lack of a better term) as having "special needs." Older children, minority children, sibling groups, physically handicapped children, medically ill children, and emotionally disturbed children all fit into this category (Brodzinsky & Huffman, 1988). Under these conditions, the transition to adoptive parenthood becomes potentially even more complicated, and deserves the attention of researchers.

SUMMARY

- Becoming a parent for the first time marks a period of change and growth. The availability of contraception has given people choices, and decisions about whether or not to parent and when is the best time are a part of the process.

- Mothers and fathers experience many changes during pregnancy, both physically and emotionally. Pregnant women must take steps to ensure as much as possible that they will have healthy babies. Avoiding sexually transmitted diseases and harmful drugs, as well as exercising, eating well, visiting the doctor regularly, and taking care of general health needs all create a healthy prenatal environment.

- Most couples participate in prepared childbirth classes to ready themselves for the birth of the baby. Being educated, supported, and aware of birthing options helps pregnant couples have more positive birthing experiences. The adjustments that parents must make in the early weeks are both difficult and joyous, and may depend somewhat on whether the infant is fussy and difficult to care for.

- Marriages must also change and grow as parents adjust to their multiple roles. Husbands and wives must remember to give each other love and care, also. Parenting classes and other parenting information can help parents learn and cope with the new demands. Social support systems are also needed to make the transition to parenthood easier.

- Sometimes people experience difficulties that prevent them from conceiving a child. They have to deal with this disappointment, and perhaps try alternative ways of becoming parents. One such way is through adoption. Although there are some special circumstances and needs, many aspects of becoming a parent are similar, whether a child is biologically conceived or adopted. Parents need information and support to make a successful transition.

CHAPTER 5

Parenting Infants and Toddlers

Parenting infants and toddlers is an exciting job that requires lots of flexibility. It is quite a challenge to keep up with the dramatic developmental changes taking place during this time. A child is born somewhat helpless, dependent upon others for food, warmth, and caring. Within two years the same child can think, walk, talk, and be very effective at getting his or her needs met. This chapter will examine the amazing transformations that occur during this important stage of development and how they affect the parenting role. Parents face many challenges as they cope with the task of parenting a little person who grows so quickly and has such diverse and changing needs. Learning about and adjusting to the newborn period is the first hurdle. Social and emotional development will be examined, with special attention being given to the issues of trust, autonomy, temperament, and the development of attachment relationships. How do parents provide an optimal learning environment in terms of both cognitive and language development? Finally, the physical development of the child, especially with regard to health and safety, will be explored.

THE PARENTING ROLE

> I feel so weird. I don't have a clue what I'm doing. I just hope the mistakes I make in my parenting are small enough that they won't come back to haunt me someday.
>
> *A first-time father*

The tasks of parenting during the infant and toddler years may have crucial importance to later parent-child relationships since basic issues of love and acceptance are involved amid many changes and adjustments. To be successful, parents must include the new baby in the family, reestablish their relationship as a couple, and find a balance between their needs as individuals and as parents. These tasks will be examined first from a theoretical perspective, and then from a research base—examining parental concerns and parental involvement during the infant-toddler years.

Theoretical Context: Parenting

Up until the time the baby is born, parents are busy preparing for parenthood. Galinsky (1987) refers to this as the *Image-Making Stage.* As Chapter 4 showed, preparenthood preparations involve making adjustments individually and as a couple to get ready for the baby. Once the baby arrives, parents enter the *Nurturing Stage* (Galinsky, 1987). The major task of this stage is to form an attachment to the baby. This includes accepting the characteristics of the baby and their new role as parents. The ease with which these tasks might be accomplished is quite variable. Research suggests that the infant's characteristics may have an impact on how parents view their competence in the parenting role; parents of infants who were perceived as more difficult and demanding experienced more negative changes in their lives. They perceived themselves as less competent parents (Roberts, 1983) and as having less personal control (Sirignano & Lachman, 1985). Certainly, these findings have implications for parental development. Parents must cope with the discrepancies between their expectations of parenthood and the reality of parenthood (Wapner, 1993).

Theoretical Context: Infants

Erikson's theory suggests that infants during the first year of life have the developmental task of establishing *trust*. Parents are the main source of providing this sense of trust so that the infant begins to expect that his or her needs will be met. The regularity with which the infant receives food, warmth, and affection affects the development of feelings and expectations that he or she will be cared for. If parents fail to provide what the infant needs, a sense of mistrust develops. Parents must become responsive to the infant's needs. A parent's ability to give responsive feedback to an infant is called *parental sensitivity*. Parental sensitivity consists of paying attention to the infant's signals, interpreting the signals accurately, and giving appropriate feedback. Sensitive parents respond contingently, which means that they respond promptly enough for the baby to feel that his or her signals caused the response. The goal of sensitive parents is to cooperate with the baby's ongoing activities rather than intruding or interfering with them.

There are two dimensions of parental sensitivity. The first is the issue of responding vs. not responding. Sensitive parents respond to their infant's signals on a regular basis, building the trust that is necessary in the attachment relationship. Some parents respond to their infants only if it is convenient for them to do so. For example, some parents ignore the infant's hunger cries during the night because they want the extra sleep and don't want to be disturbed. The other dimension of parental sensitivity is responding appropriately vs. responding inappropriately. Appropriate responses necessitate that the parent be tuned into the baby's signals to tell whether what she or he is doing for the infant is working. It is not enough to just try something, it has to be the right thing. For example, a baby might be overstimulated, and crying because he or she is tired and out of control. If parents ignore the baby's cries, they are not responding. If they try to comfort the child by bouncing the baby vigorously, they are responding inappropriately, because they have mistaken the cries of a tired, overstimulated infant for those of a bored infant. If they swaddle the baby and try to cuddle him or her close so that the baby is comforted and can fall asleep, they are responding appropriately.

Children whose parents are consistently insensitive to their signals may come to feel that they have little effect on the world. Babies need to learn to trust that others will care for their basic needs. Parents can learn to become more accurate in reading infants' signals and responding sensitively. A recent intervention study involving lower-class mothers with irritable infants showed that training was effective in enhancing sensitive maternal responsiveness (van den Boom, 1994). In addition, infants of mothers who participated in this three month intervention were more sociable, able to soothe themselves, engaged in higher quality exploration, and cried less than the infants whose mothers did not participate in the intervention.

The interaction between infants and parents can be assisted through parental awareness and attitudes. Parents can learn to use touch as a form of communication. Infants understand touch much earlier than they do speech and language. Holding infants in a calm, relaxed manner, handling them with confidence, cuddling them, and talking in soothing tones allows parents to communicate effectively with their infants. Keying into the infant's unique ways of communication by observing her or his movements, gestures, facial expressions, and body positions helps parents be sensitive to infant cues. Simply spending quality time with an infant, where the parent is totally available to and focused upon the infant will encourage sensitivity (Gonzalez-Mena & Eyer, 1980). Parents are sometimes only "half there," supervising but withdrawing mentally to daydream. It is important to build focused, quality time into the daily schedule. Infants and toddlers should be respected as individual people who have the right to have feelings and express them.

According to Piaget's theory, infants and toddlers are in the *sensorimotor period* of cognitive development. He believes that knowledge is derived from information gathered through the five senses and through motor activity. In other words, knowledge occurs through action. Children learn by doing, and are actively involved in the learning process by using their senses and their bodies. Increasing motor skills give babies an opportunity to explore and interact with everything around them—to learn about space, distance, and gravity by using their bodies.

The young child's ability to taste, touch, see, hear, and smell allows him or her to experience the world in many different ways (Wilson, 1977). Infants put whatever they can into their mouths, and learn if an object tastes sweet, sour, bitter, or salty. They use their hands and arms to bring the world to them by reaching, grabbing and pulling. Touching an object allows them to learn whether it is smooth, rough, sharp, slippery, hard, soft, furry, cold, hot, big, or small. Infants see objects close up and from a distance, and identify what is familiar and unfamiliar. They observe characteristics such as size, color, shape and function. Infants hear a variety of sounds such as giggles, laughs, cries, screams, whispers, shouts, talking, and singing. From these sounds, they begin to learn about the relationships between different tones of voice and people's feelings. The sense of smell allows them to identify objects like roses or pine trees, or various foods. People and favorite objects may also have familiar odors that comfort a child. Children use all of these abilities to process information about their environment.

Theoretical Context: Toddlers

According to Erikson, the time between one and three years of age is spent dealing with the issue of *autonomy*. Toddlers are learning to be self-sufficient in many activities, and are able to eat, walk, talk, and go to the bathroom independently. The job of the parents is to help the children feel successful in their quests for independence, since toddlers will otherwise learn to doubt their abilities and feel shame over failures. This is often easier said than done. Times where great strides occur in growth and development are often difficult to

The issue of autonomy is prevalent during the time
between 1 and 3 years of age, when toddlers are
learning to explore independently and become more
self-sufficient.
(*Bill Bachman/Photo Researchers*)

deal with. The child has the ability to run away from the parents, but is then
not able to deal with being so far away from them, and screams for them to
come and provide comfort. There is always a tension between the fear and
desire for autonomy that makes both parent and child feel as if each is being
manipulated by the other.

The cognitive abilities of the child have a great impact on parenting, both
in terms of the strategies parents use and the learning environments they provide for their children. Piaget proposes that by twelve months of age, behavior becomes intentional. Infants begin to have goals, and can find the means to
achieve particular ends in limited kinds of situations. They begin to imitate the
actions of others. As babies grow into toddlers, they begin to learn by trial and
error, taking advantage of unexpected happenings and gaining new knowledge from them. They are very interested in novelty, creating changes in the
environment so that new or unusual experiences result, often acting like little
scientists who test and explore everything around them. By twenty-four
months of age, representation occurs. This means that children can begin to
think in advance, performing mental actions instead of being tied to physical
actions. Thoughts begin to be represented using symbols, such as language.
These changes in the child's thinking are signals to parents that the child's

abilities are expanding, possibly necessitating changes in the environment to best meet newly developing needs.

Parental Concerns

The most commonly reported problems of mothers during the first year of a child's life are infant illness, infant crying, concerns about feeding and nutrition, and role conflicts (McKim, 1987). Pediatricians can always be consulted regarding the first three concerns, which will also be addressed in this chapter, but role conflicts may be particularly difficult to deal with. There are no easy answers for how mothers should adapt to the sometimes conflicting roles of individual, mother, wife, and possibly working woman. The same is true for the competing roles of fathers (Volling & Belsky, 1991).

There are minor stresses that go along with being a parent of young children. These stresses, often referred to as *daily hassles,* have been examined in the context of how they affect parenting and family functioning. Hassles consist of irritating, frustrating, or annoying demands that may affect parent-child relationships adversely (Crnic & Greenberg, 1990). They include child behaviors such as nagging, whining, interrupting, and not wanting to go to bed, as well as parental tasks such as having to continually clean up their children's messes. Interestingly enough, these daily hassles predict how satisfied parents are and how they feel about themselves (Crnic & Booth, 1991), which may have important implications for the parent-child relationship. For example, parents who feel hassled may be dissatisfied with their parenting and have negative feelings about themselves and their children. Social support networks, such as friends or family members, seem to be able to moderate at least some of the negative effects of these minor stresses (Crnic & Greenberg, 1990; Crnic & Booth, 1991).

Parental Involvement

Research prior to the 1960s often focused on the mother as the primary parent. Since then, studies regarding the role of fathers have become more prominent. Upon examining the involvement of mothers and fathers during the first two years of life, researchers have suggested that mothers and fathers often take on different roles with their infants and toddlers. Mothers tend to engage in more caregiving activities (such as feeding, burping, diapering, and bathing), while fathers tend to engage in more play activities (Lamb, 1977). When mothers do play with their infants, it tends to be more conventional play, such as pat-a-cake or peek-a-boo. Fathers, on the other hand, tend to play in more active, physical, and unpredictable ways. Fathers are as competent as mothers in caregiving activities; they just choose to do them less often. These findings have recently been duplicated in an African-American sample of fathers (Hossain & Roopnarine, 1994). Accurate and meaningful ways of measuring parent-infant interactions continue to challenge researchers, although advances in computer technology and methodology have made many improvements in obtaining information (Heermann, Jones, & Wikoff, 1994).

Each ecological context, such as the marital relationship and the work environment, must also be considered when trying to determine parental involvement. Research on a sample of white, middle- and working-class American men suggests that fathers who have positive marital relations and a supportive work environment regarding family-related issues may be more stimulating and responsive when interacting with their infants (Volling & Belsky, 1991). Similar results were found in a working-class sample of Irish men. Fathers who rated their marital relationships positively and were able to modify their work schedules in order to increase parental participation were involved in more child care tasks during the first year of the child's life (Nugent, 1991). These findings suggest that involvement may be dependent upon a complex interaction between the demands of each ecological setting.

PARENTING NEWBORNS

Wanted: Parent of Infant. Must be able to function without sufficient sleep for long periods of time. Must be able to walk the equivalent of ten miles each night without leaving the bedroom. Must put social life and sex life on hold while tending to the needs of a totally dependent, demanding, unreasonable, and very tiny boss. If this is a first-born, must have photography skills; less essential for later-borns. Must be proficient at interpreting commands in ear-piercing shrieks. Must enjoy, or at least tolerate, highly repetitive tasks: diapering, feeding, burping, diapering, feeding, burping . . .

(Moschell, 1991)

The newborn period can be one of great adjustment for new parents. Although the average newborn usually sleeps more than fourteen out of every twenty-four hours, the sleep comes in short intervals. Newborns like to eat every two to four hours, and cry a total of an hour or so each day (usually not all at once). The average newborn urinates eighteen times a day and moves its bowels up to seven times a day, although there is much variability (especially with breastfed infants). Because of these obvious caregiving demands, the newborn period can be a fairly labor-intensive experience for new parents.

Newborn Characteristics

I've never experienced any feeling quite like it. I looked at his wet, bloody, writhing little body and a flood of emotions rushed over me. It was a miracle, and I was filled with awe and gratitude. I looked up at my husband's face and saw the tears streaming down his cheeks. The world seemed to stop for those first moments when we welcomed our son to the world.

A first-time mother

Newborns look very different from what people imagine when they think of babies. The average newborn is about 7 pounds in weight (most full-term babies are between 5 and 10 pounds), about 20 inches in length (most full-term babies are between 18 and 22 inches), and are covered with vernix caseosa, an oily protection against infection, that dries after a few days. Some newborns are covered with a very fuzzy prenatal hair called *lanugo*, which drops off in a few days. Others have no hair at all. The newborn's head is about a quarter of his or her body length, and it is often misshapen and elongated from passing through the mother's pelvis. Similarly, the noses of newborns are often squashed looking since the cartilage in the nose is also malleable. Sometimes a newborn's body will be covered with bruises, or skin will be red and splotchy, yet there is nothing more beautiful and wondrous to parents than the sight of their newborn.

Parents often want to know what patterns of behavior they can expect from their newborn. Newborns spend most of their time in various phases of sleep and wakefulness known as *states of arousal* (Wolff, 1966; Fogel, 1984). There are four sleep states, forming a continuum based on characteristics such as the infant's respiration and body activity. The three wakeful states are dependent upon the baby's alertness and activity level. Knowing how these patterns of behavior are organized can be very helpful to parents in relation to planning activities and developing expectations. For example, trying to awaken an infant who is involved in a deep regular sleep may be difficult, just as trying to get a baby who is in an active awake state to go to sleep may be unrealistic. As infants give clues and establish patterns in their states, sensitive parents can respond appropriately to their needs.

Sensory Abilities

Newborns have surprised researchers through the years with their advanced sensory capabilities. Parents who are knowledgeable about the sensory abilities of newborns can maximize supportive parent-infant interactions. Parents are encouraged to use a distance of about 7–10 inches from the newborn's face when letting the baby look into the parent's face (which infants show a strong preference for doing) or when showing them a toy. Newborns can perceive shape and color (Jones-Molfese, 1977), and can follow moving light or objects by tracking them with their eyes. Parents can provide colorful shapes and patterns to interest and enrich infants, as long as they are careful not to overstimulate newborns by presenting too many things at once. Infants can locate the source of a sound and turn to look in that direction (Field, 1990), and show a sophisticated ability to discriminate between sounds (Field, Dempsey, Hatch, Ting, & Clifton, 1979). Infants like certain sounds better than others. The sound of the human voice, especially that of the mother (DeCasper & Fifer, 1980) is preferred. This underscores the importance of parents' talking to their babies.

The chemical senses, taste and smell, are well developed from birth on (Field, 1990). Newborns have a good sense of smell, and are able to discriminate among distinctive odors, turning away from unpleasant odors (such as ammonia) and turning toward those they prefer (Rieser, Yonas, & Wikner, 1976). This well-developed olfactory system is an important learning tool. By five days of age, an infant can recognize the scent of his or her mother (Cernack & Porter, 1985). Infants may use this ability to recognize familiar people with their sense of smell to enhance feelings of security. The kinesthetic aspects of touch are the most developed of the tactile senses. Therefore, infants are much more sensitive to touch that involves the whole body. For example,

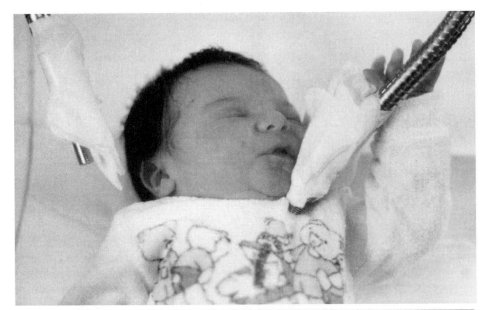

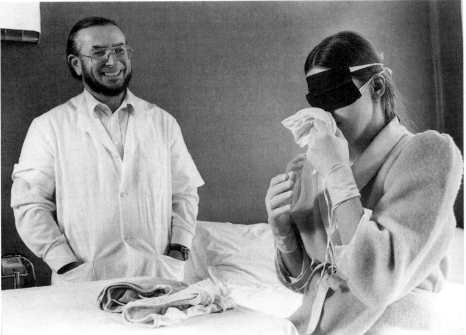

Within a few days after birth, newborns and mothers are able to recognize each other's scent, possibly enhancing feelings of security and connectedness.
(*J. Guichard/Sygma*)

parents often find that infants are much more likely to calm down if they swaddle or rock the infant, activities that stimulate the whole body (Lester, 1985).

Crying and Colic

This is the Basic Baby Mood Cycle, which all babies settle into once they get over being born:

MOOD ONE: Just about to cry
MOOD TWO: Crying
MOOD THREE: Just finished crying

Your major job is to keep your baby in Mood Three as much as possible.

(Reprinted from *Babies and Other Hazards of Sex* by Dave Barry, Copyright 1984. Permission granted by Rodale Press, Inc., Emmaus, PA 18098.)

Crying is the major form of communication available to the infant. It is used to signal needs and discomfort. During the early weeks of life, it is the only verbal means babies have to express themselves. Crying can indicate a variety of things, such as hunger, boredom, a wet diaper, being too hot or too cold, pain, loneliness, wanting something to suck, restlessness, being overtired, or being too full. Sometimes infants cry for no reason at all. The job of the parent in the caregiving role is to try to find a reason for the crying if there is one, and alleviate the cause. This can take a while, since the parent has to first learn the baby's signals and preferences, both of which are unique to each individual baby and may change over time. Usually, caregivers begin by exploring physical reasons for crying, and either feed the baby or change the baby's diaper. If these attempts do not work, there are a variety of things parents can experiment with as they attempt to meet their infant's needs. A list of possibilities is found in Box 5-1.

 ## Box 5-1 How to Soothe a Fretful Infant

1. *Movement* (Vestibular Stimulation)
   - rock in a rocking chair
   - rock in a cradle
   - use the baby swing
   - adult sways back and forth holding baby
   - ride in car

2. *Touch* (Tactile Stimulation)
   - heated water pads
   - swaddling (wrapping snugly in a blanket so limbs are held close to the body)
   - stroking an infant
   - pat infant's back
   - gently massage infant's arms and legs
   - use skin to skin contact

   - use "colic hold" position (place baby's tummy across your arm with his head near your elbow and his legs in your hand)
   - use baby carriers

3. *Sound* (Auditory Stimulation)
   - monotonous noises (clothes washer or dryer, vacuum cleaners, fans, room vaporizers, rhythmical household appliances)
   - hold baby on left side to hear heartbeat
   - soft music with a monotonous beat
   - talk to baby in soothing tones

Adapted from: Schaper, K.K. (1982). Towards a calm baby and relaxed parents. *Family Relations*, 31, 409–414. Copyrighted 1982 by the National Council on Family Relations, 3989 Central Ave. NE, Suite 550, Minneapolis, MN 55421. Reprinted by permission.

Infant crying can elicit very strong feelings in parents. There is some evidence that caregivers are biologically predisposed to answer a baby's cries, which explains the emotional pull parents sometimes feel upon hearing their baby cry. The crying is a signal, and the responsive caregiver wants to react to it. Crying in the early months of life is not an attempt on the part of the infant to manipulate or reject the parent—and it is certainly not an indication of being spoiled. Babies who are fussy simply have high need levels.

There has always been controversy about whether picking up a crying baby reinforces the crying and causes the baby to cry all the more, or if babies whose cries are promptly responded to feel their needs are being met and cry less. Research suggests that the latter is the case. Babies of mothers who picked them up soon after they began to cry did less crying by the time they were a year old than babies of mothers who responded to their infants' cries slowly or not at all (Bell & Ainsworth, 1972). It is believed that parents who respond to their infant's cries as consistently and effectively as possible build feelings of security and trust in the infant (Sroufe, 1977). The infant experiences a sense of potency with regard to her or his effect on the world, and doesn't need to cry as much later, because experience has taught the infant that the caregiver will meet his or her needs.

It can be very stressful for parents when their baby cries for prolonged periods of time and they are unable to make the baby stop. It is important for parents to remain calm, since anxious, harassed, frustrated, tense parents may begin to contribute to the cycle of fretfulness the infant is experiencing and heighten disruptive behavior (Schaper, 1982). Fathers may be particularly affected by infant crying; sometimes frustrated fathers blame mothers for not being able to stop the baby from crying. Mothers seem to be more able than fathers to cope with a crying infant without feeling personally inadequate or negative toward their spouses (Wilkie & Ames, 1986). On the other hand, fathers tend to have more difficulty than mothers with feelings of powerlessness and anxiety, which may lead fathers to feel more negative about lifestyle changes related to the baby in general. Possible coping strategies might include minimizing the overall stresses in life during these trying weeks by cutting down on the number of visitors to the home, finding someone to help with child care and household chores, and trying to sleep when the baby does to replenish depleted energy levels.

Sometimes the cries of babies are attributed to a mysterious ailment known as *colic*, which affects about 20 percent of normal, full-term infants. Colic is a catch-all term for symptoms such as extreme fussiness, sustained periods of crying (usually in the evening), and abdominal discomfort (Karlsrud, 1987). The timetable for colic is fairly predictable, beginning at two to three weeks of age and usually lasting until three to four months of age. The cause is unknown, but some suggestions for relieving the symptoms of colic involve holding the baby more erect during feeding, more frequent burping, offering a pacifier, and applying gentle pressure on the baby's abdomen. Colic is not a serious medical condition, and babies who experience colic are not sick. On the contrary, they often thrive physically and are hearty eaters who blossom into responsive, active, alert infants. But colic is an unpleasant experience for most parents, who become understandably tense amid the noise level and frustration of dealing with a crying infant. If parents are in doubt, it is best to seek a pediatrician's opinion regarding whether the baby has colic or some other possible problem. A sense of humor and being able to take a break from caring for the colicky baby occasionally are good preventive mental health measures for parents, but the best relief for colic is time. Sooner or later, the symptoms do go away.

SOCIAL AND EMOTIONAL ISSUES

Social development refers to the evolution of a system of relationships in which each person contributes to the exchange, and strong affectional feelings and mutual caring are present. Many people are puzzled when social development is discussed with relationship to infants and toddlers. After all, what could they contribute to a social relationship? The answer is quite a bit. Biological theorists believe that infants and toddlers have a number of attributes and behavioral predispositions that are very adaptive. The physical appearance of newborns seems to release a feeling of protectiveness in adults. An infant's smile is extremely endearing, and evokes a positive social response from others. Belsky & Tolan (1981) have listed many characteristics that may be important to infants' roles as "producers of their own development." These include gender, activity level, cuddliness, responsivity, physical attractiveness, alertness, affective expressiveness, susceptibility to illness, readability, and predictability. Perhaps the best example of bidirectionality in infant social exchanges is shown in the very important relationship babies develop with their caregivers.

Attachment

The existence of at least one stable, long-term affectionate relationship between a child and another person is needed in order for adequate social development to occur (Bowlby, 1969). In the past, this person has usually been the mother, but it could also be the father or another caregiver. The term *attachment* refers to a long-lasting but changing relationship between the caregiver and the infant. It takes most of the infant's first year to develop, and transforms as the infant grows and the relationship develops. For the first few months of life, the baby responds to people in general, and is not very discriminating. During the next few months, babies become more intense in their social responses, especially directing their efforts to familiar persons. The infant is able to distinguish his or her primary caregiver and tries to stay particularly close to that one person.

The next phase of attachment is particularly interesting. The clear-cut phase of attachment begins at seven to twelve months and ends around the second or third year of life. At this time, the infant is able to locomote by crawling or walking, which greatly enhances the infant's ability to seek proximity, or nearness, to the caregiver and to explore the physical environment. The infant uses the caregiver as a "base" from which to explore the world, returning to the caregiver when security is needed and then departing again.

Infants may protest or express alarm at the caregiver's departure. They use a repertoire of *attachment behaviors,* such as clinging, asking to be picked up, following, crying when left, and generally seeking and maintaining nearness, to assert their need to be with their caregiver. During this stage infants begin to show *stranger anxiety,* or the fear of people they don't know—a developmentally appropriate reaction. The caregiver is the center of the infant's world, and all others are intruders. The last phase of attachment occurs as the child begins to understand the caregiver's goals, feelings, and points of view. A more complex caregiver-child relationship becomes possible as the child is able to communicate more effectively and adjust behaviors.

There is much evidence for the concept of attachment and its importance in child development. The richness of attachment research is found particularly in the work of Mary Ainsworth and her colleagues (Ainsworth, Blehar, Waters, & Wall, 1978), using a research paradigm called the "strange situation," which consists of seven episodes of separation and reunion between twelve-month-olds and their mothers. The purpose is not to see if the infants and mothers are attached, but to look at the quality of the attachment. Three major patterns of response have been identified and described. *Securely attached* infants use caregivers as a secure base for exploration and show interest in unfamiliar people and objects in an unfamiliar setting. They show mild protest upon separation from their caregiver, but are happy upon the caregiver's return. They accept being put down, and show confidence in the caregiver's accessibility. Babies who can't seem to make up their minds when choosing between playing with toys and being near their caregivers exemplify the *anxious/ambivalent* attachment pattern. These infants tend to be wary of strangers and do not show extended exploration. They are usually upset when separated from their caregivers, and are resistant or not easily comforted when reunited with them. Babies who are anxious/ambivalent seem to feel anxiety about the caregiver's continued accessibility. Their behavior vacillates because they are unable to trust that their needs will be met. The *anxious/avoidant* attachment pattern is characterized by babies who are not upset when their caregiver leaves them with a stranger, but are quite distressed if left alone. When they are upset, they are likely to avoid approaching the caregiver, and will actively resist all efforts at being comforted. Since Ainsworth's original work was completed, an additional attachment pattern, *disorganized/disoriented* has been identified (Main & Soloman, 1986). These babies seem to have no coherent coping mechanisms, exhibiting disorganized and contradictory behaviors. They seem unable to decide if they want to approach or avoid their caregiver, making movements and then freezing in midair. Their affect appears depressed. The disorganized/disoriented pattern has been found among children who have been maltreated (Carlson, Cicchetti, Barnett, & Braunwald, 1989).

What do these patterns of attachment tell us? Securely attached relationship patterns are considered optimal, while the other patterns of relationship are viewed as problematic or deviant. The quality of attachment relationships reflects the sensitivity and responsiveness of parental behavior (Ainsworth, Bell, & Stayton, 1974). Parents who respond perceptively to the baby's signals (e.g., crying, gazing, looking away, smiling) tend to have securely attached infants. Inappropriate response on the part of the parent, or not responding at all, leads to anxious attachment.

Attachment theory suggests that the quality of the mother-child relationship is predictive of other close relationships the child develops (Park & Waters, 1989). Research has demonstrated many longer term associations based on early patterns of secure and insecure relationships, since attachment relationships may provide a working model for other relationships in life (Eiden, Teti, & Corns, 1995). Of particular interest is the research on peer relationships. Children who have secure attachments tend to have more positive peer relationships in toddler, preschool, and early school years than children categorized as having insecure attachments. Children with secure attachments have peer relationships described as more responsive, less controlling, less aggressive, and happier (Jacobson & Wille, 1986; Park & Waters, 1989). Children with insecure attachment relationships exhibited more dependent (Sroufe, Fox, & Pancake, 1983) and aggressive (Jacobson & Wille, 1986) behaviors, and were less competent in peer relationships. This appears to be especially true for boys (Lewis, Feiring, McGuffog, & Jaskir, 1984; Cohn, 1990).

Since the effects of insecure attachment relationships are not the same for both boys and girls, it is reasonable to assume that other factors intervene. Although attachment relationships are important, insecure attachments do not doom children to later problems, just as secure attachments do not always protect children from later problems (Lewis, Feiring, McGuffog, & Jaskir, 1984). An intervention study that randomly assigned anxiously attached twelve-month-olds and their mothers to a control or intervention group showed positive outcomes for both mothers and children (Lieberman, Weston, & Pawl, 1991). When compared with the control group after a year, mothers in the intervention group exhibited higher levels of interaction and empathy with their children, and children in the intervention group displayed less avoidant, resistant, and angry behaviors. Further study is needed to examine the long-term effects of intervention, and the specific needs of potentially high-risk groups.

Parenting Challenges: Attachment in an Applied Context

> We go out about twice a month. Our son cries and carries on every time we leave him with a babysitter. He grabs our legs and tries to keep us from going. We've had the same sitter since he was born, so it's not like she's a stranger. And we've never left him for more than a few hours at a time. Why is he so insecure and afraid? What are we doing wrong?
>
> *Mother of a one-year-old*

Separation anxiety is a normal reaction on the part of a young child to the departure of his or her caregiver. Behaviors that exemplify separation anxiety include a vocal protest, physical clinging, and general expressions of alarm. These behaviors are not proof that children are "spoiled," but rather that they are trying to convey loving feelings in the only way they know how. It is easiest to understand separation anxiety in the context of attachment. The caregiver is the center of the young child's world, and a special attachment relationship between the two is formed. The child feels most secure when he or she is near this special person. Children feel pain and distress when they are separated from those they love, just as an adult does. The difference is that children lack the cognitive ability to process the time and context of the separation, so they are more likely to overreact.

Since there are many individual differences in children who are "normal," one can expect variability in the length and severity of separation anxiety. However, major developmental events often coincide with a heightened sense of separation anxiety in children, which then subsides when children adjust to the changes they were experiencing. Throughout the early childhood years, children seem to seek exclusive relationships when they experience rapid developmental changes, needing lots of reassurance from a caring adult (see Box 5-2). Milestones in locomotive abilities, such as crawling and walking, or large increases in verbal and cognitive abilities during the toddler years are examples of events that may overwhelm the child. It may be frightening for children to do so many things alone that they previously needed help with. Sleeping difficulties often accompany episodes of separation anxiety. At certain developmental stages, young children need the extra reassurance from a special caregiver that they are safe and loved in order to cope with growth and change.

Temperament

> I can't believe it, but he has a personality of his own already. He was born with it, and each day I learn something new about him. He knows what he likes and what he doesn't like, and tries hard to get me to understand. No one told me parenthood would be like this. Discovering who he is brings me great joy.
>
> *Mother of a two-month-old*

 ## Box 5-2 What Parents Can Do About Separation Anxiety

1. Remember that clinging and crying at separation are urgent requests for reassurance, love, and attention.
2. Parents should *always* say goodbye to the child directly and give assurances that they will be back.
3. Minimize separation distress by helping the child become familiar with new surroundings and people before actually being left with them.
4. Parents should be understanding and accepting, but firm. Scolding, criticizing, mocking, teasing, or threatening a child over separation

distress is never a good idea.
5. Parents should resist the temptation to bribe a child for controlling or hiding their distress.
6. Parents should try to go out less often if there are multiple stresses in the child's life. But when parents do go out, prepare the child directly. Be honest and don't back down. Parents should always make the decision whether they are going or not. Don't leave it up to the child.

Adapted from: Katz, L.G. (1986, February). Coping with separation anxiety. *Parents*, 150. Copyright © 1996 Gruner & Jahr USA Publishing. Reprinted from *Parents Magazine* by permission.

An extensive body of literature pertaining to individual differences focuses on the concept of temperament. Temperament is the behavioral style of an individual—*how* the individual responds across a variety of different situations, as opposed to what he does or why she does it. Temperament is biologically based and tends to be stable over time, although aspects of it may be modified by environmental experiences (Bornstein & Lamb, 1992). In other words, all people are born with a certain temperament, but can learn to make changes that make it easier to live with themselves and others. Temperament has been examined from many different theoretical perspectives, and researchers have had to deal with measurement problems and methodological challenges, but conceptually, temperament endures as a rich, complex aspect of understanding human behavior.

The first systematic research on temperament began in the 1950s, and still continues today. The researchers involved (Thomas & Chess, 1977) proposed nine categories of temperament. *Activity level* refers to the proportion of physically active and inactive periods people have during an average day. *Rhythmicity* is the biological regularity and predictability of bodily functions such as hunger, excretion, sleep, and wakefulness. *Approach or withdrawal* focuses on a person's initial response to something new, whether it is positive or negative. *Adaptability* refers to the ease with which a person adapts over time (regardless of the initial response) to a new situation or one that has changed. *Threshold of responsiveness* specifies the intensity level of stimulation that is necessary before a person responds—sensitivity. *Intensity of reaction* is the energy level or vigor of a person's response, how mild or intense a person is. *Quality of mood* refers to the amount of pleasant, joyful, friendly behavior as contrasted with unpleasant, crying, unfriendly behavior. *Distractibility* is the ease with which a person may be diverted from an ongoing activity by extraneous outside stimuli or events. *Attention span and persistence* refers to the length of time a particular activity is pursued by a person, how long the person stays with an activity, despite obstacles encountered along the way.

Three common temperament types were then derived from the nine categories. *Easy* temperaments are characterized by regularity, positive approach responses to new stimuli, high adaptability to change, positive mood, and mild or moderate intensity. Babies with easy temperaments are the ones who quickly develop regular sleep and feeding schedules, like new experiences, are rarely frustrated, and smile much of the time. *Difficult* temperaments were characterized by irregularity in biological functions, negative withdrawal responses to new stimuli, nonadaptability or slow adaptability to change, and intense mood expressions that are frequently negative. Babies with irregular sleep and feeding schedules, prolonged adjustment periods to anything new, frequent frustration, and loud crying were considered difficult. *Slow-to-warm* temperaments are characterized by a combination of negative, but mild, intensity responses to new stimuli, with slow adaptability after repeated contact. Babies who were slow to warm were often negative about first-time experiences, but adapted when allowed to reexperience situations over and over. It is important to note that 35 percent of the babies in the study were not categorized because they did not fit into any grouping. Those that did fit were still on a continuum (e.g., somewhat difficult, very easy, etc.). Subsequent research

(Bates, Olson, Pettit, & Bayles, 1982; Buss & Plomin, 1984) has focused on the difficult temperament because of its conceptual robustness and its applications to relationship issues.

The nine temperament characteristics and the three types of temperament are important to examine, both in terms of the child's personality and the parent's personality. Identifying a child's temperamental characteristics and type may help the parent learn about and appreciate the child's individuality, as well as be aware of traits that may possibly be problematic. Putting parents in touch with their own temperaments may help them discover more about themselves and what triggers them both positively and negatively as parents. For example, an easy, relatively inactive, sedentary parent who has a long attention span may have trouble dealing with a child who is difficult, extremely active and distractible, because their approaches to life are so different. There is much variability in people's perceptions and preferences, however; someone who is perceived as difficult by one person may seem interesting to another. A person with an easy temperament may seem boring to someone else. Perceptions can greatly influence our behavior.

The *"goodness of fit" model* (Thomas & Chess, 1977) refers to how well the expectations and demands of the environment (as provided by the parent or caregiver) coincide with the capacities and behavioral style, or temperament, of the child. If the child meets the expectations and demands, there is a good chance for optimal development. If the expectations are not met, maladaptive development may occur. If you are a first-time parent and your expectation is that babies sleep most of the time, you may have some difficulties "fitting" with a difficult, fussy infant. If your expectation is that babies cry a lot, however, you may be worried when your newborn does nothing more than eat and sleep. Temperament plays a crucial role in all social interactions—with parents, children, a spouse, friends, peers, teachers, and bosses. Although the "goodness of fit" model has been postulated in relation to parenting, it could also apply to many other situations.

The original ideas about temperament have been refined and changed to fit with new information and beliefs regarding the concept, its origin, and development over time (Buss & Plomin, 1984; Rothbart & Derryberry, 1981). Cross-cultural research supports the existence of these dimensions in different settings (Super & Harkness, 1981), but the importance of the influence of temperamental traits and environmental demands on each other is a theme that remains. Environmental experiences may modify or change some traits, while reinforcing others (Bornstein & Lamb, 1992). An athletic parent may provide an environment that encourages an inactive child to change her or his natural tendencies and move around more, whereas the same child might feel reinforcement from a physically inactive parent. At the same time, strong temperamental traits may change environmental situations by having an impact upon events or settings. An active, sociable child may exude so much energy and friendliness that the usually quiet and uneventful trips to the grocery store become major social occasions where strangers stop to talk to both child and parent. Cultural factors also influence the temperament-environment dynamic. Because of social support networks and cultural parenting practices, a child with similar temperament characteristics is viewed very differently by parents in the United States and parents in Kenya (Super & Harkness, 1981). Successful interactions between the environment and individual temperament characteristics within a cultural context provide many opportunities for research.

Parenting Challenges: Temperament in an Applied Context

Our daughter is an intense, active, unpredictable child who doesn't adapt well to new situations. Every time we go to a gathering of our extended family, we feel inadequate because she fusses and never settles down. What should we do?

Father of a five-month-old

Sometimes a child's temperament is difficult for a parent to deal with on a practical level. It is important to remember that a child's temperament is not a reflection on parenting ability. Some children are easy for everyone to deal with, some are easy for some people to handle but not for others, and some are difficult for everybody. Typically children with easy temperaments give parents confidence, while difficult children drain feelings of confidence. If parents respect differences instead of trying to eliminate them, they will better accommodate the needs of the child and be sensitive to the child's abilities. A child's personality cannot be changed, but as children grow older, adaptive coping behaviors and skills can be taught to help them develop optimally.

The job of parents is to provide guidance and limits. Parents must continue to modify the environment and work with the child even when it is frustrating. The important thing to remember is not to let a child's temperament determine the effectiveness of the parent. Parents are responsible for helping children meet their individual needs within different environments with various expectations for behavior. Planning for a child's needs and helping a child feel success in places that are challenging for him or her to deal with is slow, painstaking, but necessary work. An infant who is well rested, fed, and comfortable upon entering a stressful situation, and one who is given time to adjust to new settings and people might, over time, be more able to adapt.

Social Aspects of Parenting Toddlers

Wanted: Parent of Two-Year-Old. Must have extraordinary degree of patience. Must have the ability to handle the demands of an unpredictable, negative, stubborn subordinate with delusions of grandeur. Negotiating abilities essential.

(Moschell, 1991)

When children reach the toddler stage, many parents begin to feel as if they have created a monster. Even though they have heard about the "terrible two's," they are unprepared to meet the demands easily and begin to doubt their parenting abilities. Most parents question whether the stubborn behavior they see is a passing phase or a permanent personality characteristic. To deal with these issues, we must first have a basic understanding of toddlers and their needs.

As the toddler learns to assert herself, she discovers that she is independent of her parent. She is beginning to learn that she has an impact on the world around her. That is why most toddlers' favorite words are "me," "mine," and "no." The child has expanding skills and abilities that she wants to assert, but her inability to do so at times is greatly frustrating. The frustration is so overwhelming that it is hard for the child to control. Thus, temper tantrums are more common at this stage of development. And when the child's world is changing so quickly, it becomes even more important that some basic parts remain unchanged. Testing the limits then becomes a part of daily life, just to see if the results are consistent from day to day (Rothenberg, Hitchcock, Harrison, & Graham, 1995). Routines are also a very important part of the toddler's life, since the sameness in the sequence of events is reassuring and helps the child feel more in control (Ames & Ilg, 1976). Expectations of control may lead to greater feelings of cooperation. Toddlers also have lots of energy, so avoiding boredom can lead to greater cooperation and harmony.

Many techniques can be used by parents to help make day to day living with toddlers a little easier (Rothenberg, Hitchcock, Harrison, & Graham, 1995; Ames & Ilg, 1976). First of all, avoid asking questions to which the child will automatically respond negatively. Along these same lines, don't give the child choices when he doesn't have one. "Would you like to get ready for bed now?"

CLOSE TO HOME   JOHN McPHERSON

"Ma'am, I distinctly saw you turn completely around in your seat to give that child his pacifier. I'm afraid I'm going to have to charge you with driving under the influence of toddlers."

CLOSE TO HOME © 1996 John McPherson. Reprinted with permission of UNIVERSAL PRESS SYNDICATE. All rights reserved.

is an inappropriate question unless the parent is willing to comply with and accept the decision of the child either way, whether the answer is yes or no. Instead, the phrasing, "We must get ready for bed now," is a better choice. The toddler should be given limited choices whenever possible. "Do you want apple juice or orange juice?" is one example. Toddlers are usually easy to distract, which can be helpful to the parent when disaster is brewing. Allow toddlers to do whatever they can for themselves, even if it takes them a longer time to accomplish it. Finally, remember to avoid power struggles with toddlers. Adults have both the authority and strength to make decisions about the child's life; contests designed to show it are not helpful to the child's growth and development.

COGNITIVE ISSUES

> I watch her lying there looking so intently at her mobile and I wonder what, if anything, is going on in her mind. What does she know? How can I do the best job of educating her? It's overwhelming to think that we're responsible to teach her what she needs to learn. I don't even know where to begin.
>
> *Father of a three-month-old*

Most parents feel somewhat inadequate when faced with the task of teaching their children. Luckily, much of the teaching in the infancy and toddler years comes naturally to the parent, since basic skills such as how to crawl, walk, talk, eat solid foods, and sleep through the night are learned. Some experts, however, believe parents are not doing enough to help their infants and toddlers acquire knowledge. Burton White (1975) suggests that most parents do a good job during the first eight months of life, but relatively few are able to be as effective as they should be in the eight-to-thirty-six-month period. Parents can influence and support children's cognitive development throughout infancy by providing structure for the learning environment.

Learning Activities and Materials

Parents can enhance learning by providing a *supportive physical learning environment*. The physical environment is an important vehicle for the learning that takes place, so restrictions within the infant and toddler environment should be minimized. Piaget's theory suggests that because of the way in which young children acquire knowledge, they should be surrounded by things that they can explore freely and learn from. Parents who are trying to maximize their child's exploration often put breakable things away for a few months and try to remove all of the "no's" from the child's play space. These steps ensure that there is sufficient room and opportunity for children to investigate and learn.

Parents can also provide *interesting play materials*. This does not necessarily mean expensive toys. Many parents are shocked to find their one-year-old ignoring new toys and happily playing with the box and wrapping paper after opening birthday presents. Quantity of materials is less important than quality. High-quality playthings stimulate children to be actively participating and doing things for themselves, exploring and creating, rather than passively observing. Toys, games, and activities that stimulate children to look, listen, touch, taste, and smell fit in well with Piaget's conception of the sensorimotor period. Brightly colored toys of various textures that can be put together, pulled apart, stacked, and pushed are appropriate for infants and toddlers.

When parents are selecting learning materials for young children, the following hints are helpful to keep in mind (Cohen, 1976). Toys and games should be flexible so that a variety of age-appropriate, nonsexist learning experiences are offered. Materials should be as free of detail as possible in order to encourage the child to create and imagine, simple enough that their construction can be easily comprehended, and large enough to be easily manipulated by small hands that are not well coordinated. Learning materials should also be unbreakable. Everything must be highly durable, since children give materials such hard use. Price is always a consideration, but many times a higher initial investment proves to be more economical in the long run because repairs and replacement parts are avoided. If the materials are resistant to weathering, easy to care for, and easy to store, there is less chance for breakage. Finally, the safety of an item should always be analyzed before a purchase is made, since nontoxic learning materials are a must for young children who like to put everything into their mouths. It is important that an item be designed so that injuries from sharp edges, protruding parts, and splinters are avoided. Electrical, mechanical, and thermal hazards must also be absent. Materials that are flame resistant are desirable, as well as those that are easily cleaned (see Box 5-3).

Finally, parents can provide *supportive interactions for learning.* Parents who are approachable when children are playing become resources for young children, and take on the role of consultants (White, 1975). When children at this

---

 Box 5-3 Hints on Purchasing Toys for Infants and Toddlers

1. Become an informed toy shopper, read any available information from unbiased sources (government publications, consumer reports, etc.).
2. Quality should be the number one consideration for most purchases. Toys are an investment only if you buy wisely.
3. Novelty toys are often tempting but usually not the best to buy. They typically are not well constructed. Battery-operated toys are also usually a disappointment.

4. If the toy packaging contains printed material, read it. You can find warnings for appropriate use, age groups, reputable endorsements, etc.
5. Avoid buying anything with parts small enough to be choked on and anything with sharp protruding parts.
6. Give your potential purchases a test. If you could break them easily, they are a poor choice.

Adapted from: O'Brien, M., Porterfield, J., Herbert-Jackson, E., & Risley, T.R. (1979). *The toddler center.* Baltimore: University Park Press.

age have questions or need help because they are "stuck," adults can assist them by providing immediate positive interaction and help. The teachable moment must be seized. Parents can facilitate learning by talking to the child, asking questions, and verbalizing the experience. Gradually, infants begin to associate words with their actions. Parents can also facilitate learning by being interested in what the child is showing them, or by modeling curiosity and exploratory behavior. This attention is a special gift that parents and other caregivers can provide for children, and it is essential to the love of learning.

Language Development

An important parenting task throughout the life-span is to communicate, or exchange information, with children. Evelyn Thoman and Sue Browder (1987) have written a book about how parents can understand their baby's unspoken language and natural rhythms. They compare this kind of communication to the basic arm movements, verbal expressions, and nonverbal cues used in a dance, and postulate that babies are born dancing. In other words, babies are able to communicate with people immediately if their form of communication is recognized and received. This type of communication marks the beginning of the parent-child relationship.

Language is one important form of communication. Often, infants are ignored when it comes to language abilities because for a long time, babies cannot talk. When they do begin to speak during the toddler period, they often cannot carry on coherent conversations for more than a few minutes. There is more to language than saying words or learning how to understand what others are saying, however. Language is just one form of a broader intention to communicate and share information (Fogel, 1984; Sherrod, Vietze, & Friedman, 1978).

Researchers have been exploring how parents contribute to early language development. Many aspects of language are embedded in the social interaction between the child and parent (Bruner, 1983). To communicate, infants must first learn certain aspects of conversational behavior, such as *turntaking*. Speakers usually take turns and avoid interrupting each other; therefore, babies must learn when to speak and when to listen. Even in early infancy, parents can talk to babies and wait for a response (verbal or nonverbal) and respond to the baby's sounds. Sometimes *echoing*, or repeating what the child says, even cooing or babbling sounds, can encourage language. These vocal cues, in addition to facial expressions, may be extremely important in helping infants learn language (Locke, 1994).

As infants become more able, they begin the process of learning what words do (Nelson, 1985)—how language affects others in terms of social interaction, and which words actually refer to which objects. Parents can support language through *scaffolding*, where they create a support system for learning by providing attention, guidance, and feedback that will progressively enhance the child's mastery of a task. For language development, parents often use predictable interactional routines as a framework around which interaction takes place (Ratner & Bruner, 1978), since these activities help to make the meaning of words apparent and often reinforce turntaking (Bruner, 1983). These routines include such games as "peek-a-boo" and book reading activities. Part of the benefit of these activities is *establishing joint attention* between the child and parent. The parent watches to see what the child is interested in and provides language stimulation that corresponds to the activity or object that has caught the child's attention. One way of stimulating language development is *labeling,* or identifying objects. Research suggests that children may have larger vocabularies when parents provide labels for objects their children are focused on during episodes of joint attention (Tomasello & Farrar, 1986). Trying to redirect a child's attention and teach a new word was not a successful strategy. The key seems to be for parents to relate their language to the child's ongoing activities.

From roughly eighteen to thirty months, toddlers are involved in the process of learning what particular words mean (de Villiers & de Villiers, 1992). This process is known as the *naming explosion,* because there is such a large growth in vocabulary. Parents aid this process by naming things for children at a very basic level that matches their specific abilities. As their abilities grow, parents use more complex labels. For example, when parents are talking to one-year-olds, they use words like "dog," "cat," and "money"; if they are talking to a four-year-old, they may use words like "beagle," "Siamese," and "quarters." The different levels of language parents use help children understand language and organize words into categories.

Finally, parents can encourage language development by *expanding* the child's language. This is accomplished by restating what a child has said in a more sophisticated way, thus providing a model of the next step in language development. For example, if the child speaks in one-word sentences (such as "down"), the parent replies using a two- or three-word sentence ("you want down"), reinforcing the meaning and expanding what the child has said. Parents continue to expand children's language through the school years, adjusting their expansions to the next higher levels of complexity.

Language acquisition is a complex process, which is closely interrelated to both social and cognitive development. Many aspects of language development can be encouraged by parents, as was mentioned in earlier paragraphs. A list of practical suggestions for encouraging language development in infant's and toddlers can be found in Box 5-4.

Parenting Challenges: Language Development in an Applied Context

> What's the deal with talking "baby talk" to kids? Is it really a bad example for them?

"Baby talk" is the language that people use to speak to language-learning children, and it is not a bad example. In fact, it contains modifications that make it easier for infants and toddlers to learn language, and is found in many cultures (Fernald, Taeschner, Dunn, Papousek, Boyssen-Bardies, & Fukui, 1989). These modifications include simplifying difficult pronunciations, using a higher pitched voice, using a greater range of pitch in speaking, and speaking more slowly. Changes like these make speech more interesting to young children, and they are more responsive to people who use it. The modifica-

Box 5-4 How to Encourage Baby's Language Development

1. *Talk* to the baby
   - Talk about what you see in the world around you.
   - Talk about what the baby is doing.
   - Talk about routines (e.g., waking up, getting dressed, washing hands, changing diapers, etc.).
   - Talk about your feelings toward the baby. You can never say "I love you" too many times.
   - Ask the baby questions, and pause so she knows conversation is a two-way street.
   - Express your emotions.
   - Verbalize the baby's emotions.
2. *Listen* to the baby.
   - Be interested in the baby's sounds.
   - Imitate the baby's sounds.
   - Pause after speaking to give the baby a chance to respond (either verbally or nonverbally).
3. *Play games* with the baby.
   - Play talking games, such as "peek-a-boo."
   - Play singing games, such as "pat-a-cake."
   - Play naming games, naming toys, food, body parts, and objects.
   - Do finger plays with the baby, such as "Where Is Thumbkin?"
   - Play picture games with the baby.
   - Use puppets with the baby.
4. *Sing* to the baby.
   - Sing lullabies, such as "Rock-a-bye Baby."
   - Sing nursery rhymes, such as "Baa Baa Black Sheep."
   - Sing action songs, such as "Ring Around the Rosie."
   - Sing made-up songs about the baby and his activities. Cheat and use existing songs, substituting the baby's name.
   - Sing regular songs, such as "You Are My Sunshine."
   - Expose babies to all kinds of different music.
5. *Read* to the baby.
   - Look at picture books together.
   - Read stories.
   - Look at photo albums and talk about them.
   - Look at magazines and talk about them.

tions we make when talking to babies are natural; even preschoolers can modify their speech in this way when talking to someone younger than themselves. As children grow older, the modifications continue in other ways. Adults usually speak in sentences that are one to two words longer than the sentences a child is using—again providing a model for them. Responsive parents across many cultures use these adjustments in language to encourage the development of their children; baby talk should be used appropriately and often.

PHYSICAL DEVELOPMENT ISSUES

Three short-term goals that parents of infants report are protecting children against hazards, the management of eating, and the management of sleeping (Richman, Miller, & Solomon, 1988). Parents feel responsible for keeping their infants healthy, yet many are not completely informed as to what the proper course of action is to achieve this goal. Some of the first questions to arise often center on feeding the infant: what, how much, and when. An understanding of basic infant nutrition and feeding practices is helpful. Questions regarding sleeping also arise. Illnesses, infections, and drug reactions are all worries that parents of infants have. Choosing a trusted physician to give guidance in these areas is essential. Keeping infants safe from disease and injury through preventive measures such as immunizations and safety precautions is also a part of parenting related to the infant's physical health.

Nutrition

The history of feeding infants and children is diverse and interesting reading. From a practical standpoint, the bottom line is that practices and recommendations have varied quite a bit in the last 100 years. There are still disagreements in the medical and nutritional communities about what is best. Some believe that companies who sell baby formula and baby food have had far too much influence in shaping feeding practices. Amid this confusion, one resource has been invaluable in giving a sound perspective from a developmental point of view. Ellyn Satter's (1983) book, *Child of Mine: Feeding with Love and Good Sense* has been very helpful in providing basic information. Many of her ideas will be presented in this section.

Infant Nutrition

The first major decision parents must make regarding their infant's nutrition is whether the infant will be breastfed, bottle fed, or both. The decision whether to breastfeed is a difficult and emotional choice for many women. There are many advantages of breastfeeding (Eiger & Olds, 1972). First, it is very convenient. It is always ready to use and is always the right temperature. There is no formula to mix nor bottles to wash. It is also more economical, since no special equipment is needed and formula can be costly. Since the baby controls the amount and frequency of the feedings, there is less tendency for the infant to overeat. There is less indigestion and "spit-up" because breast milk is easier to digest than other milks, but the most compelling reasons for breastfeeding have to do with the infant's health. Breast milk is ideally suited for the baby, which means that breastfed babies have fewer allergies, less diarrhea and constipation, a reduced chance of colic, fewer illnesses and infections, and fewer dental problems. Breast milk is generally the best choice; however, special circumstances regarding the health of the infant (such as lack of an adequate sucking reflex) or mother (such as an insufficient milk supply) may prevent successful breastfeeding. In addition, there are many reasons why women choose not to breastfeed. Many women find that the idea of breastfeeding doesn't appeal to them, or that they don't want to be tied down. Others report feeling uncomfortable or embarrassed, which is understandable in a society that views breasts as objects of sexual desire rather than food for hungry babies. Formula is a viable substitute for women who choose not to breastfeed. Many women use both breast and bottle feedings in an attempt to have the best of both worlds. Infants are quite adaptable to different feeding arrangements and circumstances. Emotionally positive interactions can take place during feedings with either method, as long as affectionate talking and touching occur.

The next major decision parents must make is when to introduce solid foods. There are many different schools of thought on this matter. It is commonly believed that feeding infants solid foods at an earlier age will help them sleep through the night earlier, although research has not confirmed this. Some physicians feel that early introduction of solids leads to obesity and increased allergies. The best idea is to take hints from the infant as to when the introduction of solid food and other milestones in nutrition should be initiated. Satter (1983) recommends that feeding practices be matched to the child's developmental needs. Her suggestions are found in Box 5-5.

Toddler Nutrition

Toddlers are notorious for being picky eaters, commonly rejecting foods that they previously ate with passion. Parents often shake their heads in dismay and wonder how their toddlers can survive and have so much energy when eating so little food, but toddlers seem quite able to get by even when they skip meals. Americans are prone to overeating, and may be encouraging their children to develop bad eating habits. Adults are often shocked to find out that the rule of thumb for toddler portion size is one-fourth or one-third the adult portion size, or one tablespoon per year of age (Satter, 1983). In a

---

Box 5-5 Guidelines for Feeding Infants

These guidelines recommend matching feeding practices to the child's developmental needs, instead of trying to force the infant into preconceived ideas of when foods should be introduced. The suggestions are:

1. Give the baby *only* breast milk (supplemented with vitamin D and fluoride) or formula for the first four to six months of life. There is some evidence that allergies and obesity can result from earlier introduction of solids.
2. When the baby can sit (supported) begin offering iron-fortified baby cereals mixed with formula or milk. Do this *after* the breast or bottle feeding.
3. When the baby turns his head or otherwise indicates he's full, take his word for it.
4. After baby is taking about 1/3 to 1/2 cup of mixed-in cereal a day, gradually begin offering a variety of fork-mashed, unseasoned table foods, always after the milk feeding.
5. At around eight to ten months, when the baby is able to sit alone, shows an interest in the family table, and is adept at conveying things to her mouth, start putting her up to the table at mealtime, where she can feed herself a vari-

ety of soft food that won't choke her. Offer an assortment that is likely to add up to a nutritious diet.
6. At the same time (if he hasn't already) he is ready to start drinking, with assistance, from the cup.
7. Now postpone the breast or bottle feeding until after the meal, and give formula or whole milk in a cup along with the meal.
8. As she eats more at mealtime and drinks from the cup, she will gradually lose interest in the breast or bottle and can generally be weaned, one feeding at a time, with no hassle. At this point, she is getting more of her nutritional needs from a variety of foods, and formula or breast milk becomes less important nutritionally, although it may still be important emotionally.
9. Once he is well established on table food, it is all right to switch to whole milk, or to whole evaporated milk, diluted one-to-one with water.

Adapted from: Satter, E. (1983). *Child of mine: Feeding with love and good sense.* Palo Alto, CA: Bull Publishing Co.

society such as ours, where overeating is the norm, this seems like a very small amount of food.

The goal for parents regarding toddlers' eating is to avoid power struggles over food. This includes nagging and force. Satter suggests that the parent is responsible for *what* kinds of foods are offered, *where* the child will eat and *when* food is presented, while the child is responsible for *how much* is eaten. Parents can assist toddlers in the eating process by remembering that tough and fibrous foods are difficult for young children to chew. Presenting nutritious foods already cut into bite-sized pieces and at room temperature will cut down on eating difficulties.

Sleeping

Sleeping is something many adults take for granted; however, most parents of infants and toddlers become much more interested in the concept of sleeping—for both themselves and their children. The old wives' tale to "let sleeping babies lie" comes well recommended from generations of parents. As was already mentioned, parents perceive sleeping issues to be among their "daily hassles," or low-level stresses. Questions regarding how long babies should sleep at night, when and how long they should nap, how to handle bedtime routines, how to make decisions about sleeping arrangements, and what to do when children wake in the middle of the night are common questions. Although much is known regarding sleep cycles and the physiology of sleep, there is very little research to help parents with the practical aspects of sleeping problems. Many books and parenting articles exist on this subject, but most are not backed by research.

An interesting approach to sleeping questions can be found by examining cross-cultural literature (Morelli, Rogoff, Oppenheim, & Goldsmith, 1992). The issue of the family bed, or letting infants sleep in their parents' bed, is a good example. In the United States, parents value independence. Therefore, as a culture, we assume that parents and infants should sleep separately, and bedtime routines and objects (such as stuffed animals and blankets) are used during the transition to sleep. In other cultures (for instance, among the Mayans), being close to the infants is the highest value, so it is assumed that the baby will sleep with the mother. The point is that parental values influence decision making, and what works well for one culture or family may not necessarily work for another. Absolute advice one way or another on matters of personal choice should be viewed with circumspection.

Health Issues

Parents often use medical doctors as resources and support persons for many parenting questions and problems during the infancy period (McKim, 1987). It is important for parents to establish an open relationship with their child's doctor in order to feel comfortable asking for help. This may be especially true for people with diverse educational backgrounds, since they may be less likely to ask doctors questions than highly educated parents (Koepke & Williams, 1989). Points to consider when choosing a doctor include communication skills

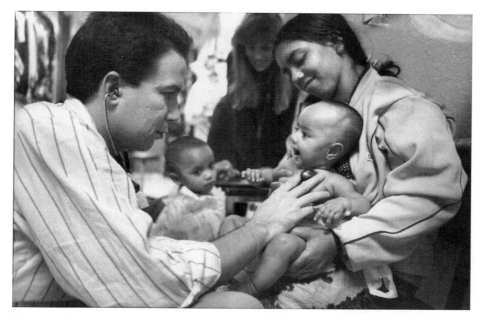

Since children's health is a major concern for parents, medical doctors are often important resources and support persons.
(Hazel Hankin/Stock, Boston)

with parents and children, location, convenience, hours, cost, philosophy, and professionalism (Gazella, 1982; Karlsrud, 1988). Being able to choose a doctor is a privilege few parents have; often, only people in higher socioeconomic groups have that choice. Many people have no choices, and many more have no access to health care at all. Choice also assumes availability, and many locations, especially in rural areas, lack physicians. Some people have limited choices in health care because of the specifications of their health insurance. These health care issues are of national concern, and are currently being debated.

Children's health is always of concern to parents. In one study, infant illness was the most frequently reported problem during the first year of life (McKim, 1987). Common ailments include colds, ear infections, rashes, intestinal problems, and teething-related complaints. During the infancy and toddler periods, parents often acquire information about health-related issues that they didn't have before. This list includes things such as when and how to administer acetaminophen for a fever, what to do if a child vomits the medicine, the proper diet for intestinal flu, when children are or aren't contagious, and when to call the doctor and when to wait (Yarrow, 1989). See Box 5-6 for suggestions regarding taking care of sick children.

A big part of infant health involves protecting children from harmful diseases that can do permanent harm physically or mentally, and may result in death. The goal is to *immunize* children so that they have a special capacity for resisting certain diseases. Common immunizations include DPT (*d*iphtheria, *p*ertussis or whooping cough, and *t*etanus or lockjaw), measles, tuberculosis,

Box 5-6 Taking Care of Sick Children

It is often stressful for parents when children are ill, since the parents themselves may also be sick, or are probably lacking sleep and are tired from caring for the sick child. From a practical point of view, it is helpful to be organized when dealing with sick children. This is especially true when talking to a doctor on the phone or taking the child to the doctor. The following tips can assist parents in getting organized.

1. Have a paper and pencil ready to take notes. Tell the doctor the name, age, weight, temperature, and symptoms of the child (what they are and how long the child has had them).

2. Parents should find out the following information from the doctor: what the parents should do, when they should do it, how much medication they should give the child (including when and for how long), what should happen if the treatment is working and when those results can be expected, what happens if the child doesn't get better, and what kinds of symptoms indicate that the parent should seek the doctor's help again.

3. As a safety precaution, keep records of any allergies the child may have to specific medications.

4. If things seem frantic in the home because of the demands of the sick child or children, many parents feel that writing down when they administered which medications to whom is essential. It is surprising how easily one can lose track of such details when one is exhausted.

Adapted from: *Parent Making: A Practical Handbook for Teaching Parent Classes About Babies and Toddlers* by B. Annye Rothenberg, Ph.D., et al. © 1995 Banster Press, P.O. Box 7326, Menlo Park, CA 94026.

---

mumps, Hib (*h*aemophilus *i*nfluenzae *b*, which causes bacterial meningitis), and polio.

Safety Needs

> **Wanted: Parent of Toddler.** Must be able to handle life-threatening emergencies several times daily while performing usual daily tasks. Must tolerate cluttered working conditions. Eyes in back of head a plus.
>
> (*Moschell*, 1991)

As soon as an infant is mobile in any way, parents face the overwhelming task of trying to provide a safe environment that is free from hazards for them. This is often not an easy thing to do. Accidental injuries in the home cause more children's deaths in our country per year than all childhood diseases combined (U.S. Consumer Product Safety Commission, 1985). The National Center for Health Statistics finds that millions of children under the age of five are injured at home each year—and many of these injuries and deaths come from "freak" happenings, such as toddlers drowning in toilets.

One successful strategy parents use to deal with safety issues is to *child-proof*, or rearrange, their homes to protect children from common safety hazards. Many parents find it helpful to follow a crawling infant or a walking toddler around the house to get perspective on the infant's view of the world and what kinds of mischief she or he can get into. Often, trouble spots become obvious. A checklist for home safety can be found in Box 5-7. Using checklists to aid in childproofing a home is a crucial safety step to take when mobile infants and toddlers are present. It is also important to remember, however, that childproofing should be used in addition to (not instead of) an attentive adult who is within sight at all times. Other strategies parents use, in addition to childproofing, are restricting the child's movement through the use of gates or playpens, and trying to teach the infant, even during the first year, what the hazards are (Richman, Miller, & Solomon, 1988).

In addition to home safety, parents must be concerned with environmental safety, such as protecting children from sunburns, insect bites and stings, and frostbite. Other safety issues revolve around the use of equipment. Car seats that ensure the safe restraint of children when they are traveling in automobiles are essential and legally required pieces of equipment. It is important for parents to be aware of controversies and issues regarding other pieces of equipment in order to make informed decisions. For example, many professionals believe the use of baby walkers is unsafe and developmentally inappropriate (Frazen & Felizberto, 1982; Wellman & Paulson, 1984). Many injuries result from walker accidents, such as falling down stairs and tipping over when the wheels become jammed. Even though most equipment is safe, parents must be aware of potential hazards and adhere strictly to age, weight, or developmental limits. Equipment use must be adjusted according to the needs of the developing child. Infant seats are wonderful in the early months, but as

---

 ## Box 5-7 Home Safety Checklist

1. Keep electric cords out of reach of children by running them under and behind heavy furniture.
2. Protect electrical outlets.
3. Keep electrical appliances and their cords out of reach so the child can't pull them down on himself or herself.
4. Be careful if anything small is dropped on a rug. Although it may be hard to see, a crawling baby finds it easily.
5. Block stairs with safety gates.
6. Pad sharp corners on furniture, stairs, and around the fireplace.
7. If matches, cigarettes, or foods such as nuts and popcorn are kept on low tables, move them out of a child's reach.
8. Watch out for breakage of glass shelves or tables when babies bang things on top.
9. Keep house plants out of reach. Many have poisonous parts.
10. Keep pots on the back burners and turn pot handles toward the back of the stove.
11. Store plastic bags and cleaning aids in high or locked places.
12. Check tablecloths. A child may be able to pull dishes off the table.
13. Many substances stored under the bathroom sink are dangerous if swallowed. Use this area for "soft storage" (towels, etc.) instead.
14. Areas containing gasoline, pesticides, paint, lawn mowers, and other tools should be off limits to children unless accompanied by an adult.
15. Block off or fence in a safe area for children to play. Spot and take care of any dangers in this part of the yard.

Adapted from: *Parent Making: A Practical Handbook for Teaching Parent Classes About Babies and Toddlers* by B. Annye Rothenberg, Ph.D., et al. © 1995 Banster Press, P.O. Box 7326, Menlo Park, CA 94026.

children grow bigger, stronger, and more active, the seats may tip over. Crib gyms hung across the baby bed are very stimulating to infants lying on their backs, but an infant just learning to sit up could fall forward and strangle in a short period of time. Strollers are great, but a child can choke to death while an unaware parent keeps on walking. Caution and good sense are needed.

Parenting Challenges: Physical Development in an Applied Context

> I am very concerned about toilet training my child. How do I know when to begin? What is the best way to go about it? How much should I push it? I am worried that I'll do something wrong.

One of the most talked about body-related issues in the toddler years is toilet training. We seem to be obsessed with this issue as a society, which is easy to understand when one looks at some of the Freudian ideas that have lingered on in societal lore. There is even controversy about whether it should be called toilet training, potty training, toilet teaching, or toilet learning (Rosenberg, 1990). Toileting is one of the first independent steps toddlers take where they call the shots; parents can force a child to go into the bathroom, but they cannot make the toddler use the toilet. One of the reasons parents get so concerned about toileting is that they find it difficult to deal with the loss of control.

Today's professionals agree that parents should wait until females are at least eighteen months old to begin the toilet training process, since that is the earliest time it is possible for the nervous system to be sufficiently mature to allow voluntary control over the sphincter muscles (Gibson, 1988). Because of maturational patterns, boys are usually not ready until even later. The average child has daytime control at two-and-a-half to three years, and nighttime control by three to four years (Azrin & Foxx, 1974). People who hear stories about children that were potty trained at ages much younger than this must realize that adults can be trained to set children on the toilet at specific times and "catch" immature reflexive responses. This does not mean that the child is toilet trained.

Starting the process of toilet training too early can be frustrating for both parent and child. Three areas of readiness can be examined to determine if a child is prepared to begin the process of toilet training (Azrin & Foxx, 1974). The first thing to look for is *bladder control*. Children who stay dry for several hours and urinate quite a bit at one time (as opposed to dribbling frequently) may be ready. Other indications are facial expressions or postures before they are about to urinate. Signs of *physical readiness* include finger and hand coordination to easily pick up objects and walking competently without assistance from room to room. These abilities are indicators of physical maturity that coincide with maturation of the sphincter muscles. The last area to examine is that of *instructional readiness*. Toddlers must be socially responsive and exhibit understanding before toilet training can be successful. Ask them to point to their nose, eyes, mouth, and hair. Ask them to stand up, sit on a chair, and walk with you to another room. See if they can imitate you in a simple task (such as pat-a-cake), bring you a familiar object (such as a toy), or put one familiar object with another (such as putting the dolly in the wagon). Children who can follow eight out of these ten simple directions are exhibiting readiness.

Parents who are most successful during the toilet training process are those who don't equate their abilities as parents or the child's intelligence with early toileting (Gibson, 1988). Each child reaches this milestone at his or her own individual rate, and parents must tune out the advice of friends and relatives and follow their own instincts about what is the best timing for their child. Older toddlers learn more quickly. Tips for parents who are involved with toilet training toddlers include being patient, cheerful, and consistent. It takes some time to learn about using the toilet, and all toddlers have accidents. Responding in anger can frighten a toddler, and expecting learning to happen when a child is experiencing exceptional stress or tension (such as moving to a new house or adjusting to a new sibling) is unrealistic. Being positive and calm can be very effective in encouraging the toddler. Talking about toileting with the child, using words and potty books to explain the process, buying new underpants that the child views as special, and providing a model can be helpful techniques.

CONTEXTUAL CLOSE-UP: HOME ENVIRONMENT

For many years, researchers have been interested in the impact of the home environment on children's development. Parents may be the most crucial influence within the home environment. Parental actions or nonactions give meaning to the environment, from the perspective of both what the environment contains and what it lacks (Bradley, 1995). This includes the emotional climate of the parent-child relationship, the physical surroundings provided by the parent, and parental encouragement of learning (Honzik, 1967).

Parents are responsible for five tasks in the home environment: sustenance, stimulation, support, structure, and surveillance (Bradley, 1995). *Sustenance* refers to biological survival, which is exemplified by parental provision of nutrition and shelter, and maintenance of health. *Stimulation* is sensory data that attracts attention and provides information. Exposure to a variety of stimulating objects and events can be beneficial (Elardo, Bradley, & Caldwell, 1975), but more stimulation is not always optimal; this task also involves parental prevention of overstimulation. *Support* refers to an environment that is responsive to the social and emotional needs of humans. Parents who provide supportive environments reinforce goal-directed behavior and give guidance and direction for functioning in other environments. *Structure* refers to the organization of the environment so that it is reasonably easy to use. Parents enhance learning by structuring predictable, orderly environments. Finally, *surveillance* refers to keeping track of the location and activities of the child, using age-appropriate parental monitoring of the environment.

Researchers (Elardo, Bradley, & Caldwell, 1975) have developed a measurement instrument called the HOME (Home Observation for Measurement of the Environment) to examine different aspects of home stimulation to determine how environment relates to cognitive outcomes for children at various ages. Parents can influence their child's development through responding to children both emotionally and verbally, organizing the environment, providing appropriate play materials, providing a variety of experiences, interacting with the child, and avoiding restrictive punishments. Although it is difficult to sort out specific environmental effects and the complex interactions between various environmental factors, the parental role within the context of the home may account for many differences in children's development.

SUMMARY

- Parents of infants and toddlers are in the *nurturing* stage of parenthood, where the major task is to form an attachment to the baby. Parents have a number of child-related concerns to deal with, as well as their own role changes.
- Infants, according to Erikson, have the developmental task of establishing trust. Trust is enhanced by parental sensitivity to infant cues. Toddlers have the task of establishing their autonomy. Parents have the task of dealing with the toddler's autonomy.
- Infants and toddlers are in the sensorimotor period of cognitive development, where knowledge occurs through action.
- Newborns have many unique characteristics and abilities. Crying is the newborn's major form of communication. Parents must learn to respond to the newborn's needs.
- Attachment is a crucial concept in parent-child relations. Infants who are securely attached use caregivers as a base of exploration, while insecurely attached infants are ambivalent, avoidant, or disorganized in their attempts to form relationships. The changing relationship between the child and caregiver may serve as a model for later relationships with peers, and others.
- Temperament, or behavioral style, is one avenue of exploring individual differences. Goodness of fit refers to how well the expectations and demands of the environment coincide with temperament characteristics.
- Parents can encourage language development through turntaking, echoing, scaffolding, establishing joint attention, and expanding the child's language.
- Nutrition, sleeping, illnesses, immunizations, and safety are issues of prime importance to infant and toddler health.
- The context of the home environment varies greatly, depending upon the parental tasks of sustenance, stimulation, support, structure, and surveillance.
- Infants and toddlers experience great strides in their growth in every area of development during the first two years of life. Parents must learn about their children's needs and personalities, as well as adjusting to their new parenting roles. All of this occurs at a time when many changes happen daily. Parenting infants and toddlers is a demanding and rewarding job.

Parenting Preschoolers

139

Wanted: **Parent of Preschoolers.** Must be omniscient, able to answer any "Why?" question while performing tasks such as driving through heavy traffic, cooking, showering, or making love. Depending on child's ability to nap, you may have to relinquish all coffee breaks. Mechanical skills needed to assemble trikes, wagons, and assorted plastic toys, usually without the instructions.

(Moschell, 1991)

As this quote demonstrates, parents find that preschool children (ages two–five years) can be both charming and challenging companions. They possess social, cognitive, and physical abilities that allow them to participate more fully in the world around them, as well as the communication skills to report these experiences and feelings. They are determined to try things out and do things for themselves. Because of these developmental changes, parents begin to have higher expectations for the behavior of their preschoolers, and are called upon to set more limits. Parents must help preschool children learn to be more independent and able, while still providing a safe environment in which they can grow. The parent-child relationship can play a crucial role in the preschool years, either as a major source of support or a major source of stress (Dumas & LaFreniere, 1993).

THE PARENTING ROLE

I asked him to please stop running in the house. Then I told him to please stop running in the house. Then I yelled at him to STOP RUNNING! Each time he replied, "Make me." He's drawing a line in the sand, and I don't know what to do about it.

Mother of a four-year-old

Theoretical Context

When children are approximately two to five years of age, parents enter into the *authority stage* of parenting (Galinsky, 1987). The transition into this stage is more gradual than the first two parenting stages, since it is more dependent upon characteristics of the developing child. In other words, the child's behavior determines when the parent needs to become more of an authority figure. It is a difficult transition, since the parent-child relationship becomes more adversarial. As children become more mobile and able, they begin to test the limits of their existence. Power and conflict become issues in the parent-child relationship. Within this context, parents face the task of accepting the responsibility of their authority over the child. They must establish, communicate, and enforce limits (Wapner, 1993). Parents must also begin to cope with parent-child conflicts by either avoiding or handling battles where the child's will is in direct opposition to the parent's will. This task presents quite a change from infancy, where the parent is mostly required to be nurturing. These experiences with setting limits help parents to realize that their child is separate from them, rather than an extension of them.

The parent must also begin to establish working relationships with other authority figures in the child's life (Galinsky, 1987). The most obvious person is the other parent. The coparenting relationships discussed in Chapter 2 continue to gain importance, as parents must work together to negotiate child-rearing issues. Common topics parents of preschoolers discuss are what to do if a child uses objectionable language or lies, what to do about defiant behavior, and what constitutes appropriate independence for this age. Teachers, caregivers, grandparents, and others may also be involved with the child. Sometimes parents must work closely with others to gain their cooperation in dealing with a particularly troublesome behavior, such as whining, in a consistent manner. The setting for interactions becomes more public with preschool children, so authority struggles are often undertaken in less than private circumstances. Many parents can relate to the added pressure of disciplining an uncooperative child in a store or restaurant. In addition, preschool children are exposed to more outside influences from the larger social world, such as peer relationships and the media (Lamb, Ketterlinus, & Fracasso, 1992). The parenting process is complicated by children's exposure to information that they are not yet able to comprehend. For the first time, many preschool parents experience the frustration of being unable to shelter their child from contact with violence, greed, and unhappiness.

According to Erikson's view of psychosocial development, preschool-aged children are in the stage of establishing *initiative*. In their eagerness to undertake many adultlike activities that appeal to them, children sometimes overstep the limits set by parents. The impatient preschooler who crosses the road by himself, or the enthusiastic preschooler who applies liberal amounts of her mother's makeup without permission are two such examples. If these introductory steps into higher level tasks fail, the result is a feeling of guilt on the part of the preschooler. The parent must therefore try to impart to the preschool child a balance of self-reliance and respect for others and their rules. Bandura (1986), a social learning theorist, refers to the child's growing sense of initiative as *self-efficacy,* a sense of being able to do things on one's own. Rapidly developing skills help preschoolers become more able, and create a sense of personal power and independence. When preschoolers realize these newly acquired abilities, they begin to separate from their parents and grow in the awareness of their existence as individuals.

Understanding the limitations of preschoolers' cognitive abilities can be helpful to parents who are trying to gain a perspective on why children act in certain ways. Piaget suggests that preschool children are in the *preoperational stage* of cognitive development. Children who are operating in the preoperational period display certain characteristics that exemplify illogical thought processes. *Egocentrism,* the inability to consider another person's point of view, is an excellent example of how a preschool child's thoughts differ from logical thought patterns. Preschoolers are aware of themselves, but are not able to take into account the perspective or needs of others. For example, young preschool children often hide by covering their face and eyes with their hands; if they can't see, then it seems logical to them that no one else can see, either. Parents who believe that preschoolers have the cognitive limitations suggested by Piaget's preoperational stage may find it easier to deal with behaviors such as selfishness and not sharing toys than parents who do not share or understand this perspective.

Transductive reasoning is a second example of illogical thought during the preoperational period. Logical reasoning consists of deduction (reasoning from the general concept to the specific) and induction (reasoning from the specific to the general concept). Transductive reasoning is illogical in that it reasons from one particular to another without taking the general concept into account. In other words, preschool children often perceive cause and effect between two unrelated events. "I was thinking mean thoughts about my brother, my brother got sick, I caused my brother to get sick" is just one of the many common scenarios preschoolers envision. Knowing that these incredible leaps in thinking occur can help parents assist children in sorting out their fears and worries.

The developmental changes experienced by preschool children influence parent-child relationships. Parents often become more directive in encouraging appropriate behavior and discouraging inappropriate behavior (Lamb, Ketterlinus, & Fracasso, 1992). The goal is for children's emerging abilities to coincide with parental demands and expectations. Luckily, the tools parents use in accomplishing their goals are much more effective with preschoolers than they were with toddlers. For example, verbal encouragement and demands may be more successful, since the child is now able to understand and communicate. Interactions become less physical and use more complex symbols, such as language. It is easier to ask a child to stop an activity than it is to get up and physically remove the child from an activity. Recent research suggests that positive affect (good feelings of love and caring) between mothers and children predicts child compliance (Kochanska & Aksan, 1995). More research is needed to further explore the relationship between affect, compliance, and children's internalization of their parents' standards.

Parental Involvement

The factors that applied to parental involvement with infants and toddlers (mentioned in Chapter 5) are still valid at the preschool age. Mothers appear to be the primary caregivers, even in dual-career families (McBride & Mills, 1993). They spend a higher proportion of their interaction time with their preschoolers in caregiving and work-related activities, while fathers spend more of their interaction time in play activities. Experiences such as parent education/play group programs for fathers and preschoolers have been effective in encouraging fathers to be more comfortable parenting and to increase the amount of responsibility they take on in their child rearing (McBride, 1990).

It has been suggested that men's parenting of preschool children is indirectly and directly affected by their wives (Grossman, Pollack, & Golding, 1988). In "flexible" families, where fathers are able to break out of their typical gender roles, men have the freedom to be different from their wives and interact with the child in ways the wives would not, as well as trying to model their parenting behavior after their wives', thus learning how to be better parents.

For example, fathers tend to like vigorous, physical, rough play, whereas fewer mothers engage in this activity. Their preference for rough-and-tumble play, however, should not prevent fathers from trying to learn how to respond sensitively to a child's hurt feelings and tears. Mothers are traditionally seen as more nurturing, but fathers can be quite capable in this area. The complexity of interactions and roles within the family system must be recognized. In essence, wives may have to give "permission" to husbands to try to expand their parenting repertoire.

SOCIAL AND EMOTIONAL ISSUES

It's like having Dr. Jekyll and Mr. Hyde in the house when he has a friend over. One minute he's mean, yelling at his friend and not sharing toys. Minutes later he's got his arm around his friend's shoulders and they are whispering and giggling like nothing bad happened.

Father of a four-year-old

Preschool-age children seem to be a study in contrasts. They can be sweet and loving one minute, and mean and spiteful the next. Young children are learning about their negative and positive social repertoire of skills, and are apt to exhibit large quantities of both. Parents have the task of helping their children process the consequences of their social acts and learn more about their individuality.

Aggression and Prosocial Development

Parents are often puzzled and upset by the aggressive, hurtful actions of their preschool child. It is helpful to try to analyze aggressive episodes by taking the perspective of the child. From the preschooler's point of view, aggression is often the solution, not the problem. Aggression can be an uninformed attempt at problem solving. For example, a three-year-old child may shove another child away from a toy because he wants to play with it. The preschooler's solution to the perceived intruder's taking the beloved toy is to shove the other child away. Because young children are largely unable to take the perspective of the other child, they do not see the moral overtones of their actions. As preschool children get older, their aggression may become more hostile and purposely hurtful. That does not mean, however, that a child is necessarily "bad" or a bully. It may just be an indication that he or she needs some help with verbally communicating his or her needs in an acceptable way, or finding positive ways to deal with frustration. Prevention (such as having duplicate toys or close adult supervision) and guidance (such as problem solving rather than punishment) may be effective strategies for parents to use in dealing with aggression in early childhood.

Parents may also want to reduce the number of aggressive models available to preschool children, both in real life and on television. Research suggests a strong relationship between aggressive behavior and viewing violence on television (Geen, 1994). If television violence does not cause aggression,

Parental modeling encourages many prosocial behaviors in preschoolers, such as
sharing, nurturing, comforting, or helping tie a shoe.
(*Robert Finken/The Picture Cube*)

which is currently being debated, it certainly encourages it. This may be especially true in children who are already prone to aggression. Because of their
limited reasoning abilities, preschool children may focus on the aggressive acts
portrayed on television, and may be unable to cognitively absorb the "good
guy, bad guy" distinctions and story lines where punishments or morals are
also provided. The effects of watching violence on television may be long-lasting, and have prompted professional organizations such as the American Psychological Association and the American Academy of Pediatrics to strongly
recommend government and parental intervention in limiting the violence
viewed by children on television.

Although many preschoolers appear hedonistic, or self-centered in their
attempts to deal with social interactions (Eisenberg, Lennon, & Roth, 1983),
they are also capable of *prosocial* behaviors—altruism or selflessness in which
the child acts out of concern for someone else. Prosocial behaviors include
sharing, comforting, compassion, helping, cooperation, sympathy, nurturing,
protecting, and kindness. For example, preschool children can be very sensitive to parental needs. Recent research on clinically depressed mothers suggests that preschool children are able to exhibit many caring behaviors (Radke-
Yarrow, Zahn-Waxler, Richardson, Susman, & Martinez, 1994).

It appears that parents can have a substantial effect on prosocial develop-ment in children. Providing explanations of how the child's actions are related to the distress they caused can lead to increased compassion (Zahn-Waxler, Radke-Yarrow, & King, 1979). For example, saying, "You hurt Cassie when you pinched her, and now she's crying. It isn't nice to hurt people." is much more effective in producing compassionate children than saying, "Stop that," with-out giving an explanation or simply punishing a child physically. This process begins to train children to have *empathy*, to experience the emotions of other people. In addition, parents who model sympathetic concern by explicitly ver-balizing their own sympathetic reactions to others are helping children, partic-ularly boys, develop sympathy (Eisenberg, Fabes, Carlo, Troyer, Speer, Kar-bon, & Switzer, 1992). Cooperative behavior can also be successfully facilitated for preschoolers through adult modeling and encouragement (Doescher & Sugawara, 1992). Everyday situations such as picking up toys provide parents with opportunities to model ("Let me help you so we can all be done more quickly") and encourage ("Can you think of some ways we could do this job together?") cooperation.

Parental Encouragement of Peer Relationships

Many recent studies have attempted to find out more about the link between parent-child relations and peer relations. An observational study of thirty fam-ilies using both home and school observations suggested that there was simi-larity between children's interactions at home and their interactions with peers (Harrist, Pettit, Dodge, & Bates, 1994). This finding indicates that if children are having difficulties in their peer relationships, practitioners might be able to focus intervention efforts on the family, which may then influence peer rela-tionships. Researchers have also demonstrated that mothers may improve children's social skills with peers by having frequent conversations with their children about peer relationships, giving them advice about problems they might be having with peers, and discussing emotions the child is feeling (Laird, Pettit, Mize, Brown, & Lindsey, 1994). For example, a mother might say things like, "Tell me about how you and Johnny got along today. How did you feel when he took your ball away from you? Maybe Johnny didn't realize how upset you were. Perhaps you could try telling him how mad you felt. Pretend I'm Johnny. What would you tell me?" According to this recent study, mothers who provided this kind of stimulation had children who were more competent with peers.

Another way parents encourage peer relationships is to *manage* these rela-tionships by taking an active role in planning, facilitating, and supervising the child's social life, as well as reacting positively to more spontaneous opportu-nities (Ladd, Profilet, & Hart, 1992). Although sometimes all parents have to do is be flexible enough to take advantage of a naturally occurring situation, such as running into a peer at the park climbing structure, managing chil-dren's peer relationships often takes time and effort. Getting to know other parents, organizing play times or trips to the zoo, and being available and tuned in to the children when they are playing together to provide help and guidance when necessary are all important tasks. This managerial role also includes discouraging a child from playing with a child the parent feels is undesirable. Parents can take advantage of both formal (preschool) and informal (neighborhood play group) contacts.

Imaginative Play

> My four-year-old daughter has an imaginary friend that she talks to frequently and who goes everywhere with us. At first we thought it was kind of cute, but lately we've been worried that maybe she has some serious personality maladjustment that causes her to try to escape from reality. What should we do?

Preschool children typically spend between 10 percent and 17 percent of their time in *imaginative play* (Rubin, Watson, & Jambor, 1978), also known as pretend play or dramatic play. Imaginative play involving other children is a training ground for social interaction. Parents can use the observation of imaginative play as a window for viewing where their child is in the development of many social skills, such as taking another person's desires into consideration and social problem solving.

Imaginative play can also be a solitary activity. Imaginary, or invisible, playmates are common companions for preschoolers. Research suggests that children who have imaginary playmates exhibit less aggressive behavior than their peers and may be more creative, cooperative, and independent (Singer, 1973). Imaginary playmates also help the child experience a feeling of control and provide outlets for strong emotions (Croft, 1979). A child might be lonely and want to have a playmate always available, or perhaps she feels helpless and her imaginary friend helps her when she is in trouble. Children who blame mistakes on invisible companions may have unrealistic demands and expectations placed upon them in their everyday life. If children are not able to perform the tasks that are being asked of them at home, they may use imaginary companions as a coping mechanism. Perhaps the imaginary friend allows them to express aggressive or angry feelings, or to practice behaviors that are later used with peers.

Parents may try to assess the function of imaginative play in their children's lives in order to gain insight into how preschoolers think and feel. Having invisible companions is not abnormal behavior for preschool-age children; these playmates are often in place because the child has an active, creative imagination.

Fears

Because preschool children are attempting to do things they have never tried before, the risks seem to be very frightening at times. Most preschool children experience many fears and apprehensions. These strong emotions are caused by the anxious concerns preschoolers have about impending dangers, real and imagined. Because of the limited reasoning abilities of preschool children, it is not always easy for them to cope with their fears logically. Children lack the life experience that helps them understand their fears. For example, parents spend a lot of time teaching preschoolers to cross the street safely. The potential danger of getting hit by a car is not always obvious to young children, who may not be able to anticipate the events that could happen in this scenario and probably have never witnessed a person being hit by a car. Because of their previous experiences receiving shots (which are actually for their protection), some preschoolers develop a fear of going to the doctor's office. Their experiences tell them that there is risk involved in that particular activity. It is therefore important for parents to try to see situations from the child's point of view and help them address their fears.

Parents sometimes feel frustrated or concerned when children are fearful for what parents see as "no good reason." These kinds of fears include such things as being afraid of monsters, or fear of the dark, and are perfectly normal for preschool children. Their imaginations are far more developed than their logical thinking. As children grow in size and experience, the world becomes more predictable for them, and they feel more control. At that point many of their fears do dissipate or become diminished. See Box 6-1 for ideas on helping children cope with fear.

 ## Box 6-1 Helping Children Cope with Fear

1. *Talk with children about their fears.* Communication can be a source of information, comfort, and encouragement. Share your own feelings so it will be easier for them to share theirs.

2. *Give children accurate information about fears.* Tell them the truth, even if it may be unpleasant. Shots at the doctor's office do hurt, and death is not like sleeping at all. Do not confuse them with explanations they cannot understand, but try to help them learn to distinguish between what is real and what is pretend. Whenever possible, prepare them in advance for situations that may potentially be frightening.

3. *Select good children's books about fears to read to children.* Books about children's fears can provide information, clarify misinformation, assure children that they aren't the only ones experiencing fear, and give them the opportunity to see how others handle fear. Coming up with solutions for a story character and talking about the character's feelings can be helpful to children who are unable to talk about their own fears.

4. *Provide creative outlets to help children verbalize feelings about fear.* Puppets allow children to work through their fears using imaginative play. Art, such as painting or drawing, allows children to express themselves physically, and perhaps verbally tell a story based on their work.

5. *Broaden children's range of skills for coping with fear.* Help children identify their potential strengths and practice problem solving so that they feel more competent. Suggest ways to help them cope with fear.

6. *Accept children's fears, feelings, and reactions.* Be supportive and understanding. Do not deny children's fears, because they are very real to them. Ridiculing or shaming children will only make them hide their true feelings. Children lack the experience, maturation, and reasoning abilities to rid themselves of many fears.

Adapted from: Croft, D.J. (1979). *Parents and teachers: A resource book for home, school, and community relations.* Belmont, CA: Wadsworth Publishing Company, Inc.
Growing Child/Growing Parent. (1983). *Growing parent: A sourcebook for families.* Chicago, IL: Contemporary Books, Inc.

Parenting Challenges: Emotional Development in an Applied Context

> My three-year-old son has a stuffed bear he calls Fuzzy that he sleeps with and carries with him wherever he goes. I'm concerned that he's too dependent on Fuzzy. He cries and becomes upset if we force him to leave Fuzzy at home. Does this mean he's a socially insecure kid? Isn't he too old to be carrying a bear around with him?

In psychological circles, Fuzzy is known as a *transitional object* (Winnicott, 1953). Stuffed animals, blankets, pacifiers, pillows, and other similar (usually soft) objects are typical transitional objects. Most professionals agree that attachment to transitional objects is not only normal behavior for young children, but can be very healthy and beneficial to their development (Passman, 1987). The purpose of transitional objects is to provide comfort in stressful situations. In other words, the presence of the transitional object helps children cope with changes between activities, shifting from one person to another, or going from place to place (Kutner, 1993). The transitional object is not a sign of dependency, but a means to help a child become more independent. Socially difficult or uncomfortable situations can become manageable when a child possesses his or her own source of comfort and security. Estimates of the prevalence and scope of transitional objects vary considerably across cultures due to differing definitions of transitional objects and subcultural values. The majority of young children in the United States, however, display at least mild attachments to transitional objects (Passman & Halonen, 1979).

Many children give up their transitional objects when they no longer feel that they need them; some do not (Kutner, 1993). Many of these attachments subside after forty-eight months (Passman & Halonen, 1979). If a parent does decide to take the transitional object away, or limit its use to a certain setting or time of day (such as bedtime), then alternative coping strategies must be provided for the young child to use in its place during transitions and stressful situations. Talking with children, teaching them to verbalize their feelings, and helping them to learn effective social skills may help them feel more comfortable and secure. Sucking can be a very effective coping mechanism for young children in stressful situations. Although most parents are comfortable with sucking as a normal and necessary activity for infants and toddlers, parents of three- to five-year-olds are often concerned about thumb sucking and the use of pacifiers at the preschool age. Parental discomfort often stems from social pressures from peers and adults who regard the sucking habit as babyish, and a concern about children's teeth and the possible need for orthodontic work. If a child stops before the permanent teeth are in (around five or six years of age), damage is believed to be minimal (Maynard, 1991). See Box 6-2 for hints on how to stop the thumb-sucking habit.

Sex Roles and Sexuality Education

Sex Roles

Sex roles are socially defined behaviors associated with being either male or female. Perhaps the best approach to discussing sex-role development in the context of parenting is that of parental awareness. Sex-role development is societally influenced in two ways. *Direct instruction* is the first. For example, in our particular society, females are often taught to be affectionate, gentle, quiet, nurturing, and emotional while males are often socialized to be aggressive, independent, active, competitive, and dominant. These attributes are often learned and promoted through play activities. Female children have historically "played house" with dolls and dress-up clothes, while males played aggressive war games with toy guns and tanks. An important message for parents is that certain kinds of play and toys can reinforce certain kinds of gender stereotypes. Awareness of this fact may influence parents to choose toys and activities that reflect individual parental values regarding the roles of men and women. For example, many parents encourage the use of toys and activities

 Box 6-2 Stopping the Thumb Habit

The following techniques can also be adapted for children who suck on pacifiers; however, most experts agree that thumb sucking is the most difficult habit to break, since pacifiers can be removed physically from the child and thumbs cannot!

1. *Enlist the child's help and support.* It is important to inform the child of your concerns and wishes, and involve the child in the decision-making process. Often, quitting is most successful when the child helps to negotiate the timetable. A child who will not agree to cooperate with a plan will probably not make any significant progress in quitting. It is difficult to force a child to stop if he doesn't want to or doesn't understand why you want him to. Avoid power struggles.
2. *Limit sucking to a particular place and time.* Depending on the individual patterns of the child, a parent might begin with a heavy-duty user by allowing thumb sucking to occur only at home. A logical choice for a more occasional thumb sucker is to start by limiting thumb sucking to the child's room and nap or bed times. It is usually easier to eliminate daytime sucking first.
3. *Give the child visual and auditory cues.* Painting a child's thumb nail red as a reminder to her not to suck, or using colorful mitts or a bandage as visual cues can be helpful techniques. Deciding on an auditory cue in the form of a code word or phrase as a no-sucking reminder could be

very effective, especially in public places where reminding the child verbally might embarrass her. For example, instead of saying "Stop sucking your thumb," a parent might cue the child with a nonsensical phrase like "What a pickle!" that they have agreed upon beforehand.

4. *Keep the child involved and busy.* If their hands and minds are busy with interesting activities, there is less time for them to focus on the thumb sucking.
5. *Offer incentives.* This approach must be carried out carefully so that it does not become a bribe. Behavioral charts keeping track of desired behaviors can be very effective for some children. A certain number of stars may translate into a toy or special privilege. Avoid using candy or other rewards that can be used up; generally, incentives that last are more helpful.
6. *Be patient.* It is a difficult habit to break, and it may take some time. Expect some backsliding in situations such as illness or stress. Think about how difficult it is for some adults to stop smoking if you're feeling unsympathetic. And remember that this, too, will pass.

Adapted from: Bernstein, L. (1994, January). Thumbs away: Common sense strategies for weaning your child from thumbs and pacifiers. *Parents*, 73–74.
Maynard, F. (1991, January). There's a thumb sucker born every minute. *Parents*, 74–79.
Copyright © 1996 Gruner & Jahr USA Publishing. Reprinted from *Parents Magazine* by permission.

that are not gender specific, such as blocks, painting, and reading children's books that do not depict gender stereotypes.

Talking to children about the roles of males and females directly is another strategy that communicates parental views to children. The level of discourse must certainly be related to the child's developmental understanding, but even preschoolers can begin to grasp complicated issues. For example, an appropriate level of explanation for a four-year-old might be: "Some people think that little boys shouldn't play with dolls. But I think it's important for you to have a doll to take care of so that you can practice being a good daddy someday."

The second way society influences sex-role development is through *modeling and observation.* Parents, of course, are very influential in the lives of their children. It is important to realize, however, that peers, siblings, and television are powerful influences as well. Commercials for toys are often depicted with all boys or all girls, reinforcing the notion that some toys are exclusively appropriate only for boys and some toys are "girl toys." Books and teachers can also have an impact on sex-role development. Misinformation from peers is difficult to counteract, even in young children. One mother described her struggle to persuade her son to wear his new shirt after his friend told him that "boys can't wear pink." Careful explanations and discussions of values and differences open the door to tolerance and diversity. It is more difficult to counteract media messages, because they are not as direct. The impact of viewing sex-stereotyped programs on young children is not known, but parents must be aware of the possible messages children might be receiving from television and movie viewing. If the majority of the television shows children watch have both males and females in more traditional roles, and the lead characters are predominantly male or encourage negative messages about females, children of each sex will take different messages regarding their roles and importance from the experience. Parents must therefore oversee children's media viewing and buffer negative messages.

Sexuality Education

Research suggests that parents want and need guidance about how and when to talk to young children about sexual issues. They are especially concerned about the timing of sexuality education (how much information is appropriate and when it is too much information too soon), society's influence on timing (children being exposed to sexual topics before they are ready), gender roles (especially with regard to masturbation), and trying to do a better job of sexuality education than their parents did (Geasler, Dannison, & Edlund, 1995). Parents indicate needing help in five areas: exploring their own values and attitudes about sexuality, addressing conflicting feelings, understanding their role as educators in this area, obtaining accurate information, and developing ways to communicate this information (Alter & Wilson, 1982).

Normal sexual development begins at birth, a notion that conflicts greatly with the common misconception that sexual development starts in adolescence. Infants are capable of pleasurable self-stimulation. Three-year-olds continue the exploration of their bodies, naming the different parts and trying to figure out how males and females differ. Bathroom activities, such as urination

Calvin and Hobbes

by **Bill Watterson**

CALVIN & HOBBES © 1987 Watterson. Dist. by UNIVERSAL PRESS SYNDICATE. Reprinted with permission. All rights reserved.

and defecation, are of great interest. Preschool children are notorious for entertaining each other with bathroom humor, which often consists of saying the word "poop" and giggling uncontrollably. Along with the independence of toileting, the concept of privacy begins to form and be encouraged by parents. Children learn that there are some things that are appropriate to do in public places, and some things that one should do away from others. By four years of age or so, there is an increased interest in sexual activity. This development corresponds to an increased interest in everything else, too, since preschoolers at this age have high levels of curiosity overall. Masturbation is still common, but some sex play between children is also normal.

It is important for parents who are feeling disturbed by incidents of sex play to realize that the motivation for this behavior is just normal curiosity on the part of the children, who are equally as interested in a variety of things such as dead birds and how much food one can put into his or her mouth at one time. Sex play does not have the same meaning or connotation for young children as it does for adults. Many parents choose to continue to talk about appropriate and inappropriate sexual behavior, and reinforce the concept of privacy so that children learn what is acceptable in society. This is an extension of the same lessons that help young children learn that loud burping and picking one's nose in public are also not well-received practices.

Most preschoolers ask endless questions, and eventually get around to the topic of where babies come from. This is especially interesting to the preschool child who is about to have a new sibling. There are many books for preschool-level children on this topic, presented in words that preschoolers can understand. Sometimes parents find it helpful to read the books themselves, whether or not they decide to share the book with their child, just to get an idea of how to answer certain questions or approach certain topics in an age-appropriate way. Sex education is an ongoing conversation, not just one discussion. Simplified answers are given at early ages, with more details provided as children get older.

Sexual messages can be very confusing in our culture, and it takes some time for children to learn all of the rules. For example, many preschoolers struggle with its "being okay" from a societal perspective to wear a swimming suit in public, but not being okay to run around outside in only underwear

(Calderone & Ramey, 1982). It is crucial to keep the lines of communication open regarding the topic of sex. Healthy patterns can be established early and drawn upon as the years progress. Remember that if parents do not answer children's questions about sex, someone else (who is probably much less qualified and who may provide misleading information) will. Some guidelines for talking to preschoolers about sex include being prepared for obvious questions, clarifying questions children have so that it is clear exactly what is being asked, keeping answers simple and complete, using correct words for body parts and functions, and encouraging open communication about sexuality and related topics (Geasler, Dannison, & Edlund, 1993).

COGNITIVE ISSUES

I just love Annie's curiosity about everyone and everything around her. Why is the grass green? Why do cats purr instead of bark? Where does the sun go at night? How does the car know when to go forward and when to go backward? The questions come rapidly and without warning. I'm not sure I give very good answers; sometimes I don't know and other times I can't explain it on her level of understanding. But, to be perfectly honest, sometimes I just get tired of responding to the endless stream of questions.

Mother of a three-year-old

Preschoolers are known for their insatiable curiosity about everyone and everything. They are notorious for asking "why?" every chance they get. Taking advantage of this natural time for learning provides a challenge for parents who are trying to provide the most beneficial and appropriate experiences for their children. This section deals with preschoolers' learning abilities and the issues that surround this area of development.

Learning Activities and Materials

Given the varied cognitive abilities of preschool-aged children, many parents are unsure what to do in order to best provide a good learning environment. The answer depends upon the parents' philosophy about how children learn and what children need. Some parents believe that children will learn just fine with no extra parental stimulation for learning. Other parents sign their children up for prestigious preschool programs, or specific classes in an area of interest such as music, art, or sports. Music lessons, gymnastics programs, and swimming instruction are a few examples of the many opportunities commonly available to preschoolers. Many parents believe that teaching children to read at an earlier age will help them excel in future academic endeavors, while others believe this puts too much pressure on young children. There is much professional debate as to which opportunities are best for preschool children, and how much is too much and what is too little.

It is clear that young children can learn skills, such as reading, at very early ages. Is it advantageous for children to learn academic skills at earlier ages? The answer seems to be no, since there is no evidence that early instruction has lasting benefits. Children's ability to learn these complex skills doesn't mean they should learn them, because there may be some negative side effects. Elkind (1987) calls formal instruction of young children in academic subjects "miseducation," and claims that such endeavors put children at risk for short-term stress and long-term personal damage to self-esteem and attitudes toward learning. Research suggests that mothers who strongly believe in early formal academic instruction may be "pressuring" their children (Hyson, Hirsh-Pasek, Rescorla, Cone, & Martell-Boinske, 1991), possibly leading to superficial rote knowledge (Sigel, 1987), performance anxiety, and less positive attitudes toward learning (Gallagher & Coche, 1987). It is suggested that these effects might be even more apparent if fathers who emphasized early formal education were studied (Hyson, Hirsh-Pasek, Rescorla, Cone, & Martel-Boinske, 1991). Leading experts in the field of child development seem to be in agreement that these efforts to inappropriately force formal instruction on young children are more for the parents' feelings of success than for the benefit of children (Brazelton, 1987b; Elkind, 1987).

What is a reasonable goal for parents of preschoolers with regard to academic skills and learning? Perhaps the best possible answer is to motivate interest, excitement, and enthusiasm for learning. This is not difficult to do, since preschoolers are eager to discover and learn on their own; however, parents must provide supportive, nonpressured environments (Elkind, 1987) and become effective teachers (Taylor, 1985). They must learn to be attentive listeners, giving children the opportunity to talk, ask questions, make observations, and answer questions. It is tempting to talk to children of this age rather than with them, but communication is a two-way venture. Sharing activities with children, providing them with opportunities to explore and discover motivates interest in learning. Being available to children at those "teachable moments" is crucial, extending White's (1975) idea of the parent as consultant to the child. Whenever possible, children's questions should be answered as they come up. Just as children look up to parents, parents should model their own sense of awe and wonder for their children.

Reading to children is an especially important activity. A school district in South Carolina implemented a program of personal shared-book experiences (two to three children with one adult) in their kindergarten classrooms. Literacy awareness and competence on a readiness test increased 10 percent overall from the previous year (Brown, Cromer, & Weinberg, 1986). In another study, the home literacy environment (measured by questions such as the frequency of shared picture book reading, number of picture books in the home, and duration of a recent book reading experience) accounted for 12 percent to 18.5 percent of the variability in Head Start children's language scores (Payne, Whitehurst, & Angell, 1994). In other words, literacy in the home had an important impact on children's vocabulary and language skills. Research involving African-American Head Start mothers and their children in joint reading tasks showed that low-income African-American mothers use teaching strategies (such as adjusting their teaching to the child's level of competence) that are very similar to those of middle-class mothers (Pellegrini, Perlmutter, Galda, & Brody, 1990). These studies, considered altogether, show the important impact parents can have on their children's literacy and interest in learning by simply reading to them.

School

Many parents begin to struggle with the issue of formal schooling for their child when he or she is three or four years of age. Since schooling is not mandatory for this age group, parents must inform themselves about the pros and cons of this decision. Should children attend preschool? Even the experts cannot agree. The experience can be beneficial if the quality of the preschool is good, but if the home environment is also of high quality, then preschool may not be necessary. If the answer is yes, what kind of preschool should it be? There are nearly as many choices as there are preschools. Should the preschool be academic or socially oriented? Large group or small group? Public or private? Teacher-directed or child-directed? The choices create confusion for many parents. In addition, there is always the matter of cost. Often, preschool is expensive. With the exception of programs like Head Start, which are aimed at low-income populations, parents must provide the payment for these services. Each individual family must decide, based on their unique circumstances, whether preschool is an option. Some suggestions for how to make these decisions are found in Box 6-3.

At the end of the preschool years, there is great interest in kindergarten on the part of parents and children. Attending kindergarten is a big step, even for children who have been involved in full-time care outside the home. Entrance into kindergarten marks the beginning of the school-age years, where children accept increased responsibility at each stage of maturity. It is the first of many public transitions that occur, and parents often view the event as a significant

Although there are many diverse choices within preschool programs, most educators agree that reading to children is an important activity in both the home and school. (*Paul S. Conklin/Monkmeyer*)

one, in which they must begin to "let go" of their children to other societal institutions and expectations (McClelland, 1995).

Because this event is so significant symbolically, much time and energy has been spent in looking at the transition to kindergarten and formal schooling. The U.S. Department of Health and Human services has compiled a pamphlet to help families ease the transition from preschool to kindergarten. Many of their suggestions are practical and helpful to parents who are trying to prepare themselves and their children for school. First, parents are encouraged to educate themselves and become as knowledgeable as possible about the kindergarten experience. Parents are urged to collect information about the school their child will be attending, such as the address, name of the principal, telephone number, and dates for registration. Kindergarten "round-ups" or other orientation sessions that the school may plan for incoming parents are very important. Talking with school personnel (including teachers and principals) about the kindergarten program and the role of parents in the school, or asking any other pertinent questions is a good idea. Arranging a visit to the new school before the first day can be time well spent, because it makes both parent and child more comfortable. Building the child's confidence about going to school by reading stories about this topic can be helpful, as well as discussing the child's new activities and schedules.

Trying to meet other parents of children who will attend kindergarten, and letting the child meet new classmates prior to school opening can cut down on

---

 ## Box 6-3 The Preschool Decision

Some good reasons for a child to go to preschool:

1. To encourage self-identity (a life of his or her own).
2. To promote self-reliance and independence.
3. To gain mastery of basic rules and routines.
4. To develop language and communicate more effectively.
5. To provide exposure to books, art, and play materials that may not be available at home.
6. To meet and learn to get on with other children.
7. To practice using his or her body effectively.
8. To improve fine motor skills.
9. To enjoy freedom of action in a place designed and geared to his or her age.
10. To become closely acquainted with warm, caring adults outside the family.

Some not-so-good reasons for a child to go to preschool:

1. Everyone is doing it.
2. The child lacks discipline or is having problems.
3. It will give the child a fast start on academics

for kindergarten.
4. The child is too attached to you.

Some good reasons not to send a child to preschool:

1. You're enjoying having your youngster around and you're not quite ready to give that up, even for half a day.
2. Good preschool in your area is expensive and you can't afford it.
3. Your child has plenty of opportunities to play and socialize with other children.
4. Your youngster doesn't want to go.
5. You don't like the preschools in your area.
6. You feel you and your spouse are providing your youngster with good preschool experiences.

Adapted from: *The preschool handbook* by Barbara Brenner. Copyright © 1989 by Barbara Brenner. Reprinted by permission of Pantheon Books, a division of Random House, Inc.

anxiety for everyone involved. Recent research shows a modest relationship between maternal social support (mothers who have friends and relatives who provide help or emotional assistance) and children's school adjustment (Pianta & Ball, 1993), suggesting that parental networking can reduce or buffer the stress involved in this change for some families. Once school starts, volunteering in the kindergarten classroom can be a wonderful and rewarding way to help ease the transition for both parent and child.

Language Development

> I spent the first two years trying to teach her how to talk, and now that she can hold her own in a conversation, I find myself wishing for a moment of silence.
>
> *Father of a four-year-old*

As most parents know, preschoolers are excellent conversationalists. Because they are just learning the rules of grammar, however, preschool children tend to make predictable mistakes. Understanding the normal course of language development often helps parents feel more at ease with their child's language abilities. For example, the most common mistake children make is to *overgeneralize,* or overregularize grammatical rules. In other words, preschoolers apply the rule to every case without exception. For example, one rule is to add "s" when forming a plural, such as ball/balls. Another is to add "ed" to a word to indicate past tense, such as walk/walked; however, the plural of "foot" is "feet," not "foots," and the past tense of "go" is "went," not "goed." Preschool children can often be heard saying those words, even though they have not heard adults say them. Eventually, they begin to identify the exceptions.

Parents can play an important role in the expansion of their child's vocabulary. Preschoolers have the ability to learn language rapidly through a process known as *fast mapping* (Carey, 1978), where they quickly understand the meanings or partial meanings of previously unknown words. These words are usually learned through hearing an adult use them in context once or twice—which certainly makes a case for parental involvement and encouragement in learning.

Parents can also facilitate another major task in preschool language development. During this time period, children begin to understand how words relate to one another in a meaningful context (de Villiers & de Villiers, 1992). They must discover the similarities and differences in the meanings of words and begin to group them into different levels of organization, or hierarchies. This is much more difficult than learning basic-level vocabulary words. For example, one hierarchy might be my pet Spot, dalmatians, dogs, mammals, living things. The complexity of these hierarchical categories is very difficult for children to organize. Parents, however, influence this process by providing explicit information about why objects form categories at different levels (Callanan, 1985). Using strategies such as saying, "All of them together are mammals," can help a child understand these difficult concepts.

Parenting Challenges: Language Development in an Applied Context

> Our four-year-old stutters quite a bit when he talks, and we're worried about it. Should we take him to a speech specialist of some kind? We correct him when he does this, but we don't know what else we can do at home to help him.

Parents are often concerned when children have difficulty speaking clearly. It is reassuring to know that most children have some problems in this area during the preschool years. There are so many things to say and think about that preschoolers commonly stutter and stammer, repeating words or parts of words while engaged in conversation (American Academy of Pediatrics, 1995). Their new cognitive skills allow them to think faster than their minds can translate these thoughts into language. Hesitation between words, repetitions, and habits such as saying "umm, umm" are transient ways for preschoolers to "buy" the time they need to organize their thoughts and put them into coherent words.

Speech pathologists usually advise parents to avoid becoming overly concerned at this point. Correcting children, or making them become more self-conscious about their mistakes, can create nervousness, exacerbate the stuttering, and lead to more serious problems. Patient listening on the part of the parent will allow the child to slow down and feel confident that he or she will be listened to no matter how long it takes.

PHYSICAL DEVELOPMENT ISSUES

> I can hardly believe how much Tommy has changed in the past few months. He isn't so sturdy and round any more. He's gotten taller and slimmed down. His little potbelly is gone! The toddler look has disappeared; he's starting to look like a real kid.
>
> *Mother of a three-and-a-half-year-old*

Although physical changes are less dramatic in the preschool years than they were in infancy, important transformations are still occurring within the child's body. Children are usually healthier than they were in the infant and toddler years, thanks to the further development of the immune system and respiratory-circulatory changes that increase physical stamina. Although children's growth rate slows down between ages three and six, bones and muscles continue to grow steadily, making children stronger and more able to perform a variety of gross motor and fine motor skills. Because of the slowed growth rate, children in the preschool years eat less than they did in the previous three years. Changes in appetite often concern parents, and many worry that they have a "picky eater" on their hands. Nutritional needs at this time are fairly easy to satisfy, however, so if the child is energetic and active there is usually no need for concern. Since children are eating proportionately less food, however, it is especially important to serve nutritional snacks. Raw vegetables, fresh or dried fruits, whole-grain crackers, dry low-sugar cereals, fruit juices, milk, peanut butter, and cheese are healthy suggestions (Satter, 1983).

Sleep Problems

Parents of preschoolers must commonly face sleep disturbances such as *night-mares* and *night terrors*. Both are common in preschool-age children, but handling each requires a different strategy. Nightmares are "bad dreams" that contain such frightening ideas or images that they wake the person up. The causes may be emotional, resulting from the processing of various experiences or feelings (Murray, 1990). For example, watching a scary show before bed can trigger an emotional response that may lead to a nightmare in young children. Strategies parents have found to be successful in dealing with nightmares include cuddling, a drink of water, a night light, and lots of reassurance (Kutner, 1993). Children sometimes remember their nightmares, so it might be helpful to talk about them the next day or draw the images to make them less frightening. Since preschool thinking is not logical yet, it is often difficult for children to draw the line between fantasy and reality, which can cause more anxiety. Some researchers have found that having the child think of a new ending to the nightmare that isn't scary will help him or her feel better, and may keep the nightmare from reoccurring.

Night terrors are physiological in nature. The child may have his or her eyes wide open and look like he or she is awake, but be partially awake and partially asleep (Murray, 1990). Night terrors are a result of being unable to make the transition smoothly from deep sleep to REM (rapid eye movement) sleep, because of the preschooler's immature nervous system (Kutner, 1993). They usually occur one to four hours after falling asleep, last between five and fifteen minutes, and may have a genetic basis—although environmental factors such as a lack of sleep when changing a nap schedule may also contribute (Helligman, 1992). Children do not remember night terrors, and are usually not able to be comforted when having them. Because children cannot remember their night terrors, these occurrences are probably much harder on the parents who witness them, since they are unable to help or soothe their child. The best course of action during a night terror is to make sure the child doesn't hurt himself; comforting words or trying to wake the child may make the episode last longer (Helligman, 1992). Most children outgrow night terrors by age six or so.

Enuresis

The medical term for bedwetting is *enuresis*, which refers to repeated urination in clothing or in bed. Most children between the ages of three and five years are able to stay dry both day and night, although occasional accidents can happen. Enuresis is a concern only if it occurs at least twice a month in children five years of age or older. This affects about 7 percent of five-year-old boys and 3 percent of five-year-old girls (*DSM* IV, 1994).

Parents often feel frustrated with bedwetting problems, and are uncertain about the course of action they should take to deal with this issue. Enuresis is an unconscious act beyond a child's control; therefore, punishment and blame are not effective (Berg, 1991). Family history is a strong predictor of bedwetting, since most children who are affected have one or more close relatives who also wet the bed (Fergusson, Horwood, & Shannon, 1986). Most children will outgrow this problem in time without any specific intervention or help; however, many behavior modification suggestions, such as devices that wake children when they begin to urinate, are available. These treatments seem to have variable results, with few clues as to why some children (approximately 10 percent) are still unsuccessful in overcoming this problem (Gustafson, 1993).

CONTEXTUAL CLOSE-UP: SIBLING RELATIONSHIPS

Siblings provide an interactional context within the family structure that may influence many areas of development. Every family is a complex network of interactions, and how parents treat children individually and as a group influences the overall functioning of that network. Parents of more than one child soon learn that they must not only parent each child, but must parent the relationship between children. One of the most puzzling issues facing parents is why some siblings get along and why others fight and argue (Dunn, 1985). Much of the research on siblings does not address the challenges parents must face and the concerns they have about how to help siblings get along and develop positive relationships (Schachter & Stone, 1987). This is an especially complex issue when children's differing developmental levels are considered. For example, sibling conflicts between young children are often about possessions and objects (such as toys), but adolescent sibling conflicts often have multiple causes that are not always obvious (Raffaelli, 1992).

Parents often choose to have a second child while their first child is in the preschool years. There are many complex adjustments that take place within the family when another child is added (Dunn, 1995). For preschool children, it is not uncommon to experience jealousy. Parental interaction time, which was once theirs alone, must be shared. Anger and attempts of one sibling to control the other sibling's behavior are also problems (Kramer & Baron, 1995). Parents can take an active role in minimizing negative effects of a sibling through careful planning and providing emotional reassurance. Modeling appropriate behavior may improve and encourage warmth between siblings. Although the causes of linkages between parent-child relationships and sibling relationships are unknown, research suggests that positive interactions and warmth in parent-child relationships is related to positive interactions and warmth in sibling relations (Furman, 1995). The same is true for conflict and hostility.

It is not possible for parents to eliminate all conflict between siblings in the home. Fortunately, there may be some benefits to the inevitable bickering between siblings. Social development, as evidenced in negotiating and managing conflicts, may be promoted through nonaggressive sibling conflict (Hartup, Laursen, Stewart, & Easterson, 1988). Because of the limitations in research, many things remain to be learned about the intricate nature of parenting siblings. Families with diverse ethnic traditions and family circumstances warrant more research in examining the full range of family interactions and needs.

SUMMARY

- Parents of preschool children are in the authority stage of parenthood, where they must establish, communicate, and enforce limits. In addition, parents must work with other authority figures in the child's life.
- Preschool children have the developmental task of establishing initiative, according to Erikson. Self-efficacy, or the sense of being able to do things on one's own, is also developing.
- Preschool children are in the preoperational stage of cognitive development. This stage is characterized by egocentrism and transductive reasoning.
- When aggressive behaviors occur, parents should try to understand the child's motivations. What is the child trying to work out?
- Prosocial behaviors of preschoolers include sharing, comforting, compassion, helping, cooperation, sympathy, nurturing, protecting, and kindness. Parents can train children in empathy skills through modeling and encouragement.
- Preschoolers spend much of their time playing. Parents encourage peer relationships by providing healthy interactions at home, conversing with children about their peers, giving children advice, discussing a child's emotions, and managing peer relationships.
- Sex roles are the socially defined behaviors associated with being either male or female. Sex-role development is influenced through direct instruction and modeling-observation.
- Preschoolers have growing vocabularies, thanks to fast mapping. They commonly overgeneralize grammatical rules. Parents help children understand how words are related to one another in a hierarchical way.
- Nightmares and night terrors, as well as enuresis, are issues that parents may encounter during the preschool years.
- Parenting siblings is a difficult job, since sibling relationships change over time. Encouraging and modeling warmth and positive interactions within the parent-child and sibling relationships is important.
- Although the rapid growth of the infancy period is over, preschool children continue to gain steadily in each area of development. Their new social, cognitive, and language abilities allow them to gain new experiences, which will influence how they feel about themselves and others and set the framework for how they will approach later developmental tasks.

Parenting School-Age Children

THE PARENTING ROLE
> Theoretical Context
>
> Parental Concerns

SOCIAL AND EMOTIONAL ISSUES
> Self-Esteem
>
> Parenting Challenges: Self-Esteem
> in an Applied Context
>
> Peers

COGNITIVE ISSUES
> Cognitive Competence
>
> Creativity
>
> Morality
>
> School
>
> Parenting Challenges: School Issues in an
> Applied Context

TEACHING RESPONSIBILITY
> Chores
>
> Self-Care
>
> Parenting Challenges: Teaching Responsibility in an Applied Context

PHYSICAL DEVELOPMENT ISSUES
> Sports
>
> Childhood Obesity

CONTEXTUAL CLOSE-UP: ENTERTAINMENT
TECHNOLOGIES
> Television
>
> Interactive Entertainment

SUMMARY   **161**

BOXES

162

Wanted: **Parent of Elementary School-Aged Child.** Chauffeur's license essential. Overtime includes evenings at PTA meetings, school pageants, soccer games, paper drives, and other activities you swore you'd never become involved in. Your job includes being social secretary, responsible for scheduling child's birthday party, gymnastic practice, music lessons, soccer practice, and current list of best friends.

(Moschell, 1991)

Parents of school-age children are often on the run trying to keep up with their competent, active, involved, and on-the-move children. School-age children are engaged in many activities that keep their minds and bodies busy. Although they are more self-aware and may experience some feelings of stress in reaction to high expectations, most elementary school children experience these years as a time of emotional calm relative to other periods of development. They are focused on learning the skills—reading, writing, and math that will allow them to be successful functioning members of their culture. School is the focus for many social, as well as academic, activities. School-age children explore friendships in more depth, as greater periods of time are spent in the company of peers. Learning to be responsible for themselves and accountable for more complex tasks at home and school are all part of growing up for school-age children.

At each stage of parenthood, mothers and fathers must balance the need for separateness from their children with connectedness to their children. Although this is true in the *nurturing* and *authority* stages, the independence versus involvement questions are more compelling when parenting school-age children. This stage sets the framework for these same questions of connection and separation to be reexamined when children are adolescents and young adults. Parents must rethink and possibly revise their own theories of child-rearing as they prepare for the challenges that await them.

THE PARENTING ROLE

She looks so grown up, waiting for the school bus with her backpack on. I'm glad she likes school, but I can't help but feel sad that she spends so many hours of the day away from us with people we don't know. I miss her.

Mother of a first-grader

Theoretical Context

Preschool children live within the confines their parents provide for them most of the time. They have access to the outside world, but only if their parents take them there. School-age children are capable of going places on their own and doing things without their parents. Because of children's exposure to different experiences, the parental task is to help children translate the meaning of their encounters with the world. Galinsky (1987) calls this the *interpretive stage* of parenthood, where parents must answer questions, provide information, and help children form values. Within this process, parents must interpret themselves to their children, and help children develop their own self-concepts. These tasks necessitate that parents do a reality check on their perceptions of the child, so that they are reflecting the child's individuality and not the parents' hidden agenda. They must also assimilate other people's perceptions of the child—especially those of teachers. This stage requires ongoing judgments on the part of the parents regarding what information to share with the child, and what to withhold.

Parents of school-age children are most effective when they engage in *co-regulation* (Maccoby, 1984). Co-regulation simply means that parents and children cooperate, share responsibility, and have mutual respect for one another. This transitional arrangement acknowledges that the parents supervise and guide the child, but that the child is capable of taking part in decision-making processes. The use of co-regulation in parenting is supported in the research literature. Physical coercion and directing children are not as effective as monitoring and verbal mediation (Patterson & Dishion, 1988; Maccoby, 1984). Research also suggests that when mothers use direct strategies, children are defiant; when they use reasoning strategies and suggestions, children tend to negotiate (Kuczynski, Kochanska, Radke-Yarrow, & Girnius-Brown, 1987). Parental agreement on child-rearing issues may be crucial to the success of co-regulation, since parental agreement facilitates family problem solving (Vuchinich, Vuchinich, & Wood, 1993).

School-age children are in Erikson's stage of *industry*, where children are learning to be competent and productive in mastering important academic and social skills. Learning to read, write, do math, make friends, participate cooperatively in groups, and communicate effectively with adults are some of the tasks at which school-age children are seeking competence. Failure to achieve industry in these areas leads to feelings of inferiority, feelings that they are unable to do anything well. The role of the parent, then, is to promote responsible behavior, monitor leisure-time activities, learn about the child's friends, and deal with problems at school.

The tasks that are expected of industrious school-age children coincide with Piaget's stage of *concrete operations*, where children start to use symbols in a sophisticated way to carry out mental activities. These logical skills often evolve through a series of transitional phases that allow children to master these difficult cognitive concepts over time. By the end of this stage, however, children can classify, seriate, decenter (taking all aspects of a problem into account), and understand other people's points of view. The parental role is to seek activities that promote intellectual development and to participate in the child's cognitive growth (Sternberg & Williams, 1995).

Parental Concerns

Maccoby (1984) identified four concerns parents of school-age children have, all revolving around children's diligence and achievement. The first concern is their worry about how involved they should be in their child's school work. The second worry is whether they should require their children to do chores.

The standards of performance they should demand in all areas is the third concern. Finally, they worry about the extent to which they should monitor their child's social life. These concerns will be addressed in this chapter.

Based on a white, middle-class sample of 362 parents of eight- to twelve-year-olds, five kinds of problem behaviors that cause friction in the home were identified (Teglasi & MacMahon, 1990). First, angry outbursts and emotional upsets were explored. This consisted of children yelling, sulking, crying, complaining, and acting irritable when upset or angry. Next was joylessness or apathy, which consisted of an unwillingness on the part of the child to try new activities, learn new things, and meet new people. The third kind of problem behavior was low self-direction, where the child wasted a lot of time and was forgetful of school responsibilities and chores, needing constant supervision. Self-reproach was the fourth problem, where the child worried too much, expected too much, and put too much pressure on himself or herself. The last problem behavior mentioned was oppositionalism or aggression, where the child was easily provoked into teasing, fighting, and arguing. The researcher involved in this study suggested that parents examine patterns of behavior, taking individual temperamental differences into account, in an effort to respond in the most appropriate way. Research suggests that monitoring, affection, and teaching on the part of parents help to prevent behavior problems (Maccoby, 1984).

SOCIAL AND EMOTIONAL ISSUES

> He's so busy now. Two nights a week he has basketball practice, and one night a week he has piano. Throw in some play time with friends and homework, and his time is fairly scheduled. But he seems happy; all of the activity seems to agree with him.
>
> *Mother of a nine-year-old*

Few research studies focus on socioemotional issues between parents and school-age children (Lamb, Ketterlinus, & Fracasso, 1992). Most of the research on this age group focuses on parents' influence on achievement and the effects of peers, teachers, and schools on children's development. There are many important developments, however, that take place as school-age children begin to discover more about who they are and what their particular strengths and weaknesses are. They begin to measure themselves in relationship to others. Although they experience some stresses, most children learn to cope and grow as they approach and prepare for the adolescent years.

Self-Esteem

The exact age at which children become self-aware is unknown, although evidence shows that by the end of the second year of life, toddlers seem to have a firm concept of self (Stipek, Gralinski, & Kopp, 1990). *Self-concept* is the cognitive understanding of a person seen from that person's own point of view. These concepts change with age and development as children's thinking

Common activities of school-age children, such as
dance classes, may influence children's self-esteem
through the process of social comparison with peers.
(Laima Druskis/Photo Researchers)

becomes more advanced. *Self-esteem* is an emotional response to self-concept,
and is the result of the value (both positive and negative) attached to self-
descriptions. In other words, self-esteem is the child's evaluation of the qualities she perceives herself as having. If she is satisfied with the person she is
and feels that she has many strengths, she has high self-esteem. If he dwells on
what he perceives to be his negative qualities or inadequacies, he has low self-
esteem. Self-esteem comes from an overriding feeling of satisfaction or dissatisfaction with oneself.

Although there are a number of complex measurement issues and controversies in the study of self-esteem, evidence suggests that parents may play a
crucial role in how children evaluate themselves. Parents who are loving,
accepting, have clear standards of behavior, and allow the child to participate
in making decisions have children with high self-esteem (Coopersmith, 1967;
Lamborn, Mounts, Steinberg, & Dornbusch, 1991). This is not necessarily a
causal relationship, but this type of parenting does co-occur with high self-
esteem children. Some researchers (Felson & Zielinski, 1989) believe that the
relationship between parental support and children's self-esteem is bidirec-

tional; in other words, supportive parental behavior influences a more positive self-esteem in children, and children with higher self-esteem perceive their parents' behaviors as more supportive.

Another influence on self-esteem in the school-age years is the process of *social comparison,* in which children seek information regarding how competent they are when compared with their peers. This behavior begins around age six and increases as children get older (Stipek & Mac Iver, 1989). Children often differ in self-esteem in key areas because their skills vary. The areas chosen as important vary with the values of the social community. Parents can be important sources of information regarding the child's competence, and can be instrumental in communicating values regarding how important it is to be competent in various areas. For example, if athletic prowess is valued, or high achievement in school is rewarded by teachers and peers, clumsy children with learning difficulties may experience low self-esteem in that setting. Parents can help children by mediating the social comparison process.

Parents can contribute to children's positive self-esteem. Clinical evidence suggests that four requirements must be fulfilled in order for children to experience positive feelings about themselves (Clemes & Bean, 1990). First, children have to have a sense of *connectiveness,* a feeling that they are part of a group, can relate to other people, and are important to others. *Uniqueness,* or a sense of being special and different, is the second requirement. Next is a sense of *power,* which means that children feel that they can influence what happens in their lives. The last requirement is *models,* or human examples that help children establish meaningful values, goals, and ideals. Parents can be instrumental in helping children build high self-esteem in each of these areas by providing a strong model for values, using co-regulation, and communicating their love and caring to the child.

Parenting Challenges: Self-Esteem in an Applied Context

Although his scores are very high, my son missed the cut-off by several points and didn't get chosen to be in the special program available at school for gifted learners. Unfortunately, both of his best friends got in. He's very angry and upset, and feels very bad about himself. What can we do to help him?

Father of a ten-year-old

Children experience stress in their lives, just as adults do. The role of the parent is to help children deal with the challenges and demands of life in constructive ways. School-age children have many self-concerns that cause them stress, such as not meeting personal goals, questions about their competence and abilities, and self-esteem needs (Humphrey, 1988). Any one of these problems or a combination could influence situations involving unfavorable social comparisons. It may be helpful to ask the child about his perception of what he can do to cope with this situation, since research has suggested that children who perceive themselves as capable of controlling their stress attempt to change the stressful circumstances or cope with them in different ways (Compas, Banez, Malcarne, & Worsham, 1991).

Parents can help to reduce stress by helping children improve their personal resources, such as self-esteem, communication skills, the ability to set realistic expectations, decision making, and problem-solving skills. The parent's and child's values will be clarified in this process. Being excluded from a special school program is a relevant example. Both parent and child must ask themselves the following questions. Is it realistic for the child to enter the program next year? Do they believe that the child can do better on the test next time through increased studying? Do they believe the child is doing great as he is, shouldn't pressure himself to try to get in, but should emphasize the skills he already has and concentrate on developing those? Exploring both the parent's and the child's understandings of this event through listening and emotional support can be effective in leading to values clarification and action. During this process, parents should be aware that they are role models, providing the child with coping strategies and approaches.

Peers

We often have five or six kids here playing on the weekends. He wants to be with his friends, and we want to know who these kids are that are so important to him. It works out fine, except it gets pretty noisy at times.

Mother of an eleven-year-old

School-age children often have very different social opportunities today than their parents did at similar ages. More socialization occurs in organized settings, such as after-school care or competitive sports, than informal neighborhood settings. Mobile families may mean that children have less social contact with extended family. The peer group becomes extremely important in middle childhood; children spend more time with other children and away from their parents and families. Parents are aware of the important role peers play in their children's development, but have concerns about undesirable peers, and whether a child's friends are good or bad influences.

What can peers do that parents cannot? Peers help children form attitudes and values during the school-age years. Friends are a filter through which children sift what they learn from their parents to help them decide what to discard and what to keep. In other words, peers are a testing ground for parent-derived values. Peers also offer emotional security and comfort at a level parents sometimes cannot because peers have shared thoughts and experiences. The adult perspective is different because of life experience; parents are likely to dismiss an embarrassing incident as insignificant in the big picture of life, while peers understand how awful a social blunder can feel. Finally, peers help children learn how to get along in society. Children must learn when to adjust individual needs and desires for those of others, and when to stand firm in their values and beliefs.

Most parents want their children to be successful in their peer relationships. Not all children are equally sought after as peer companions; some are more popular than others. Popularity is a measure of the extent to which a child is regarded by others as a worthy social partner. Parents know that peer acceptance is a powerful predictor of psychological well-being. Early peer difficulties often indicate later maladjustment (Parker & Asher, 1987; Hymel, Rubin, Rowden, & LeMare, 1990).

Researchers estimate popularity with sociometric techniques—measures by which each child in the same classroom is asked to evaluate how likable she finds each of her peers. Currently, measures such as these have been used to describe five levels of social acceptance in interpersonal behavior (Coie, Dodge, & Coppotelli (1982): popular children, average children, rejected children, controversial children, and neglected children. Some evidence suggests that extreme classifications are more stable over time, so popular children tend to remain popular and rejected children tend to remain rejected (Coie & Dodge, 1983). A closer look at these two extremes is warranted.

Popular children usually exhibit consistent cooperative and friendly social behavior, and tend to be effective problem solvers, good communicators, and natural leaders. They are also more helpful, sympathetic, and sensitive toward their peers (Dekovic & Gerris, 1994). *Rejected children,* on the other hand, are actively disliked. Their behaviors are usually negative, with high rates of aggression, conflict, and distractible or disruptive behavior. They also tend to be more concerned about themselves than they are about their peers. Although much variation exists over time, assessments of peer acceptance tend to be moderately stable for rejected male children who exhibit aggression (Cillessen, van IJzendoorn, van Lieshout, & Hartup, 1992). *Neglected children* are at an increased risk of becoming "rejected peers" at a later age. These "socially invisible" children are not disliked, but unliked. They engage in low rates of peer interaction of any kind, often play alone, and are regarded as shy. Shyness is correlated with loneliness, depression, and low self-esteem in older school-age children—traits that are associated with rejection in middle childhood (Rubin, LeMare, & Lollis, 1990).

As was mentioned in Chapter 6, parents can do many things to encourage and support healthy peer relationships. One key to success in peer interactions may be to start early. As children become more familiar with each other, they may begin to interact more frequently, intensely, and competently. Children who are more socially competent may be able to maintain friendships over time (Howes, 1990). A recent study found that children who entered kindergarten with peers they had known in nursery school liked school better and showed fewer symptoms of anxiety than children who were more unfamiliar with the children in the class (Ladd & Price, 1987). Making new friends is also related to higher school performance (Ladd, 1990). Parents may be able to assist children who are either rejected or neglected by peers; interventions used to help unpopular children are mostly based on social learning models. Strategies include coaching, modeling, and reinforcement of positive social skills such as how to initiate peer interaction, cooperate in play, and respond to others in a friendly way.

COGNITIVE ISSUES

I remember when reading seemed so painful for her. Each word came out slowly, as if she were sounding it out. She made the same mistakes again and again. Then, she suddenly seemed to catch on. She's been reading independently ever since.

Mother of a seven-year-old

Children in middle childhood are often eager to learn and experience new things. Providing a learning environment includes understanding children's abilities and needs so that enough, but not too much, help is given in order for them to succeed. Parental fostering of cognitive competence, creativity, and morality in school-age children is addressed, then the section ends with a focus on school issues.

Cognitive Competence

Parents are often uncertain about how to foster cognitive competence in their children. Recently, Robert Sternberg and Wendy Williams, two experts in the field of cognitive development, compiled a list of strategies for parents to implement to improve their children's competence (Sternberg & Williams, 1995). The seven lessons for parents for developing their children's cognitive abilities can be found in Box 7-1. They see the role of the parent much like that of a coach; parents should watch, guide, and stay involved, but not do activities for the child.

Creativity

Fostering creativity is an important aspect of providing a learning environment, and is especially crucial in the school-age years, when so much emphasis is put on school achievement and finding the "right" answer. School-age children often lose faith in their own creative talents because of their awareness of their peer's abilities. Ask any group of preschoolers if they are good at drawing, and every single hand goes up. Ask the same question of a group of fifth-graders, and you are lucky to get one or two hands.

 Box 7-1 Seven Lessons for Parents for Developing Their Children's Cognitive Abilities

Lesson 1: Teach children that the main limitation on what they *can* do is what they tell themselves they *can't* do.

Lesson 2: It is more important that children learn what questions to ask, and how to ask them, than that they learn what the answers to questions are.

Lesson 3: Help children find what really excites them, remembering that it may not be what really excites you, or what you wish would really excite them.

Lesson 4: Encourage children to take sensible intellectual risks.

Lesson 5: Teach children to take responsibility for themselves—both for their successes *and* for their failures.

Lesson 6: Teach children how to delay gratification—to be able to wait for rewards.

Lesson 7: Teach children to put themselves in another's place.

Taken from: Sternberg, R.J., & Williams, W.M. (1995). Parenting toward cognitive competence. In M.H. Bornstein (Ed.), *Handbook of parenting:* Vol. 4. *Applied and practical parenting*. Mahwah, NJ: Lawrence Erlbaum Associates. Page 260. Reprinted by permission.

Parents must advocate for creative children, who may get negative messages from the outside world. Creative children often have a good sense of humor and are very playful, which sometimes gets them into trouble in a classroom setting (Sisk, 1987). Children who think creatively have insight, imagination, and innovative reasoning abilities. Other characteristics include being open to new experiences, the ability to play with ideas and take risks, and the ability to lose oneself in a task (Callahan, 1980). Being able to generate new ideas is one aspect of successful leadership, especially when paired with other skills such as organization and goal setting (Edwards, 1994).

It is crucial that parents model creative behavior themselves, and provide a creative environment in the home. In their book *How to Raise a More Creative Child*, Belliston and Belliston (1982) give parents concrete suggestions for accomplishing this goal (see Box 7-2).

Morality

> I overheard my ten-year-old son Seth talking with a friend of his. The friend was offering my son a piece of candy that he had taken from our local grocery store. Seth took the candy and said, "Thanks," but seemed unconcerned that he was eating stolen property. Now I'm worried that I've failed to teach him right from wrong. What should I do?

Morality is a set of principles or ideals that help individuals distinguish right from wrong and to act on this distinction. It involves three basic components: moral affect (the emotional need of the child to internalize parental moral standards), moral reasoning (a rational process that coincides with cognitive development and changes in thinking), and moral behavior (acceptable responses that are situation-specific and are learned through direct instruction and observation). Many experts believe that moral development is an aspect of social cognition, where both cognitive maturity and social interaction with peers and adults is needed for development to take place.

 ## Box 7-2 Providing an Environment That Promotes Creativity

1. Establish a creative atmosphere in your home. Be encouraging when children want to create. Be excited about the creations they show you.
2. Set up places where children can create.
3. Set up times when children can create.
4. Provide tools and a work bench for the child to work with creatively.
5. Provide materials for creativity, such as fasteners, glue, scissors, paper, wheels, popsicle sticks, rubber bands, crayons, paint, and chalk.
6. Buy appropriate toys for creativity, such as Legos, Erector sets, blocks, Lincoln logs, and Tinkertoys.
7. As much as possible, refrain from using TV.
8. Listen to dramatic programs on the radio so that children can mentally participate and create mind images.

Taken from: Belliston, L. & Belliston, M. (1982). *How to raise a more creative child.* Allen, TX: Argus Communications. © 1982 Marge and Larry Belliston.

Studies show that parents can promote moral development by encouraging children to state their position, after which the parents present a new perspective containing higher order moral reasoning in a supportive way (Walker & Taylor, 1991). It might also be beneficial for children to talk to friends, since moral discussions with peers can stimulate thoughts about parents' ideas and their own ideas about moral issues (Kruger & Tomasello, 1986).

School

School is a major focal point in middle childhood; therefore, the impact of school issues on the parent-child relationship is an inevitable part of parenting. All parents want their children to do well in school, but parental beliefs differ regarding what "doing well" is and how the parent can promote school success. For example, research suggests that American-born parents value autonomy over conformity in their school-age children, while immigrant parents in the United States are more concerned that their children conform rather than be autonomous (Okagaki & Sternberg, 1993). Cultural context and individual parental beliefs influence how parents feel about their children's schooling. This section will deal with two issues that overlap school and home. The first is parent-school relations, and the second is homework.

Parent-School Relations

The relationship between the school and home is a crucial one. The collaboration and cooperation between these two primary environments is essential to the optimal development of the child. The National Association of State Boards of Education Task Force (1988) recommends that parents be partners in the education of their children by observing and volunteering in classrooms, being involved in decision making regarding programs, and exchanging ideas and information with teachers. These are worthwhile goals, but how can they be attained? Parents seem to be less available than they were in the past. Changing family structures and lifestyles have made it difficult for single parents and working parents to participate in the school process (Coleman, 1991). Multicultural diversity in families also must be recognized in planning for parent participation. Certain kinds of oral and written communication from schools may alienate or confuse parents whose native language is not English or who struggle with their own illiteracy problems (Herrera & Wooden, 1988).

How important is parental involvement? Research suggests that children of parents who are more involved in school activities do better in school than children whose parents are less involved (Stevenson & Baker, 1987). A study of inner-city, low socioeconomic children (95 percent African American) showed that parental involvement during the second year of school was reflected in higher grades and achievement scores, as well as lower retention rates (Marcon, 1993). Parents tend to be more involved when children are younger than when children are in the upper elementary grades. Some believe that parental involvement in the classroom increases parents' appreciation of teachers (Galen, 1991). Being in the actual classroom situation helps parents gain perspective regarding the difficulty of the teacher's job. Conversely, parental involvement may also influence teachers' perceptions of the child's abilities, contributing to higher expectations of achievement (Marcon, 1993).

Parent-teacher conferences are usually scheduled twice a year. These meetings can cause anxiety on the part of both the parent and the teacher. It is helpful for parents and teachers to meet in an informal setting first, such as an open house or a PTA event prior to conference time. Of course, teachers must organize materials to get ready for conferences, but parents also must prepare for conferences; they must think about their child's strengths and weaknesses, and identify questions they might have. Jotting these questions down and asking the important ones first (in case time runs out) are essential parent strategies. Some suggestions for questions parents might want to ask teachers are found in Box 7-3. If possible, both parents should attend conferences so that both parents are clearly informed and involved. This is especially important in families with joint custody arrangements. Parents should be prompt for conferences as a courtesy to the teacher and all of the other parents.

Homework

An important aspect of the parent-school partnership is parental involvement in learning activities at home (Connors & Epstein, 1995). Parents are children's first and most influential teachers; therefore, parental attitudes toward school, behavior at school, school work, and home learning activities are crucial in helping children form their own attitudes regarding these subjects. The goal, of course, is for children to be internally motivated to learn and achieve

---

Box 7-3 Questions for Parents to Ask Teachers

1. How is my child progressing in his or her growth and development? Ask to see examples of your child's work. Ask the teacher for examples of your child's social skills.

2. What types of motivators and rewards are used to reinforce my child's growth and development?

3. What is my child's classroom behavior like (e.g., listening, following directions, participating in class activities, attitude, work habits)? Ask the teacher for specific examples of your child's classroom behavior.

4. What are my child's most and least favorite activities?

5. How is my child's progress assessed? How often is my child assessed? Ask to see copies of the assessment instruments.

6. What types of rules is my child expected to follow in the classroom? How is my child informed of these rules? What consequences follow when my child breaks a rule?

7. How often is homework assigned? What role would the teacher like me to play in helping my child with homework?

8. What special services (e.g., after-school care, physical health screenings, tutoring, counseling, sick care) are provided by the school?

9. How can the school help me locate community services should my child need help with his or her academic work or behavior?

10. How can I help my child continue to do well in school?

11. How can I help the teacher to accomplish the classroom goals that he or she has set for the year?

12. How does the school keep parents informed about schedules, policies, events, and problems? Is there a classroom newsletter?

Taken from: Coleman, M. (1991). Planning for the changing nature of family life in schools for young children. *Young Children*, 46, 15–20. Copyright 1991 by NAEYC. Reprinted by permission.

THE FAMILY CIRCUS®   **By Bil Keane**

"You misunderstand. I'm a
homework consultant, not a
homework subcontractor."

*Reprinted with special permission of King Features
Syndicate.*

in school. Parental behavior that is supportive and encouraging can be instrumental in the realization of this goal; however, the operative words are *supportive* and *encouraging*. Recent research suggests that parental surveillance of homework (reminding children to do their homework, making sure it is complete, overseeing and helping in its completion) contributes to children's being dependent on external factors to motivate them rather than on internal motivation (Ginsburg & Bronstein, 1993). Since this sample was mostly white, middle-class families from New England, generalizability of these findings is in question.

Since homework becomes an important part of family life during the elementary school years, ways in which parents can be involved with homework, but not overly controlling, are needed. Homework is largely the responsibility of the child, but parents can be instrumental in setting limits within which the child can function. The patterns set up at this time may influence study habits in the middle school and high school years. An environment where homework and learning activities in the home are valued, television watching is limited, and bedtime is stable can enhance learning in the home.

To help parents set up an environment conducive to homework, specific suggestions from *The Elementary School Handbook* (Oppenheim, 1989) include the following: A routine time should be set in the daily schedule for homework to be done. A workspace should be established that is quiet and free from distractions, as well as organized so that supplies are easy to find. Children may need help in clarifying what the assignment is asking them to do, or in organizing the tasks to get them done. Parents should be aware of how long average assignments should take so that realistic amounts of time are allowed. Parents who convey their expectations to children as suggestions rather than directives may have more success (Koestner, Ryan, Bernieri, & Holt, 1984). Families must make a decision based on their own needs regarding the involvement of parents in homework.

It is interesting to examine cultural differences in homework. American children spend less time in school and fewer hours doing homework than children in many other countries. Recent research suggests that Chinese children were assigned more homework, spent more time doing homework, received more help with their homework from family members, and had more positive attitudes about homework than Japanese and American children (Chen & Stevenson, 1989). Japanese children were second in amount, time spent, and attitudes. Both the Chinese and Japanese children perform very well on academic achievement tests in cross-national studies of math and science, while American children's performance is mediocre. More research on the effectiveness of homework is needed to evaluate which approaches might improve children's education in the United States.

Parenting Challenges: School Issues in an Applied Context

My seven-year-old daughter often wakes up in the morning and says that she doesn't want to go to school. Lately she has even been complaining that her stomach hurts. I keep telling her that she's not really sick, but this seems to upset her more. This has caused a lot of stress and has made mornings very unpleasant. What should I do?

"School phobia" is quite common in the early elementary grades. It is often accompanied by physical symptoms such as stomachaches and headaches. The symptoms are real, and children actually experience physical discomfort. Parents who successfully combat school phobia acknowledge the child's distress, but focus on the cause of the symptoms instead of the symptoms themselves. Parents must ask the child what it is that is bothering him or her about school. Sometimes there is a concrete problem to be dealt with, such as a substitute teacher. Often, though, there is no one specific problem. It may be an accumulation of different changes; new classmates, an unfamiliar routine, unpredictable situations, schedule changes in home activities, worries about schoolwork, worries about peer acceptance, and fatigue are some of the many possibilities.

Parents must provide reassurance to children that they will help them deal with whatever problems exist; however, a clear message that the parent expects the child to attend school is also appropriate. Communication with the child regarding problems, brainstorming solutions, and following up with a discussion after school are all possible strategies for parents to employ. Enlisting the teacher's help and cooperation is always an option if the problem persists. For most children, school phobia is a fleeting problem that disappears as quickly as it appeared.

TEACHING RESPONSIBILITY

> There are days when I feel that teaching this child to be responsible isn't even a possibility. He can't find his shoes before school in the morning, he forgets his glasses at school half of the time, and he never gets his chores finished unless he's reminded frequently. It takes me twice as long to get him to do things as it would take me to do them myself.
>
> *Mother of a ten-year-old boy*

Teaching someone to be responsible is a difficult task. This is the task of parents, however, since increased freedom and responsibility must go hand in hand with expanding social and cognitive abilities during middle childhood. For example, being able to read traffic signs and follow safety rules responsibly gives children the freedom to ride their bikes. Much of the parenting that occurs during the elementary school years involves making decisions about freedom and responsibility. Trying to ascertain when a child is ready for certain activities, when to let a child learn a lesson the hard way and when to intervene, and finding out how much freedom is too much are the tasks facing parents.

The household task of setting the table is a common chore that parents assign to school-age children in an effort to teach them responsibility and cooperation. *(Jerry Howard/Stock, Boston)*

Chores

Household chores are a common responsibility of children in our culture. Estimates show that by nine or ten years of age, over 90 percent are involved in regular chores (White & Brinkerhoff, 1981). Early chores require children to assume responsibility for themselves, such as picking up their own toys and keeping their rooms clean. This evolves into doing work that benefits the whole family—first by helping a parent and then by taking over the chore from the parent. School-age children most commonly participate in house cleaning and food preparation tasks (Cogle & Tasker, 1982). Parents report that they assign chores to promote responsibility and foster character building, although teaching children to develop skills and needing help are also reasons that are frequently cited. Research does not necessarily support the premise that household chores teach children responsibility, since the literature is inconclusive on this point (Goodnow, 1988). Chores may help in the development of prosocial and cooperative behavior, however, and may also improve cognitive skills and strategies such as problem solving and decision making. More studies are needed to investigate the benefits of household chores on the development of children.

To be successful, parents must believe strongly in the benefits of performing household tasks, since it is often quite an undertaking to get children to actually do their chores. Children need clear rules that are enforced in a caring, consistent manner (Clarke, 1993). A reminder device (other than the parent) is beneficial, such as a chart or checklist in a prominent place (like the door of the refrigerator). Persistence on the part of the parent is also essential, so that children eventually get the message of what the expectations are for their behavior. Finally, helping children break down bigger tasks into smaller steps can teach them to plan and be efficient in managing their time. It is unrealistic to expect perfection from children, and it is wise to be careful in using criticism. If it is a task of such importance that it must be done flawlessly, a child of this age should probably not be doing it.

Self-Care

Probably the biggest issue regarding responsibility and the school-age child is the decision of when a child can stay home without adult supervision. The definition of a *self-care child* is one "between the ages of approximately 6 and 13 who spends time at home alone or with a younger sibling on a periodic basis" (Cole & Rodman, 1987, p. 93). Conservative estimates show that there are between 5 and 10 million self-care children (Long & Long, 1982). Research suggests that 76 percent of self-care children spend after-school time home alone, while 15 percent of self-care happens in the morning before school and 9 percent happens at home in the evenings after 6:00 PM (Rodman & Pratto, 1980). For additional information regarding positive and negative aspects of self-care, see Chapter 13.

It is difficult for parents to know when to begin to let children stay home alone, without adult supervision. Certainly, individual differences must be taken into account, since maturity levels vary greatly at these ages. Although there is no consensus as to age, some professionals believe that eight years old is a minimum age where a child could respond to self-care demands appropriately from a developmental point of view (Cole & Rodman, 1987). This does not mean that all eight-year-olds would have sufficient skills. An informal survey of parents, teachers, and doctors suggested that children younger than ten are not prepared for this responsibility, although most eleven- and twelve-year-olds can probably be on their own for a couple of hours ("On Their Own," 1989). Box 7-4 contains information to help parents determine whether a child is ready to be home alone.

 ## Box 7-4 How to Know If a Child Is Ready to Be Home Alone

The following guidelines represent minimum requirements parents may use to evaluate the readiness of their child for self-care.

Physical A child should be able to:

1. Control his body adequately so that he is not susceptible to injury while moving around the home.
2. Manipulate locks and doors so that she will not be locked in or out.
3. Operate safely any equipment to which he will have access while alone. This might include the stove, blender, or vacuum cleaner. If it isn't safe to operate, he shouldn't have access to it.

Emotional The child should:

1. Be able to comfortably tolerate separations from adults for the length of time required without much loneliness and fear.
2. Not exhibit a pattern of withdrawn, hostile, or self-destructive behavior.
3. Be able to handle usual and unexpected situations without excessive fear or upset.
4. Be able to follow important rules without always "testing the limits."

Cognitive The child should:

1. Be able to understand and remember verbal and written instructions.
2. Solve problems without relying on irrational solutions.
3. Be able to read and write well enough to take telephone and other messages.

Social The child should:

1. Be able to solicit help from friends, neighbors, and designated helpers when appropriate.
2. Understand the role of police, fire fighters, rescue squads, and other community resources.
3. Be willing and able to call in those resources when needed.
4. Be able to maintain friendships with other children and adults.

Family Readiness The parents or guardians should:

1. Maintain some level of communication with and supervision of their children, even if they are not physically present.
2. Be available for emergencies or designate several adults who will be.
3. Be stable enough to provide emotional security for their children.
4. Provide training for their children in the special issues that may arise in self-care.

Community Suitability The community should:

1. Be reasonably safe in fact and perceived as safe by all family members.
2. Provide a variety of care options so that families can make appropriate choices based on their changing needs and circumstances.

Adapted from: Cole, C., & Rodman, H. (1987). When school-age children care for themselves: Issues for family life educators and parents. *Family Relations*, 36, 92–96. Copyrighted 1987 by the National Council on Family Relations, 3989 Central Ave. NE, Suite 550, Minneapolis, MN 55421. Reprinted by permission.

Planning can be an essential part of children's staying on their own successfully. Programs developed by educators to teach self-care skills usually concentrate on basic safety, time management, and self-reliance skills (Koblinsky & Todd, 1989). Behavioral rehearsal and active practice have been suggested as the most effective teaching strategies. Practicing what to say if someone calls on the phone, or role-playing what to do in case of an emergency (such as an illness or a fire) can better prepare children for situations that may come up than simply talking about these issues with children. Having rules regarding having friends over, how much TV can be watched, and which appliances can be used in the parent's absence are helpful. Posting a list of emergency numbers by each phone, preparing a household emergency kit with first-aid supplies and a flashlight, and regularly reviewing all safety rules are also essential preparation strategies ("On Their Own," 1989).

Parenting Challenges: Teaching Responsibility in an Applied Context

> My seven-year-old daughter wants to have her own money to spend. Is it too early to start giving her an allowance? How much should we give her? Should it be tied to chores? What are the advantages and disadvantages?

Most parents feel that it is appropriate to start giving allowances sometime during the child's elementary school years. Parental reasons for doing this vary, although training children to be increasingly independent and responsible is a frequently given explanation (Feather, 1991). It is often a solution to the problem of children's wants; children want things, but must learn that they cannot have everything they want. By giving them money for the extra things they want, parents teach them to make their own decisions, and consequently, to learn to live with their mistakes when they make the wrong choices. Children begin to learn the difference between needs, desires, and goals, while also learning to set priorities. It is a wonderful way for children to learn the value of money and to practice math skills.

Each family is unique and must establish its own criteria for allowances, such as how much money is a reasonable amount, how often it is given, and what are the expectations from the parent regarding the use of the money. The amount usually starts out small for a younger child, with simple expectations for its use (e.g., candy, or a matchbox car). As the child gets older, allowances tend to increase, and more complex tasks are expected. The child may be asked to save a certain proportion of his allowance, or to give some of her or his money to a worthy cause or church each month. Older children with more expensive wants may experience having to wait until they have saved up enough money before purchasing something special. Allowances given at regular intervals allow children to plan within a stable financial framework, learning needed money management skills. Bad choices at an early age may help children become more knowledgeable consumers later in life. All of these lessons are applicable to skills needed in adulthood, but they are practiced in safety since necessities are already provided by parents.

There are differing opinions among people who give parenting advice regarding many aspects of allowances. Although none of these opinions is research based, some commonalities can be found. First, most agree that linking regular household chores to an allowance or payment is not a good idea. Similarly, paying a child for "good" behavior is also not recommended. Chores and appropriate behavior are not negotiable, and children should not expect payment for them. Last of all, parents are cautioned against giving children advances on their allowance. Deficit spending is not a good habit to get into—even for children.

PHYSICAL DEVELOPMENT ISSUES

It is so much fun to watch them play soccer now. I remember when she was in kindergarten all they did was chase the ball. They couldn't stay in their positions because the temptation to try to be where the ball was overcame any attempts at coaching. But now they play their positions well and execute as a team. What a difference five years can make.

Father of a fifth-grader

Children in the elementary school years seem to come in all shapes and sizes, differing greatly in height, weight, and body shape. Growth rates average about two to three inches and seven pounds per year until the adolescent growth spurt, although there is some variability between children of different races, ethnic backgrounds, and socioeconomic levels. School-age children are generally healthy, although respiratory infections are common, given the close surroundings of children in school settings. Children during the elementary school years usually have good appetites and eat well to support the steady growth and activity demands on their bodies (Williams & Caliendo, 1984).

Sports

Part of the school-age child's quest for industry and involvement with peers leads to participation in organized sports such as baseball, softball, soccer, basketball, swimming, and gymnastics. Inappropriate handling of competitive sports at early ages can cause children to "burn out," or abandon athletics permanently. A community-based organization called Parents and Coaches in Sports (PACS) proposes the implementation of coaching strategies that are more child-centered, instead of being centered on the outcome of the game. They suggest that three out of four children who play sports as younger children will not be playing team sports when they are teenagers because of negative experiences—too much emphasis on winning, criticism from parents and coaches, and not enough playing time.

Parents must ensure that children are not in abusive situations while participating in sports activities. Active abuse occurs when children directly experience harsh actions from adults that result in feelings of low self-esteem, fear, or failure. Passive abuse occurs if the child observes another child receiving this same treatment. Parents are urged to refrain from becoming overinvolved,

Participation in organized sports, such as little league
baseball, is evidence of the school-age child's industry and involvement with peers.
(Alan Carey/The Image Works)

and to examine their own motives in competitive situations. Don't expect a
child to live out the lost dreams of the parent. Offering money or rewards for
winning or making the most points makes the activity more of a job or obligation, and less fun. Parents must make informed decisions regarding children's involvement with sports.

Childhood Obesity

> My eight-year-old daughter is fairly chubby. We were hoping she would out-
> grow it, but it seems to be getting worse. This isn't a surprise, since my hus-
> band and I are also a little on the heavy side. The doctor says we need to help
> her change her eating and exercise habits, but we feel she's too young to be on
> a diet yet. What should we do?

Childhood obesity has become a growing health concern in the United
States. Since fat children usually do not "outgrow" it, they become fat adults
who are at risk of a variety of health problems that include high blood pressure and diabetes (Kolata, 1986). Given this information, medical professionals
are recommending that obese children change their eating and exercise habits
earlier in their lives. Parental involvement in this process is crucial, since
behavioral changes are more effective when parents also participate in the
process (Epstein & Wing, 1987). If parents stop buying tempting but unhealthy
foods, and do not reward good behavior with treats, children can be more suc-

cessful in changing eating habits. If parents limit the amount of time television is watched by the child, model physical exercise themselves, and encourage more vigorous activities, exercise habits can be changed. Treatments for childhood obesity do not involve "fad diets"; they usually do not center around one food or fasting. Instead, children learn to make healthy choices in their eating, such as avoiding high-calorie foods and sweets, and eating more reasonable portions or amounts.

Cultural beliefs and societal attitudes in the United States often equate being thin with being beautiful (Feldman, Feldman, & Goodman, 1988). Since obesity among schoolchildren is increasing (Gortmaker, Dietz, Sobol, & Welher, 1987), there may be negative psychological consequences, in addition to physical concerns, for a growing number of children. Parents may be required to help their overweight children deal with teasing, lack of popularity, and low self-esteem.

Although no one knows the exact causes of obesity, there is evidence to suggest that people can have a genetically inherited predisposition to being overweight. Environmental factors such as eating too much and exercising too little can aggravate and accentuate the problem, however. Trying to teach children healthy eating and exercise habits may help them be healthier adults.

CONTEXTUAL CLOSE-UP: ENTERTAINMENT TECHNOLOGIES

Exposure to technological diversions in the form of television and interactive entertainment is a common experience for today's school-age child. How much and what kinds of experiences children have vary quite a bit, and may lead to differing developmental outcomes. Parents are called upon to make choices about the extent of children's participation in technological activities. This section contains a brief review of the literature in this area, highlighting points for parents.

Television

Television plays a significant role in children's lives in the United States. There are more TVs than there are toilets; 99 percent of homes have television sets and over half of the homes have more than one (Van Evra, 1990). Children view three to six hours per day, and spend more hours watching TV by age eighteen than they spend in school. Parents are justifiably concerned about what their children are viewing—acts of violence, sexual acts or references to sexual acts, sex-role stereotypes, racial stereotypes, age-related stereotypes, and advertisements that entice children to push their parents to make more purchases. Critics say that even the best TV does more harm than good because it takes away play time, family time, and sleep time, and it contributes to childhood obesity. Children who watch a lot of TV are more passive, less creative, and less verbal, and they have fewer social skills.

Many professionals (Van Evra, 1990; Dorr & Rabin, 1995) agree that parents must take steps to help their children manage the television problem. The first thing parents should do is *limit the amount of TV watched.* Suggestions include planning ahead what to watch, putting the TV in a room that is used infrequently, avoiding using the TV as a babysitter, planning one night a week with the TV off, finding other leisure activities, and reading more. The second step is to *monitor content.* Only about a third of the homes in the United States dictate to children which shows they can and cannot watch. Unrestricted television viewing introduces children to adult problems before their time, and may not be appropriate. Children should be encouraged to watch only good programs. Last, parents should *discuss and watch* shows with children. Talking to them and keeping them company can help children understand the content of programs more effectively, and can give parents an opening for discussions about sexuality, values, violence, and other important topics.

Interactive Entertainment

Interactive entertainment (video games) has become an increasingly popular form of enjoyment for children. Very little is known, however, about the effects of these games on the developing child. Parents must give consideration to potential positive and negative aspects of both short- and long-term use. Most of the research that exists on this topic is cognitively oriented, documenting that video games improve spatial abilities (Subrahmanyam & Greenfield, 1994), mental rotation time and spatial visualization time (Okagaki & Frensch, 1994), and hypothesis testing through problem solving and discovery (Greenfield, Camaioni, Ercolani, Weiss, Lauber, & Perucchini, 1994). Many believe that video games are a form of cognitive socialization that prepares children for a future where computer skills are crucial (Greenfield, 1994).

Very little is known, however, about the social impact of video games. Researchers have explored the implications of children's viewing violent acts on television; now they must explore the effects of being a part of the violent acts, especially with regard to virtual reality, where representational realism increases (Greenfield & Cocking, 1994). Preliminary results using young adult subjects suggest that participants have higher physiological arousal and aggressive thoughts than observers when playing a violent virtual reality game (Calvert & Tan, 1994). Since males play more video games than females, they may be more at risk for adverse effects. Perhaps the development of more nonviolent games would reduce some of the negative effects and encourage more females to gain the cognitive benefits. Research on the differential effects of aggressive games for children should also be explored.

Finally, parents should consider basic issues regarding the sedentary nature of this activity. It can be argued that children who are spending hours in front of a video game have the same risks as children who watch too much TV. Inactivity can lead to obesity, the solitary nature of the activity can lead to social isolation, and time spent with video games is time that isn't spent reading, drawing, playing music, and so forth. Parents must weigh the positive and negative aspects and make their judgments accordingly.

SUMMARY

- Parents of school-age children are in the interpretive stage of parenthood, where they must answer questions, provide information, and help children form values. Co-regulation encourages parents and children to share responsibility for behavior and decisions.
- School-age children are in Erikson's stage of industry. They are busy, industrious, and eager to learn skills in every area of development. Parents play a crucial role in helping children have high self-esteem by being loving and having clear standards of behavior.
- Peers are important to school-age children in many ways. Parents want their children to be successful in peer relationships, and have special concerns when children are rejected or neglected by their peers.
- School is a major focus in middle childhood. Parent-school relations and homework issues must be addressed within individual and cultural contexts.
- Taking responsibility for chores and self-care are steps of growth for school-age children.
- Sports and obesity are two issues pertaining to school-age children, and may impact on their future development.
- Television and video games have positive and negative aspects. Parents must review the possible effects on children, and consider limiting and monitoring their exposure.

Parenting Adolescents

W anted: **Parent of Teenager.** Must have extraordinary degree of patience. Knowledge of current fads and slang helpful. You will be treated as if you have lost some or all of your mental acuity, but don't panic! Ability to fade into the woodwork at appropriate times a plus. Driver's license no longer necessary, since teen will inevitably have car when you need it, or it will be out of gas.

(Moschell, 1991)

Parenting adolescents is a job that requires much flexibility. Multiple developmental changes in affect, behavior, and cognition occur within multiple contexts, resulting in many challenges for both adolescents and parents. Parents have the difficult and sometimes contradictory task of trying to encourage independence on the one hand, while attempting to provide responsible supervision on the other. Families must transform in response to developmental events. Steinberg (1988) refers to the changes that take place over a period of time as normative realignment, because the process has temporary periods of disequilibrium, movement, and adaptation. To make parenting tasks even more complex, parents are often trying to assist adolescents with issues pertaining to identity and physical change at a time when the parents themselves may be experiencing similar stresses in midlife (Silverberg, in press). Many parents report feeling least competent and effective during the stage of parenting adolescents (Ballenski & Cook, 1982). Part of the difficulty for parents lies in foreseeing the future and adequately preparing adolescents for adult roles (Hamburg & Takanishi, 1989; Small & Eastman, 1991).

The period of adolescence seems to be lengthening in our society (Hamburg & Takanishi, 1989). Traditionally, adolescence consisted of the teen age years, from thirteen to eighteen. Contemporary definitions of adolescence now include the preteen years, since eleven- and twelve-year-olds are maturing earlier and social problems such as drug abuse and sexual experimentation are occurring in these younger age groups. On the other end of the spectrum, nineteen- to twenty-two-year-olds are often considered to be adolescents because most of them do not yet possess adult roles or responsible positions. For the purposes of this chapter, we will focus on issues related to parenting adolescents of all ages.

THE PARENTING ROLE

Sometimes it seems like everything about him is changing all at once, and I don't even know him anymore. We just keep talking things over so I can keep up with where he's at.

Mother of a 15-year-old

Theoretical Context

According to Galinsky (1987), parents of adolescents are in the *interdependent stage* of parenthood. During this time, parents have the major task of forming a new relationship with the teenage child, while also struggling with the process of finding fresh solutions to the recurrent authority and communication issues. Parents seek a balance between connectedness and separateness, where adolescents may express their individuality while remaining attached to family members (Grotevant & Cooper, 1986). Setting limits and giving guidance are main issues during this time period. Redefinition of the relationship must include the parent's acceptance of a child's separate identity and sexuality. In addition, of course, this stage is permeated with concerns about the child's impending entry into the world as a young adult (Wapner, 1993).

According to Erikson, adolescents are trying to figure out the answer to the question "Who am I?" In this stage of psychosocial development, the task is to establish a unique and independent *identity*. The alternative to establishing an identity is role confusion, where adolescents are either "mixed up" about who they are and what they want to do or have made no efforts to explore what their future roles might be. Identity involves developing a sense of purpose, clarifying long-term plans, clarifying values, knowing who you really are, and pinpointing where you are headed. This process includes establishing a sexual, ethnic, social, and occupational identity. Obviously, establishing an identity is a gradual, lengthy, complex, flexible, and adaptive process that does not begin or end in adolescence. Late adolescence, however, is an especially important time because physical, cognitive, and social development is advanced enough to allow a sorting and synthesizing process to occur,

Thinking becomes more logical in Piaget's stage of formal operations, where adolescents are capable of hypothesizing and problem-solving in situations such as a chemistry experiment.
(John Eastcott/Yva Momatiuk/The Image Works)

which incorporates childhood experiences and constructs a pathway to adulthood.

According to Piaget, sometime between age twelve and adulthood, young people become capable of logical thinking, which psychologists call *formal operational thinking.* When individuals can think in abstract ways and deal with hypothetical situations, they are in Piaget's stage of *formal operations.* Cognitive development in adolescence involves thinking in ways that are more advanced, efficient, and effective. Teens are more able to think about possibilities, moving from the specific to the abstract, generating alternative explanations in a systematic way. They are able to think through hypotheses in problem-solving situations, to deal with hypothetical situations that are contrary to fact, and to reason through "if-then" propositions. Finally, adolescents can think about religion and philosophy, and explore the world of social cognition; they can think about themselves and their interpersonal relationships.

It takes awhile for both the adolescent and his or her parent to adjust to the fact that the teenage child is in possession of such powerful cognitive tools. Explanations that have been given by parents in the past and accepted by the child are now often questioned. Teens suggest arguments that parents may not have considered, possibly challenging the parent's ideas. Parents should also be aware that, although adolescents are capable of high-level thinking and abstraction, they do not always apply these skills at home. Just like adults, adolescents do not always engage in logical thinking.

Parental Behaviors

Parenting Styles

As Chapter 2 explains, four basic styles of parenting based on dimensions of responsiveness and demandingness have been suggested. They are *authoritative, authoritarian, permissive,* and *uninvolved* parenting styles. Many research studies have examined which parenting styles have the most favorable outcomes for adolescents. The literature seems to suggest overwhelmingly that the authoritative parenting style is the most successful in a number of different areas. Adolescents who characterize their parents as authoritative are more competent in psychosocial areas and school achievement, and score lower on measures of distress and problem behaviors (Steinberg, Elmen, & Mounts, 1989; Lamborn, Mounts, Steinberg & Dornbusch, 1991). Although examples of authoritative parenting can be found across various ethnic groups and socioeconomic classes, it is important to be aware of differing socialization goals and parenting behaviors within different cultures (Spencer & Dornbusch, 1990; Darling & Steinberg, 1993). The relationships between ethnicity, poverty, and parenting style need to be further studied in order to understand contextual variations (Holmbeck, Paikoff, & Brooks-Gunn, 1995).

The authoritative parenting style, as introduced in Chapter 2, is characterized by three parenting behaviors: warmth, balance of power, and demandingness (Baumrind, 1978; Small & Eastman, 1991; Holmbeck, Paikoff, & Brooks-Gunn, 1995). *Warmth* consists of the emotional closeness and connectedness of the parent-child relationship. The task of the parent during the adolescent years is to continue to provide warmth and acceptance during these years of change and growth. *Balance of power* specifies how parents practice democratic parenting by involving children in family decision making and allowing them to express their opinions. Parents must constantly adapt to the changing abilities of the adolescent, knowing when he or she is ready for the responsibility of additional freedom. Joint decision making, especially with regard to issues of autonomy and control, is necessary. *Demandingness* refers to the reasonable, clearly communicated standards or expectations parents have for their child's behavior. Authoritative parents are able to enforce rules firmly and consistently without being coercive. Taken together, these parenting behaviors are the crux of the authoritative style.

Other Parenting Practices

An important part of parenting adolescents is *parental monitoring* (Small & Eastman, 1991; Holmbeck, Paikoff, & Brooks-Gunn, 1995), which involves parental supervision and awareness of where the child is, what the child is doing, and with whom. Research suggests that adolescents who receive this kind of parental involvement in their lives show higher levels of self-esteem and less delinquent behavior than do adolescents whose parents do not monitor their activities (Patterson & Strouthamer-Loeber, 1984; Patterson, 1986). In addition, parental monitoring serves a protective function. Adolescents with parents who monitor them are less likely to find themselves in situations where unwanted sexual activity (such as date rape or sexual coercion) may occur (Small & Kerns, 1993), are less likely to be susceptible to pressure from peers engaging in delinquency (Curtner-Smith & MacKinnon-Lewis, 1994), and are less likely to use tobacco (Melby, Conger, Conger, & Lorenz, 1993). Societal changes such as working parents, less cohesive neighborhoods, and the tendency of people to interact mainly with others who are similar in age may contribute to the difficulty of monitoring adolescents.

Modeling is an important parenting practice, and is effective in the transmission of values as well as behaviors and skills (Small & Eastman, 1991; Holmbeck, Paikoff, & Brooks-Gunn, 1995). Parents who give their time and resources to needy causes, for example, may find their adolescents similarly involved in charitable work. *Providing information* is also a crucial aspect of parenting adolescents, especially in areas where there are health risks (Holmbeck, Paikoff, & Brooks-Gunn, 1995). For example, female adolescents who can communicate with their parents about sexual issues such as birth control are at a lower risk for sexually transmitted diseases and teenage pregnancy in both white (Luster & Small, 1994) and black (Murry, 1994) samples.

Parental Concerns

There is a misconception that parent-adolescent relationships are characterized by intense conflict and turmoil, instead of closeness and harmony (Steinberg, 1990), but large surveys suggest that the majority of adolescents continue to rely on their parents for advice, support, and emotional intimacy (Maccoby & Martin, 1983: Lamb, Ketterlinus, & Fracasso, 1992). Although severe conflict happens only in 5 percent to 10 percent of families (Steinberg, 1990), minor but persistent conflict occurs between virtually all parents and adolescents (Montemayor, 1986). Bickering is more likely to occur during early adolescence than middle or late adolescence (Steinberg, 1990). Using ethnicity as a descriptive category to highlight cultural diversity in families, Table 8-1 shows percentages of parent-adolescent conflict in ten areas. Overall, conflict appears to occur more frequently over everyday things like chores and school than larger issues, such as sexual behavior (Barber, 1994).

Conflict resolution can be an instructive experience if it takes place in the context of a warm parent-child relationship (Small & Eastman, 1991). Families who are supportive of their adolescents' development promote successful negotiation of disagreements, keeping conflict low and improving parent-adolescent relationships (Rueter & Conger, 1995). Disagreements may provide opportunities for discussion and communication about important issues (Steinberg, 1990), although sometimes these opportunities are missed when either the parent or teen leaves and does not resolve the conflict. Adolescents' participation in these discussions may give them a clearer view of their parents' beliefs and values, since what they assume their parents think may be in error (Brody, Moore, & Glei, 1994).

SOCIAL AND EMOTIONAL ISSUES

> He's so moody. One day he comes home from school on top of the world, hugging me and talking a mile a minute. The next, he barely grunts as a greeting, heads straight for his room, shuts the door, and doesn't come out until supper. It's impossible to predict what he'll be like.
>
> *Mother of a 14-year-old*

Parents of adolescents often struggle while trying to help children cope with the emotional aspects of teenage life. Adolescence is often a time of feeling up one minute and down the next. On the one hand, teens are exploring self-concept, self-esteem, and sexuality in the effort to decide identity issues. On the other, the social world of adolescents is a busy one, full of people and activities. Parents have the task of accepting the importance of peers during this time period. It is sometimes difficult for parents when their adolescent chooses to confide in a friend and not in them. As adolescents begin to understand more about themselves, they begin to understand more about their relationships with others, allowing intimate, meaningful friendships to evolve. This section explores the social and emotional context of adolescent interactions and the role that parents play in these contexts.

Identity

The quest for identity is a lifelong process. Parents themselves continue to make revisions and changes as they continue to grow. Adolescence, however, is a particularly important time for identity issues to be addressed in a meaningful way. All children go through a process of identification, where they incorporate aspects of other people's personalities into their own. Parents are

TABLE 8-1. Parent-Adolescent Conflict
(*Row percentages of parent-adolescent conflict by ethnic group*)

Topic of Conflict	Never	Monthly	Weekly	Up to Daily
Helping around house				
White	21	28	37	14
Black	35	22	27	16
Hispanic	52	14	23	11
Family relations				
White	47	22	21	10
Black	67	14	12	7
Hispanic	64	13	14	9
School				
White	50	25	18	7
Black	68	16	10	6
Hispanic	76	10	11	3
Dress				
White	51	28	17	4
Black	56	20	17	8
Hispanic	61	16	17	6
Money				
White	58	24	15	3
Black	71	14	11	5
Hispanic	81	7	8	4
How late child stays out				
White	62	25	11	2
Black	66	18	12	4
Hispanic	77	12	10	1
Friends				
White	63	28	8	2
Black	64	21	11	4
Hispanic	67	17	14	2
Boyfriend/girlfriend				
White	79	14	5	2
Black	77	13	6	5
Hispanic	84	8	6	2
Substance use				
White	88	8	3	1
Black	97	2	1	1
Hispanic	94	2	3	1
Sexual behavior				
White	92	6	1	1
Black	92	5	1	2
Hispanic	96	2	1	1

Taken from: Barber, B.K. (1994). Cultural, family, and personal contexts of parent-adolescent conflicts. *Journal of Marriage and the Family,* 56, 375–386. Copyrighted 1994 by the National Council on Family Relations, 3989 Central Ave. NE, Suite 550, Minneapolis, MN 55421. Reprinted by permission.

It is helpful for parents to recognize that clothing choices are part of the adolescent struggle between forming a unique identity and conforming to the peer group. *(Michael Siluk/The Picture Cube)*

influential models in this process, as are teachers, siblings, and peers. Identification occurs mostly in bits and pieces during early and middle childhood, and the pieces are then integrated into a coherent balanced whole by late adolescence. The analogy often used to explain this process is that of a quilt. Patches are acquired along the way, but are not sewn together yet. Later, they are interconnected into a pattern that makes that particular quilt unique.

The planning and putting together of these "quilt pieces" takes time and effort. Parents may assist the building of a sense of identity by being supportive and tolerant of the experimentation process. Many psychologists in the United States believe that adolescents need a *psychosocial moratorium.* This concept, proposed by Erikson, suggests that adolescents need a time-out from excessive responsibilities and obligations that might restrict the young person's pursuit of self-discovery. Adolescents in the United States, for example, are urged to stay in school for an extended period of time so that they have more opportunities to think seriously about their plans. Without this chance to explore, experiment, and choose among options for the future, adolescents may not realize all they are capable of becoming. Although the idea of a moratorium may be ideal, it is not a choice for many young people who lack the economic freedom to take time off. This does not mean these adolescents won't develop an identity, but some of their potential may be lost (Steinberg, 1993).

The goal in pursuing identity issues is *identity achievement,* where adolescents have undergone a crisis or exploration and made a commitment (Marcia, 1980). Parents can facilitate the achievement of identity by trying not to interfere in the process and by being aware of problems that can inhibit identity achievement. Some of these include *identity confusion* (an incomplete sense of self due to lack of exploration), *identity foreclosure* (the premature establishment of a sense of identity before sufficient role experimentation has occurred) or *negative identity* (the selection of an identity that is obviously undesirable in the eyes of significant others and the community). Such identity problems may affect autonomy, intimacy, sexuality, and achievement. Sometimes identity problems have their roots in the quality and nature of parent-adolescent relationships. A negative identity is often a form of rebellion against parents, for example, the overachieving, successful parents who have a child with no ambition or ability to stick with a job or school. Identity foreclosure may occur in the case of an overeager parent who really wants a lawyer, or a doctor, or some other parent-chosen occupation in the family.

Parents who want to be supportive of an adolescent's search for identity can facilitate identity development by helping adolescents to feel connected while allowing them to be individuals. Adolescents may be more able to explore identity issues in families where disagreements are permitted. Differentiation is encouraged if the adolescent is allowed to develop his or her own opinions (Holmbeck, Paikoff, & Brooks-Gunn, 1995). It is particularly important that parents be supportive of the special challenges minority adolescents face in their search for identity, since feeling torn between the culture of origin and the standards of the majority culture can be challenging and confusing (Phinney, 1990).

Parenting Challenges: Identity in an Applied Context

> My 15-year-old son seems to think that certain brand-name clothes are the most important things on earth to have. But some of the styles are absolutely ridiculous. He likes the clothes that look like someone else has already worn them for a few years. We object to spending good money on clothes that make him look like a bum. Should we let him have the clothes he wants, or insist that he wear things that are more practical?

During adolescence, flaws of any kind are a big deal. Adolescents have to learn to accept themselves as they are; however, that is very difficult to do when bodies are changing so rapidly. Often, adolescents have to become comfortable with pimples, gangly bodies, and prominent noses. They have an idea of attractiveness that they would like to meet, but their bodies will not cooperate. That is why clothes are so important within this age group. Clothes are one thing that adolescents can control about their appearance; their bodies won't conform, so they find acceptance wearing clothes that look like everyone else's or that are socially acceptable to peers.

Many parents of adolescents struggle with issues surrounding clothing, shoes, and hair styles. Parents have one idea of how their children should look, while the teens involved, in an effort to express their individuality and fit in with peers, have another. Researchers have found that there is often a generation gap between parents and teens in matters such as clothes, music, and leisure activities. Conflict over these issues seems to stem from differing perceptions of what the problem is and who has authority or jurisdiction over the problem (Smetana, 1989). Parents usually view clothing disputes as a matter of convention ("People don't wear jeans to church") while teens view clothing as a matter of personal taste ("Maybe you wouldn't wear jeans to church, but I want to. Why should my choice bother you?"). Effective strategies to deal with such problems include trying to understand each other's point of view and finding joint solutions.

Peers

> She's with her friends all of the time. Even when she's home, she's on the phone with one person or another. It takes hours for them to make their plans of who is going where and with whom. I feel like I need to make an appointment if I want to talk with her.

Mother of a 17-year-old

Peer relationships become more important and intimate in the adolescent years (Savin-Williams & Berndt, 1990). Peers begin to share thoughts and ideas with their friends, in addition to activities. Peer interaction among adolescents is organized around two structures (Brown, 1990). The first is *cliques,* small groups of same-age, (usually) same-sex individuals who are friends and share common activities. The average group size is around five or six, but a clique may have anywhere between two and twelve individuals involved. The clique provides the adolescent with a social setting for interaction where people know each other fairly well. Many social skills in communication, leadership, and friendship are learned within this context. The structure of cliques changes from early adolescence to later adolescence (Dunphy, 1963). Preteens and young teenagers usually engage in activities within their same-sex cliques, followed by a transitional period in which boys' and girls' cliques get together, but do not mingle very much. As middle adolescence approaches, a shift towards mixed-sex cliques becomes more dominant. These are usually interest or activity based. During this period of time, the emphasis is on friendships. By late adolescence, the peer group breaks off into sets of couples, which becomes the most common mode of social activity. This is where adolescents develop intimate opposite-sex relationships.

The other structure that organizes peer interactions in adolescence is the *crowd.* Crowds are large groups of individuals who have a similar reputation and stereotyped identity even though they may not actually know each other very well. The labels differ from school to school, but typical crowds are "jocks," "nerds," "brains," "preppies," and "wannabe's." These labels provide a big contribution to the adolescent's self-concept. Crowds also change over time, and decline in importance as the teen moves into late adolescence (Brown, 1990). Crowds provide an identity for young and middle adolescents who are still searching for and experimenting with their true identities. As middle and late adolescence approaches and individual identity emerges, the adolescent has less need for the crowd association.

Parents often feel that they no longer have input into their adolescents' peer relationships. Research suggests however, that parenting practices may have an indirect influence on adolescents' peer group affiliations (Brown, Mounts, Lamborn, & Steinberg, 1993). Parental monitoring (knowing where the child is, whom she or he is with, and what they are doing) may have an impact on the adolescent's peer-related choices. The parental practice of joint decision making within the context of a balance of power is also associated with adolescent behaviors that, in turn, relate to membership in certain adolescent crowds. Although more research is needed to delineate these parental influences on peer groups, the fear that parents are replaced by the peer group in adolescence appears unfounded.

Adolescent Depression

Depression occurs in people of all ages. Some people have depressive symptoms, while others experience a much more severe disorder known as *clinical depression.* The majority of adolescents do not have major problems with depression, but approximately 20 percent become extremely depressed and require clinical intervention (Hauser & Bowlds, 1990). Unfortunately, in our society teen problems are often not taken seriously because we think that its "normal" for teenagers to feel disturbed and experience many ups and downs. There is a misconception that adolescents will "grow out of it." Parents must recognize that this is a difficult time for teens, as they must adapt to changes in their physical appearance, new expectations of others, and new social roles. The extensive self-examination and introspection that must be undertaken to establish a coherent sense of identity can be a painful process. Such societal changes as increasing divorce rates, high mobility, and an unpredictable job market have made adolescence an even more difficult period, leaving many teens feeling helpless, confused, and pessimistic about the future instead of having a healthy sense of themselves.

Depression is not a minor fluctuation in self-esteem, but a prolonged, intense sense of hopelessness and frustration. Parents must be particularly tuned in since many teens mask their depression with extreme restlessness or fatigue. Adolescents have a difficult time admitting their helplessness to themselves as well as to others. Sometimes adolescents become so depressed that they consider suicide. Depressed mood is strongly related to suicidal behaviors for both sexes, although it is a better predictor for females (Bettes & Walker, 1986). Unfortunately, suicide rates of adolescents in the United States have skyrocketed in the past thirty years (Tomlinson-Keasey & Keasey, 1988). Suicide is the second leading cause of death among teenagers, although some experts believe that many accidents (the number-one cause of death in adolescents) are questionable, and may actually be suicides. People often mistake the precipitating event of a suicide as the reason for it, but in most cases it is usually the last incident in a long chain of events, and is the most desperate of a series of attempts to cope with life. More females attempt suicide than males, but males outnumber females in the number of suicide-related deaths because they tend to use more lethal methods.

Clinical models of adolescent suicide suggest that failure to compete successfully and social isolation may lead to feelings of extreme hopelessness and, eventually, suicide (Holinger & Offer, 1982). In addition, a suicide contagion effect (the "copycat" suicide) has been identified in adolescents who are highly suggestible and vulnerable. These adolescents are eager to imitate models that give them permission to go ahead with what they were already thinking anyway.

There are several things parents can do to help adolescents cope with depression and possible suicide. Some effective strategies include creating

---

 ## Box 8-1 Warning Signs of Suicide

1. *A previous suicide attempt.* Anyone who has made a previous attempt at harming himself or herself is always considered at high risk of another attempt. Many teens who are not sure of their decision to take their lives may lead up to a serious attempt through a series of self-destructive acts. Most suicides (60 percent) follow failed attempts.

2. *Talk or thoughts of suicide or death.* Anytime a teen begins to talk of suicide or seems to concentrate on thoughts of death, the situation may be critical. People believe that teens threaten killing themselves to get attention or "get their way." Most parents are not in the position to make professional judgments, so any threat or discussion must be taken seriously.

3. *Changes in personality or mood.* Parents must take depression seriously. It is hard to judge if a teen is just "down" or in intense emotional pain because she or he is in the midst of immense physical and psychological change. A quick recovery can be a sign that the adolescent has decided to take his or her life.

4. *Changes in eating or sleeping patterns.* Many people who are under stress respond with changes in eating patterns (either eating more or less) or in their sleeping patterns (sleeping more, less, or at different times than usual).

5. *Withdrawal from friends and activities.* Any change in involvement with either friends or activities may signal danger, since both are so important to teens. Pulling away from social involvements may be an indication of the teen's energy level.

6. *Taking unusual risks.* All teens take risks as a part of learning about themselves, but if they take risks that offer serious danger to themselves or others, parents have to investigate why this is happening. For example, a series of "accidents," reckless driving, and other such behaviors are signals that the teen has little regard for life.

7. *Drug abuse.* This category includes the overuse and abuse of both alcohol and other street or prescription drugs. The teen who needs to artificially change the way he or she feels is in trouble. Parents must look beyond the symptom to the cause. Drug abuse may be an attempt at self-treatment, but loss of control may be passive suicide.

8. *Final arrangements, giving away prized possessions, making peace with friends.* Teens who are ready to leave this life feel they have no need for possessions and must make arrangements for the people and things that are important to them.

9. *Recent loss.* Loss of important persons, positions, or possessions can trigger a suicide attempt. This includes death or separation because of divorce, loss of a job, or loss of prized possessions. For teens, it is often a break in a sexual relationship that precipitates a suicide. Relationship breakups are relatively common, which often blinds parents and teachers to the pain and depression they may cause. Teens sometimes need a sympathetic shoulder rather than platitudes such as "there are other fish in the sea."

open channels of communication by being available to listen, acknowledging the child's feelings, offering positive feedback and encouragement, and creating episodes of pleasure that break up the usual routine with something exciting. Prevention training provides alternatives for parents that may help them be more able to identify depression, deal with depression using problem-solving techniques, and promote social competence to meet adolescent needs (Petersen, Compas, Brooks-Gunn, Stemmler, Ey, & Grant, 1993). Perhaps the most important role for parents is awareness of risk. Parents must be able to accurately assess signals the adolescent may be giving regarding a contemplated suicide. Nine warning signs of suicide are found in Box 8-1. Finally, parents must be particularly involved in combating the contagion effects of suicide by helping adolescents cope with the suicide of a friend or relative.

COGNITIVE ISSUES

> He is constantly questioning everything I say and arguing with me. And the thing that really gets to me is sometimes he's got a good point, and my reasoning is faulty or not well thought out in some way. I hate it when that happens. He's just getting too smart for his own good.
>
> *Frustrated father of a 17-year-old*

The cognitive changes accompanying the adolescent's growth spurt lead to advanced critical thinking on the part of the adolescent, which enables the parent and child to discuss issues on the same level. The teenager goes from childlike thinking, where everything is black or white, to a belief that everything is relative. Problem-solving abilities gradually improve, and evaluation strategies become more complex (Holmbeck, Paikoff, & Brooks-Gunn, 1995). The arguments and difficulties that can ensue are often exasperating to parents, who begin to feel that their adolescent questions everything for the sake of aggravation. In addition, parents must deal with the eventuality that adolescents, having profound thoughts of their own, no longer idealize parents and their views. Parents often console themselves during this potentially stressful

For Better or For Worse®   **by Lynn Johnston**

FOR BETTER OR FOR WORSE © 1990 Lynn Johnston Prod., Inc. Reprinted with permission of UNIVERSAL PRESS SYNDICATE. All rights reserved.

period with the knowledge that the processes involved in adolescent thinking provide good practice for adulthood.

Providing a learning environment for the active and demanding adolescent mind is a formidable task for parents who want to prepare their children for later life. Strong, supportive parent-child relationships often facilitate academic achievement (Maccoby & Martin, 1983). Simple things, such as the organization of the home and helping with school assignments, may help parents facilitate learning and achievement (DuBois, Eitel, & Felner, 1994). Parents who engage in intellectual conversations with their teens, allowing an exchange of ideas with a minimum of conflict may contribute to cognitive advances.

Adolescents experience periods of extreme self-absorption known as *adolescent egocentrism* (Elkind, 1967). Adolescents do not believe everyone thinks similarly to themselves, like their preschool compatriots. They do, however, have a sense that the psychological universe revolves around them. In fact, adolescents may have difficulty believing that others are not thinking something about them. This concept is known as the *imaginary audience*. Adolescents typically imagine themselves to be under tremendous scrutiny at all times from everyone around them. They believe others are as admiring or critical of them as they are of themselves. It is helpful to perceive how they are thinking—to understand the adolescent perspective. If a person believes that each and every pimple will be noticed and scrutinized by each and every person one runs into, self-consciousness becomes more understandable.

Another outgrowth of adolescent egocentrism is a concept known as the *personal fable,* which is of more concern to parents. This is the adolescent's belief that since so many people are interested in him or her, she or he must be special and unique. This kind of magical thinking leads adolescents to believe that they are not subject to the same rules as everyone else—that they are immortal. Adolescent risk-taking activities, such as unprotected sex, substance abuse, or delinquent behaviors can be seen in light of the personal fable. Adolescents simply believe that they are somehow protected, and that bad things will not happen to them. As was mentioned previously, parents may have an impact on adolescent risk-taking behaviors by closely monitoring adolescent activities within a warm and supportive environment. In addition, parents may act as positive models for their children, since adults are not immune to taking risks and believing that they are invulnerable. For example, a parent who smokes two packs of cigarettes a day, or drinks alcohol and then drives home may be also be exhibiting evidence of the personal fable, and that parent is certainly providing a negative model for adolescents.

PHYSICAL DEVELOPMENT ISSUES

It seems like it happened overnight. My chubby little girl with rosy cheeks and pigtails is now a slender young woman with breasts and makeup. It's just hard to get used to.

Mother of a 15-year-old

Adolescents are in a period of rapid physical growth. At a time when they may prefer to be invisible, bodily changes are intense and as a result, quite noticeable. Height, weight, and shape transformations occur in both sexes, in addition to hair growth, voice changes, and increases in sweat and oil production glands. Because of these rapid physical changes, the health needs of the adolescent are also increased. Legal and illegal drug use, sexually transmitted diseases, and eating disorders are real threats to the adolescent's well-being. This section will address these physical development and health issues.

Adolescent Physical Development

Adolescence is a time of many physical changes. Broadly speaking, "puberty" is used as a collective term to refer to all the physical changes that occur in the growing girl or boy passing from childhood to adulthood. Changes include a rapid acceleration in growth, which results in dramatic height and weight increases; further development of the gonads or sex glands (which are the testes in males and the ovaries in females); the development of secondary sex characteristics (changes in the genitals and breasts, the growth of pubic, facial, and body hair, and the further development of the sex organs); changes in body composition, specifically, in the quantity and distribution of fat and muscle; and changes in the circulatory and respiratory systems, which lead to increased strength and tolerance for exercise.

There may be a down side to all of the physical changes adolescents experience. Extreme physical growth may translate into high percentages of malnourished teens, who often are eating a diet that is high in sugar and carbohydrates but low in protein. In addition, fatigue is often a problem, since teens often don't get the sleep they need.

Physical Changes and Social Development

Physical changes may have implications for social development. For example, acne, which affects around 85 percent of teens at some time or another, can affect self-image, which may in turn affect social relationships. The production of hormones and changes in hormonal levels can definitely affect moods, contributing to increased irritability and negativity (Buchanan, Eccles, & Becker, 1992). This could easily lead to more unpleasant parent-child interactions.

The timing of physical changes and puberty can define the social environment of the adolescent. People often react differently or expect different things from early and late maturers because their timing differs from that of the majority of their peers (Steinberg, 1993). Given that there are so many diverse contexts in which development takes place, it is obvious that many different social consequences are possible. Parents and teachers must be particularly watchful of the effects of early and late maturation on the social and emotional needs of adolescents. Not being "on time" with peers can make many things much more difficult. Parents can be particularly helpful in finding alternative sources of status for teens, such as academic achievement or special talents or activities. A recent report to Congress suggests that adolescent health could be improved if adolescents had more recreational opportunities, and more opportunities for community service (Dougherty, 1993).

Health Issues

Adolescents have greater access to potentially life-threatening activities than ever before (Hamburg & Takanishi, 1989). Parents are worried because of the exposure teens now have to these potentially dangerous activities and influences (Small & Eastman, 1991). Drug use, sexual activity resulting in sexually transmitted diseases that may be fatal, and eating disorders are just three of parents concerns regarding adolescent health issues.

Drug Use

Drugs are a confusing subject in our culture. Drugs of all kinds are used, although some are specified as "legal" and others are deemed "illegal." A line is drawn between "legitimate use" and "abuse." It is all right for adults to use drugs, but it is upsetting when people experiment at earlier ages. Society says drugs are bad, but then glorifies them as vehicles for having a good time or being "cool." No wonder there is confusion among adolescents as to drug use; the messages being sent are often contradictory.

Drug use in adolescence can have a long-term negative effect on health. It is also clear, however, that a majority of adolescents experiment with drugs of one kind or another. Outcomes are dependent upon which drugs are used and how frequently. We know that excessive long-term use of cigarettes and alcohol puts people at risk for cancer, heart disease, and liver and kidney damage. Some evidence suggests that early experimentation with these substances is particularly harmful because young adolescents lack judgment and maturity to use drugs safely or moderately (Baumrind & Moselle, 1985). Alcohol, tobacco, and marijuana are the most popular drugs used by teenagers. Abuse of drugs and alcohol in adolescence is associated with problems such as depression, delinquent activities, and unprotected sex (Newcomb & Bentler, 1989).

Laurence Steinberg (1993), an expert in the area of adolescent development, has thoroughly reviewed the literature and proposed four risk factors for substance abuse. First, people with personality characteristics such as anger, depression, impulsivity, and achievement problems are more likely than their peers to abuse drugs and alcohol. Adolescents with distant, hostile, or conflicted family relationships (as opposed to nurturing families with close relationships) are more likely to have problems with substance abuse. Individuals with drug and alcohol problems are more likely to have friends who also use drugs, both because of peer influence and a common interest. Last, adolescents who are at a susceptible point in their own psychological development may be more influenced to use drugs than they would be at other times that are less transitional. Substance abuse is more likely if the adolescent has many risk factors. Parents may try to prevent substance abuse by monitoring teen behavior, providing them with accurate information, and providing a supportive, open home environment.

Sexually transmitted diseases (STDs) are spread by sexual contact. The rates for STDs are very high among adolescents, which may be tied to both their ignorance and their risk-taking behavior. Included in this list are chlamydia, gonorrhea, genital warts, herpes simplex, syphilis, and acquired immune deficiency syndrome (AIDS). The subject of "safe sex" has become even more prevalent in recent years since the proliferation of the AIDS epidemic, as it is incurable at this point and results in death. Most parents find subjects related to sexual matters difficult to talk about with adolescents. Suggestions for parents to consider when talking to an adolescent about AIDS are found in Box 8-2.

Parenting Challenges: Health in an Applied Context

I'm worried about my teenage daughter. She used to eat us out of house and home, but now she eats like a bird. At first, her weight loss looked good, and she got lots of positive attention for it. But I'm concerned she's carrying it too far, as she's getting down to skin and bones. I've talked to her about it, but she doesn't think that there is a problem. What should I do?

Many adolescents diet. Parents need be alarmed only if the dieting behavior becomes extreme or obsessive. A small number of adolescents (estimates are 2 percent to 3 percent) suffer from an eating disorder known as *anorexia nervosa,* which often begins with dieting behaviors that eventually become obsessive. Of that number, between 2 percent and 8 percent actually die of self-starvation (Herzog, Keller, & Lavori, 1988). Typically, the anorexic becomes preoccupied with talking about or preparing food, but does not eat. In addition, most anorexics have a totally unrealistic perception of what they look like; they are unable to see how thin they are. Other symptoms are a cease in menstruation for females, hair loss, overactivity, and irritability.

Anorexia nervosa is much more common in females than males, and is most common in white adolescent girls. The cause of this disorder is not known, although physical factors (such as a chemical deficiency in the brain), personality factors (such as perfectionism), psychological factors (such as fear of sexuality and growing up), family factors (such as dysfunctional family patterns in dependency and conflict), and environmental factors (such as societal pressures to be thin) have all been suggested as possibilities. It is unknown which factor or combination of factors is responsible.

If a child is suffering from an eating disorder of any kind, it is important for the parent to seek professional help immediately. Denial is often a part of this disease, so it is difficult for the teen to get help on her own. Parental monitoring and paying attention to adolescent behavior is important. Self-help groups are often used in addition to medical treatment. Since there is increased risk of depression and depressive symptoms with eating disorders, this area is also addressed during the course of treatment.

Box 8-2 Talking with Adolescents About AIDS

TALKING WITH PRETEENS

Children at this age are going through all the changes of puberty. They are concerned about their bodies, their looks, and what is normal. For some young teens, this time marks the start of dating, early sexual experiences, and trying drugs.

Because of the strong social pressures that begin at this age, it is important that you talk about AIDS, regardless of what you know about your children's sexual or drug experiences. As a concerned parent, you must make sure your children know about prevention NOW. During the changes of puberty, preteens are very curious about sex and need to be given basic, accurate information. They need to know what is meant by sexual intercourse, homosexuality, and oral and anal sex. Preteens need to be told that sex can have consequences, including pregnancy and HIV infection. They should be told why sexual intercourse is not healthy for children, and why it is a good idea to wait to have sex. They need to know how HIV is transmitted, and how it is not transmitted, and how to prevent transmission, including talking about condoms. This may seem like a difficult task, but it will give you a chance to teach your children the values that you hope they will adopt in their lives. It is also the time to let your children know that they can come to you with their questions about AIDS or sex.

TALKING WITH TEENS

Teenagers and preteens should be told that the best way to prevent HIV is by not having any type of sexual intercourse or using any type of drugs. Parents should share their family values about premarital sexual intercourse.

Many parents want to tell their children to wait to have intercourse at least until they are no longer teenagers; however, most teenagers are not waiting. The majority of Americans are having intercourse by their twentieth birthday.

Therefore, most parents also want to make sure that their children can protect themselves. We can explain to our children that if they are going to be involved in sex, they must protect themselves against teen pregnancy and HIV.

Parents can talk to teens about the full range of sexual behaviors that people find pleasurable. Many of these activities are "safe sex"—they cannot transmit HIV or cause pregnancy. This means talking to your teens and preteens about kissing, handholding, caressing, masturbation, and what some call "outercourse," sexual behaviors that do not involve penetration.

Social pressure to try sex or drugs can be very strong for teens. Therefore, at this age, regardless of their personal experience with sex or drugs, all young people must know:

- Not having sexual intercourse (abstinence) is the best method of HIV prevention. It is also the best method of prevention of sexually transmitted diseases and pregnancy.
- Long-term monogamy with an uninfected partner is as effective in preventing HIV infection as abstinence. Long-term monogamy means for one's whole adult life, not going steady for a few months.
- Teenagers who are going to have sexual intercourse must use condoms for each and every act of intercourse, including oral sex, anal sex, and vaginal intercourse. Only latex (rubber) condoms should be used, and they should be used with a foam, jelly, or cream, with the chemical nonoxynol-9.
- Teenagers should avoid all drugs and alcohol. Drugs and alcohol impair good decision making and may suppress the immune system. Sharing needles of any kind puts people at risk of HIV; that includes IV drug use, skin-popping, steroids, ear piercing, and tattooing.

Taken from: SIECUS (Sex Information and Education Council of the U.S.). (1989). *How to talk to your children about AIDS*. New York: SIECUS and NYU. Reprinted with permission of SIECUS, 130 W. 42nd St., New York, NY 10036.

Working is a common context in which adolescent development takes place in the United States. Recent estimates have suggested that prior to graduation, the majority of high school students have some school-year work experience (Greenberger & Steinberg, 1986). Much attention has recently been given to the possible outcomes working may have for adolescents who are employed during the school year. Not surprisingly, the impact of working depends on many variables, including the type of work, how many hours are worked per week, and how the experience of working affects the other areas of the adolescent's life.

There are several different levels of work available to adolescents. They could have informal part-time employment, such as babysitting or newspaper delivery, or formal part-time employment, where they work a regular number of hours after school, evenings, or weekends. Most jobs available to adolescents pay only minimum wage, for example, in restaurants or retail sales. Surprisingly, most of the time adolescents spend on the job is spent with other adolescents who either work there also or who are customers (Greenberger & Steinberg, 1981). The jobs performed by adolescents are usually not intellectually stimulating and tend to be very repetitive, although the stress of intense time pressure is common (Greenberger & Steinberg, 1986).

Interestingly enough, commonly held beliefs regarding the benefits of work are not always true for the adolescent population. One would assume that a teenager working and making several hundred dollars a month would be learning valuable lessons in money management. Unfortunately, few adolescents save any percentage of their earnings, or help with family household expenses. Instead, teenagers seem to be indulging themselves in materialism—spending money on expensive clothes, stereo equipment, entertainment, drugs, and alcohol (Greenberger & Steinberg, 1986). If teens are working more than twenty hours a week, school work, extracurricular activities, and family time tends to be adversely affected, and rates of drug, alcohol, and tobacco use go up (Steinberg & Dornbusch, 1991). Students often try to protect their grades by cutting corners, copying homework from friends, and taking easier courses.

Parents and adolescents must sit down together and weigh the potential costs and benefits of working. What are the adolescent's goals? What will the money be used for? How many work hours are being considered? What kind of job is it? In answering these questions, decisions can be made in the best interest of the teenager.

SUMMARY

- Parents of adolescents are in the interdependent stage of parenthood, where they have the task of allowing the adolescent to be separate, while still maintaining connectedness.
- Parental monitoring, the parental supervision and awareness of where the child is, what the child is doing, and with whom, is an important parenting practice.

- Modeling positive behaviors and providing information are effective parenting practices for adolescents.
- Parent-adolescent relationships are not usually characterized by intense conflict, but minor, persistent bickering occurs between virtually all parents and adolescents.
- Parents can assist adolescent identity formation by being supportive and allowing exploration.
- Although peer relationships are much more independent in the teen years, parents may still indirectly influence adolescents' choices of peers.
- Open communication, encouragement, prevention, and problem solving are some of the techniques parents may use with depressed or suicidal adolescents.
- Adolescent egocentrism, in the form of the imaginary audience and the personal fable, lend insights into adolescent thinking and risk taking.
- The timing of physical development may influence the social environment and pressures on the adolescent.
- Health issues of adolescents include drug use, sexually transmitted diseases, and eating disorders.
- Adolescents and their parents must weigh the pros and cons of the adolescent work environment before making decisions in this area.

CHAPTER 9

Intergenerational Relationships: Parenting Adult Children, Grandparenting, and Parent-Caring

The term *intergenerational relationships* describes the connectedness between generations. Today, the parent-child relationship typically endures for an unprecedented amount of time, with many families experiencing 50 years or more of togetherness (Hagestad, 1987). The "children" are adults during most of this time, yet almost all of the parenting literature focuses on the first eighteen years of the child's life. Although information is limited in many of these areas, the focus of this chapter will be on what happens after the child grows up. What is it like to parent adult children? The specific challenges posed in parenting young adults, and the changes that occur when children leave home, will be explored. The special problems that are encountered and require resolution if children leave home and return will also be examined. How does grandparenthood differ from parenthood? Finally, we will investigate issues related to parent-caring, and how intergenerational themes extend across adulthood into old age.

PARENTING ADULT CHILDREN

> **Wanted: Parent of Adult.** You have spent the past two decades dispensing help, advice, and criticism. Now you have the hardest job of all: stopping all of the above unless asked.
>
> *(Moschell, 1991)*

Even though the most active years of parenting are over when the child leaves home, parenting continues throughout the life span. Parents often feel they have a big investment in their children's lives, and they may feel success or failure, based on their children's accomplishments or difficulties (Pillemer & Suitor, 1991a). Even very elderly parents are affected by the problems their adult children are experiencing (Pillemer & Suitor, 1991b). New aspects of the parent-child relationship come to light as the years pass by, and parenting roles change as children and parents grow older. Eventually, dependency patterns may begin to shift, although most parents continue to support and give to their children as long as they are able (Lewis, 1990). Parents seem to derive gratification from helping their adult children, whether it is providing money for educational expenses, assisting with a down payment on a house, or just giving advice and support (Rossi & Rossi, 1991).

Parenting Young Adults

> It's so hard to know whether we're being fair or not. It's true that he pays us rent, although it is very reasonable. And he is an adult, and does have the legal right to drink. But it is still my house, and I don't approve of drinking. His mother and I don't want women visiting with him in his bedroom, either. I realize his lifestyle is his choice. But it doesn't match our values, and we expect certain standards of behavior from someone who is living under our roof.
>
> *Father of a 23-year-old son*

Parenting young adult children poses a special challenge since it is often necessary for parents to let go of certain tasks and responsibilities at a time when they are unsure whether their child is prepared and competent to take them over. Many young adults are still involved in the identity process—learning who they are and what they want out of life. They may also be forming emotional attachments to significant people outside the family. According to Erikson, the task of young adulthood is to develop close relationships, or *intimacy* with others, as opposed to experiencing isolation from meaningful relationships. Children will make many decisions during the young adult years that will have far-reaching effects in their lives. It is often difficult for parents to step back and allow their children to make these choices.

Leaving Home

When children grow into adults and leave the nuclear family, parents begin to reorganize their lives. The *empty nest transition* begins when the first child leaves home and continues until the last child leaves. For some parents this may be a difficult period of adjustment. Parents who have focused almost exclusively on the needs of their children may experience personal and marital crisis. Other parents, who may not have been as attentive to their children, sometimes feel depression and regret over the missed opportunity. Some parents have very few difficulties with the transition, and enjoy their new freedom (Lowenthal & Chiriboga, 1972). Often couples go through a period of adjustment where they reestablish their personal goals and marital commitment, thereby creating a new lifestyle. It is normal for parents to feel some sense of loss when their children grow up and leave home. Reports of parents who feel anxiety, sadness, mild depression, and emptiness are not uncommon (Giddan & Vallongo, 1988). Making the necessary life adjustments when children leave home takes time and flexibility.

Galinsky (1987) describes this phase of parenthood as the *departure stage*. The tasks of parenthood at this stage are to redefine identities as parents with grown-up children, to accept the separateness and individuality of adult children, and to maintain connections with them. Connectedness is an integral part of the parent-child relationship at this particular time. Connectedness consists of empathy, closeness, communication, concern, and respect (Frank, Avery, & Laman, 1988). Research involving a fairly representative national sample (minority groups, people living in large metropolitan areas, and people with less education were slightly underrepresented) showed that closeness with parents predicted psychological well-being in young adults (Amato, 1994). This was especially true for fathers. Young adults who reported greater feelings of closeness to their fathers also reported that they were happier, more satisfied with their lives, and less distressed. This study exemplifies the importance of the parent-child relationship beyond the childhood years.

Years ago, young adults usually remained in the parental home until marriage. Because of economic demands, rites of passage such as marriage or independence are occurring later, taking up to ten years longer than before. Currently, however, even though many young adults are delaying marriage, they are leaving the parental home to live in nonfamily arrangements (Goldscheider & Waite, 1987). The different paths for leaving the parental home are so diverse and numerous that no one nonfamily arrangement (such as group quarters, housemates, or cohabitation) accounts for the majority of young people (Thornton, Young-DeMarco, & Goldscheider, 1993). Leaving home has become a process, as opposed to a discrete event. It is not an easy task for young adults to gain autonomy physically, emotionally, and financially as they leave home and enter the adult world. Young adults are facing a different set of problems today, and the lines between adolescence and adulthood are becoming more blurred (Littwin, 1986). The transition to adulthood may necessitate a pattern of going away and coming back during the early adult years, all within the context of complex decision making and expectations involving both parents and young adult children (Goldscheider & Goldscheider, 1993).

Expectations on the part of both the adult child and the parent can influence attitudes regarding living arrangements. Most young adults who are seniors in high school expect that they will be independent, leave their parents' homes, and reside in their own homes or apartments before they get married (Goldscheider & Goldscheider, 1989). When this doesn't become a reality, disappointment can occur. Some parents have these same expectations, while others are not ready to give up their parental influence over the daily lives of their children. In general, parents are more concerned that sons move out and be given opportunities to be independent than daughters. Perhaps this is because recent research shows that females leave the parental home earlier than males, usually as the result of marriage (Mitchell, Wister, & Burch, 1989), making it less of a long-term issue.

A recent study of young white adults showed that two-thirds of the total time between the ages of fifteen and twenty-three years, they used the parental home as their primary residence (Thornton, Young-DeMarco, & Goldscheider, 1993). For twenty-one- to twenty-three-year-olds, 40 percent continued in this pattern. More research is needed to see if these figures are accurate and generalizable to other populations. Such factors as culture, ethnicity, sex of the child, regional differences, family characteristics, financial resources, and economic issues (unemployment, e.g.) are all variables that need further exploration (Buck & Scott, 1993). There are indications that growing up in stepfamilies or single-parent families and having larger numbers of children in the family leads to earlier home-leaving (Mitchell, Wister, & Burch, 1989), possibly because of family crowding and finances. Adopted children and children living in nonparental situations (such as in foster homes or with other relatives) are also more likely to leave home prior to age nineteen (Aquilino, 1991).

Parenting College-Age Children

Educational needs and training may be one reason why the early adulthood years are marked by transitions in and out of the parental home. Of course, this affects a narrow segment of the population, since not all young adults go to college. But it is definitely a transitional time, and can be thought of as a mediating step between living at home and leaving home. The college experience can be thought of as "living away from home" (Buck & Scott, 1993).

Many parents don't know how to proceed with their parenting once a child is eighteen and has graduated from high school. They recognize their child's need for independence and don't want to interfere, yet they know the child is not yet ready to be totally on her or his own. Very little research information is available on continuing the parenting role at this time. There are some indications that parental social support and a nonconflictual relationship between the mother and father are important factors in the transition from adolescence to young adulthood in a college sample (Holahan, Valentiner, & Moos, 1994). Norman Giddan and Sally Vallongo (1988) have written a book that illuminates parenting issues from a practical and conceptually sound perspective. They perceive the role of the parent during these years to be one of *supportive consultant and facilitator.* To perform in this new role, parents must explore the changes that are taking place in their parenting and their lives.

As a child becomes an adult, parents must gradually switch from being in control and telling children what to do to allowing children to assume responsibility for their own actions. The loss of control parents experience is not always comfortable. It can be difficult not to know who the child's friends and teachers are or be able to monitor how many hours the child is studying. Open and effective communication, as well as a sense of emotional connectedness before the college entrance transition may reduce parental stress after the transition (Anderson, 1988). Parents who have put emphasis on preparing children for adulthood often have the opportunity to watch the lessons come to life within the context of the child's growth. Coping skills, practical life skills (such as laundry and cook-

Many parents see the task of helping a high school senior choose a college to attend as a transitional step to their role as a supportive consultant and facilitator.
(*John Coletti/The Picture Cube*)

ing), and the ability to use consumer skills in making educational decisions all lead to emotional readiness for the college experience. On the other hand, problems in the home (such as alcoholism or sexual abuse) can also follow a child to campus. The emotional burden of coming from a dysfunctional family will not go away just because the child no longer lives at home physically.

Parenting college-age children often requires a low-profile approach. Clinical information suggests that the new relationship between parent and child is more successful if it is based on mutual respect, trust, concern, and love (Giddan & Vallongo, 1988). Relationships that are free of conflict and allow communication are sometimes difficult to attain, however, since the child may be feeling ambivalent about parental involvement of any kind. The college years are a time of self-discovery. During this process, children try on different lifestyles and test their own beliefs, even though they may conflict with parental values. Many parents experience a sense of rejection at this point, and feel that they do not belong in the child's life. Counselors at the college level, however, suggest that parents are needed as a buffer of love and confidence for college-age children (Giddan & Vallongo, 1988).

When college students run into difficulties, they often ask their parents for help. It is tempting for parents to come in and solve the problems, showing the child and themselves how much they are still needed. Many college professors have amusing stories to relate regarding parental inquiries about a student's grade. Clinicians suggest that a more productive approach might be for parents to avoid the urge to "rescue" the child, and instead help the child find appropriate sources of assistance (Giddan & Vallongo, 1988). Independent problem solving within an atmosphere of parental concern and confidence can be facilitated. Most college students enjoy their college years, and continue to grow throughout this period of time without serious problems. When severe problems are encountered, however, the parent may have to take a more active role in helping the child. Situations that may require parental intervention are problems with alcohol and drugs, eating disorders, sexual problems and diseases, academic failure, crime, depression, and potential suicide.

The Not-So-Empty Nest

Increasing numbers of adult children are returning to the home they grew up in after leaving to establish homes of their own. There are many reasons for this increase, including unemployment, low salaries, high housing costs, educational needs, and divorce (Clemens & Axelson, 1985). Since divorce rates are so high in the United States, it is interesting to examine the effects this may be having on living arrangements. Table 9-1 shows the percentage of young adults living with relatives after divorce or separation (Glick & Lin, 1986).

Findings from a study with a large national sample suggest that adult children living with their parents after divorce or separation may present a particularly vulnerable situation for the parent-child relationship. Parents were more dissatisfied with the living arrangements if divorced or separated children (and possibly grandchildren) were present in the home as opposed to never-married children with no dependents (Aquilino & Supple, 1991). The likelihood of continuing dependency, both emotionally and financially, may be contributing factors to dissatisfaction and conflict. It is interesting to note that

TABLE 9-1. Percentage of Young Adults Living with Relatives After Divorce or Separation

	Percentage Living With Relatives by Age			
	20–34	20–24	25–29	30–34
Separated and/or divorced Total	23%	40%	23%	17%
Separated and/or divorced Men	28%	52%	28%	21%
Separated and/or divorced Women	18%	34%	19%	10%

Source: U.S. Bureau of the Census, 1985.
Taken from: Glick, P.C., & Lin, S.L. (1986). More adults are living with their parents: Who are they? *Journal of Marriage and the Family,* 48, 107–112. Copyrighted 1986 by the National Council on Family Relations, 3989 Central Ave. NE, Suite 550, Minneapolis, MN 55421. Reprinted by permission.

this particular sample overrepresented African Americans, Mexican Americans, and Puerto Ricans at a rate double that of the general population. Perhaps young adults with lower socioeconomic status have fewer options when their marriages dissolve, placing more of the burden on the parents. These trends should be examined in future research studies.

Lifestyle differences may create stressful situations for families where young adults are living in the parental home (Glick & Lin, 1986). Since the decision to live together is a mutual one, the parent and child must negotiate responsibilities in the context of the shared household (Aquilino & Supple, 1991). Areas of possible conflict include curfews, substance use, personal and household responsibilities, and money (Clemens & Axelson, 1985). Most parents are unwilling to have the living arrangement continue indefinitely, since it may put considerable stress and strain on some marital relationships. Some people feel that they have not done their job as parents until their last child has left the parental home and is independent (Aldous, 1978). Therefore, parents of children who are off schedule may experience a sense of personal failure. The majority of parents are satisfied with the arrangement, however, as long as the quality of the parent-child relationship is good, with few conflicts and more shared activities to enjoy (Aquilino & Supple, 1991).

Parent-Child Relations in Later Life

I'd be lying if I said I didn't miss them. But I've come to enjoy the peacefulness of our lifestyle more and more. My husband and I have more leisure time now, and we both have hobbies we like to pursue. We love going to visit our children in their homes. We're still able to experience what their lives are like and share with them. We try to help out in whatever ways we can, but we no longer feel responsible for them. Its more of an equal relationship, a friendship.

An "empty nest" mom

Very little is known about parent-child relationships in later life. There seems to be a gap in both research and theory between the focus on parenting children who are not yet adults and the focus on relationship between elderly parents and their children (Hagestad, 1987). The intervening decades have been largely ignored; however, parent-child relationships do exist during this long stretch of time, and some sketchy theoretical and empirical information is available. In this section, later-life parenting relationships will be explored. The qualities and patterns in these relationships will be investigated to tie together salient aspects of the parenting relationship during this time.

Later-Life Families

Families "who are beyond the child-rearing years and have begun to launch their children" are referred to as *later-life families* (Brubaker, 1983, p. 9). They consist of parents who are middle aged or older, with adult children (Brubaker, 1990b), and perhaps elderly parents and grandchildren as well. Later-life families have several unique characteristics. First, they are *multigenerational* (Brubaker, 1990a). Families are affected by the number of generations represented, since each generation has its own needs and abilities. Four-generation families are not all that uncommon in today's world (Shanas, 1980). Multigenerational social systems that work well are valuable to all of the family members involved. Elderly parents, parents, adult children, and grandchildren can all benefit from exposure to the joys and struggles each generation is facing. For example, adult children in the midst of demanding careers may appreciate the perspective of the parent who is at the end of his or her career, or may even be retired. In turn, the grandchild may be making decisions that relate to choosing a career, and may benefit from a broader perspective on the issue.

Later-life families also have a *lengthy family history* of coping patterns, communication, and experience (Brubaker, 1990a). Some of the history may be positive, and healthy ways of communicating and dealing with difficulties may have evolved. But past experiences may also be negative, with much unfinished business that adds to stress in later life. Traumatic life events, such as having lived with alcoholic parents, or having suffered through a child's drug addiction, will not easily be forgotten. The backlog of family experiences will color the interactions people have in their later years. If family strives for respect, however, positive aspects of the family can be strengthened and negative experiences can be minimized. Parent-child relations may be enhanced by an understanding of, and respect for, the challenges and joys the adult child is experiencing. A list of practical tips for parents on getting along with adult children is found in Box 9-1.

Finally, later-life families are experiencing many *new life events* (Brubaker, 1990a). Retirement, grandparenting, and widowhood, are part of the normal aging process and begin to influence family interactions. Some of these new life events are wonderful; for example, retired grandparents can spend more time with grandchildren. Other events, such as the death of a family member or a debilitating illness, may have a negative impact on the entire family system. Support and reciprocity between the generations may provide the necessary linkage for dealing with later-life changes more effectively.

CHAPTER 9
*Intergenerational
Relationships:
Parenting Adult
Children,
Grandparenting,
and Parent-Caring*

Later-life parent-child relationships seem to be characterized by reciprocity, where the help and services that are exchanged between parents and adult children are perceived as being relatively equal (Rossi & Rossi, 1991). The contributions of each partner may be different, but the exchanges feel mutually satisfying and beneficial. It is believed that as adult children mature and take on roles that are more similar to their parents', there will be better mutual understanding and closer relationships between the generations (Bengtson & Black, 1973). A recent research study using a large nationally representative sample found that 80 percent of the participating adult children (who were in their thirties) reported an emotionally close relationship with their parents (Lawton, Silverstein, & Bengtson, 1994).

A conceptual framework that helps to explain the lifelong affection and connectedness found in the parent-child relationship is supported by an extension of attachment theory (introduced in Chapter 5) over the life span. The child's attachment does not end in late childhood or adolescence, but persists throughout life in a somewhat modified form (Bowlby, 1979). Although separation from the parent is part of the normal course of development, the desire to be close and stay in contact continues. Adult children often feel preoccupied with thoughts about their parents, either missing their company or feeling concern for their well-being. This is especially true during times of stress, when adult children seek the understanding, security, emotional support, comfort, or help of their parents (Cicirelli, 1991). Attachment behaviors in adulthood become more verbal in nature, and include visiting, telephoning, and writing letters (Cicirelli, 1983). At times, the attachment becomes symbolic, and the adult child simply thinks about what the parent would say or advise in a similar situation (Cicirelli, 1991).

In general, later-life families seem to be satisfied with their relationships. The family usually continues to be a vital, contributing support group that provides enjoyment and help (Brubaker, 1990b). For example, adult daughters who have a positive relationship with their mothers experience less anxiety and

---

 ## Box 9-1 Getting Along with Your Adult Child

1. Don't try to dominate or manipulate.
2. Don't give unsolicited advice; don't meddle.
3. Be helpful.
4. Treat your child as an equal.
5. Don't have unrealistic expectations of your child.
6. Don't reproach your child for things that happened in the past.
7. Don't complain habitually.
8. Take an interest in your child's and grandchildren's lives but retain your own interests, too.
9. Don't criticize your child's lifestyle or parenting style.
10. Don't overuse one child's help and emotional support.
11. Try to solve your own problems.
12. Be considerate.
13. Cultivate your sense of humor.

Taken from: *A Picture of Health* St. Peter's Medical Center, New Brunswick, NJ.

depression than those who have a poor relationship with their mothers (Barnett, Kibria, Baruch & Pleck, 1991). In turn, adult children can help parents be open to new life experiences, learn new skills, and take risks (Cicirelli, 1991). If older parents stay involved with life, they may be able to challenge negative stereotypes about aging and experience more enjoyment in their later years. Healthy later-life family relationships seem to work well for both generations.

GRANDPARENTING

If I had known grandchildren were so much fun, I would have had them first!

T-shirt slogan

Most major decisions in a person's life are of a voluntary nature, such as when to get married and whether to have children. Grandparenthood, however, is beyond the individual person's control. It happens automatically whenever a person's child becomes a parent. Estimates show that 77 percent of all persons sixty-five years or older are grandparents, and 51 percent are great-grandparents (Hagestad, 1988). Grandparents are a diverse group, and it is difficult to make generalizations about them; many different factors can affect grandparenting,

Without the pressures of parenthood, grandparents often have the freedom to relax and enjoy their grandchildren.
(Erika Stone)

such as health, occupational changes, family involvements, and personality factors (Troll, 1985). In today's world, the stereotypical image of a grandmother sitting in her rocking chair with fresh-baked cookies on a plate beside her, waiting for her grandchild, may be joined by the image of a grandchild waiting for the grandmother's aerobics class to be finished so that they can walk to work together!

Despite the diversity among grandparents, some aspects of the grandparent-grandchild relationship have remained unchanged throughout the years. Many people are retiring at age sixty-five, and therefore have more leisure time to enjoy being grandparents (Aldous, 1985). Because of their stage in life, grandparents may have more relaxed time to spend with grandchildren than parents do. And without the pressures inherent in parenthood, grandparents have the freedom to be connected with grandchildren, simply loving and enjoying them. Although there may be many racial and ethnic differences between and within groups of grandparents, one study (Kivett, 1993) has suggested that black and white grandmothers are very similar in the affection and positive regard they have for their grandchildren. Perhaps commonalities within the grandparenting role transcend other differences.

Responsibilities and Roles

Grandparenthood provides middle-aged and older adults with a meaningful and valued role, as well as a chance to relive parts of their lives (Kivnick, 1982), but the privileges of grandparenthood also bring responsibilities. It is the responsibility of both grandparents and parents to keep the lines of communication open, especially regarding troublesome issues. Most Americans believe in the "norm of non-interference" (Cherlin & Furstenberg, 1985), which suggests that grandparents should not interfere with parents' rearing of grandchildren. Learning to be tolerant of lifestyle differences and tactful about giving advice may help to improve intergenerational relationships (Kornhaber, 1986). It is also important to be aware of showing favoritism to some grandchildren over others. Many grandparents are willing to admit they have a favorite grandchild, and it certainly isn't necessary for grandparents to have equally intense ties to all of their grandchildren (Cherlin & Furstenberg, 1985). Most grandparents, however, strive to give equal time and love to their grandchildren, and to avoid hurting them whenever possible (Kornhaber, 1986).

There is some evidence that the most important role of the grandparent is that of *family watchdog* (Troll, 1983). In other words, grandparents are often vigilant watchers, trying to ensure that the family system as a whole is maintained. In times of transition or crisis, they respond if and when they are needed. For example, grandparents may be helpful to new parents in terms of helping them with the work of parenting, possibly affecting the adult children's view of their new responsibilities (Fischer, 1988). Some researchers see grandparents as a possible avenue for ameliorating the negative impact of such family disruptions as divorce, alcoholism, and other pervasive social problems (Denham & Smith, 1989). The message seems to be that when something goes wrong in families, many grandparents are ready to step in and help.

215

CHAPTER 9
Intergenerational
Relationships:
Parenting Adult
Children,
Grandparenting,
and Parent-Caring

Another important role grandparents play is that of *nurturer.* In their role as head of the family, grandfathers are usually seen as nurturing family values and philosophy. They serve as heroes or mentors to the rest of the family (Kornhaber, 1986). Grandmothers are often considered the "heart" of the family, and are emotional leaders in the nurturing role. A child's self-esteem can be positively affected by the grandparent's unconditional love and affirmation (Cherlin & Furstenberg, 1985). These loving, caring interactions are not only beneficial to grandchildren, but may also benefit the morale and mental health of the grandparent (Kivnick, 1982). Nurturing grandparents provide a safety net for their grandchildren when parents either fail or experience difficulty. Grandparents can help indirectly by supporting the parents or directly by caring for the child. Grandparents are often relied upon to provide advice and a role model for parents (Thompson, Tinsley, Scalora, & Parke, 1989).

Grandparents also play the role of family *historian.* They can give grandchildren a sense of family history and belonging by relating stories from the past (Cherlin & Furstenberg, 1985). Friends, relatives, houses, and ways of life from former times can come to life through a grandparent's words. A feeling of pride and excitement may be fostered that enhances a child's identity as part of a close-knit group. Values and traditions can be passed along to children as a part of their heritage (Thompson, Tinsley, Scalora, & Parke, 1989), and children can also gain insights about their parents from the grandparent's perspective. Being able to picture what their parent was like as a child, or the challenges the parent had to overcome may be helpful growing experiences. In return, grandchildren provide grandparents with a link to the future.

Finally, many grandparents take on the role of *companion* to their grandchildren. There are many social aspects to the grandparent-grandchild relationship. Grandparents may share activities like joking around, watching TV, talking, discussing the grandchild's problems, giving advice, taking trips together, and teaching skills or games (Cherlin & Furstenberg, 1986). Grandparents can be important attachment figures to their grandchildren, and their support might help mediate a grandchild's adjustment during a difficult period of transition (Creasey & Koblewski, 1991). These strong feelings of closeness grandchildren feel for grandparents do not seem to diminish as the grandchildren grow older (Kennedy, 1991), although grandchildren may spend less time with them (Creasey & Koblewski, 1991). Box 9-2 lists some of the reasons grandchildren feel close to grandparents.

Factors Influencing Involvement

Since people are living longer, one might expect that grandparents would be more important in their grandchildren's lives than ever before in our history. There is much potential for the older generation to influence the younger generations, but families vary in the importance they place on kinship (Fischer, 1988). The American kinship system is so flexible that grandparents have very diverse relationships with their grandchildren; some are actively involved, while others are passive and distant (Cherlin & Furstenberg, 1985). The timing of grandparenthood and the chronological age of both the grandparent and grandchild helps to determine the amount of contact grandparents have with

Box 9-2 Top Ten Reasons Why Grandchildren Feel Close to Grandparents

Three hundred ninety-one undergraduate students were asked to respond to twenty-nine statements (where 1 = not characteristic and 5 = very characteristic) describing reasons why they felt close to their "most close" grandparent. The top ten reasons for closeness are:

1. My grandparent is an enjoyable person to be with.
2. My grandparent has expressed special interest, love, and appreciation for me.
3. I have great admiration for my grandparent—the attitudes and values or the things my grandparent has accomplished.
4. I can relax and feel comfortable around my grandparent.
5. My grandparent helps me feel proud of myself.
6. I know my grandparent will always be available to help me or encourage and support me.
7. My grandparent listens and understands me and treats me as an individual.
8. My grandparent's admiration makes me want to be a credit to my grandparent.
9. My grandparent expresses much affection for me with words and hugs.
10. My grandparent has taught me many things.

Taken from: Kennedy, G.E. (1991). Grandchildren's reasons for closeness with grandparents. *Journal of Social Behavior and Personality*, 6, 697–712. Reprinted by permission.

their grandchildren (Roberto, 1990). Each grandparent is an individual, and may have a beneficial, harmful, or neutral impact on a grandchild (Denham & Smith, 1989). What determines the extent and pattern of involvement between grandparents and grandchildren?

There is much confusion centered around the appropriate levels of grandparent involvement. The middle generation (the parent) plays an important role in determining the influence of the grandparent. Adult children's attitudes toward older people, the quality of the adult child–aging parent relationship, and the adult child's expectations for the role of grandparents affect the grandparent-grandchild relationship (Barranti, 1985). In other words, the adult children's feelings and attitudes toward their aging parents are transmitted to their children, either consciously or unconsciously. Recent research suggests that if the relationship between the parent and grandparent is less than optimal, the grandparent-grandchild relationship is negatively affected both in terms of relationship quality and the frequency of contact (Whitbeck, Hoyt, & Huck, 1993; King & Elder, 1995). Many studies report that grandchildren tend to have closer ties with maternal grandmothers than with their other grandparents (Fischer, 1988), which makes sense given the strong ties between adult daughters and their mothers (Lawton, Silverstein, & Bengtson, 1994). The diversity of our culture, however, often leads to individual exceptions to broader generalizations. For example, children from farm families often have high-quality relationships with paternal grandparents (King & Elder, 1995), possibly because of male-centered patterns of inheritance in rural areas.

The relationship between the parent and the grandparent may mediate the relationship between the grandchild and grandparent (Kivnick, 1983). This is not necessarily something the generations are even aware is going on. Parents act as "gatekeepers" who can encourage, allow, or restrict the access of grandparents to grandchildren (Fischer, 1988). Young children are especially vulnerable to this kind of mediation because they are unable to pursue relationships on their own. Mothers are particularly powerful gatekeepers, since they tend to be the primary caretakers. By avoiding a parent or parent-in-law, they may be intentionally or unintentionally depriving their child of the opportunity to be with a grandparent.

The idea of the parent generation as gatekeeper is recent, and can be traced to the Great Depression. When families had to become more mobile for economic reasons, many intergenerational interactions were disrupted. A "new social contract" (Kornhaber, 1985) emerged, suggesting that parents have the power to determine the extent of emotional attachment between grandparents and grandchildren. Many people are in the process of advocating for grandparental rights and an end to that contract. Their belief is that the vital connections between grandparents and grandchildren must be reestablished to strengthen families (see Box 9-3).

Grandparents of Divorce and Remarriage

There are two ways for grandparents to be affected by divorce and remarriage. One is for the grandparents themselves to get divorced and, perhaps, remarried. This describes a small, but increasing number of couples who divorce after twenty to forty years of marriage (Kalish & Visher, 1982). The second and more common way in which grandparents are affected is as parents of a child who divorces or remarries. When this situation occurs, grandparents often face special problems and challenges relating to their grandparenting.

The divorce of an adult child disrupts the established links in the extended family system, thus necessitating a renegotiation of relationships. Many factors, such as who has custody of the child, influence the grandparents' role following divorce. If a grandparent's divorced child does not retain physical custody of the children, it is often difficult for a grandparent to maintain a relationship with the grandchildren (Kalish & Visher, 1982). Grandparents have the right to sue for visitation in every state, although statutes regarding how the courts decide who has visitation privileges vary greatly from one state to another (Purnell & Bagby, 1993). Until recently, grandparents often lost these cases because of the reluctance of judges, attorneys, and mental health professionals to acknowledge the importance of the grandparent-grandchild relationship (Kornhaber, 1985). There are no legal ties between grandparents and a child's former spouse, so courts rarely provided grandparents with visitation rights (Kalish & Visher, 1982). The current trend, which is growing in popularity, is for the courts to recognize the uniqueness and importance of the grandparent-grandchild relationship (Purnell & Bagby, 1993).

Since the typical custody pattern in the United States usually translates into children living with their mothers, the ties between paternal grandparents and their grandchildren are often weakened (Cherlin & Furstenberg, 1985). Maternal grandparent relationships, however, are usually maintained or even strengthened. Some grandparents become heavily involved in their children's lives after a divorce in an attempt to help lessen problems with child care and finances (Aldous, 1985). Research suggests that grandchildren from families

Box 9-3 Long-Distance Grandparenting

This isn't how I imagined it would be. I want my three-year-old grandson to feel close to me, but I'm afraid I'll always be a stranger to him. There's 2,000 miles between us, and visiting once or twice a year just isn't enough time to build a relationship.

This story is familiar to many grandparents in the United States. Increased mobility has led many families away from the traditional living arrangements of the extended family. But distance doesn't have to be the end of the grandparent-grandchild bond. Many families live far away from one another and maintain close emotional ties, just as others live close to one another but never get together. A little creative effort and adaptability can lead to rewarding grandparenting relationships, regardless of the miles. There are many ways to keep in touch. Here are some suggestions for long-distance grandparents.

1. *Telephone Calls*

Telephone calls are essential to maintaining a long-distance relationship with a grandchild. There is great joy in being able to communicate one on one. The cost of phone calls to a grandchild is a worthwhile investment with many returns. Gift certificates are a thoughtful gift for those on limited budgets.

2. *Letters*

Many people don't write letters because they're too busy or they don't know what to say. No excuse is good enough for not writing a grandchild. It doesn't matter if the letters are short or unexciting because a grandchild knows the love that is being conveyed with every word. For many people, its easier to write about their feelings than it is to verbalize them, and the beauty of a letter is that it can be read and reread. Some grandparents complain that their grandchildren never write to them, but letters inspire other letters. Perhaps grandchildren need a positive model of what fun letters can be to receive and send.

3. *Cassette Tapes*

Grandparents can use cassette audiotapes to share the things they would like to be able to do with their grandchild if they lived closer together. Reading stories, singing songs, or just talking familiarizes the grandchild with the grandparent's voice and begins an ongoing conversation of friendship between the generations.

4. *Photographs*

Photographs are a way of sharing lives. A grandchild can "see" the grandparent doing various activities that she or he enjoys. Many grandparents like to share family history with their grandchildren, which can be easily done by looking up some old negatives of pictures and having prints made. The pictures can fit right into the envelope along with the letter or tape telling the story. Photographs can help nurture the closeness of family members.

5. *Videotapes*

Videotapes are the closest thing to being there in person. Perhaps a grandchild can watch Grandma make the cookies that are being sent, or reexplore a favorite place the grandchild enjoyed during their last visit. If spending the holidays together isn't a possibility, Grandpa can show the grandchild all of the wonderful decorations. Videotapes are limited only by the imagination of the user. They are wonderful ways of communicating with a grandchild long distance, and can be a priceless treasure.

who have experienced divorce or stepfamily life report close relationships with grandparents and spend greater amounts of time with them (Kennedy, 1991). The critical variable in determining the extent of these intergenerational contacts seems to be the adult child. If emotional aid or tangible help is needed, grandparents usually make every effort to give what they can.

The picture becomes even more clouded when stepgrandparenting is discussed. Again, the parent and stepparent mediate the relationship between stepgrandparent and stepgrandchild. Stepgrandparents are usually acquired

219

when the stepgrandchild is older, so there isn't as much time for a relationship to develop. Researchers have found, however, that 48 percent of stepgrandchildren view the relationship as important, and 63 percent desire more contact with the stepgrandparent (Sanders & Trygstad, 1989). This attests to the strength and importance of the grandparenting relationship.

PARENT-CARING

> One day I just just looked across the table at my dad and realized that he was an old man. And I knew the time was coming for me to pay my dues.
>
> *Son of a 79-year-old man*

Parent-caring refers to the assistance children give to their parents as the parents grow older and require some help (Archbold, 1983). As parents age, usually at some point after they enter their 70s, the exchange of help between the parent and child generations may begin to be less balanced (Rossi & Rossi, 1991). There is, however, still an exchange that goes in both directions. In western societies, most elderly parents continue to derive satisfaction from giving whatever they can to children and grandchildren.

Conceptually, parent-caring fits into the theoretical context of attachment, since protective behavior is complementary to attachment behavior (Cicirelli, 1991). Adult children respond to a parent's illness, needs, or life changes by trying to help so that the parent survives and the emotional bond is preserved. Other motivations for parent-caring may include feelings of obligation and duty based on cultural norms, or an equitable exchange that balances help given and help received over the years. Regardless of why this assistance occurs, parent-caring is a fact of life for many adult children in today's society.

There are multiple reasons why parent-caring is more of an issue today than in the past. First, there have been major *demographic changes* in our society. There are more individuals over sixty years of age than ever before (Pedrick-Cornell & Gelles, 1982) due to medical advances in the last fifty years. This makes having two or three postretirement generations in a family a fairly common occurrence—one that will be even more prevalent in the next twenty years (Douglass, 1983). The older elderly tend to be women (Lang & Brody, 1983). At the same time, birth rates in our country have declined, so there are fewer adult children to care for more aging parents (Hirschfield & Dennis, 1979). Parent-caring is a relatively new and intense responsibility (Pedrick-Cornell & Gelles, 1982).

The *physical needs* of the elderly have also changed in ways that have an impact on parent-caring. Even though people are living longer, they are not necessarily living independently or in good health. It is true that there is a huge diversity in the health and self-sufficiency of the elderly population. To help sort out this confusion, a classification of the elderly as "young-old" and "old-old" (Cohen, 1983) was adopted, and has since been modified. Distinguishing between people who are active and vigorous, and those who are frail and ill, regardless of age, is also a way to describe this diverse population (Neugarten & Neugarten, 1987).

It is projected that a larger population of elderly people in the old-old category will require higher levels of personal care for longer and longer periods of time (Douglass, 1983). About one in fifteen of the old-old group of elderly need long-term care, as compared with one in fifty of the young-old group (Pedrick-Cornell & Gelles, 1982). Some experts believe that nursing homes and other long-term care facilities cannot be built or maintained in sufficient numbers for them to be a realistic solution to this kind of need (Douglass, 1983). Even the community-based elderly population (those living in their own homes) require some assistance with daily living and personal care activities, such as shopping, meal preparation, and visits to the doctor. Estimates of assistance vary from 25–33 percent (Stoller, 1983) to 68 percent (Dunkle, 1985). Much of this help comes from relatives.

Political pressures also contribute to the issue of parent-caring. The rapid increase in the number of persons over age seventy-five has made long-term health care one of the most critical policy issues to be addressed (Montgomery, Gonyea, & Hooyman, 1985). At the same time, there has been a decline in federal funds for formal programs, thus increasing the demands on family members to provide support services (Stoller, 1983), and to use family resources as a hedge against the rising costs of health care (Montgomery, Gonyea, & Hooyman, 1985). The system of services available to the elderly provides little economic support for families with parent-caring responsibilities. For example, less than 1 percent of Medicare and Medicaid are spent on home health services (Archbold, 1983).

Demographic changes, the physical needs of the elderly, and the current political climate have contributed to the growing concern of many adult children regarding the care of their aging parents. There is definitive evidence that the family is the main source of help to older people in need of emotional support or concrete assistance (Lang & Brody, 1983). At the same time, social service and health professionals are concerned about the family's capability to provide long-term care and the consequences of caregiving for the family (Montgomery, Gonyea & Hooyman, 1985).

Issues from the Aging Parent's Perspective

> My greatest fear is that I won't be able to take care of myself. I don't want to end up in a nursing home. Who does? But I would definitely choose to go there before I'd allow myself to become a burden to my children.
>
> *A 79-year-old father*

There are many emotional issues involved when parents begin to age and adult children are needed to assist them. From the aging parent's perspective, *communication* is the most important aspect of the intergenerational relationship (Hirschfield & Dennis, 1979). Aging parents desire increased communication between their children and themselves, particularly regarding family issues such as maintaining family ties and having relationships with grandchildren. Another important issue is *independence*. Aging parents want to maintain their independence financially, emotionally, and physically for as long as possible. They fear dependency because they do not want to become a "bur-

221

CHAPTER 9
*Intergenerational
Relationships:
Parenting Adult
Children,
Grandparenting,
and Parent-Caring*

den" to their children. Awareness of the dependency issue is so acute that only half of the elderly are accurate in their perceptions of how much aid they receive from their children; the other half tend to overestimate the amount (Walker, Pratt, Martell, & Martin, 1991). Because of their desire to remain competent, they become frustrated if their level of functioning requires that they have help. Unfortunately, this frustration and dissatisfaction with their own abilities often translates into a negative perception of the caregivers' behaviors (Dunkle, 1985). This can lead to conflict and bad feelings between the adult child and aging parent.

Another important issue for aging parents is that of *utility* (Hirschfield & Dennis, 1979). Aging parents have the desire to feel useful and needed. In this country, the tendency is toward serial (or sequential) family responsibility rather than reciprocal arrangements. Each generation is responsible for each succeeding generation (Cheal, 1983). The elderly do not want the middle generation to be providing for their children and parents at the same time. They want to continue to benefit their children even into advanced old age. Elderly parents and their children must struggle to find a balance between giving and receiving care so that a mutual but flexible pattern of caring and being cared for can evolve (Silver, 1993). Some elderly people have the economic resources to assist their children financially or to give expensive gifts. At all ages, parents are much more likely to provide a home for adult children than the reverse (Aquilino, 1990). There are many other ways to give, such as contributing services to the household (e.g., cooking, washing, or housework), providing companionship, or babysitting. The most important aid aging parents give may be psychological in nature, such as love, information, and advice (Walker, Pratt, & Oppy, 1992). These noneconomic contributions can help the elderly avoid depression and enjoy feelings of self-esteem (Dunkle, 1985).

Issues from the Adult Children's Perspective

> No matter what I do, it isn't enough. I know it's tough to get old and have aches and pains, but I can't change that for her. I keep telling myself it's not my job to make her happy. She has to do that herself.
>
> *A 50-year-old son*

The most dominant and pervasive issue in intergenerational relationships from the perspective of the adult child is *guilt*. The middle generation is often caught between the competing responsibilities for the older and younger generations, requiring that priorities be set (Silverstone, 1979). Adult children must commonly make choices between their own families, their parents, and their own personal needs (Hirschfield & Dennis, 1979). Unreasonable demands on the part of parents can intensify the difficulties adult children experience. They also feel a sense of responsibility for their parents' well-being, sometimes wanting to repay parents out of a sense of duty to them. Frequently, however, they cannot improve their parents' general satisfaction with life. The aging parents' unhappiness with their lack of income and mobility may result in loneliness and depression—dissatisfactions that are not easily addressed. The middle generation often responds with feelings of helplessness, resentment, and guilt.

Adult children must adjust to role changes as parents age and dependency needs shift.
(Susan Lapides/Design Conceptions)

223

CHAPTER 9
Intergenerational
Relationships:
Parenting Adult
Children,
Grandparenting,
and Parent-Caring

The second issue adult children must deal with is adjusting to the *role changes* within the intergenerational relationship. There is a shift in dependency needs. Caretaking used to be the role of the parent, but now parents may have some physical, emotional, or financial dependency on their children. Some people refer to these changes as "role reversal," however this term is an oversimplification of the complex changes in the parent-child relationship (Lang & Brody, 1983). Having an aging parent is not like raising a child. Needs are more variable and irregular in the aging phase of life and are not always predictable. They also tend to be continuing or progressive needs, as opposed to the transitional needs of children. The dependencies of children in our society are accepted and expected, but there are no legitimate standards of dependency for the elderly. Also, the responsibility for an aging parent may last longer than the original parent-child dependency period when the adult children were young (Douglass, 1983). Parental caregiving may especially conflict with the expectations of leisure and independence from family responsibilities in the retirement years (Stoller, 1983). Successful role changes must take place with great sensitivity and be based on feelings of mutuality and shared responsibility (Peterson, 1979).

Adult children also need *information* on normal age-related changes so that they can make better decisions when dealing with the problems of their aging parents (Hirschfield & Dennis, 1979). It is important to be able to distinguish between the physical, cognitive, and emotional changes that take place as a function of age and the abnormal or pathological changes that indicate more serious problems. Consulting with a physician or specialist is the best course of action. It is unrealistic to expect people who are not medically trained to be able to distinguish between age-appropriate forgetfulness, Alzheimer's disease (the most common cause of mental deterioration in the aged), and brain dysfunctioning which, when properly diagnosed, may be treatable. Adult children need to know what to expect, not just for their parents' sake, but in projecting their own aging process.

Parent-Caring Options

> All I know is she took care of me when I was little and couldn't care for myself. The least I can do is return the favor and do my best to pay her back for all the great things she's done for me.
>
> *A 58-year-old care provider*

A central issue in intergenerational relations is *involvement* (Hirschfield & Dennis, 1979). What will the actual role of the adult child be in relation to the aging parent? Adult children must systematically examine what they are willing and able to do and how much they are willing to have parent-caring be a part of their lives. The decisions made often reflect a lifetime relationship with the parent. Personality differences and conflict do not disappear with age, and may even intensify. Family members can be caring and responsible, however, even when they are not emotionally intimate (Silverstone, 1979). The adult child's current roles, responsibilities, values, and life goals will influence the amount of involvement.

All aspects of parent-caring affect women in our society more than men (Spitze & Logan, 1990). In fact, parent-caring may be an intensification of an already existing intergenerational pattern of giving aid (Walker & Pratt, 1991). The typical caregiver in our society is the adult daughter or daughter-in-law, and there are a number of important issues that must be addressed in relation to her. She is often referred to as "the woman in the middle" because she is middle-aged, in the middle of generations (many have adolescent children during this time of life), and in the middle of many competing responsibilities (Lang & Brody, 1983). Most of these women are working outside the home, and their job is a financial necessity to the family; however, few significant changes in the traditional division of labor for household and domestic tasks have occurred (Stoller, 1983). Therefore, the length of the woman's work week has increased, because after working her job, she comes home and does the cooking, housecleaning, laundry, and so forth. When the responsibility of an elderly parent is added, it usually means there is no leisure time at all. Life becomes a series of complex time allocation decisions between work, children (and possibly grandchildren), spouse, household tasks, and parents. These events often occur when women are facing their own aging process and are experiencing depleted physical energy and health. Current research is beginning to focus on factors that may mediate the stress women are experiencing, such as having children in the home who also help with the elderly parent's care (Stull, Bowman, & Smerglia, 1994).

Although women are still the major providers of care for the elderly, recent studies suggest that men are taking an increasingly bigger role (Teltsch, 1992). It is estimated that men (husbands, sons, sons-in-law, and brothers) provide about a third of the care for the elderly. The change seems to be a result of economic, political, and cultural changes. Some believe that men have been taking a more active role because women are becoming saturated with their caregiving duties, yet the need for caregiving continues to increase. Solid information regarding what kinds of care men provide is lacking, although some preliminary data show that it is more likely to be intermittent (such as grocery shopping or helping with finances) than full-time, personal, hands-on care. As the burden of caregiving increases, services are needed to prevent and alleviate the strain for both men and women and strengthen their caregiving efforts.

There are two parent-caring roles; the *care provider*, who identifies the services the parent needs and then performs them, and the *care manager*, who identifies the needed services and manages their provision by others (Archbold, 1983). Socioeconomic status and employment are the major factors influencing the decision regarding parent-caring roles. Care managers usually have a higher SES than care providers. Income usually determines whether services can be purchased or must be personally provided. The amount of money a person has determines how many services can be purchased and gives families more options and more access to professionals. Care managers are usually employed full time and have a good earning potential. Among working women, care managers are usually employed in socially valued careers that allow them to delegate parent-caring without too much internal conflict or guilt. Women who perform jobs that are less valued by society often experience more feelings of obligation to be care providers.

Both care providers and care managers may become overwhelmed with the activities of parent-caring, but the tasks and problems of each group differ substantially (Archbold, 1983). Care providers spend their time and energy in the physical care of the parent, and often have very little time for focusing on the parent's psychological or social needs. Care managers devote a great deal of time trying to find and keep appropriate service systems for their parents. They put more thought into the parents' social activities, such as going places or providing entertainment. The consequences of parent-caring are difficult to assess. Both groups of caregivers felt satisfaction with their efforts, although care providers identified fewer benefits than care managers. Both groups, however, experienced many costs in connection with their caregiving (Archbold, 1983; Montgomery, Gonyea, & Hooyman, 1985). Care providers felt decreased freedom, lack of privacy, and constant daily irritation. Care managers experienced career interruptions and financial difficulties due to the tremendous expense of the services. The time and energy required by parent-caring activities created stress for both groups. These demands caused difficulties in their sibling relationships, and especially in their marital relationships (see Box 9-4).

Several approaches have been identified as useful strategies for addressing the stresses of caregiving (Zarit & Eggebeen, 1995). The first is education—helping families understand the parent's problems and the available alternatives for dealing with them effectively. Second, it may be possible to improve management of the care situation by supplying a wide range of social and behavioral activities to help the parent and relieve the caregiver strain. Third, an evaluation of the amount or type of help provided by family members may

Box 9-4 Warning Signs of Caregiver Stress and Depression

1. Difficulty falling asleep or remaining asleep at night.
2. Waking up early in the morning feeling anxious and irritable.
3. Marked changes in appetite, either toward overeating or loss of appetite; substantial weight changes.
4. Increased use of sleeping pills, other medications, alcohol, or caffeine.
5. Uncharacteristic short-temperedness, crying, or agitation.
6. Delay or neglect of vital physical needs.
7. Decreased resistance to illness.

8. Difficulties with concentration and attention.
9. Loss of energy or fatigue.
10. Subdued mood; expressionless face or flat tone of voice.
11. Rough handling and other signs of impatience in giving care.
12. Recurrent thoughts of death or suicide.

Reprinted with the permission of the Free Press, a division of Simon & Schuster from *Taking Care: Supporting Older People and Their Families* by Nancy R. Hooyman and Wendy Lustbader. Copyright © 1986 by The Free Press.

mobilize family resources and encourage positive changes. A recent exploratory study suggests that caregiving partnerships or teams may provide more comprehensive and cooperative family caregiving than one primary caregiver (Keith, 1995). Finally, stresses in caregiving can be lessened by bringing in new resources. Community programs can be valuable in reducing caregiver strain.

Using Community Resources

> It's so difficult to know where to go to find the help you need and get it all figured out. I didn't even know about half of what was available until mom got so sick.
>
> *A 64-year-old son*

The most frequent questions adult children and aging parents have center on the awareness and effective use of community resources. They have to determine which services they need and where they can find them. To obtain this information, some sort of assessment of the elderly person's capabilities is needed so that accurate decisions regarding needed services can be made. After assessing the elderly person's level of functioning, all of the possible types of help or services elderly people may need should be examined so that the overall picture of what is available can be provided. Of course, medical, dental, and nutritional needs must be acknowledged. A list of other suggestions is found in Box 9-5.

Services are most easily located through information and referral agencies such as the Office on Aging, which is a comprehensive planning agency designed to provide an efficient service delivery system to the elderly and to serve as an advocate for the concerns of older people. Senior centers, home-makers' services, home health care services, nutritional programs, transporta-

Box 9-5 Types of Help or Services Elderly Parents May Need

1. *Homemaking.* Help with the basic task of daily living, including meal preparation, cleaning and laundry, shopping for needed foods, clothing, and so on.
2. *Housing.* Help with the parent's housing may involve taking the parent into the child's home or providing all or part of the cost of other living quarters, such as a house, apartment, or room.
3. *Maintenance.* Help with the repair and upkeep of the parent's living quarters.
4. *Income.* Help with all or part of the income the parent needs to live on in the usual or desired manner, whether in the form of money or goods.
5. *Personal Care.* Help with bathing, dressing, grooming, or moving about.
6. *Home Health Care.* Help with any special medicines, treatments, massage, exercise, or other care at home.
7. *Transportation.* Taking the parent or helping the parent with transportation for needed or desired activities.
8. *Social and Recreation Activities.* Providing social and recreation activities for the parent, or helping the parent to carry out such activities. They may include entertaining or being entertained by others, public activities, meetings, and sports.
9. *Psychological Support.* Help to parents on a psychological level, including communication of warmth and affection, sense of caring for the parent's welfare, listening, discussing, and giving advice.
10. *Employment.* Helping the parent to find a job, or helping the parent to market his or her goods or services.
11. *Spiritual.* Helping the parent with the observance of a religious faith through attending services, home rituals, discussion, and prayer.
12. *Bureaucratic Mediation.* Helping the parent in transactions with government agencies, businesses, or arranging some service.
13. *Reading Materials.* Providing, or helping the elderly parent to procure, desired reading materials, such as newspapers, books, and magazines.
14. *Career Education.* Helping the parent to get training to enter a new occupation after retirement. The child may provide informal training or may help the parent to acquire formal training from some other source.
15. *Enrichment.* Helping the parent to learn new hobbies, arts, crafts, and other interests that will enrich the elderly person's life.
16. *Protection.* Helping the elderly person to protect person and property against criminals and physical danger.

Taken from: Cicirelli, V.G. (1984). Marital disruption and adult children's perception of their siblings' help to elderly parents. *Family Relations*, 33, 613–621. Copyrighted 1984 by the National Council on Family Relations, 3989 Central Ave. NE, Suite 550, Minneapolis, MN 55421. Reprinted with permission.

tion programs, and geriatric day care facilities are common services available to families as they need various types of help.

There is a great need for public policies that assist adult children in the care of their aging parents instead of removing caregiving responsibilities from them (Cicirelli, 1991). Flexible work schedules and leave periods might allow adult children to maintain their jobs while also managing caregiving activities. Formal care services, under the direction of the adult child, could be used to supplement the family care system rather than replace it. Social structures must be modified and educational programs implemented that will support long-term informal family care.

Dealing with Death

> The funeral was the most unreal experience I've ever had. The whole service is foggy in my mind. Afterwards, the people at the church provided a meal for the family. As I looked around at my mother and siblings, I couldn't believe we were eating. My father was dead and gone from us, and we were talking about the weather.
>
> *A 40-year-old daughter*

For many people, one of the most difficult subjects to deal with is death. In earlier times, death was a part of daily life. Now people are more removed from death, since health care professionals and morticians often care for the dying or dead rather than family and friends. Recently, there has been a push for more understanding about death and dying. Researchers have been surprised to find that many dying people welcome the opportunity to talk about death (Kubler-Ross, 1969).

In the normal course of life, most children must deal with the death of their parents. Usually the loss of a parent earlier in adulthood triggers more distress than when the parent is at an advanced old age (Cicirelli, 1991). The potential loss of a parent is obvious by midlife, and by that time children have observed their friends' loss of parents (Pratt, Walker, & Wood, 1992). The grief an adult child experiences at the loss of a parent is another indicator of the adult child's attachment to the parent (Cicirelli, 1991). In situations where the

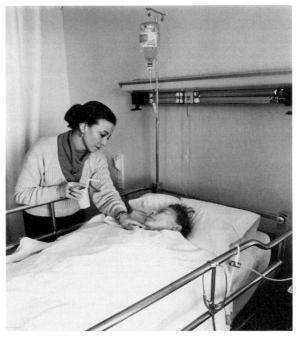

Most children must deal with the death of their parents at some point, experiencing the grief and facing the difficult task of adjusting to life without them.
(Joel Gordon)

death of an elderly parent is known to be near, children often begin to anticipate their grief, preparing themselves for the loss by grieving while the parent
is still alive. Adult children may lack support for this difficult experience, suggesting the need for possible intervention (Pratt, Walker, & Wood, 1992).

CHAPTER 9
*Intergenerational
Relationships:
Parenting Adult
Children,
Grandparenting,
and Parent-Caring*

Grief usually follows a predictable pattern, although there is some variability involved. Although the phases of the grieving process are not necessarily orderly, immediate reactions to loss can be distinguished from long-term
responses (Bouvard, 1988). *Shock and protest* or denial is usually the immediate
response when a loved one dies. Many people experience a sense of unreality
or numbness as they feel the pain of separation. It is not unusual to feel a need
to relive the details surrounding the death. Crying can be very helpful in dealing with the sadness. A period of *disorganization* usually follows, during which
familiar routines, habits, and roles become disrupted. Profound sorrow can
lead to feelings of depression, sadness, anger, and guilt. People in this phase of
grief often experience sleep disturbances and fatigue. Eventually, a period of
reorganization or recovery occurs. Sadness is still felt, but the intensity is diminished.

As they mourn, children must face the difficult task of adjusting to life
without the parent. With time, however, many children find that they carry
their parents with them in numerous ways. The strength of the parent-child
bond endures beyond the death of the parent.

SUMMARY

- The parenting role continues even when children become adults. The tasks
  during this stage of life are quite different, and bring their own challenges
  and rewards. This phase of parenthood is known as the departure stage.
  Parents must learn to let go of their offspring and adjust to children's adult
  status, even when events require a child to return to the home of origin.
- Although little information is available about parent-child relationships in
  later life, there is evidence of reciprocity and attachment between adult
  children and their parents.
- Parents must acquire the skills for becoming grandparents, adapting to the
  new joys and demands that come with the role. Although grandparents
  are a very diverse group, they play a vital role in keeping families strong
  and connected.
- As parents grow older, adult children must often begin to give their parents some assistance. The type and extent of this help is dependent on
  many factors. Complex issues and options must be explored to balance the
  needs of the elderly parent with those of the adult child so that a satisfying resolution can occur for both generations.
- Dealing with the death of a parent is a developmental milestone that children must face. Grieving and trying to gain a better understanding of
  death in general is just another step in the growth of the parent-child
  bond.

PART THREE

Special Topics
in Parenting

Single Parenting, Divorce, and Stepparenting

Although much of the research on parenting has involved intact families, the reality is that a growing number of children are raised in families that have been formed outside of marriage or as a result of marital transitions. For example, recent data indicate that more than half of all children under the age of eighteen will spend some part of their childhood residing in a single-parent household (U.S. Bureau of Census, 1992). These changes in families affect adults, children, and parent-child relationships.

This chapter explores child rearing across various family structures, including parenting alone, nonresidential parenting, and stepparenting. A number of significant questions are addressed. How does the experience of raising a child as a single parent differ from that of coparenting with a supportive spouse? In what way does the divorce process influence parent-child relationships before, during, and after the breakup? When new parenting coalitions are formed through remarriage, how do the new family structures support or impinge upon the child's relationships with biological parents? What are the effects of multiple transitions on family members? Because family structure and marital transitions influence parents' emotional state, available social supports, and economic resources, parenting behaviors and child outcomes are also affected.

SINGLE PARENTING

In the United States more than 26 percent of children under the age of 18 live in a household headed by one parent. Figure 10-1 shows how this statistic has changed in recent decades and how family structure varies as a function of

FIGURE 10-1. Children by presence of parents: 1970 and 1992. *U.S. Bureau of Census (1993).*

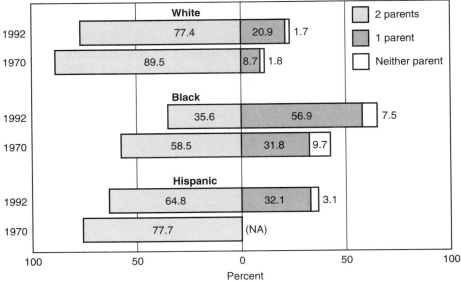

ethnicity. Current projections estimate that 40 percent to 70 percent of white children and 90 percent of black children born in the 1980s will spend some time in a single-parent home. This rapidly growing population is a diverse group, encompassing parents and children of all social classes, races, and age groups (Hernandez, 1993).

Transition to Single Parenthood

Some parents have never had the experience of coparenting, while others have had to adapt to parenting alone after losing a spouse through divorce or death. Some children are born into single-parent families, while others experience them after having lived in two-parent families. These different transitions will affect parent-child relationships in the single-parent household.

The most common pattern is that of individuals becoming single parents following divorce. More than 40 percent of single mothers fit this description. These individuals become parents with the intention of sharing child-rearing responsibilities, and then find themselves in changed circumstances, often raising their children with little or no help from the former spouses. The conflict that surrounds separation and divorce, as well as the changes in daily routine experienced by parents and their children, can make the transition to a single-parent home after divorce very difficult for all concerned.

In some families, the death of a parent results in a widowed parent carrying on alone. For many, this change in marital status and family structure comes without warning, as when a woman dies in childbirth, leaving behind a newborn child. For others, terminal illness gives warning that a single-parent household is in the family's future. Although the surviving parent then has an opportunity to plan for single parenthood, the stress-filled months of waiting can take their toll. Widowed single parents must simultaneously cope with their own grief, help their children deal with a significant loss, and assume sole responsibility for child rearing.

A less obvious type of single parent is the one who is still married but parents alone because the spouse is unavailable due to work or incapacitation. This occurs when one parent is serving in the military, works overseas, is imprisoned, or is institutionalized for health reasons. The transition to this status may be sudden, or it may have been an established pattern from the time the children were born. Although the day-to-day life of the children and the residential parent do not include the unavailable parent, he or she may be consulted when major decisions about the child's welfare must be made.

A large number of women experience out-of-wedlock births. In 1992, more than 23 percent of never-married women between the ages of eighteen and forty-four had children (U.S. Bureau of Census, 1992). Generally, these are unplanned pregnancies in which the mother decides to carry the baby to term and keep the child. The majority of single mothers are very young, with teenage pregnancy reaching epidemic proportions in some sectors of American society. The topic of teenage parenting will be discussed more extensively in Chapter 12.

A small, but increasing number of older, financially capable women are choosing to become parents outside of marriage. Recent census data indicate that 8.3 percent of never-married women in managerial or professional posi-

When older, financially stable women choose to parent alone, they may find little societal support but significant pleasure in their new role.
(Erika Stone)

tions fit this description (U.S. Bureau of Census, 1992). In many cases the "biological clock" is running out and they do not want to forgo the parenting experience for lack of a partner. The transition to parenthood is a painstakingly thoughtful process for these women, and is often plagued by a lack of support from friends and relatives. Many of these women become pregnant by utilizing a sperm bank and artificial insemination, while others carefully choose someone they know to father the child. Adoption is another option for single women who wish to become parents. Unlike other single parents, never-married parents are not simultaneously coping with single parenting and the loss of a spouse through divorce or death.

Challenges of Parenting Alone

"One parent can model only one gender role, give so many hugs, offer so much discipline, and earn so much money." (Clarke-Stewart, 1989a, p. 61). Although many parents succeed in parenting alone, there are some difficulties inherent in this family structure. As a group, single parents suffer role overload and economic difficulties. They tend to have high rates of poverty, low educational levels, and high mobility—characteristics that make the parenting process more stressful.

Even in two-parent families in which one parent assumes most of the child care responsibilities, the less-involved parent can provide emotional support, a role model, a source of income, and an adult presence. Single parents must find other sources of emotional and practical support. Simple procedures, such as taking a babysitter home when children are sleeping, require more advance planning in one-parent households.

There are cultural differences in adaptations to single parenthood, in part, because of family attitudes. For example, one study found that in Mexican-American families, extended families were not very supportive of divorced or separated women. At a time when these women needed to rely more on others for help, the negative reactions of family members made the transition to single parenthood more difficult (Wagner, 1988b). As a result, the Mexican-American single parents gradually increased their dependence on friends, and those who did not follow this pattern found themselves more socially isolated (Wagner, 1988a).

The effects of social context were also illustrated in a study of single mothers from working-class backgrounds in Ireland. During pregnancy, unmarried women experienced cultural rejection and were depressed—factors that placed them at risk for parenting problems. However, cultural attitudes were more positive after the child was born. These new mothers were no longer depressed and they displayed positive interactions with their infants (Nugent, Greene, Wieczoreck-Deering, Mazor, Hendler, & Bombardier, 1993). Research with different cultural groups highlights the complex relationship between context and single parenting.

Over time and with adequate support, single parents gain confidence in their ability to manage alone and their children adjust. There may be some advantages to being a single parent. The emotional closeness that may develop between single parent and child is noteworthy. Many single mothers and fathers report that they like being solely responsible for choosing the influences that will guide their children's development. Those who are able to make parenting decisions alone, without conflict and compromise, believe that they have more control over the values that are being imparted to the child. When their children succeed, parents who have engaged in child rearing without a coparenting partner may feel a unique sense of accomplishment.

Single Mothers

Most single parents (86 percent) are mothers. Because women tend to have lower levels of educational attainment, less-developed job skills, and lower wages than men, their families are often plagued by financial difficulties. Figure 10-2 shows the levels of family income associated with different family structures.

Two routes to single motherhood are particularly likely to be accompanied by inadequate or decreased income: teenage pregnancy and divorce. Recall from Chapter 1 that poverty indirectly affects parenting because it determines where the family can afford to live, what types of material comforts they have, and whether they can purchase services to reduce stress. Researchers studying family violence have concluded that single mothers have a higher risk of child abuse because of their poverty, not because they are parenting alone (Gelles, 1989).

When single mothers work outside the home, role overload is compounded. Single employed mothers have little time to spend on household

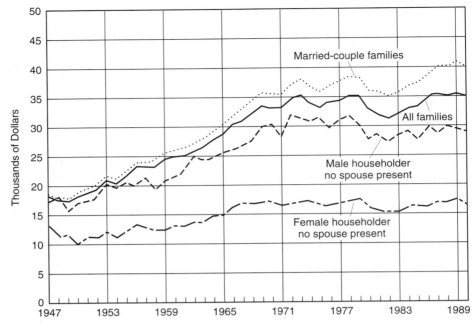

FIGURE 10-2. Median family income, by type of family: 1947 to 1990 (in 1990 dollars).
Source: U.S. Bureau of the Census, Current Population Reports, P23-181, "House-
holds, Families, and Children: A 30-Year Perspective" U.S. Government Printing
Office, Washington, DC, 1992.

tasks, child care, and personal interests. They tend to divide their time
between work and children, neglecting their own social and recreational activities. This trend may have long-term consequences for their parenting skills
(Sanik & Mauldin, 1986).

The majority of research on single mothers originally focused on the
effects of father absence for boys. Studies suggested that without a close
father-son relationship, boys were at risk for developing behavior problems
and less-masculine traits (Biller, 1981). More recent studies have looked
beyond sex-role identity to parent-child interactions in the home, finding that
single mothers, especially those who are recently divorced, do have more
problems disciplining their sons. These mothers tend to make inconsistent and
ineffective efforts to control their sons, and boys react with aggression and
noncompliance. A frustrated mother might then resort to more authoritarian
techniques, only to find that this approach escalates the unpleasant cycle of
interaction (Hetherington, 1988, 1989).

Single mothers often lack adequate social support. If they are poor, have
numerous child-rearing responsibilities, and must work outside the home,
they generally do not have the time or the energy to make friends. However, because single mothers constitute a large group in society, they are
more likely than men to see and know other women who face the same
challenges.

Single Fathers

239

CHAPTER 10
Single Parenting,
Divorce, and
Stepparenting

Although the number of single fathers with custody of their children has increased in recent decades, this family form still constitutes only 14 percent of all single-parent families (U.S. Bureau of Census, 1993). Like mothers, these men suffer role overload as they try simultaneously to fulfill the homemaking, child-rearing, and breadwinning roles of a family. Single fathers have shown that they are capable of performing these tasks, and most feel competent as single parents (Risman, 1986).

Because men tend to have stronger work histories and higher status jobs, single fathers do not suffer financially in the same way that single mothers do. However, because of their added parenting responsibilities, career advancement is often slowed and they may not attain their full earning potential. A single father may find that he cannot take advantage of opportunities for working overtime or that he must turn down a much-deserved promotion if it involves a more time-consuming job.

Since it is uncommon for fathers to have custody of their children, their reasons for assuming this role may affect their success and satisfaction with parenting. A man may choose to become a single parent because he is emotionally attached to the child or because he believes his ex-wife is unfit. Fathers who have fought for custody and won describe the father-child relationship in very positive terms. If the child's mother did not want to continue parenting, the father may feel trapped or he may view himself as a savior who will rescue the child. Many single fathers today want custody of their children and this motivation bodes well for their satisfaction and success (Risman, 1986).

One of the reasons that single fathers succeed is that they are more likely to parent older children. Infants and toddlers, who require more physical caregiving, are usually raised by mothers. Boys, rather than girls, are more often cared for by single fathers. When fathers do raise daughters, they report more insecurity about their parenting abilities. They are especially ambivalent about providing appropriate guidance when their daughters reach adolescence, and are uncomfortable dealing with sexuality (Greif, 1985; Santrock, Warshak, & Elliot, 1982).

Single fathers may have fewer social supports than single mothers do. Because they constitute a smaller group and because men are less likely to avail themselves of social networks, single fathers may be parenting in isolation (See Box 10-1). Unless they actively seek out other single fathers through formal groups, they are unlikely to encounter them by chance. The major source of support for a single father may be his own parents, the child's grandparents. Because single fathering is uncommon, society generally regards the man who undertakes this role as exceptional. As a result, he may receive praise for performing the same tasks that a single mother does without recognition.

Children in Single-Parent Households

When divorce and unwed pregnancy were less common and less socially acceptable, there was more stigma attached to the single-parent status. Children were labeled "illegitimate" or described as being from "a broken home," terminology that reflects negatively on the child's worth. Because of the growing numbers of single-parent families, children are more likely to know peers with a similar family structure, and they do not feel as stigmatized as they may have in previous decades.

Studies of children in single-parent households have shown that they differ from children in two-parent households in a number of ways. First, they usually assume more responsibility around the house. This can have either positive or negative effects on the developing child. When the child is given a reasonable number of age-appropriate tasks, development is enhanced. However, when children are expected to assume adult tasks that interfere with normal children's activities, they resent the burden and may rebel (Hetherington, 1988).

Box 10-1 Support for Single Parents

Although social support is important for all parents, it is particularly significant for the well-being of single parents. The physical and emotional burden of assuming multiple roles and responsibilities can be detrimental to both the parent and the child. If there is anything to be learned from the experience of single parents, it is that these mothers and fathers need support from others in order to thrive. The support may be instrumental (e.g., sharing child care, financial assistance) or emotional (e.g., an adult to talk with about child-rearing concerns). Some sources of support might include the following.

EXTENDED FAMILY AND FRIENDS

When relatives and friends can be counted on for instrumental and emotional support, single parents and their children are not as burdened. For example, if grandparents can be called to help with the children when a single mother is sick, or if friends are willing to carpool to children's activities, the daily routine is not as stressful. As long as these people do not undermine parental authority or cause the parent to feel inferior, support is generally welcomed. Also, children benefit from knowing that they can depend on a number of people.

COMMUNITY SUPPORT

A variety of community agencies can offer appropriate support to single parents. Child care centers often serve as extended families, becoming partners in child rearing and serving as a source of child development information when questions arise. A Big Brother/Big Sister program can provide regular contact with another adult for the child. Churches can offer single parents spiritual support and a social network. Schools must be sensitized to the needs of single parents so that they can support the parenting process. Teachers must be realistic in their expectations regarding parental participation, and flexible when it comes to scheduling conferences. It is a mistake for parents to keep their marital status a secret, especially when the child is experiencing transitions such as separation, divorce, or remarriage. Schools can be instrumental in teaching all children that structural variations in families are acceptable.

OTHER SINGLE PARENTS

Either through formal groups such as Parents Without Partners or via informal networks, single parents can help each other. Having similar needs, they may be able to share resources for the common good. In some communities, single parents have organized cooperative child care and discussion groups about parenting alone. Informal liaisons are also sources of support. For example, one single mother student with a preschool child found a kindred spirit in another woman in a similar situation. They relied on each other as emergency backups and decided to vacation together with their children.

Children in single-parent homes also have more power in family decision making. Single mothers are more likely to listen to their children's opinions and yield to their demands. More egalitarian parent-child relationships are characteristic of single-parent families. These relationships may be mutually supportive—or they may be parasitic—with the child being emotionally burdened by a parent who needs an adult confidant (Hetherington, 1988).

In contrast with two-parent families, single parents grant their children more autonomy. For example, they are more likely to allow their children to stay up late (Zill, 1988). Single parents monitor their children's behavior less closely, knowing less about where they are and who they are with (Hetherington, 1988). This tendency is noteworthy, given research on parenting practices that suggests poor monitoring puts a child at risk for developing antisocial behaviors (Patterson et al., 1989).

Some psychologists have suggested that children in single-parent homes may be more androgynous, having both masculine and feminine characteristics regardless of their gender. Since the single parent often fulfills multiple roles, he or she is likely to be modeling androgeny for the children (Demo & Acock, 1988).

Are the effects of being raised in a single-parent household long-lasting? The poverty that characterizes many single-parent households may curtail opportunities for the children far into the future. A recent research study has shown that adults who were raised by single mothers tended to have lower educational, occupational, and economic attainment than their peers raised in two-parent households (Keith & Finley, 1988). Their adult relationships are also less satisfying (Lauer & Lauer, 1991).

Some children seem to fare better if they are raised in a family headed by the same-sex parent. Boys often have problematic relationships with their single mothers, but boys in father-headed households are more socially competent and mature. Similarly, girls from single-mother homes show better social and emotional adjustment than girls living with single fathers (Lee, Burkham, Zimilies, & Ladewski, 1994; Santrock et al., 1982). These findings suggest that the same-sex parent model is particularly salient for many children, but more research on this topic is needed.

DIVORCE

The instability of marriage in contemporary society is illustrated by American divorce statistics. The divorce rate in the United States has more than doubled since 1960, giving this country the highest divorce rate in the world. Approximately one-half of all marriages end in divorce (U.S. Bureau of Census, 1992). As a result, a growing number of disrupted families have experienced the marital conflict associated with separation and the difficult transition from a two-parent to a one-parent home. Both of these factors affect parenting skills (Cherlin, Furstenberg, Chase-Lansdale, Kiernan, Robins, Morrison, & Teitler, 1991). Divorce alters parental responsibilities, strains parent-child relationships, and leaves lasting impressions on many children.

Marital Conflict

The impact of marital turmoil on parent-child relationships prior to separation or divorce has been documented (Emery, 1982). As parental energy is directed at marital conflict, parenting skills suffer. When parents are preoccupied with the spousal relationship, depressed about their failing marriage, or involved in an extramarital affair, they tend to spend less time with their children and to be inconsistent in their reactions to them. Although children may distract parents from the spousal problems, they can also aggravate the conflict.

A longitudinal study that followed children in intact families from age three through fourteen found that many years prior to parental separation, boys exhibited impulsive and undercontrolled behavior (Block, Block, & Gjerde, 1986). Causality cannot be determined by these correlational results, but a bidirectional model of influences seems appropriate. Having a son with difficult behavior may increase marital stress and the likelihood of divorce. An alternative interpretation suggests that the boys' behavior is an outcome of the conflict. It is possible that predivorce conflict adversely affects children long before parents themselves realize that the marriage will terminate. The effects of persistent parental conflict are also highlighted by studies of intact families in which children display negative behaviors (Peterson & Zill, 1986). These findings suggest that marital conflict has detrimental effects on children even when parents stay together.

When marriages are terminated, the divorce process is generally adversarial. Each spouse hires an attorney to represent his or her best interests as they divide common property and redefine parenting responsibilities. Children can become pawns in this process, often being asked to testify on behalf of either parent. While the adversarial approach might secure the best tangible outcomes for participants, the process can intensify conflict and destroy what is left of relationships. In some states there has been a trend toward *divorce mediation,* a cooperative method of settling divorce-related disputes that relies on direct communication and negotiation between the spouses. It is believed that mediation places less strain on postdivorce family relationships. Some professionals have suggested that this approach is particularly appropriate when issues of child custody, support, or visitation are in question, because the coparental relationship will continue long after the divorce agreement is signed (Emery, 1988).

Children's Reactions to Divorce

Children's reactions to parental separation and conflict will vary according to their relative maturity and social supports (Wallerstein & Kelly, 1980). Toddlers and preschoolers lack the cognitive abilities to understand the meaning of divorce. They may be confused and illogically conclude that the separation is their fault (e.g., "Daddy is leaving because I didn't pick up my toys"). Because of their limited levels of understanding, younger children are more likely to deny that separation is occurring or to fantasize about parental reconciliation. When they are told that parents no longer love each another, they may become fearful of losing parental love themselves or of being abandoned.

Their egocentric thinking may also lead them to believe that they are causing the mood swings their stressed parents are exhibiting.

Preschool children are likely to feel angry, guilty, and rejected when they learn about the divorce. It is not uncommon to see very young children regress to infantile or acting-out behaviors (e.g., bed-wetting, tantrums, fears). Unfortunately, young children have few sources of support outside the family that they can rely on when parents are psychologically unavailable or preoccupied, although grandparents and other extended family members may be stabilizing influences (Hetherington & Camara, 1984).

School-age children have better coping skills and more extrafamilial support than their younger peers do. Their more advanced cognitive skills enable them to understand divorce as a result of parental problems, so they are less likely to blame themselves. However, their more sophisticated level of understanding also deprives them of using denial or fantasies as coping mechanisms. Their emotional reactions to the loss may be very intense and they can become preoccupied with the sadness and the anger. Because school-age children have larger social networks, they have more resources to rely on when they are stressed. Peers and adults in a supportive school environment can provide the necessary buffer when divorce makes family life painful and uncertain.

Adolescents have adult-like reasoning abilities, so they are more likely to understand why parents are divorcing, especially if they have witnessed marital conflict. Although their cognitive abilities enable them to understand that children are not to blame for divorce, the fact that they can see both sides of an argument makes them more vulnerable to loyalty conflicts. Parents who would not expect a young child to take sides might not hesitate to involve adolescents in parental conflict and request their support (Johnston, Kline, & Tschann, 1989). Older children may be embarrassed by divorce, especially because it calls attention to parents' sexuality at a time when they are struggling with their own sexuality.

Some adolescents deal with the pain of divorce by trying to comfort either or both parents, while others cope by withdrawing from family relationships. With close friends to confide in and greater involvement in the world outside the family, these older children have more resources to support them when parents are divorcing.

Because of these varying developmental needs, parents must take special care when informing children about parental divorce. Box 10-2 offers suggestions for dealing with children's needs when a decision to separate has been made.

Some studies suggest that family disruption has such a profound impact on children that they remember the event with sadness years later (Wallerstein & Kelly, 1980; Wallerstein & Blakeslee, 1989). Although these findings have attracted much media attention, research methodology must be evaluated when considering their generalizability. Data were collected from a clinical sample of divorced families seeking therapy. Factors that weaken the research design include an upper middle-class population, a reliance on retrospective reporting, and the lack of a control group.

There is no doubt that divorce is an emotional issue for the children involved, but there are individual differences in their reactions. The process also affects outsiders. Children from intact families who witness marital tran-

Box 10-2 Telling Children About Separation and Divorce

Although children's various developmental levels and individual personality characteristics will affect their reaction to the news that their parents are divorcing, there are certain guidelines for informing children that may be applicable to all. The following information is an attempt to translate research findings into practical advice and may help parents to undertake this difficult task:

1. It is important to tell children as soon as a decision is made, especially if other people are privy to this information. Many parents dread this task, since they have probably tried to protect children from marital conflict. Most children will be surprised by the news, but others will not. It is damaging for a child to hear rumors about a marital breakup from other children or adults, because it will undermine the trust they have in their parents.
2. When children are initially informed, both parents and all siblings should be present. This scenario may be emotionally difficult, but it will reinforce to the children that the parental decision is mutual and that they will not be asked to side with either parent. Later, parents should be available to talk privately with individual children who will have varying reactions and degrees of understanding.
3. Use language that children will understand. Clearly state that the reason for divorce is marital discord and that the child is not the cause. Avoid blaming the other parent by stating that this decision has been made by both parents. Although your feelings about your spouse may be less than positive, remember that nothing is gained by negative comments about someone your child loves.

4. Reassure children that they are still loved by both parents. The fragility of relationships becomes frighteningly apparent to children when their parents separate. The concept that the marriage will end, but parenting will continue, is a difficult one to grasp.
5. Children of all ages need to know what the immediate impact of divorce will be on their own lives. When will they see the noncustodial parent? Will they still have contact with extended family members? Will they live in the same household or will they be moving? Will their siblings be separated from them? Answers to these concrete questions will provide a sense of stability at an otherwise confusing time.
6. Be aware of resources available to assist children experiencing marital transitions. Many good children's books about divorce have been written in recent years. If parents have been involved in counseling, children might be invited to sessions to air their feelings. Some community agencies organize peer groups for school-age children and adolescents to share the experience of being caught up in marital transitions.
7. Telling children about parental separation is not a single event. As children process the information presented to them at the initial discussion, they will need follow-up discussions that include the opportunity to ask questions and express feelings. Their understanding of divorce and the way it will affect them personally will evolve over time, and parents must be available to talk and listen as needs change.

sitions among friends and relatives may worry about the stability of their own parents' marriage. When parents argue, children from stable families may fear the possibility of divorce.

Child Custody

After divorce, provisions for child rearing must be made. Custody decisions determine the child's living arrangements and parental rights and responsibilities. Prior to the mid-nineteenth century, fathers were often awarded custody of their children upon divorce, because children were considered property that belonged to the father and because only fathers were financially capable of supporting them. This reality made the consequences of divorce very severe for mothers. With the idealization of motherhood in the current century, the tides turned and the popular belief was that it would be cruel to deprive a child of maternal care. Fathers were left by the wayside. In the 1970s, dissatisfaction with the maternal advantage resulted in application of the "best interest of the child" standard, so that neither parent would be favored solely on the basis of gender. Joint custody is a more recent phenomenon that attempts to give both parents equal opportunities to continue parenting (Derdeyn & Scott, 1984). The actual custody decision may be less important than parental satisfaction with the custody arrangement. When parents are satisfied, they have better relationships with ex-spouses and more harmonious coparenting (Arditti & Kelley, 1994).

Noncustodial Parents

After divorce, some parents become less involved in the child's life. The noncustodial parent may or may not share parenting responsibilities. The typical pattern is for the noncustodial father to diminish contact with his children within one or two years after separation (Seltzer & Bianchi, 1988). A national study (Furstenberg & Nord, 1985) revealed that nearly half of all children did not see their nonresident fathers for over a year, and those with more frequent contact still did not have a regular routine. Sometimes this happens because he loses interest; at other times the children's lives become so involved that they do not want to make the effort required to continue visitation. Contact with a noncustodial parent tends to be social (i.e., going on trips, to a ball game, to a movie) rather than instrumental (i.e., helping them with homework). For "Disneyland fathers" parenting is a series of special events, instead of a relationship based on regular interaction. One teenager described herself as a "convenience child" because she felt she was involved in her noncustodial father's life only when it was convenient for him.

Custodial mothers complain that they are overburdened with child-rearing decisions. Some resent the effort they expend to maintain the relationship between children and the absent biological parent. One mother said she was tired of carrying a video camera to every school event just because the non-residential father could not find time for his children. Research tells us that coparenting among formerly married couples is more myth than reality. It is the parent with whom the child resides who assumes major parenting responsibilities (Furstenberg & Nord, 1985).

Why do noncustodial parents diminish their involvement with children over time? In an effort to gain a better understanding of noncustodial parents, one research study focused on reasons divorced fathers had infrequent or no contact with their children (Dudley, 1991). The largest number cited their former spouse as an obstacle, either because the divorce had been so adversarial or because they continued to fight. Others mentioned personal problems such as drug abuse or a lifestyle that did not include children as the reason for diminished contact. Another group cited geographic distance as a problem.

Finally, some fathers said that it was more difficult to maintain contact with teenage children who had lives of their own (Dudley, 1991).

For boys living with single mothers, continued contact with a noncustodial parent seems to be quite important. In a study of elementary school children from divorced families, boys who had a good relationship with the noncustodial father were better adjusted. Frequent visitation was associated with the best father-son relationships (Guidubaldi, Cleminshaw, Perry, Nastasi, & Lightel, 1986). Similarly, adolescents are more likely to get advice from their fathers when visitation is frequent, and this leads to higher levels of satisfaction among sons (Barber, 1994).

Noncustodial mothers are a distinct minority, and they report a lack of support for their status (Arditti & Madden-Derdich, 1993). Mothers who give up or lose custody of their children are likely to feel guilty about being forced into such a decision. Even when they relinquish control voluntarily, it may be because they feel emotionally or financially unprepared to support a family. Mothers bring unique strengths to noncustodial parenting, because they tend to be successful in maintaining mutually satisfying relationships with their children through visitation, letters, and phone contact (Furstenburg & Nord, 1985).

The noncustodial parent is often under court order to pay child support, but many do not. The economic deprivation of single mothers is sometimes blamed on the noncustodial father's failure to pay court-ordered support. Fathers who withhold payments often resent having no control over child-rearing decisions or how the money will be spent. Also, fathers who are denied visitation rights will often withhold payments. Sometimes noncustodial parents fall on hard times and are unable to pay, but custodial parents may feel that this is an unalterable commitment. Some states use a fixed percentage formula for assessing the noncustodial parent's financial responsibility. This approach links the child's economic well-being to both parents' income and does away with continual legal battles to change support payments. Noncustodial parents who pay support on a regular basis are communicating an important message of caring to their children (Bronstein, Stoll, Clauson, Abrams, & Briones, 1994).

Joint Custody

Although most children in the United States reside with mothers after divorce, there has been a trend toward *joint legal custody.* This arrangement assures that both parents have the right to continue to be involved in parenting decisions affecting the child. Fathers with joint custody are more likely to maintain contact with their children and are less likely to discontinue financial support. They tend to participate in the children's activities and share parental decision making with the child's mother (Bowman & Ahrons, 1985). Another advantage cited is that this arrangement relieves the burden and stress of single parenting and, thus enhances parental well-being (DeFrain, Fricke, & Elmen, 1987).

Because studies of joint custody generally show positive effects for parents and children, many states have suggested making it the legally preferred arrangement. Unfortunately, most studies of joint custody have used families who actively sought this arrangement, which may be the reason for the positive results. However, in families in which custody status and visitation are disputed, joint physical custody may not be desirable. A longitudinal study of 100 California families found that children suffer under these conditions (Johnston et al., 1989). When adversarial parents had more frequent access to children, the children were more emotionally troubled and behaviorally disturbed. These children witnessed more verbal and physical aggression between the parents and were marred by it. It is clear that there are differences between families who voluntarily choose joint custody and those who are forced to accept this arrangement, and that social policy makers must not make broad recommendations based on studies of a limited population.

With *joint physical custody*, children have two homes and alternate living with each parent. The arrangements are varied, with children changing living quarters daily, weekly, seasonally, or annually. In a few families, the children live in one home and the parents move in and out during their time of primary responsibility. Obviously, multiple residences can present logistical problems for children, including leaving important possessions at one home or the other, making sure friends have both phone numbers, and keeping both parents informed of important activities and schedules. Joint residential custody is particularly attractive to parents living in the same school district, more affluent families, and those who have been cooperative in the early stages of the separation and divorce. Parents who are able to negotiate joint physical custody also tend to be less critical of an ex-spouse's parenting practices (Pearson & Thoennes, 1990).

Most divorcing parents assign physical custody to the mother, but allow both parents to maintain legal custody. The age and gender of the child predict the level of visitation to the nonresidential parent. Infants and toddlers are less likely to spend time away from the mother than are preschool and school-age children. Divided residence between parental households is also less common for adolescents, who have stronger ties to school and peers (Maccoby, Depner & Mnookin, 1988).

Effects of Divorce on Children

Children are affected by divorce in a number of ways. They may lose contact with a parent and other relatives, suffer economic distress, change routines, witness hostility between their parents, and be subjected to inadequate parenting and unstable role models (Kalter, Kloner, Shreier, & Okla, 1989; Wallerstein & Corbin, 1989). Not all children react in the same way to parental separation. A child's gender, age, and behavioral characteristics may temper the effects of family disruption. Some outcomes are immediate while others emerge over time.

The most common types of disturbances that children manifest in divorced homes are poor impulse control, increased aggression, noncompliance, and achievement deficits (Amato & Keith, 1991; Cherlin et al., 1991; Hetherington et al., 1989). For example, studies of school-age children reveal that those who had experienced family disruption were more likely to be experiencing academic problems (Kinard & Reinherz, 1986), and were often characterized by antisocial behavior (Demo et al., 1988).

When these disturbances are found, they are related to the custodial parent's inadequate parenting skills—not simply an outcome of divorce itself (Hetherington, 1989; Kalter et al., 1989). It generally takes two to three years for families to settle into developmentally appropriate parenting patterns after marital disruption, so children are more likely to exhibit behavioral and emotional problems during this early period. However, for some families problems persist. Since the effects of divorce on children are mediated through the parent, children suffer when the parents are not adjusting well.

A longitudinal study identified specific home environment factors that influence children's postdivorce adjustment after the initial crisis stage (Guidubaldi et al., 1986). These included child-rearing style of custodial parent, home routines, and parental satisfaction with child rearing. School-age children who were socially maladjusted, unhealthy, and performing poorly in academics were most often subjected to authoritarian parenting practices. When a divorced parent was working or trying to establish a social life, irregular bedtimes and more television viewing were common. The beliefs of single parents may also influence the developmental outcomes of their children. Divorced mothers who believe that they do exert some control over their children and that their parenting practices will influence child outcomes are more likely than other divorcees to have children with high self-esteem, good physical health, and few psychological problems (Machida & Holloway, 1991).

Virtually all studies showing that children suffer from divorce find that the effects are most severe and long lasting for boys and for children with difficult temperaments. It is apparent that these groups are more vulnerable to stress in general, but there may be factors related to divorce that are particularly salient. For example, boys are more likely to witness parental fighting and may suffer more when consistent authoritative parenting is lacking. Also, because adults perceive boys as sturdier than girls, they may give them less support during stressful periods. Temperamentally difficult children are less adaptable to change and are more likely to suffer from the multiple stressors that accompany divorce. (Hetherington, Stanley-Hagan, & Anderson, 1989).

It is also significant that most boys are in mother-custody homes, and that mother-son relationships continue to be problematic long after other stabilized divorced families have settled into healthier patterns. One study found that single mothers nagged their sons and complained about their behavior (Hetherington, 1988). They tended to spend less time with sons than with daughters and felt more emotionally distant from them. School-age sons accurately describe their own behavior as aggressive and noncompliant. They also report spending more time with peers than with adults, and realize that their mothers have little control over their behavior (Hetherington, 1988). These negative outcomes are not as likely to be found when boys reside in father-custody homes (Santrock et al., 1982).

In contrast, girls in mother-headed divorced families tend to have amicable relationships with their mothers and do not manifest as many behavioral problems. However, when girls reach puberty and begin dating, mother-daughter relationships are often strained (Hetherington, 1988). As they become older adolescents and young adults, daughters of divorce are troubled by the model of their parents' relationship. Because they identify with their mothers, they may have problems with intimacy and trust (Wallerstein & Corbin, 1989).

The long-term effects of divorce are apparent when adult populations are studied. For example, the economic consequences of divorce mean that children are more likely to attain less education and have a lower occupational status. They also have problems with adult relationships, marrying earlier and divorcing more frequently (Keith & Finley, 1988). Paradoxically, adults who grew up in disrupted families tend to seek out intimate relationships, but often describe these relationships as deficient or lacking. This may be because they are modeling parental dating behavior or because they have a stronger need for intimacy, given the losses they have suffered as children (Lauer & Lauer, 1991).

If biological parents continue to quarrel after divorce, are children adversely affected? A recent study suggests that the way in which divorced parents resolve parenting conflicts predicts children's adjustment (Camara & Resnick, 1989). Those who could negotiate and compromise when they disagreed (i.e., about where the child should go to school, how to deal with the child's misbehavior, or where holidays would be spent) have children who are emotionally healthy. Even in families in which levels of parental conflict had been high with respect to divorce issues, developing cooperative relationships as parents was possible and important for their school-age children. Similarly, studies suggest that when ex-partners engage in cooperative coparenting, their adolescent children have fewer psychological problems (Bronstein et al., 1994; Forehand, Neighbors, Devine, & Armistead, 1994).

In looking at children of divorce, E. Mavis Hetherington (1989) has labeled them "winners, losers, and survivors," depending on how effectively they weather the transitions in family life related to divorce. In her longitudinal study that followed children from age four to age ten, some children emerged apparently unscathed, as competent and caring children six years after divorce. Others were described as competent, yet manipulative—capitalizing on parental conflict for personal gain. The most maladaptive group included aggressive children with low self-esteem.

Clearly, divorce does not have the same effect on all children. Longitudinal studies done in the United States and Great Britain indicate that some of the negative outcomes often attributed to divorce may more accurately reflect predivorce conflict, behavior problems, and achievement difficulties (Cherlin et al. 1991). It is hoped that future research on this topic will delineate which children will be adversely affected by marital conflict and divorce, and what can be done to protect them from this adversity. Similarly, new studies may help parents and policy makers better understand which children under what conditions will have the most positive adaptations when their parents' marriages deteriorate (Hetherington et al., 1989).

STEPPARENTING

The trend toward remarriage following divorce has meant that many adults and children must adapt to life in stepfamilies. It is estimated that 75 percent to 80 percent of divorced parents remarry, and many of these second marriages subsequently end in divorce. As a result, life in any one family structure is often temporary and children experience a series of family transitions over time.

Remarriage as a Transition

When new families are formed through remarriage, household rules are restructured and roles are negotiated. Parenting relationships in the early stages of remarriage are different from those that are eventually established. Initially, stepkin may be veritable strangers who lack a shared history. Unlike biological families, most newly formed stepfamilies have not yet established the emotional bonds that provide a basis for weathering turmoil.

When remarriage occurs, children are forced to give up their hopes for parental reconciliation. Any fantasies they may have had about reuniting the biological parents and the family are shattered. Children may be emotionally troubled because they are unsure about their relationships with adult family members. A child who has developed a close bond with the single parent during the years between marriages may feel displaced by the new marital partner. She or he may also be wary about accepting the new stepparent for fear that this will be viewed as disloyalty toward the noncustodial parent.

The newly married couple is faced with the difficult task of trying to nurture their marital relationship while simultaneously dealing with an instant family. The redivorce rate in remarriage is higher when there are children (White & Booth, 1985). Psychologists speculate that the marriage suffers because parents spend so much time on child-related concerns that they do not have an opportunity to devote time to solidifying their relationship (Pill, 1990).

Recall from Chapter 1 that a good marital relationship is often associated with successful parenting. For stepfamilies, this maxim does not necessarily apply. Remarried couples reporting the highest levels of marital satisfaction and closeness are the same ones that have the highest levels of parent-child conflict (Hetherington, 1988). Focusing on the spousal relationship may undermine the needs of the parental relationship.

Parental well-being often improves with remarriage, and this can have a positive influence on parenting skills. For most single mothers, remarriage means a significant improvement in their financial status, a reduction in task overload, and a more ordered household routine (Hetherington & Carama, 1984). One such woman reported that, with the support of her new husband, she was able to be more consistent in setting limits for her children than she had been when she was parenting alone.

When both parents bring children to the remarriage, potential problems are noted. Conflicts related to finances, stepsibling rivalries, and parental favoritism of biological children are common. Couples often wonder whether having a child together will help "cement" the marital bond and facilitate family development. A recent study suggests that a shared biological child does not seem to make any difference in stepfamily relationships. Neither the marital bonds nor the stepparent-stepchild bonds appear to be affected by the addition of a shared child (Ganong & Coleman, 1987).

The desirable level of emotional connectedness among family members may be different for stepfamilies. Although nondivorced families function better when members have very strong feelings of attachment for each other, stepchildren appear to benefit from a more moderate emotional connection, especially if they are participating in two households. Psychological flexibility enables them to celebrate holidays and enjoy vacations with a large network of people without feeling guilty or disloyal (Pill, 1990).

Life in stepfamilies requires continual and deliberate effort, and constant attention to the evolving relationships. Over time, stepfamilies do develop a shared history and a sense of connectedness. Stepparents acquire a sense of belonging, stepchildren no longer feel that they are living with a stranger, and all may begin to care about one another. These changes will influence the type of parenting that is possible or desirable at a particular time in the life cycle of the stepfamily (see Box 10-3).

Parenting a Spouse's Children

Clinicians working with stepparents have identified common emotional issues that plague relationships with a spouse's children. Stepparents often feel hurt, frustrated, and disappointed because they fail to instantly establish a loving relationship with their newly acquired stepchildren. Over time they may become angry with stepchildren who refuse to reciprocate love. Guilt is also common, with stepparents often feeling that they have failed when stepchildren continue to reject them (Nelson & Levant, 1991). Stepparents sometimes express the wish that they could have been part of the child's life at an earlier stage. They feel that if the child had been younger when the remarriage took place, they might have enjoyed closer emotional bonding and they could have had a stronger influence on the child's values (Pill, 1990). In stepfamilies, the biological parent is often caught between spouse and child. They are buffers, trying to protect family members from their negative emotions about each other.

There are two contrasting models regarding the relative roles of stepparents and nonresident biological parents. Working in clinical settings, some psychologists suggest that stepparents and biological parents form "parenting coalitions" (Visher & Visher, 1989). By parenting cooperatively and joining forces to make child-rearing decisions, these mutually supportive coalitions

For Better or For Worse®   **by Lynn Johnston**

FOR BETTER OR FOR WORSE © 1988 Lynn Johnston Prod., Inc. Reprinted with permission of UNIVERAL PRESS SYNDICATE. All rights reserved.

Box 10-3 Easing the Transition to Stepparenting

When a single parent remarries and a stepfamily is formed, the feelings of adults and children must be considered. Someone who has never parented may have idealized notions of what it will be like, or may be dreading the thought of becoming a parent overnight. Stepparents who bring children to a second marriage may worry about how they will meet the needs of their biological children while trying to develop a relationship with a spouse's children. Children who have enjoyed a great deal of autonomy in a single-parent family and those who have a relationship with a noncustodial parent may be confused about how to relate to this new adult in their lives. A certain degree of instability is expected as the new family interacts and makes decisions about living arrangements and daily routines. A successful transition to stepparenting may be facilitated if the following issues are considered:

1. It helps to discuss feelings in advance. Plans for remarriage must include opportunities to explore the child's feelings about the new adult in the family, as well as the couple's feelings about assuming new roles. Discussing ambivalence, resentment, or excitement helps both parties understand each other.
2. Wedding plans should include the children. Some may wish to participate in the ceremony while others prefer to be spectactors. Some couples delay a honeymoon trip until several weeks after the wedding so that children do not feel they are being abandoned because of the new relationship. Others include children in some of the postwedding vacation plans.
3. If possible, begin life after remarriage in a new setting. Neutral territory helps minimize feelings of being an outsider or being invaded. Do not overlook the needs of nonresident stepchildren, who need separate space to give them a sense of belonging in the new home. One stepmother described her unique housing requirements—large common areas to accommodate two sets of children, an extra bedroom that could be furnished in a dormitory style where three stepsons could sleep on alternate weekends, and many shelves and drawers so that each child and each adult could have a special place for personal belongings.
4. Children must decide what they will call the stepparent. Usually they feel comfortable with first names, but younger children who have no contact with a biological parent may be pleased to have someone to call "Dad."
5. Do not interfere with the child's relationship with the noncustodial parent. Although it may seem threatening to have the "real" father as a lurking influence, recognize that in most cases the child benefits from this contact. Attempting to replace the biological parent is unrealistic. Instead, recognize the uniqueness of the stepparent role and nurture it.
6. Neither stepparents nor stepchildren can expect that they will be instantly loved. Falling in love with a woman does not guarantee that you will be enthralled by her children. At the outset the goal must be for stepkin to get to know one another. As family members develop communication skills and an interest in each other, the stage will be set for the development of affection.
7. Preconceived ideals can interfere with an appreciation for the individuality that stepkin bring to the family. Remarriage is a blending of family traditions, resources, and values. Just as any newly married couple bring with them ideas from their families of origin, stepparents and stepchildren have personal histories that must be acknowledged and dealt with. Stepfamilies often try to incorporate familiar routines into the stepfamily, realizing that over time they will develop their own special traditions and rituals.
8. Although a previously overburdened single parent may welcome a supportive coparent into the family, the stepparent must proceed with caution in areas of discipline. Until some sort of bond between stepparent and stepchild has been established, it is best to let the biological parent handle discipline. During this period the stepparent can be a source of emotional support for the biological parent and as a couple they can discuss ideas about discipline. Over time children will accept the coparenting role of the stepparent.

provide the child with guidance from three or more caring adults. This scenario might also reduce conflict and power struggles between parents and stepparents. Another model, based on empirical research, suggests that the introduction of a stepparent reduces the involvement of the nonresident biological parent. From this perspective parenting is more sequential, with no more than two adults actively participating at any one time (Seltzer & Bianchi, 1988; Furstenberg & Nord, 1985).

Stepparent relationships are not clearly defined. Although stepchildren may benefit from their involvement, their approach must be sensitive to the affectional ties that the child has with the nonresident biological parent (Zill, 1988). It is not unusual for a stepparent to feel defeated and confused when trying to accomplish this seemingly impossible task.

Single Parenting, Divorce, and Stepparenting

Stepfathers

Because children of divorced parents generally reside with their mothers, remarriage creates many stepfathers. Initially, stepfathers are likely to adopt a "disengaged" parenting style; that is, they are minimally involved in controlling and monitoring their stepchildren's behavior. If they have never parented before, they tend to be more adult-oriented and do not spend much time and effort on child rearing (Hetherington, 1988).

During the first two years of remarriage, stepfathers are often emotionally distant from their stepchildren, especially if they have been rejected by them. They may support the mother's attempts to discipline, but they do not generally confront children directly. Over time, warmer relationships develop with stepsons, but conflicts with stepdaughters may increase. Only when stepfathers become more accepted by their stepchildren are they able to adopt an authoritative parenting style and take a more active role in child rearing. If they attempt to do this sooner, they are ineffective (Hetherington, 1989).

Stepmothers

The residential stepmother is uncommon, but the image of the wicked stepmother is familiar from fairy tales. Although this negative image is unwarranted, there is evidence that stepmothers take on a difficult parenting role with few positive role models.

Unlike stepfathers, new stepmothers seldom adopt a disengaged stance. They are more likely to take an active interest in their stepchildren, especially with daughters. Relationships with stepchildren may be strained because stepmothers try too hard too soon (Clingempeel & Segal, 1986).

Stepdaughters may be living with their fathers because they have more problematic relationships with their biological mothers. These difficulties may adversely affect a daughter's ability to form a trusting relationship with a new female parenting figure. Research studies have found that regular contact with a biological mother complicates the child's relations with the stepmother. More frequent visits from the noncustodial mother are associated with more friction between a stepmother and a stepchild. The stepmother who takes over when the biological mother has died experiences fewer problems (Furstenberg & Nord, 1985; Clingempeel & Segal, 1986).

Remarriage may be greeted with uncertainty and mixed emotions by children.
(April Saul)

Effects on Stepchildren

Remarriage is another transition to which children must adapt, and many initially react to the disequilibrium with behavior problems. The cumulative stress associated with divorce, single parenting, and remarriage can take its toll on stepchildren. The stepchild's risk for developing behavioral and emotional problems is strikingly similar to that of the child from a single-mother family. Studies have found that children are more negatively affected if there are multiple transitions; more problems are found in children who have experienced several remarriages. On a more positive note, behavior problems generally subside over time, and the benefits of family stability and increased income have been observed as positive influences on stepchild development (Peterson & Zill, 1986).

The age of the child will influence relationships with stepparents. Younger children are more likely to accept the stepparent, while early adolescents will challenge any authority that the stepparent attempts to exert. Also, preoccupation with sexuality may make the early adolescent less understanding of parental displays of affection. Some researchers have suggested that adolescent children are upset if, at a time when they are trying to establish their own separate identity, they are required to devote effort to a new family identity (Pill, 1990). Older adolescents are less likely to be bothered by the entry of the stepparent because they are readying themselves for departure from the home. They may actually be relieved that they do not have to worry about leaving the parent alone (Hetherington et al., 1989).

Remarriage affects daughters and sons differently. When children in same-sex single-parent homes enjoy positive parent-child relationships, these same children may be most vulnerable to the transition into the stepfamily. In the first two years following remarriage, mother-daughter conflict is high. Those daughters who enjoyed close relationships with their single mothers become more demanding, hostile, and coercive when their mothers remarry (Hetherington, 1988). Daughters often resent a new stepfather. They may feel that they have adjusted well to living in a single-parent household and not want to disrupt the close relationship they have formed with mothers.

In contrast, sons living with single mothers often benefit from the involvement of a caring stepfather, especially if they have been caught up in a conflict-driven, authoritarian relationship with mother. Boys who acquire a stepfather and girls who acquire a stepmother may not find the transition detrimental, if their prior relationships with custodial parents have been troubled (Santrock et al., 1982).

Because 35 percent of remarriages involving stepchildren end in divorce, the effects of multiple marital transitions must be considered. A study of preadolescent boys from lower-class and working-class families found that the risk for poor adjustment increased each time their mothers divorced or remarried. These findings may suggest that there are cumulative effects for children when conflict is repeated, or that those with poor parenting skills are also more likely to rush into new relationships (Capaldi & Patterson, 1991).

Questions have been raised regarding the relationship between stepkin if the marriage is terminated. Unless stepparents have legally adopted stepchildren, they generally do not have any ongoing parental rights. Although they may have formed a bond with the children and have been responsible for parenting them, it is difficult to secure visitation rights. In amicable divorces, however, the child's wishes to continue seeing the stepparent are often respected. Child development specialists with an interest in public policy have asked whether these nontraditional parenting relationships should be legally protected (Thompson, 1991).

The ability of children to deal with the complexity that results from multiple marriages and remarriages is notable (Furstenberg & Nord, 1985). It is not unusual to hear a child describe a person who "used to be my grandmother." When biological parents divorce, children often learn that regardless of what happened to the marriage, parenting continues. However, when a second marriage fails, it becomes painfully obvious that significant relationships with other parenting figures and extended family may not have such an enduring quality. Children in this situation may become anxious about the possibility of losing other stepkin and, in the future, they may be wary of forming relationships with potential family members.

SUMMARY

- The traditional family structure headed by two biological parents living together in one household is no longer the predominant pattern in the United States. Parenting and child development are influenced by the number and types of parents involved, as well as by the number and nature of the marital transitions that the family experiences.

- Single parenting, by choice or by default, is a difficult task. These parents are generally plagued by role overload, inadequate financial resources, and minimal social support. Parent-child relationships and developmental outcomes for children are most positive in single-parent homes with the same-sex parent.
- When separation and divorce occur, both parents and children are emotionally distressed and family functioning is disrupted. However, within two to three years following this structural change, most family members are able to adapt to their new life unless there is continued conflict or another transition.
- Not surprisingly, children's reactions to marital transitions are not uniform. Consistent with other developmental research, the divorce literature suggests that boys and children with difficult temperaments have the most difficulty coping with the stress.
- Custody arrangements can increase or decrease stress and conflict. Noncustodial parents tend to diminish contact with their children over time, and many do not contribute financially to their children's support. Joint custody offers a vehicle for continued involvement of both parents, but may work only when parents are able to overlook their differences and cooperate on child-rearing issues.
- Stepparenting is a special case of parenting and the relationships do not necessarily follow the same rules as those in nondisrupted families. Stepfathers, in particular, are advised to spend time establishing a relationship with the stepchildren before becoming involved in disciplining stepchildren. During this time, it is most helpful to offer support to the mother as she takes primary parenting responsibility for her biological children. Stepmothers have a more difficult time finding their appropriate role, especially when the biological mother is still involved with her children.
- The amount of parental conflict, the cumulative effect of multiple transitions, the availability of instrumental and emotional support for both parents and children, and the amount of time that has elapsed since the disruption will determine the quality of the parent-child relationship. If parents can maintain an authoritative parenting style while guiding children through transitions, children and parents will benefit.

CHAPTER 11

Parenting Children
with Special Needs

All children bring unique characteristics to the parent-child relationship. A child's mental level, temperament, physical capabilities, and appearance will influence the parenting process. Some children have such "special needs" as delayed development, chronic health problems, or exceptional abilities. Although these children have much in common with their normally developing peers, their parents may face some atypical challenges.

In recent years, parents of children with special needs have received much attention from researchers and policy makers. There has been a trend away from institutionalizing children with disabilities and toward providing support that enables a child to be reared by the family at home. There has also been a new recognition that children with exceptional talents require special supports in order to thrive, thus broadening our definition of "special needs." Social science research has pointed to parent involvement as an important factor in enhancing the development of disabled and gifted children. At the same time, legislation has given parents new rights and responsibilities regarding the educational programming that their special needs children receive.

This chapter presents information about the special roles that parents assume in nurturing their children with disabilities. Caregiving duties, responsibility for the child's education, and parenting stresses are altered by the child's uniqueness. Family dynamics are also affected; relations between spouses, with siblings, with extended family, and with the community can be strained. This chapter offers an overview of the research findings on parents of disabled and gifted children and provides insights into the ways in which these findings translate into daily life issues for families of children with special needs.

PARENTING CHILDREN WITH DISABILITIES

A historical look at research on parents of children with disabilities indicates that these studies have followed a pattern similar to more general parenting studies. Early investigations focused on the effect of mother on child, trying to identify maternal behaviors that "caused" the disability. The next wave of research acknowledged the contribution of the atypical child's characteristics to mother-child interactions. Assuming that factors such as the child's impaired motor abilities, lack of eye contact, and hyperactivity might also be viewed as "causes," researchers began examining the effects of different types of disabilities on maternal stress and satisfaction. Fathers were ignored at first, and then considered only as an indirect influence on mothering. The relationships between fathers and their children with disabilities were eventually examined and later a family systems approach that recognized the interdependence of parenting, child development, and marital relationships emerged. The current trend is to examine the family with a disabled child as a whole, with an understanding that the development of the child and his or her parents depends on factors both within and beyond the family system. Interventions have moved away from a deficit approach, that focused only on remediating the child's problems. Instead, contemporary interventions are based on a more comprehensive model of the parenting process that recognizes the strengths of children with disabilities and of their parents (Bristol & Gallagher, 1986).

Altered Roles

All parents assume a variety of roles and responsibilities in relation to their children. They are nurturers, caregivers, educators, disciplinarians, advocates, and advisors. When children have disabilities, some of these roles and their timing may be altered.

Caregiver

As noted in Chapter 5, the greatest demands for physical caregiving occur in infancy and toddlerhood. During this period, children are dependent on parents for assistance with feeding, dressing, transportation, and protection from danger. Over time and with development, the children become more autonomous and capable of caring for their own needs. This pattern does not necessarily follow when children have disabilities. There may be a protracted period of caregiving, because some children are unable to engage in self-care, due to their physical or mental disabilities, while others take longer to learn these skills. It is not surprising that most of the stress experienced by parents of children with disabilities is attributed to caregiving demands (Beckman-Bell, 1981).

Some children with physical disabilities may not have the coordination or strength necessary to feed themselves, dress themselves, or even move from place to place without assistance. Some children with mental disabilities may not have the cognitive capacity needed to understand simple commands or to follow through with routine self-care. Children who are medically fragile because of conditions such as seizure disorders, hemophilia, or diabetes may be at a safety risk in situations that pose no problems for normal children. For parents, these scenarios may translate into years of worry and fatigue. Ironically, the physical demands often become more difficult as the child grows older and larger, because a five-year-old is more of a challenge to carry than a small infant.

Caregiving often involves attending clinics or programs to obtain medical and educational services for the child with a disability. As a result, family routines and time allotments are altered. Increased caregiving needs may indirectly impose a financial burden on the parents. This occurs when one parent must forgo employment to care for the child or when the disabled child needs special diets, equipment, transportation, or medical operations.

Educator

Parents teach their children both formally and informally. Their role in transmitting information and assisting in development of skills cannot be underestimated. As the chapter on school-age children revealed, the supportive role of the parents when children participate in formal schooling is also important. For the parent of a child with disabilities, collaboration with educational institutions has special significance. The educational role of parents has been emphasized by recent laws requiring educators to work with families. See Box 11-1 for a description of the legislation.

Box 11-1 Legislation for Parent Advocates

During the past twenty years U.S. public policy has supported special needs children and their families in many ways. National legislation has been enacted as a result of the work of many parent advocates, and these laws have changed the lives of children and their families.

PUBLIC LAW 94-142: THE EDUCATION FOR ALL HANDICAPPED CHILDREN ACT OF 1975

This legislation marked a new philosophy in American education. It assures that *all* school-age children, regardless of abilities and disabilities, are entitled to a free, appropriate, public education. The law also states that the education must be provided in the "least restrictive environment," which means that children are not automatically segregated into groups of disabled. An important component of the law is that it requires that *parents* be included in the process of developing an individualized education plan (IEP) for the child, and parents must consent to the plan before the school can proceed with it. This act gave parents legal ground to negotiate with school systems.

Although this landmark legislation guaranteed parents the right and responsibility to be active participants in their children's education, it is basically a *child-centered law.* Parent participation is included because it will improve services for the child. The role of the parent is to be the child's advocate, assuring that the IEP is implemented.

PUBLIC LAW 99-457: EDUCATION OF THE HANDICAPPED ACT OF 1986

This law was an amendment to PL 94-142, which extended its rights and privileges to younger children not yet in school. This law recognizes the interdependence of child development and family functioning, and broadens the scope of public responsibility to include serving the needs of the family and the child. Recognizing the contribution of the family system to developmental outcomes, it legislates an individualized family service plan (IFSP). The IFSP includes not only an assessment of the child's functioning and needs, but also a statement of the family's strengths and needs. More important, it empowers parents to define their own needs, rather than having a professional determine what is wrong with the family. Parents have a right to determine which goals are most important for the child and for family functioning.

It is evident that this recent legislation is more *family-focused.* In keeping with the current emphasis on a contextual approach to child development and parent-child relations, PL 99-457 recognizes that the most adaptive approach is to work with the family system. Taken together, the two laws safeguard the rights of children with disabilities and their families, while addressing the needs of both.

Because research on children with disabilities has shown that home teaching can have a positive influence on early development, parents have been expected to teach specific skills, carry out home therapies, and work with professionals to enhance the child's physical and intellectual development. Many intervention programs focus on training parents to work with children, but not all parents have the interest or the ability needed to assume the educator role (Turnbull & Turnbull, 1982). The parent-child relationship is affected in subtle ways by parental teaching. Observations of parent-child interaction have shown that, even in unstructured settings, parents of children with disabilities often assume managerial and teaching roles (Stoneman, Brody, & Abbott, 1983). In comparison with parents of normally developing children, these parents are more controlling and less playful (Floyd & Phillippee, 1993). Although many essential skills can be taught during play, if every interaction is structured as a lesson, there is a danger that the joy and spontaneity of the relationship will be lost for both the parent and the child. An alternative approach, relationship-focused intervention, encourages parents to be less directive and more observant with their children (Mahoney, 1988). The goal is to facilitate child development via sensitive, routine parent-child interactions, rather than structured lesson plans.

Advocate

Although all parents are advocates for their children, this role has a special meaning for parents of children with disabilities. As parents become better informed about their child's condition through professionals, experience, and other parents, they realize the advocacy role that they must play throughout the child's life (Vadasy et al., 1986). Although parents may look forward to the time when their child enters school and is eligible for a full range of special education services, they soon realize that when special education services increase, so do their advocacy responsibilities (Farran, Metzger, & Sparling, 1986). Parents are expected to monitor the child's program to determine whether the school placement is appropriate. They must be well informed about appropriate goals and objectives, laws, and special services in order to advocate. Although advocacy has often been seen as a middle-class activity, new efforts have been made to empower lower-class parents to assume this role (Kalyanpur & Rao, 1991).

Identity as a "parent of a child with special needs" is reinforced by advocacy activities. In the advocate role, parents have numerous contacts with professional services that are diagnostic, educational, and therapeutic. They also are encouraged to work on public policy issues that will improve the well-being of all children with disabilities and their families. Indeed, many of the legislative changes described in Box 11-1 that have benefited this population have come about as a result of hard-working parent advocates.

Emotional Reactions

Most parents, regardless of social class or cultural background, want their children to be happy and successful. New parents have dreams and fantasies about their child's future accomplishments, and they take pride in their child as he or she develops. When a child is disabled, dreams are shattered and hopes are dashed. The high value that society places on intelligence, physical beauty, and physical skills make parents' acceptance of their child's disabilities difficult.

Patterns of Acceptance

Investigations focusing on parental acceptance have suggested two models to explain the way in which parents come to terms with their children's disabilities. The first model is a stage theory, with parental acceptance emerging after parents have progressed through three predictable emotional stages. The initial stage is described as a period of shock and possible denial. As the shock fades and denial becomes less logical, parents enter a period of emotional disorganization. During this time the parent is grieving and can become immobilized by anger, guilt, resentment, or sadness. Finally, parental grieving wanes; parents adjust to the reality of the situation and accept their role in relation to the child. Parents who cannot accept the child's disability become stuck in one of the first two stages (Turnbull & Blacher-Dixon, 1980), a situation that adversely affects parental well-being. For example, one study found that when mothers of preschool children with disabilities continue to ask "Why me?" several years after the diagnosis, they scored lower on a measure of personal well-being (Shapp, Thurman, & DuCette, 1992).

Although this sequence of emotional reactions describes the experience of some parents, it may be too simplistic to be applied to all cases. An alternate theory suggests that parental grief will reappear throughout the life span of the child as new challenges emerge (Wikler, 1981). Discrepancies between parental expectations and child achievement occur repeatedly for the parent of a child with disabilities. This may happen when the child fails to meet common developmental milestones, such as walking or leaving home, or when a younger sibling surpasses an older child. In either situation, parents may feel stressed by the reminder that their child is not following a normal developmental pattern.

Stress Milestones

In addition to these developmental markers that elicit negative emotions, other stressful events are unique to parents of a child with disabilities. These include the initial diagnosis, attempts to secure appropriate services, the child's transition to a new service program, discussions of institutionalization, and decisions about guardianship (Wikler, 1981).

The *diagnosis* of a child's disability is a painful event in the life of a parent (Bernheimer, Young, & Winton, 1983). Sometimes the news is sudden and unexpected—the reaction shock and disbelief. The parent may feel the need to seek a second opinion from another professional, hoping that there has been a mistake. In other cases, the diagnosis confirms a parental suspicion that something is wrong with the child. Although saddened by the diagnosis, parents may also feel somewhat relieved to know that there is a problem, that the child's behavior is atypical, and that they are not to blame. A diagnosis brings with it the need for parents to know more about the child's condition and prospects for the future. As they acquire this information, parents may feel anxious about the child's uncertain future and ambivalent about their new identity as parents of a special needs child (Waisbren 1980).

One way in which parents deal with grief brought on by the diagnosis is to try to help the child by *securing appropriate services.* Unfortunately, this process can be stressful for parents because therapy, education, respite, and recreational services are often provided by separate agencies. There may be disagreement among professionals about the best way to intervene with the child, and parents may feel burdened by the responsibility of making these decisions. The best programs can have long waiting lists, resulting in frustrating delays (Bernheimer et al., 1983).

Children inevitably move from one set of service providers to another as they grow older. These *transitions between programs* can represent stress crises for parents. The family often becomes emotionally attached to the professionals with whom they interact. If they have developed a mutually trusting relationship, the parents may resent having to begin again with new people. Faced with new service choices, the parents must again select among various options or face the reality of limited services at the next stage. For example, one of the most difficult transitions for families is when the child with disabilities enters the public school system at three years of age. Dealing with this bureaucracy and advocating for services is often stressful (Bernheimer et al., 1983).

Parents of a severely disabled child may have to confront the possibility of *institutionalizing the child*. Discussions about institutional placements are anguishing, forcing parents to think about child, parent, and family needs. Parents are generally pleased with the facilities they choose; however, few will relinquish their child without feeling the pain of giving up a part of themselves (Blacher & Baker, 1994). Although deinstitutionalization and increased community support has been beneficial for many families, it may fuel feelings of guilt among those parents who opt for an institutional placement because they feel that they cannot cope with the child's disability. If raising a child with disabilities at home is now the norm, those who choose otherwise may feel that they have failed as parents.

Appointing a guardian, someone who will care for the disabled child when the parent dies, is also an emotionally difficult task. Provisions for the future must be made early if the parent realizes that there is little chance that the child will ever be able to live independently. Knowing how exhausting and emotionally draining their caregiving role is, parents may wonder whom they can ask to take on this responsibility.

The quotations in Box 11-2 describe in parents' own words the emotional issues they often confront when parenting children with disabilities.

Stress and Coping

Although much of the literature about parenting children with disabilities focuses on the negative effects on the family, it is clear that not all families respond in the same way. In fact, a large-scale study of parents of school-age special education students revealed that more than half reported no parenting stress (Palfrey, Walker, Butler, & Singer, 1989). What makes some families vulnerable and others resilient in the face of unusual child stressors? One model of family adaptation suggests that a parent's response to the stress of having a child with disabilities depends on three factors: child-related stresses, coping resources, and the family ecology (Crnic, Friedrich, & Greenberg, 1983).

First, the *number and intensity* of child-related stresses are important. Various studies have found that parents experience greater parenting stress when the child is male, lacks communication skills (Frey, Greenberg, & Fewell, 1989), or is multiply handicapped (Palfrey et al., 1989). Severe disabilities are more likely to affect family life in areas such as child care, parental employment, and vacation plans (Palfrey et al., 1989). A parent who feels stigmatized, exhausted because of additional caregiving demands, socially isolated, and burdened by the financial costs of treatment may have more difficulty than a parent who has only one of these issues to confront. Data from families of children with retardation show that out-of-home placements generally follow a gradual buildup of child-related stress and are unrelated to the child's age or level of retardation (Blacher & Baker, 1994).

Box 11-2 Parents of Children with Disabilities Talk About Their Feelings

The following quotations from parents of children with disabilities give us insight into their feelings at various points in time. Their words poignantly reveal some of the trials they must endure and the way in which everyday situations may elicit intense emotional reactions.

ANGER: Father of a son with microcephaly upon learning of the diagnosis: "I feel like I've been ripped off."

GUILT: Father of a multiply handicapped son who is searching for the cause of his child's disability: "If only I had driven faster when we were on our way to the hospital. Then the birth might have gone more smoothly and my son may not have suffered from a lack of oxygen. Perhaps he could have been normal."

FRUSTRATION: Mother of preschooler with cerebral palsy describing the stress she feels when the child is evaluated periodically:

"Martha has a slight speech and language delay and that makes it difficult in terms of cognitive and other evaluations. I guess I should say it makes it difficult for *me* because I know what lies behind those snappy black eyes. It's rather upsetting when I walk into an evaluation with a detailed list of things she does that indicate her intelligence only to have my list discredited because the items do not conform to some little checklist they have."

SADNESS: Mother of a five-year-old child with Down syndrome who is trying to cope with a younger sibling's developing skills: "Just when I thought I had adjusted to Lana's condition and was taking pride in her progress and accomplishments, her younger brother began to acquire skills that she hadn't mastered. It was so easy for him!"

DISAPPOINTMENT: Mother of a toddler with cerebral palsy who must decide on new equipment: "Joan is outgrowing her stroller and, therefore, I must face the difficult decision of having to select an appropriate wheelchair. I have to keep reminding myself that she'll get out of the darned thing when *she's* ready. Still, it's hard to take."

DESPAIR: Mother of four children whose seven-year-old daughter is undergoing leukemia treatment: "How do I cope? Sometimes I feel like giving up. I cry and tell my husband that I just can't go on. I can't watch Jennifer suffer with no guarantee that she will be cured. I lose hope. Then I decide that before I give up I'd better make supper for the kids, and life goes on."

ENVY: Mother of teenage boy who is severely impaired: "I look at our neighbors with teenagers. They have reached the stage of parenting when they can come and go without constantly worrying about their kids. They can go out for dinner, a movie, or a walk by themselves. I know now that we'll never have that freedom. We'll always have to be thinking of Christopher."

ANXIETY: Father of a multiply handicapped son who worries about his son's uncertain future: "Who will care for him after I'm gone?"

Source: Author's clinical work with parents.

Parental perception of the difficulty is important, because various parents interpret the same condition in vastly different ways (Gabel, McDowell, & Cerreto, 1983). For example, if parents of a child with mental retardation use only nondisabled children as a frame of reference, they are likely to be continually discouraged by the child's slow progress. If instead they look to special needs children as a comparison group, they may feel relieved that their children are making educational progress and remaining physically healthy (Frey et al., 1989). Educated parents, with higher aspirations for themselves and their children, tend to feel more stressed by the child's condition (Palfrey et al., 1989).

The second factor, *coping resources* available to the parents, can determine how successfully parents weather the storm. These resources may include parental health, social support, income, personality factors (sense of humor, feelings of self-efficacy), or religious beliefs. Coping may be facilitated by different resources at different points in time. When caregiving demands are intense, parental stress might be relieved by additional help in the home. If the financial resources or social support are not available to provide such respite, adaptation may be more difficult.

Finally, the *family ecology*, the context within which the parents experience the child, will make a difference. The context includes factors such as cultural beliefs, the neighborhood attitude toward people with disabilities and the presence of disabled individuals in the work place. Family adaptation may be easier when parents live in a community with excellent educational facilities and a commitment toward integrating people with special needs into everyday life.

Figure 11-1 summarizes this model of family adaptation.

The Family System

An important assumption of this text is that the parenting process evolves over time as the parent, the child, and the social context change. The experience of parenting a child with disabilities must also be considered from a life-

FIGURE 11-1. Family adaptation.
Source: Crnic, K.A., Friedrich, W.N., & Greenberg, M.T. (1983). Published by the American Association on Mental Retardation.

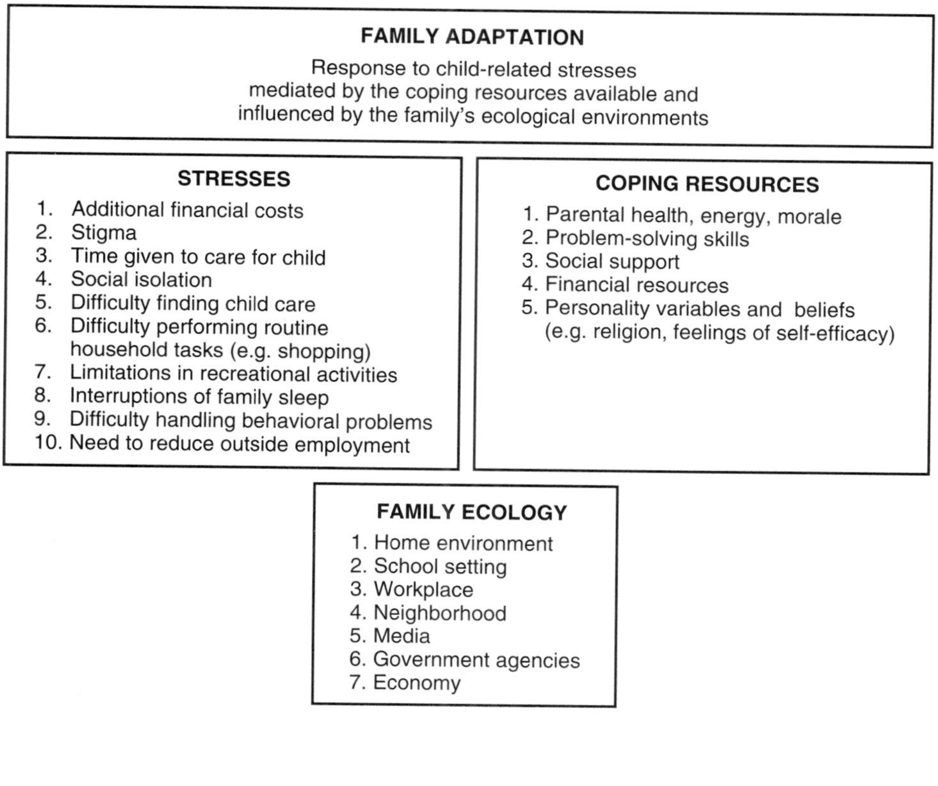

FAMILY ADAPTATION

Response to child-related stresses
mediated by the coping resources available and
influenced by the family's ecological environments

STRESSES	COPING RESOURCES
1. Additional financial costs	1. Parental health, energy, morale
2. Stigma	2. Problem-solving skills
3. Time given to care for child	3. Social support
4. Social isolation	4. Financial resources
5. Difficulty finding child care	5. Personality variables and beliefs
6. Difficulty performing routine household tasks (e.g. shopping)	(e.g. religion, feelings of self-efficacy)
7. Limitations in recreational activities	
8. Interruptions of family sleep	
9. Difficulty handling behavioral problems	
10. Need to reduce outside employment	

FAMILY ECOLOGY

1. Home environment
2. School setting
3. Workplace
4. Neighborhood
5. Media
6. Government agencies
7. Economy

span perspective, rather than as an isolated event (Beckman, 1984). Although parents of infants with special needs are still grappling with issues of acceptance, doubts about their own caregiving competence, and uncertainty about the future, they are also more optimistic than parents of older children with special needs. They expect a baby to be dependent, so the reality of the child's deficits may not be evident until major developmental milestones are not achieved. In contrast, parents of older children with disabilities worry about problems with peer relations, either because the child lacks social skills or because others reject those who are different (Miezio, 1983).

It is sometimes difficult for parents of children with disabilities to move through the parenting stages described in Chapter 1. For example, parents may fail to take on a more authoritative role with their disabled preschooler if they feel sorry for the child or fail to recognize that the child is capable of meeting reasonable demands. Parents of adolescents and adults with disabilities may have difficulty relinquishing control if they have been totally responsible for the child's well-being during childhood. The move toward independence may be threatening for parents whose identity has been defined by the child's needs for many years (Miezio, 1983).

There are differences between mothers and fathers with regard to emotional issues, coping styles, and cognitive experiences of raising a child with disabilities. As they do in all families, factors such as the number of parents, the quality of the marital relationship, the presence of nondisabled siblings, and the way in which the social support networks function will also affect parenting in families with disabled children.

Mothers and Fathers

Parents of children with disabilities are often more traditional in their gender roles, possibly as a result of difficult life circumstances. Mothers are more likely to give up outside employment to devote time to the special needs child (Schilling, Schinke, & Kirkham, 1985). Because they engage in more caregiving, they are more likely than fathers to experience physical exhaustion and parenting stress. Mothers tend to be more emotionally vulnerable and prone to guilt when something is wrong with their children (Featherstone, 1980). Although mothers are more burdened with caregiving, they are also more likely to develop a network of potential support persons because of their involvement with intervention services.

Fathers have more difficulty accepting the disability and are more likely to deny the seriousness of the problem at first (Schilling et al., 1985). They are particularly stressed when a boy has a disability, perhaps because expectations for sons are higher or because fathers traditionally engage in joint recreation with their sons. Fathers, who are less involved with daily caregiving, can more easily use avoidance as a coping strategy (Frey et al., 1989). Their reactions to the child's disability tend to be less emotional and more pragmatic. Fathers worry about the child's lack of success in the adult world and the need to provide for long-term economic support. Their pessimism about the child's future increases over time (Vadasy, Fewell, Greenberg, Dermond, & Meyer, 1986).

Fathers are less likely to have extensive social support networks. Whereas mothers discuss their trials and tribulations with friends, relatives, and organized support groups, fathers tend to rely only on the mother to discuss the child (Schilling et al., 1985). When support programs are available for fathers, participants feel less isolated, less depressed, better able to make decisions regarding their children, and more satisfied with their parenting role (Vadasy et al., 1986).

Few fathers stop working because of their children's disabilities, but their careers may be affected in other ways. The need to maintain a secure income and adequate health insurance can restrict a father's ability to change jobs. Even promotional transfers may have to be forgone if a new location does not have appropriate supportive services for a child with disabilities (Schilling et al., 1985).

In a study of families with young developmentally disabled children, the strength of the marital bond and the couple's ability to work together as a team determined the family's adjustment. Neither the severity of the disability nor the child's temperament was as important to family functioning as the quality of the marital relationship (Trute, 1990). Although a child with a disability could potentially "cause" a divorce, marital quality prior to the child's diagnosis is a key factor. Research suggests that a marriage that is faltering before the birth of a child with disabilities is less likely to be able to survive the parenting stresses previously described (Belsky, Lerner, & Spanier, 1984).

Single and married parents raising children with disabilities share similar goals and frustrations (Schilling, Kirkham, Snow, & Schinke, 1986). However, because single parenthood is often associated with social isolation and financial constraints, these families may be more stressed.

Siblings

The presence of a child with disabilities in the family changes the relationship between parents and nondisabled siblings. As mothers and fathers struggle emotionally, financially, and educationally to meet the needs of the child with disabilities, they may not be as available to other children in the family. School-age children with disabled siblings, especially girls, spend more time doing household chores and child care than their peers do. They also report more frequent arguments with their mothers. It is unclear whether this happens because overburdened mothers are less patient, or because there are more opportunities for conflict with parents when the sibling has greater responsibility for household and caregiving tasks (McHale & Gamble, 1989).

When parents fail to enforce rules or to discipline their children with disabilities, siblings may feel resentful and dissatisfied. In addition to differential treatment, they may experience the drain on the family's financial resources that the disability causes. They also may be embarrassed by the sibling and tired of explaining the disability to friends. Despite anger and resentment, siblings may feel that they cannot express negative feelings about a brother or sister who has a disability for fear of distressing the parents (Gabel et al., 1983).

Parents' self-esteem related to child rearing may come mostly from the accomplishments of nondisabled siblings (Farran, Metzger & Sparling, 1986). This puts pressure on siblings to succeed and to fulfill all their parents' hopes and dreams for the next generation. Some siblings feel trapped by the disability, because they realize that they will be responsible for caring for the child after the parents are deceased. However, a recent study suggests that many

Although children may be required to assume more caregiving responsibilities when siblings have disabilities, there are also opportunities to develop empathy and respect for individual differences.
(*Ursula Markus/Photo Researchers*)

siblings are willing to assume caregiving responsibilities in the future, but their parents are reluctant to have them do so (Griffiths & Unger, 1994).

On a more positive note, children whose siblings have disabilities may have a greater appreciation of their own well-being and capabilities. There is some evidence that they are more empathic and tolerant of differences in others. Family relations may be less strained when parents give siblings the information they need to understand the disability, to respond to inquiries from others, and to interact with the child with disabilities. Tension between the nondisabled child and other family members may be reduced if siblings are allowed to have an identity apart from the disability (Gabel et al., 1990).

Context and Social Support

The social and cultural context within which parents and their disabled children develop has changed markedly in the last few decades. For example, the development of new technologies has extended the life expectancy of many children with disabilities, but this trend has also created ethical dilemmas for parents making medical decisions for their children. Another trend, the movement away from institutionalization and toward "normalization," encourages parents to rear children with disabilities at home with community support. It is hoped that this movement will lead to more acceptance of individual differences within the community and foster social support for the parenting of special needs children.

Members of the extended family are the most obvious sources of support for parents of children with disabilities, but grandparents and other relatives may be immobilized by their own grief when a child is diagnosed. Grandparents react from a dual perspective. As parents themselves they may worry that their adult children will be burdened by a special needs child. As grandparents they must cope with the loss of the fantasized "ideal" grandchild. When extended family members are angry and sad, or when they cope with the news by denial and blaming, parents are robbed of much-needed support. For a father whose child has a disability, his relationship with his own parents is very important. If they are supportive, he will be better able to cope with the identity and stresses of raising a child with disabilities (Waisbren, 1980).

The cultural context will influence how various families experience a child's disability. The beliefs and practices of different cultural groups contribute to parents' understanding of the child's problem, to their ideas about what caused the disability, and to their attitudes toward intervention. Cultural beliefs may lead parents to view disabilities as the work of evil spirits, bad luck, or a punishment for parental wrongdoing. These differing perspectives will influence a parent-child interaction and social support. Although the dominant American culture bases its intervention services on an optimistic belief that change is possible, other cultures may be more fatalistic and view intervention as futile. When seeking help for their children with disabilities, some parents may view folk healers and spiritual remedies as more important than educational and therapeutic services (Lynch, 1992).

Parents of children with disabilities often feel isolated within their communities. It may be difficult for them to maintain friendships because of the time and energy they expend caring for the disabled child. If they feel stigmatized by the child, parents may avoid social contact. Isolation also occurs when neighbors avoid the family because they do not understand or cannot accept the disability (Parke, 1986). Parents may be shunned because of misinformation. For example, if neighbors do not understand that Down syndrome is a genetic disorder, they may wrongly assume that the child's disability has been caused by parental alcoholism. Although parents may have a need to be accepted by the community at large, they often benefit from sharing their thoughts and feelings in self-help groups with other parents of children with disabilities.

Professionals who work with the child and the family can be sources of support or stress. Offering caregiving advice, providing accurate timetables for development, and finding appropriate services for the family are ways in which professionals alleviate parental stress. Parent-professional relationships that are based on mutual respect, that focus on family strengths, and that take into account differences in parenting styles are most supportive (Kalyanpur et al., 1991). If service providers can help parents to establish their own ongoing support systems, they may become less dependent on professionals over time (Farran et al., 1986). Parents may feel stressed by intervention programs that fail to recognize parental needs (Kazak, 1986); some professionals blame parents for the child's problems. Rather than labeling stressed parents as weak, it may be more important to examine the adequacy of the social and economic support systems that could help the parents cope with the physical burdens and economic strains of caring for a disabled child (Lipsky, 1985).

THE CHALLENGES OF PARTICULAR DISABILITIES

Although there are common themes running through the experience of all parents of children with special needs, certain disabilities require special adaptations and are likely to cause special types of stress for parents. In the following sections, types of special needs are discussed in an effort to give examples of the ways in which parenting changes in response to particular child problems. A continuum of disabilities exists, as does a range of parent responses. As we take a closer look at prematurity, physical disabilities, mental retardation, and learning disabilities, a variety of parenting issues are explored.

Premature Infants

Approximately 10 percent of all births result in premature infants, born too early or with a low birth weight. Some causes of prematurity are unknown, and therefore beyond the control of expectant parents; however, inadequate prenatal care and poor maternal nutrition are the primary culprits, so prematurity is often a preventable problem. Unfortunately, the lack of health care for low-income families in the United States means that lower-class, uneducated, and impoverished women are more likely to have premature infants.

When a baby is born early or dangerously underweight, the child's development and the parenting process are at risk. Parents of premature infants are affected by the infant's physical characteristics, the professionals who immediately intervene to treat the child, and the support networks that may or may not materialize. Although the child's medical history will affect outcomes, the parent-child relationship has been found to be the major influence on the premature infant's development (Sammons & Lewis, 1988).

The transition to parenthood for those experiencing preterm births is usually sudden and unexpected. In full-term pregnancies, the last trimester is a time of preparation and of gradually coming to see oneself in the parenting role. When the pregnancy is precipitously ended and a fragile child is delivered, most parents are unprepared. For parents who were highly invested in natural childbirth, there may be a feeling of loss and disappointment. When sharing postpartum hospital rooms with mothers who have their babies with them much of the day, they may feel out of place and unsure of their role. Although no longer pregnant, mothers may not feel like "real" parents when sharing their technologically dependent infant with the medical staff (Sammons & Lewis, 1985).

To a greater extent than in full-term births, the premature infant's needs become central and the parents' needs are secondary. The major concerns of the mother focus on infant survival (Pederson, Bento, Chance, Evans, & Fox, 1987). Uncertainty regarding the child's survival and future abilities causes much anxiety, and may threaten the parents' willingness to invest themselves emotionally in a child they may lose.

Emotions are amplified by the atmosphere of the neonatal intensive care nursery (NICU), where parents may spend much time after the premature birth. Although medical intervention often leads to unusual separation of parent from infant, this does not necessarily cause long-term interference with attachment (Parke, 1986). Parents are advised to become involved in caregiving while the child is still in the NICU, to begin developing a relationship and to learn important skills that will be needed when the child is taken home. The transition from hospital to home is a significant milestone for most parents of premature infants, often filled with excitement, fear, and self-doubt (Sammons & Lewis, 1985).

Because the birth of a premature infant is an ambiguous event, extended family and friends may not visit the new parents or send baby gifts. Mothers who have the support of their husbands, their parents, or their church or synagogue seem better able to cope with the emotional issues surrounding the event (Pederson et al., 1987). Unfortunately, some potential sources of support may become negative influences. For example, the grandmother with strong beliefs that medical technology should not save high-risk children may never visit the NICU and may warn that such a child will bring only pain and suffering. When friends express sympathy for the parent and pessimism about the child's potential development, a mother's fears and sense of personal failure increase (Zarling, Hirsch, & Landry, 1988).

Preterm babies are generally less responsive than full-term babies, and the burden of maintaining parent-child interaction falls disproportionately on the parents (Parke, 1986). Parents must learn to read subtle physiological signals, being careful not to overstimulate the premature infant. The infant often cannot suck and look at the same time, so the positive feedback that many parents receive during a feeding session will be lacking (Sammons & Lewis, 1985). Biologically triggered responses, such as the social smile, will emerge more slowly in the premature infant. This means that parents must wait longer for the type of reinforcement that parents of full-term babies receive.

Labeling a child as premature immediately changes the caregiving environment because of stereotypes related to the label. To study the bias against prematurity, researchers give mothers an opportunity to interact with unfamiliar full-term infants that are arbitrarily labeled as either "premature" or "full-term." Mothers rate "premature" infants as less attentive, slower, less smart, quieter, and more passive than full-term infants (Stern & Hildebrandt, 1984). Similarly, when mothers interact with unfamiliar four-month-olds, they are less likely to touch the "premature" infant. If they believe that the baby is "full-term," they offer more advanced toys (Stern & Hildebrandt, 1986).

Fathers tend to be more emotionally involved with the premature infant than they anticipated. Studies of father participation also reveal that they are more likely to engage in caregiving tasks, such as taking the infant to the physician, bathing her or him, or consoling the infant after a nighttime waking. This is in contrast to fathers of children with other types of disabilities, who may be more avoidant (Parke, 1986).

Uncertainty about the future often plagues parents for many months and years after the child's medical problems have been resolved. They may experience a haunting feeling that some residual damage will hinder the child's development later on. Parents must adjust their expectations for the child's skill development. The practice of judging the child's abilities by the due date rather than by the birth date (using the "corrected age") for the first couple of years allows parents to judge the child more realistically.

Physical and Sensory Problems

Many physical and sensory disabilities are diagnosed at an early age, often at birth or during the first year of life. This timing means parents have fewer opportunities for denial and the parent-child relationship is affected by the disability from the outset. Despite early diagnosis, optimistic parents may hope that motor difficulties will mean delays but not complete dysfunction, that blindness is only partial, or that medical treatment will be discovered to cure the disease.

Parents of children with orthopedic problems must learn about special handling, positioning, and equipment. They often become in-home therapists for their young children, following prescribed exercise routines in an attempt to optimize development. As the child grows older and still lacks independence, physical caregiving demands and parental stress tend to increase. Although all parents must think about whether certain places are appropriate for children, those whose children have mobility problems must also consider whether a setting is accessible. A child's physical disability affects vacation plans and the ability to secure child care (Palfrey et al., 1989).

Most physical problems are visible and difficult to hide. Parents and their disabled children may feel stigmatized by things such as facial disfigurement, a wheelchair, or unavoidably messy eating routines. Siblings may feel embarrassed and sad when strangers stare or neighbors avoid the disabled child. Faced with ambivalent public reactions and the exhausting task of transporting nonambulatory children, some families isolate themselves. This deprives the parent and other family members of much-needed social support and recreational activities.

When a child has a disability, it may be difficult for both parent and child to develop a realistic view of the child's limitations and capabilities. Yet not doing so may cause a parent to become unnecessarily overprotective, and the child's self-concept may suffer. One clever mother developed a photo essay describing how her preschool daughter's leg braces were made, so that the child could share this information with her classmates and allay fears. As the four-year-old described her weak leg muscles and peers tried on the braces, there was no doubt that her self-esteem was intact. Parents will gain a new awareness of the physical disability when body image and peer acceptance become crucial issues for their children during school years and adolescence. Parents may have to work harder to facilitate a child's contact with peers and participation in age-appropriate activities, such as after-school clubs and shopping to choose clothing (Miezio, 1983).

Children with sensory deficits experience the world differently. A blind child does not see or respond to the parent's smile, and the hearing-impaired child is not soothed by a lullaby. When these children are unresponsive to vocalizing, smiling, and gesturing, parents may become discouraged, with-

Parents of this hearing-impaired child must learn to appreciate the child's unique way of interpreting the world. Sensitivity to subtle signals and communication that relies on the other senses may enhance parent-child interaction.
(Alan Carey/The Image Works)

drawn, or hostile toward them. It is possible to teach parents to recognize and appreciate different signals from their children. For example, if the mother of a blind child understands that the child is seeking social interaction when she searches for someone with her hands, the mother can respond to the child appropriately (Fraiberg, 1975).

When a child is chronically or terminally ill, parents may be shocked by the diagnosis and feel threatened by the responsibility of becoming medical managers. Since parents are supposed to be able to protect their children from physical harm, life-threatening illnesses pose a challenge to parental self-esteem. Parents of a medically fragile child must learn to be realistic about the child's condition, balancing necessary restrictions with opportunities for promoting social and intellectual development. Common pitfalls for parents include becoming overprotective, adopting a custodial role, or having unrealistically low expectations for the child (Shapiro, 1983).

Some illnesses are controllable and not life threatening if certain guidelines are followed. For example, diabetes can be controlled through diet and medication, asthma attacks may be averted if warning signals are heeded, and the risks associated with hemophilia can be minimized if dangerous situations are avoided and emergency routines practiced. When children are afflicted with these conditions, parents have a responsibility to teach them how to monitor themselves so that they can become appropriately independent.

When children are seriously ill, decisions about medical treatment weigh heavily on parents. The balance between the child's quality of life and the best medical course may be difficult to judge. The parent who realizes that a decision to proceed with chemotherapy will cause the child to suffer longer may feel responsible for the child's pain. Parents of medically fragile children may vacillate between denial and mourning. They may be unrealistically optimistic about the child's chances of survival, or emotionally withdrawn in order to protect themselves from an inevitable loss (Shapiro, 1983). When parents provide care for chronically ill children at home, mothers and fathers report increased levels of emotional distress (Leonard, Brust & Nelson, 1993).

Losing a loved one is never easy, but there are unique issues that make the death of a child particularly difficult. The unnaturalness of a child's death, unexpected social reactions, a grieving spouse, and problems relating to surviving children are factors that affect parental grief (Rando, 1985). The various coping strategies adopted by parents when they lose a child influence long-term adjustment (Videka-Sherman, 1982). Some try to escape the pain by avoiding thoughts about the child, an approach that is not adaptive over time. In contrast, others become preoccupied with thoughts about the child to the extent that no other thoughts or actions are possible. Preoccupation can immobilize the grieving parents, making it impossible for them to get on with their lives; however, if preoccupation leads to involvement with a sympathetic support group and altruistic behavior toward others in the same situation, depression is reduced over time. Box 11-3 describes some of the issues that parents confront when their child dies.

Mental Retardation

A diagnosis of mental retardation is generally not made at birth and, therefore, parents can carry their hopes and dreams for the child's future with them as they begin establishing the parent-child relationship. When the child fails to achieve developmental milestones, parents may become anxious, but professionals are reluctant to commit to a diagnosis until the child is older and can be properly tested. Even when a child is born with a clearly identifiable syndrome known to be associated with retardation, it is difficult to give parents an accurate prognosis. For example, retardation in children with Down syndrome may be mild, moderate, or severe. The belief that a retarded child's level of intellectual attainment is affected by environmental stimulation places a great deal of pressure on parents.

Parent-child interaction is altered when the child is retarded. Because these children are generally less responsive than their normally developing peers, parents must work harder to establish and maintain interaction. Researchers have shown that parents of children with Down syndrome are very responsive to their children's behavior, and yet they receive less feedback for their efforts than do parents of nondisabled children (Stoneman et al., 1983).

Confronted with a retarded child, many parents feel failure, lack of competence, and social isolation. Because children with mental retardation look and act differently, parents may feel self-conscious in public. Sometimes an innocent question by a clerk in a store ("How old is your daughter?") can be

Box 11-3 Coping with the Death of a Child

It is unnatural for a child to die before a parent. No matter what the age of the child, infant or adult, parents today do not expect to outlive their children. Unlike earlier times, when infant mortality was high and disease a constant threat, society now expects to be able to control most medical and safety issues. When a child dies today, parents may feel that they have failed to protect their child from harm. The death of a child means the loss of hopes and dreams for the child's future, and parents feel that they have lost a part of themselves. The unnaturalness of a child's death reminds parents of their own mortality.

Unfortunately, support networks may fail to comfort the bereaved parent. Friends often say the wrong things or try to avoid the issue completely. Unhelpful comments include those that criticize the child's medical care, make reference to the possibility of replacing the child with another, or trying to make positive comments about the loss (e.g., "It's probably for the best."). It is not uncommon for other parents to avoid the griever because they do not know what to say or because the situation makes them uneasy and fearful for their own child's life. Self-help groups, such as The Compassionate Friend, give parents who have suffered similar losses an opportunity to console each other. In fact, there is evidence that those who choose to become involved in such groups are those who are most preoccupied and overwhelmed when the child dies (Videka-Sherman, 1982).

Married parents have difficulty because the primary support person, the spouse, is consumed by his or her own grief and unable to offer support. Partners may become angry with each other because they grieve in different ways or they go through emotional highs and lows at different times. Sometimes parental anger leads to blaming each other for the loss of the child. (e.g., "If you hadn't let him go out that night, he wouldn't have been killed in the accident." "When I first noticed her pale color and wanted to take her to the doctor, you said not to worry."). Spouses are a continual reminder of the lost child they shared. Even couples with good histories of effective communication find their relationship strained in the face of this unusual stressor.

It may be difficult for grieving parents to relate to their surviving children, because they find themselves faced with the difficult task of maintaining their parental role at the same time that they are relinquishing it. If they are consumed with sadness, they may not have the energy to invest in everyday parenting responsibilities. Alternatively, they may become overprotective of their surviving children and place undue pressure on them to fulfill all of their unrealized hopes and dreams. Siblings often feel a pressure to fill the void left by the dead child (Rando, 1985).

Although the intensity of the grief may subside over time, parental mourning does not necessarily diminish entirely. It is common for bereaved parents to experience upsurges many years after the child's death. Some of these relapses are predictable, because bereaved parents tend to mark times when the child would have passed various milestones—graduation, marriage, and so on. There are also moments that hit the surviving parent unexpectedly—coming across an old photograph of the child, seeing the child's favorite dessert in the supermarket, and other such events (Rando, 1985).

misinterpreted by the parent as criticism ("Why is she acting like that if she's four years old?"). As children get older and the gap between them and their peers widens, the retardation becomes more of a reality for the parent and child.

It is sometimes difficult for parents of children with mental retardation to step back and allow independence. Parents worry that strangers will ridicule or take advantage of their less-capable children. One adaptive parenting response is to teach children rules of physical closeness so that they will know how to protect themselves from sexual exploitation. Because of the high value placed on intellectual achievement in our society, individuals with mental disabilities are less likely to succeed in conventional terms. At some point, even the most optimistic parents must confront the reality of the retarded child's limitations. This sentiment is revealed in the poignant words of the mother whose son is severely retarded, "As hard as he tries, he is still destined for scholastic failure, social rejection, and an inability to live independently, marry, or have children." (Farran et al., 1986).

Learning Disabilities

The largest category of children receiving special education services are classified as learning disabled (LD). Children with learning disabilities have academic difficulties that cannot be attributed to low IQ, physical impairments, or emotional problems. Parents are concerned about appropriate educational support, a child's self-concept, peer relations, the child's future in an achievement-oriented society, and the inordinate amount of time they must spend assisting the child with daily routines and school-related tasks (Waggoner & Wilgosh, 1990).

Unlike other problems, learning disabilities are generally not identified until school age. By then, the child has probably experienced a number of failures and the parent may have been frustrated by the child's inability to complete tasks. If the learning disability goes undiagnosed, parents and educators may attribute poor performance to laziness or misbehavior. Because the cause of a learning disability is generally unknown, parents may feel guilty when the problem is diagnosed, wondering if they have contributed in some way to the child's difficulties.

In the daily family routine, the child's confusion and lack of understanding may cause conflict in parent-child interactions. A child who cannot understand a complex direction may have to have the task broken down. A well-organized home environment with predictable routines can aid the child's faulty memory, helping him or her keep track of chores, clothing, and homework.

Parents of children with learning disabilities often find that much of their time is devoted to the child's education. As advocates, they must be sure that the child is receiving appropriate support in the school and that teachers are aware of the child's special learning style. Assisting the child with homework can be time consuming and frustrating. Extracurricular activities must be carefully chosen to avoid potentially frustrating and ego-deflating situations for the child.

Because they have experienced repeated failure and confusion both in the academic world and in accomplishing everyday tasks, children with learning disabilities may need more praise, approval, and reinforcement than other children. To enhance the child's sense of self-worth, the parent can structure and highlight success experiences for the child. For example, the child who cannot read might be praised for being helpful or for having a sense of humor.

Focusing on the child's strengths rather than on the disability builds self-esteem.

An emotionally difficult task for parents of children with learning disabilities is dealing with their children's problems in relating to peers. Parents report that friends tend to be younger and less mature than age-mates, which is probably appropriate given the child's lack of social skills. When children with learning disabilities are ridiculed for being "dumb," "stupid," or "clumsy," their parents also suffer. School-age children who have learning disabilities are often painfully aware of their problem. When they are educated about their disability and understand that they can compensate for the problem in learning situations, they may be realistic about their strengths and potential. Children with disabilities and their families will also benefit if the public—adults and children alike—is sensitized to individual differences.

The invisible nature of learning disabilities and their relatively late diagnosis make it difficult for parents to gain the social support available to those of children with other disabilities. Parents must work through feelings about their own self-worth, try to enhance the child's sense of self-esteem, and spend extra time working with the educational system.

PARENTING GIFTED CHILDREN

At first glance, it may seem strange to include a section on parenting gifted children in a chapter that has dealt predominately with families of the disabled. However, children who are exceptionally intelligent or those who have unusual creative talents also present parents with unique challenges and opportunities. How does it feel to have a gifted child and what parenting practices appropriately nurture these children?

Labeling

The term "gifted" conjures up both positive and negative images. On one hand the parent of the gifted child is envied. What could be better than having a bright, talented youngster who understands academic work without effort and who appears to be destined for success in later life? On the other hand, academically gifted children are stereotyped as having few social skills and being too serious for their years. Another problem with identifying children as gifted is that our society is ambivalent about elitist labels (Keirouz, 1990).

Most parents are fairly accurate in assessing their child's exceptional abilities. In fact, studies have shown that parents may be better than teachers at recognizing giftedness because they have more opportunities to observe the child's abilities (Silverman, Chitwood, & Waters, 1986). Whereas a teacher's perspective is often limited by the large group and by classroom activities, a parent views the child in a variety of situations and has the advantage of long-term observation. The task persistence and intellectual curiosity of a child may be apparent only in less structured circumstances without time constraints.

Calvin and Hobbes   by Bill Watterson

CALVIN & HOBBES © 1992. Watterson. Dist. by UNIVERSAL PRESS SYNDICATE.
Reprinted with permission. All rights reserved.

Labeling a child as gifted affects family relationships. In some families, parents disagree about the child's giftedness. Fathers are more likely to underestimate the child's abilities and to feel that mothers are exaggerating. When this happens, the resulting marital tension can adversely affect the parenting relationship (Cornell, 1983).

In studies of middle- and upper-class families, most parents describe their relationship with their gifted children as emotionally close, and they express very positive feelings about the child (Colangelo & Deltman, 1983). However, it is possible for the gifted child to wield an inordinate amount of power if his needs and wants become central. The label may result in extra family attention to the gifted child and an imbalance of power in the family system (Keirouz, 1990).

One problem that parents struggle with is their relationship with nongifted siblings. They may underestimate the abilities of their nongifted siblings, which can result in lower self-esteem and poorer adjustment for these children (Cornell, 1983). However, the negative effects of labeling on nongifted siblings may not be long term. Five years after the labeling, these children appear to accept the fact that a sibling's abilities are exceptional and do not express negative feelings about him or her (Colangelo & Brower, 1987).

Causality

Are gifted children the product of particular family characteristics or parenting styles? Studies of gifted school-age children have found that their parents tend to be intelligent, assertive, independent, conscientious, and persistent (Fell, Dahlstrom, & Winter, 1984). Adults with these characteristics may be very positive role models for and educators of their gifted children. These parents are more likely to be well educated, middle- or upper-class individuals with economic advantages that may nurture their children's giftedness. It is also true that gifted children tend to come from smaller families, and that they are often firstborns or only children who have benefited from adult attention (Clark, 1983). When compared with families of nongifted children, families of gifted children place a higher value on free expression of thoughts and feelings among family members, are more likely to be involved in non-competitive recreation, and are more interested in intellectual activities. Parenting styles tend to be authoritative, with minimal emphasis on rules and regulations (Cornell & Grossberg, 1987). These characteristics are probably more important than social class, since more than one-fourth of all gifted children are from lower-class or working-class families (Webb, Meckstroth, & Tolan, 1982).

Certain gifted children have been found to be underachievers and researchers have investigated the role that parents play in this phenomenon. Underachieving gifted children often have parents who are more rejecting and hostile, as opposed to warm and nurturing. Gifted children do not thrive when parents pressure them to achieve or set unrealistic goals for them. If gifted children feel valued only for their exceptional accomplishments and do not have warm and accepting relationships with parents, they are likely to be underachievers. Indifference to a child's special talents is also related to underachievement. A potential problem in lower-class families is that outstanding intellect may be considered nonconformist behavior. If the subculture does not value education or upward mobility, the parent may convey this message to the child by not reinforcing his or her intellectual curiosity or academic achievement (Clark, 1983).

Parenting Concerns

A gifted child influences parental self-concept, parent-child interaction, and parent-community relations. In the same way that parents of children with disabilities must focus on the child rather than the disability, parents of gifted children must learn to appreciate the child apart from his or her exceptional talents.

When parents realize that their child is gifted they may feel confused and uncertain about their role in nurturing the child (Saunders & Espeland, 1986; Keirouz, 1990). Some parents worry that they will not be able to meet this child's special needs, while others feel threatened by the child's knowledge and abilities. The gifted preschooler may have a high level of curiosity that results in an unending stream of questions. The gifted school-age child may understand concepts that baffle adults. It can be exhilarating to try to keep up with a quick mind—or it may be intimidating. Parents may be overwhelmed by the responsibility of helping the child reach his or her potential, and some may even feel guilty and inadequate. A few parents may envy their gifted or talented children; frustrated scholars or would-be composers may feel pride tinged with jealousy as they watch an exceptional child succeed.

Parent-child interactions are affected by the parent's perception of the child. Some parents have difficulty disciplining their gifted children, because they see them as so advanced. Precocity can enable the young child to make logical arguments to counter parental demands. If parents fail to place appropriate limits on the child's behavior, their increased tolerance for the child's demands can result in behavior problems (Keirouz, 1990). Forgetting that there is generally a gap between intellectual and socioemotional development, parents may not offer a gifted child the emotional support that he or she needs to negotiate social interactions. Parents may be confused when children are appropriately childish, because they are accustomed to mature responses in other domains. It is unreasonable to expect that a very verbal two-year-old will never have a tantrum.

Although as a group gifted children do not fit the "social misfit" stereotype, certain traits of gifted children may predispose them to socioemotional problems that are slightly different from those experienced by typical children. For example, an extremely bright nine-year-old girl who is fascinated by the internal combustion engine may find it difficult to locate peers with similar interests. The exceptionally talented five-year-old boy may be more logical than his age-mates in attempting to solve social disputes on the playground and may be frustrated by their inability to see the situation more accurately. Parents of a gifted teenager must understand that the child's perfectionism, awareness of others' high expectations, and gap between cognitive and emotional development may make her or him more prone to depression (Delisle, 1990).

Parental encouragement may be more important for gifted girls than it is for gifted boys. Since academic success, particularly in traditionally masculine academic areas such as math and science, is risky behavior for many girls, the support of both parents is particularly important. Sex stereotyping may be implied by parental behavior; fathers tend to be involved in quantitative areas and mothers tend to encourage verbal areas. These behaviors can inadvertently hinder exceptional mathematical ability in girls (Raymond & Benbow, 1989).

Participation by parents in the world outside the family is also influenced by the gifted or talented child. Many parents feel isolated and unable to relate to the issues confronting parents of more typical children (Saunders & Espeland, 1986). Parents who are trying to nurture a child's exceptional talents in music or athletics may find their lives consumed by the child's practice routine, and have little time for other community activities. Some parents are wrongly accused by neighbors and relatives of exaggerating their children's abilities, of pushing their children, and of being elitist (Keirouz, 1990). Joining a support group for parents of gifted and talented children brings them together with others with similar needs.

In the same way that parents of the disabled are advocates for their children, parents of the gifted and talented are concerned with finding appropriate educational placements for their children. Although this need is explicitly protected by legislation, many parents dislike the advocacy role they must assume. In an era of dwindling resources, special programs for the gifted may be perceived as unnecessary and in competition with funding for other special education programs. However, research indicates that gifted children may become underachievers or develop behavior problems if they are not appropriately challenged in school (Clark, 1983). Because parents of gifted children tend to be conscientious and intelligent, they are potentially good allies for teachers who want parents to elaborate on the child's educational experience in the home (Fell et al., 1984).

- Parents of special needs children are affected by many of the same factors common to other parents, but they also face unique challenges. When a child has a disability, the parents' behavior, self-concept, and relations with others are affected. The amount of time and energy devoted to caregiving increases, while educational issues take on new importance. Parents often assume an advocacy role as they attempt to secure appropriate services for their children, thereby reinforcing their identity as "parents of special needs children."

- The task of parenting a child with a disability can also be emotionally difficult. Although mothers and fathers experience their roles differently, both may react with sadness, guilt, anger, or a sense of failure. Over time and with development, the parent-child relationship changes. There may be times of optimistic acceptance and periods of renewed sorrow. Adaptation at any point in time will depend on the number and type of child-related stresses, the parents' coping resources, and the family ecology.

- Social support plays a major role in helping parents cope with the demands and uncertainties of parenting a child with a disability. Unfortunately, when family and friends are uncomfortable with the child, parents lose an important resource. Some parents find that professionals and formal support groups offer guidance and emotional support. The cultural context, including the availability of services and attitudes of acceptance, can help or hinder the process of parenting a disabled child.

- Most gifted children have intelligent parents who are responsive to their children's interests and who take pride in their children's accomplishments. When parents pressure a child to excel or exploit a child's talents, the parent-child relationship is threatened. If parents neglect or belittle a child's special abilities, the child may become an underachiever. The innate abilities of gifted children are nurtured when parents provide a stimulating cognitive environment coupled with appropriate social and emotional supports.

CHAPTER 12

Parenting in High-Risk Situations

In the same way that children's characteristics influence the parenting process, mothers and fathers bring unique strengths, weaknesses, and personal histories to the parent-child relationship. A parent's age, habits, and abilities have an impact on child-rearing behavior. Similarly, the ecological context within which parents and children interact can nurture or threaten development. In most families, ordinary parent characteristics combine with favorable environmental conditions to produce normal parenting patterns. However, in other families normal patterns are disturbed because of adverse personal and environmental factors (Sasserath, 1983).

This chapter focuses on parenting under less than optimal circumstances and begins by describing the concept of risk and protective factors. The literature on adolescent parents, substance-abusing parents, and parents with disabilities is reviewed in order to highlight themes associated with parenting in high-risk situations. For each of these groups, there tend to be multiple risk factors that threaten the parent-child relationship, but there are also potential protective factors that can buffer the impact of adversity.

The final sections of this chapter consider the causes and consequences of child maltreatment. Intervention strategies and public policy issues that pertain to high-risk groups are discussed in an effort to provide insight into the ways in which parents who are at risk for dysfunctional parenting can be identified and given the support and assistance they need.

RISK AND PROTECTIVE FACTORS

Risk factors are conditions or circumstances that make healthy development difficult. These include such parental characteristics as poor mental health, substance abuse, or immaturity. Such environmental characteristics as low socioeconomic status, a dangerous neighborhood, or lack of community services also compromise child rearing. However, none of these individual risk factors alone necessarily causes parenting problems. Rather, a risk factor increases the likelihood that something will go wrong with the child-rearing process and that children or parents will be adversely affected. When a family is subjected to several risk factors, the probability of poor outcomes increases significantly (Belsky, 1980). Unfortunately, this "multiple risk" scenario is quite common, because in many contexts risk factors tend to occur together. For example, a parent who abuses substances may find it difficult to hold a job. The resulting economic instability may increase the likelihood that a family will be homeless or living in an unsafe neighborhood with poor schools.

Two environmental risk factors deserve special mention because of their increasing significance in American society: poverty and violence. As noted in Chapter 1, the economic well-being of families is an aspect of the parenting context that affects how well the physical and psychological needs of children and adults are met. Unmet medical needs, substandard housing, inadequate nutrition, and a sense of helplessness contribute to the lower quality of life for poverty-stricken families. When the primary needs of parents are unmet, it is more difficult for them to recognize and be responsive to their children's needs. Poverty increases the likelihood that several risk factors will simultaneously influence the parenting process and that the effects will be cumulative (Halpern, 1990). The chronic stress associated with poverty undermines parent-child interaction and interferes with child-rearing goals (Huston, McLoyd, & Garcia Coll, 1994). The significance of this problem is reflected by recent statistics showing that more than 21 percent of children in the United States live below the poverty line, with a disproportionate number of those numbers representing ethnic minority groups (U.S. Bureau of Census, 1992).

The violence pervading some communities is another risk factor that threatens child rearing. One of the most important responsibilities of parenthood is protecting children, and yet parents living in dangerous surroundings feel frustrated by their inability to fulfill this basic function. Parents who fear for their own safety may be emotionally unavailable to their children. Others may become overprotective of their children and unable to allow age-appropriate independence. In violent communities, neighbors may be unavailable to support one another because they are so preoccupied with their own survival (Osofsky & Jackson, 1993/1994).

Under high-risk conditions some families suffer tragically while others seem to survive and grow. What makes family members resilient in the face of adversity? *Protective factors* are characteristics of individuals or circumstances that reduce the risk of developmental difficulties. Factors such as the personality of the individual parent or child, the presence of nurturant friends, or the availability of community services can buffer the effects of a high-risk context, enabling parents and children to thrive despite potentially damaging situations (Rutter, 1990). One of the contributions that parenting research has made to the well-being of families is that it has identified protective factors and suggested ways to counteract risk. When protective factors are not naturally occurring, policies and programs can be implemented to serve as a "safety net," thereby decreasing the likelihood of poor outcomes for parent and child.

ADOLESCENT PARENTING

Although the overall birth rate in the United States has declined steadily during the past two decades, the birth rate for unmarried teens has risen during this same period (see Figure 12-1). Of particular concern is the marked increase in teenage parenting among "young teens," those under the age of fifteen (Hayes, 1987; Osofsky, 1990). Most teen pregnancies (80 percent) are unplanned and unwanted. Although there is a higher incidence of teen pregnancy among African Americans, white teenagers in America are also more likely to become parents than their counterparts in other countries. In fact, they are four times more likely than their peers in Sweden to bear a child (Jones et al., 1986).

Early childbearing can put both parent and child at risk, but not all are adversely affected. How well they adapt is affected by parent characteristics including social background, personal abilities, and life plans. The support provided by informal social networks and formal intervention programs can also be an important factor. Finally, the life course of the family after the birth, such as additional children, marital decisions, and employment history, will influence parenting outcomes (Furstenberg et al., 1987).

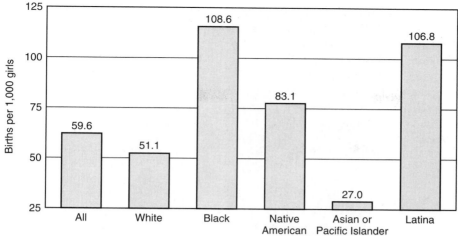

FIGURE 12-1. Teen births and ethnicity of mother, ages 15–19, 1993. Far higher poverty rates and weaker basic academic skills among Black and Latina teenagers are key reasons why their teen birth rates are much higher than those of whites. *Reprinted with permission from (November 1995)* CDF Reports, *the monthly newsletter of the Children's Defense Fund. Latina data added by author from National Center for Health Statistics (1995).*

Teen Parents

Although adolescent parents are found in all segments of society, many are poor, single mothers with low levels of education who depend on public assistance. It is this group that has been targeted by researchers, and therefore our knowledge of teen parenting under other conditions is limited. For example, few studies tell us about teen mothers who continue to enjoy the benefits of a middle-class lifestyle. This research bias must be kept in mind as the risk factors associated with adolescent parenting are outlined below.

Does early childbearing lead to poverty and academic failure, or is it these risk factors that increase the likelihood that an adolescent will become a parent? Although it is difficult to separate cause and effect, researchers have found that girls from low SES families who lack self-esteem and have poor grades in school are more likely than their peers to become teen parents (Rickel, 1989). For example, one study revealed a high incidence of undetected learning problems among teen mothers, and suggested that early parenthood may be an alternative to school failure for these girls (Rauch-Elnekave, 1994). In contrast, girls who choose to terminate an unplanned pregnancy or release a child for adoption tend to be academically motivated, from higher SES homes, and are optimistic about the future (Rickel, 1989). The fact that teens with the fewest skills and bleakest futures are more likely to have babies creates a high-risk parenting situation.

When teens become parents, they may suddenly be judged by adult standards rather than adolescent standards. This forced maturing and sudden role change can be stressful. Like their babies, immature parents are struggling to

Courtesy of the Children's Defense Fund.

survive, develop, and grow. Having a baby obviously complicates the normal course of adolescent development. The teen mother may be suddenly cut off from peers and their leisure activities, but she does not comfortably fit in among older mothers (Rickel, 1989). Economic difficulties and the demands of child rearing can make the daily life of an adolescent parent stressful. Young mothers who want to stay in school or seek employment are often thwarted by the need to piece together complex child care arrangements. Also, under these conditions the mother may have little time to spend with her children.

In interactions with their infants, many teen mothers are responsive and nurturant. Others fail to match their responses to the child's developmental needs. They may have inappropriate expectations for their babies, either over-estimating or underestimating their competencies. For example, teen mothers may expect "too much too soon," trying to make an infant hold a bottle and sit before the child is biologically ready. Paradoxically, they also have a tendency to "expect too little too late," becoming more controlling of a child's activities during the toddler years when the child is being appropriately independent. These patterns may be due to the mother's immaturity, her lack of knowledge of child development, or stressful life circumstances (Osofsky, 1990).

Research has revealed that the period immediately following the birth of the first child and the development of the family until the child enters school is a particularly stressful period for teen parents, as it is for all parents. However, it is important to determine if the effects of early childbearing are temporary or long-lasting. A seventeen-year follow-up study of more than 300 lower SES mothers in Baltimore found that there was a "recovery process" for some early childbearers. A majority of the mothers in the study eventually completed high school, found employment and managed to escape earlier dependence on public assistance. As young adults they were far better off than they had been during the period immediately following childbirth. However, most did not do as well as they might have done when compared with young women from similar backgrounds who did not experience early childbearing. This suggests that teen parenthood does not doom the teen mother to failure, however, it does make child rearing much more challenging and may "set limits" on potential achievements (Furstenberg, Brooks-Gunn, & Morgan, 1989).

Much less is known about teen fathers. Fewer young boys become parents, because half the children born to teen mothers are fathered by adult men. Among adolescent fathers, social class differences predict involvement. White middle-class youth who plan to go to college and pursue careers do not want to sacrifice these goals for parenthood. Consequently, they may encourage a girl to terminate her pregnancy or believe that the teen mother is responsible for the child she chooses to bear. In contrast, black teen fathers often show partial involvement with the mother and child, continuing some contact without assuming full responsibility (Rickel, 1989). Although marriage can be an important path to economic security and recovery for early childbearers, most married teens are economically disadvantaged. It may be very difficult for two teenagers with limited education to make enough money to support a family (Furstenberg et al., 1987).

Children of Teen Parents

Babies born to teen mothers are at a higher risk for prematurity, low birthweight, and developmental delays. It is poor nutrition and inadequate medical care, not physiological immaturity, that causes these problems. A recent study of nonpregnant black and white female adolescents revealed nutritional deficits (Sargent, Schulken, Kemper, & Hussey, 1994). Because many teen mothers come from disadvantaged backgrounds, their access to prenatal care may be limited. Young and inexperienced, they may not fully understand how a junk food diet, smoking, and drugs can jeopardize their unborn children. Studies of middle-class teens have shown that those who receive adequate prenatal care do not have an unusually high risk of birth problems (Rothenberg & Varga, 1981).

Most infants of teen mothers develop normally, but developmental problems may begin to emerge during the preschool years. Behavior problems such as aggressiveness and poor impulse control are often observed in boys raised by teen mothers (Chase-Lansdale, Brooks-Gunn, & Paikoff, 1991). Lower levels of school achievement are also evident, but not for all groups. Children from poor families with high levels of stress are less likely to achieve (Furstenberg et al., 1989). Also, the mother's intelligence and educational level are important factors. More intelligent teen mothers who complete more grades of school are likely to read to their children and provide enrichment activities for them. These experiences contribute to a child's elementary school success (Barratt, 1991).

When children of teen mothers are adolescents, they continue the pattern of school failure and often engage in early sexual activity. This contributes to the intergenerational cycle of adolescent pregnancy whereby the daughter of a teen mother is more likely to become an early childbearer herself. Ironically, teen mothers often state that their most important goal is to help their children avoid their mistakes, especially early parenthood (Furstenberg et al., 1987).

The Role of Social Support

The beneficial effects of social support on teen parenting have been studied extensively. For example, teens who can rely on their extended families for help with child-rearing problems provide better home environments for their children (Stevens, 1988). Those with inadequate support systems are more likely to reject their infants (Colletta, 1981). There are three possible sources of social support for a teen mother: family, father, and peers.

Child care and parent training are the two forms of support often provided by a young mother's family. A study of black inner-city families revealed different ways in which the intergenerational relationship can be structured (Apfel & Seitz, 1991). The most common pattern is when mother and grandmother jointly share responsibility for the child. This arrangement enables the teen mother to complete her education and to share major decisions regarding the child with someone. In other families, boundaries are more clearly drawn, with either the teen parent or the grandparent taking primary responsibility. However, the model of support that seems to have the best long-term benefits is when the grandmother serves as a "mentor" to her daughter. In these families, grandmothers help their daughters adjust to the parenting role by teaching them necessary skills; however, they also encourage the teens to gradually assume more responsibility when competence and confidence increases. Teen mothers who experience this mentoring model have good relationships with their infants and with their own mothers.

Teen mothers often live with their families of origin. This arrangement has positive effects if it is limited to the first few years of child rearing, because it allows that very young parent and her child to benefit from nurturing and skillful grandmothers. However, when coresidence exceeds five years, mothers tend to be less self-sufficient and more dependent on welfare (Furstenberg et al., 1987). It is also important to note that living with a dysfunctional or impoverished family of origin may not be supportive, because grandparents in these situations may be unable to provide the stable environment that teen parent and child need (Rickel, 1989; Chase-Lansdale, Brooks-Gunn, & Zamsky, 1994).

The fact that teen fathers are not encouraged to take an active parenting role minimizes their potential as a source of support. Many teen mothers, overwhelmed by the demands of child rearing, lack the time and energy needed to develop relationships with other men who might offer emotional support. A longitudinal study of high-risk teen mothers revealed that those who had stable live-in relationships with men were more likely to have securely attached infants. In contrast, the emotional bond between mother and child was more likely to be troubled when relationships with men were unstable or nonexistent (Egeland & Farber, 1984).

Peer support may be most available in minority subcultures in which many other young girls also have children. In white middle-class communities where adolescent parenthood is less common, teen mothers may be more isolated from peers (Rickel, 1989). Social interaction among teen mothers may occur through school-based programs that bring young mothers together. Here they have an opportunity to talk with others who share their experience.

Public Policy

As a group, teenage parents have received attention from educators and public policy makers. Interventions aimed at reducing the risks associated with teen parenting have been developed. Offering prenatal care to reduce the medical complications associated with early childbearing, discouraging school dropout, providing vocational assistance, offering parenting classes, and encouraging adolescent parents to delay additional pregnancies are approaches that have been tried. Some programs offer one or more of these

When high schools provide child care for the children of teenagers, both mothers and children benefit. Mothers are more likely to finish high school and children's development is stimulated by educational programming.
(Carrie Boretz/The Image Works)

components, while others have attempted to be comprehensive. Planners must consider the unique needs of young parents with regard to self-esteem, coping strategies, cognitive maturity, and decision-making skills.

Child care has been found to be a key component of support for teen mothers. Providing free educational day care from birth for the children of disadvantaged single teenage mothers has been linked with positive outcomes for both mother and child. One study revealed that mothers who had access to this service were more likely to finish high school, continue postsecondary training, and become self-supporting. Their children benefited from the educational programming, scoring higher on cognitive skills tests than did children whose teen mothers had not had access to free day care (Campbell, Breitmayer, & Ramey, 1986).

A demonstration project providing comprehensive services in New Haven, Connecticut, yielded long-term benefits for low-income teens and their children. Beginning during pregnancy and continuing until the child was thirty months old, families received extensive medical care, home visits, day care, and periodic developmental examinations. Participants were more likely to become financially self-supporting. Parents enjoyed nurturing relationships with their children, and their children were more likely to succeed in school. These positive effects were still evident ten years after the program ended (Seitz, Rosenbaum, & Apfel, 1985).

A policy that helps mothers delay subsequent childbearing reduces risks for both mothers and children (Furstenberg et al., 1987). Special public schools for pregnant teenagers have been successful in this regard. In one such program, low-income African-American students who attended for more than two months after the birth of their first child were less likely to have another child during the next six years. Program officials speculate that these results may be due to program support during a period of time when the teen mothers are making decisions about contraception and sexual activity after pregnancy, as well as the positive effects of finishing high school (Seitz & Apfel, 1993).

Community responses to teenage parenthood have changed over the past several decades. Teens are no longer discouraged from continuing school and infant child care is now more available. These trends have opened up opportunities for young mothers earlier in their children's development. However, we do know that teen mothers with long-range goals and life plans are more likely to use these community resources, making the best of a difficult situation for themselves and their children (Hayes, 1987). If those with severe educational deficits are at greatest risk for dropping out of school and becoming permanently reliant on public assistance, this group must be targeted for special attention. Thus far, the needs of adolescent fathers have been ignored. Programs that focus on education and job training for disadvantaged males may be another way to reduce the risks associated with teen parenting (Furstenberg et al., 1987).

In addition to providing support for teen parents, social policy makers must explore ways of reducing the number of unplanned pregnancies among adolescents. Box 12-1 describes approaches to this problem.

┌───┐

Box 12-1 Reducing Adolescent Pregnancy: Policy Implications

When compared with other industrialized countries, the United States has one of the highest rates of adolescent pregnancy. The risks associated with teen parenthood are well documented and, although ameliorative services to teen parents and their children can make a difference, they are extremely costly and may be difficult to implement. Prevention efforts aimed at delaying early sexual activity and improving contraceptive use among sexually active teens have been recommended (Hayes, 1987).

Sex education programs have worked on changing attitudes about early sexual involvement and have promoted abstinence as a safeguard against premature parenthood and sexually transmitted disease. A comprehensive parent education program that begins in kindergarten and continues throughout childhood and adolescence is needed. These programs must deal not only with the biology of reproduction, but with the emotions and responsibilities that accompany parenting. Some programs must target young boys, a group that may not receive accurate informal information about sexuality and contraception.

Cross-cultural research has identified factors that are associated with lower rates of adolescent pregnancy (Jones et al., 1986). Countries with lower levels of poverty and national health care programs have fewer pregnant teens. This may be because teens have access to free or low-cost contraceptives. In the United States, when family planning clinics have been established in inner-city high schools, teens have been more likely to delay their first sexual experience and have avoided pregnancy when sexually active.

Cultural attitudes, specifically an openness about sex as a part of human development, are also linked with a lower incidence of teen pregnancy. Although the general public in the United States is outraged about the high numbers of teen parents, adolescents receive contradictory messages about sexual activity. Sexual themes are used in advertising, music, and television shows, yet taboos against premarital sex result in teens' receiving minimal support and guidance with regard to sexual decision making. In contrast, European nations have high rates of teenage sexual activity, but low rates of adolescent pregnancy and childbearing because there are not the same kinds of mixed cultural and political messages.

Reprinted with permission from *Risking the Future: Adolescent Sexuality, Pregnancy, and Childbearing.* Copyright 1987 by the National Academy of Sciences. Courtesy of the National Academy Press, Washington, DC.

PARENTING AND SUBSTANCE ABUSE

When parents abuse alcohol and other drugs, they are more likely to have problems raising children. In all socioeconomic groups, substance abuse affects pregnant women and their unborn children. In addition, the characteristics of substance abusers and their chaotic environments have indirect effects that put the parent-child relationship at risk.

Addicted Parents

The personal characteristics associated with problem drinking and substance abuse include low self-esteem, emotional immaturity, depression, and social isolation. The context in which addicted adults engage in child rearing is often plagued by unemployment and unstable home environments. Poverty is common, and addiction can be so compelling that parents will use what money they have on drugs rather than on food, shelter, and clothing (Hawley & Disney, 1992). This profile does not bode well for successful parenting.

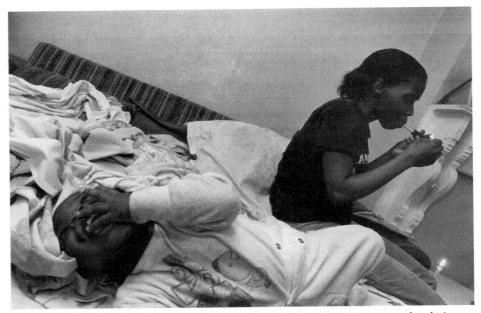

Adults who abuse substances often provide unstable home environments for their children. This mother is so focused on her addiction that she ignores her crying child's needs.
(Eugene Richards/Magnum)

The stress of child rearing can contribute to an increased dependency on alcohol and drugs. As in other high-risk situations, an escalating cycle of inappropriate parent-child interactions may develop. For example, parents who are drunk may be unresponsive to children's needs. When a child cries to gain the attention of the caregiver, the drunk parent may lash out with an angry response and drink more to cope with the anxiety of a stressful situation. The connection between substance abuse and child maltreatment has been established, with as many as 40 percent of child abuse cases involving substance abuse (VanBremen & Chasnoff, 1994).

Women who abuse drugs often neglect their health. As noted in Chapter 4, poor nutrition and a lack of prenatal care put the child and the parent at risk. Although some children are clearly harmed in utero by substance abuse, parents differ in their willingness to accept blame for a child's drug-related disability. Some parents deny that the child has a problem as a way of denying their own addiction problem. Other parents feel guilty and angry. For a group that tends not to accept responsibility for their actions, this recognition that the drinking behavior has contributed to the child's problems may be seen as positive. However, because they cannot heal the child, accepting blame may also result in feelings of frustration and depression and more maternal drinking (Weiner & Morse, 1992).

In families where only one parent has a substance-abuse problem, the other parent may be able to provide the stability children need. More often, however, the spouse is too busy accommodating the partner's addiction and neglects child-rearing responsibilities. Unfortunately, in stressed families where the father is a problem drinker, mothers tend to offer inconsistent discipline and are less supportive of their young adolescent children (Roosa, Tein, Groppenbacher, Michaels, & Dumka, 1993).

Effects on Children

The influence of parental substance abuse on children is both physiological and psychosocial. Although much attention has been focused on the adverse effects of drugs on the developing fetus, equal consideration must be given to the effects of dysfunctional parenting on the child. Sometimes research has failed to specify whether children have been directly affected by drugs in utero, or whether they have been indirectly influenced by parental addictions that result in poor child-rearing environments.

Prenatal exposure to drugs is associated with prematurity, low birth weight, and symptoms of drug withdrawal. A disorganized nervous system can make caregiving more difficult. Irritability, jitteryness, and inattentiveness make these children more difficult to feed and soothe. Such behaviors put infants at risk, especially with parents who are consumed by their own addictions.

The long-term effect of prenatal exposure to drugs is an area of concern, but a complex topic to study. As noted in Chapter 4, the timing and intensity of teratogens during the prenatal period will influence outcomes. It is sometimes difficult to get reliable information regarding these variables from addicted mothers. Although the popular press has painted a bleak picture regarding the future of children who suffer prenatal cocaine exposure, research showing that this phenomenon causes permanent damage is lacking. For example, one longitudinal study found that when the early environment was appropriate, children outgrew their early symptoms of drug exposure by age two and showed few drug-related cognitive deficits. This study points to the postnatal environment as a more important determinant of child outcomes (Chasnoff et al., 1992).

In contrast, the lasting effects of fetal alcohol syndrome (FAS) have been demonstrated. Mental retardation, facial deformities, and developmental delays are typical of FAS children. For these children, the quality of the home environment can either increase the likelihood of disability or buffer the child from risk (Hawley & Disney, 1992).

It is not unusual for children to be neglected by their drug-addicted parents, either abandoned at the hospital or unattended in the home. Neglect can result in children's assuming adult-like responsibilities at a very young age or becoming rebellious to get attention. Children who blame themselves for parental addiction problems experience failure repeatedly when they are unable to fix the situation. As adults, children of alcoholics are often plagued by low self-esteem, have trouble forming relationships, and are prone to addictions themselves (Woititz, 1983).

Intervention

Policy makers have taken many approaches to the problems of substance-abusing parents. Prevention education and outreach take place through schools, community-based programs, and public service announcements. The warning labels on liquor bottles and informational posters in public places are efforts to convey essential facts to large numbers of people. In an attempt to intervene early and provide appropriate prenatal care, many hospital clinics have developed special programs to treat pregnant women with a history of substance abuse (Hawley & Disney, 1992).

Parent education programs can be designed to address the specific concerns of addicted populations and their children. If a child has been affected by prenatal exposure to drugs or alcohol, parents must understand the child's difficult behavioral characteristics. For example, parents of infants with FAS may need to explore ways of intervening without picking the child up, because such a response tends to intensify the child's restlessness. They also need information regarding typical growth and feeding problems so that they can avoid becoming too frustrated when the child does not follow a normal developmental course (Weiner & Morse, 1992).

The link between recovery and parenting has been studied. Parents who lose custody of their children because of their addiction, or those in danger of losing them, are often motivated to seek addiction treatment; however, planning an intervention to treat both addiction and parenting simultaneously may be difficult. The methods used by substance-abuse counselors are often rigid and punitive, whereas parent educators tend to take a more supportive stance. If program planners recognize that recovery will result in improved parenting and that strengthening parenting skills will aid in recovery, both goals will be addressed and considered equally important (VanBremen & Chasnoff, 1994).

Interventions with children of addicted parents can support development and indirectly influence the parenting relationship. Children who are affected by prenatal drug exposure may need intervention to stimulate growth and learning. If children can experience positive interactions with alternate caregivers, they may become more animated and less depressed. This change in a child's affect can sometimes pull the mother into a more expressive relationship with the child. Children who have been overly responsible because of their caregiver's addiction need opportunities to experience a "normal" childhood and the comforts of a responsive environment (VanBremen & Chasnoff, 1994).

Some of the more successful interventions have taken a comprehensive ecological approach to treating the mother-child dyad that is threatened by substance abuse. Because substance abuse is not an isolated problem, a "one-stop shopping model" that offers addiction treatment along with other vital services may be necessary. Box 12-2 describes one such program that makes extensive outreach efforts, treats both mother and child, and includes a variety of services at one location.

PARENTS WITH DISABILITIES

With the societal trend toward deinstitutionalization of people with disabilities, there is an increased likelihood that children with disabilities growing up

Box 12-2 A Model Program for Drug-Addicted Mothers and Their Children

To minimize high-risk parenting among drug-addicted mothers, intervention programs must offer extensive services for both parent and child. Operation PAR (Parental Awareness and Responsibility) in St. Petersburg, Florida, is an exemplary program that recognizes the specific needs of this population. First, persistent counselors have an aggressive outreach program that includes going to food stamp offices to find prospective clients and making repeated offers of help. When they are willing to consider help, mothers find that a full range of maternal health services and social support services are provided at one location, a "one-stop shopping" model. Options include residential treatment, outpatient counseling, a weekday treatment plan, detoxification, child care, transportation to and from treatment, residential facilities for mothers and children, and training in parenting skills. An important prevention component of the program is that it also focuses on reducing the risk of future pregnancy for its clients.

Although research on the effectiveness of this program is lacking, the model does use strategies tailored to the needs of the drug-addicted mother. For example, the intervention acknowledges that both the mother and the child need assistance. When Operation PAR was first developed, it focused solely on the mother and attrition rates were much higher. Also, the nature of drug abuse makes it difficult for clients to commit to and coordinate services for themselves or their children. The case management component of the program addresses that issue. Finally, this is an ecological intervention that recognizes the extensive help that high-risk parents need to manage their parenting role in the context of their chaotic lives. Participation and effectiveness increase when the parent, child, and context are taken into account.

Taken from: Hawley, T.L., & Disney, E.R. (Winter 1992). Crack's children: The consequences of maternal cocaine abuse. *Social Policy Report,* 6(4), Society for Research in Child Development.

in the community will become parents. Parents with disabilities may be at risk because they lack certain skills or experiences that facilitate nurturance, but they also suffer from limiting societal attitudes. Although some parents with disabilities will fail in child rearing, others are successful parents, and it is important to understand what makes the difference (Greenspan & Budd, 1986). Unfortunately, there are few role models for this group of parents (Baskin & Riggs, 1988).

Mental Retardation

The developmental history of a mentally retarded adult may present some problems for parenting. Issues related to sexuality, parenting, and social role development are often ignored when raising a child with mental retardation. For example, they may not have been taught problem-solving skills necessary to make decisions related to parenting, such as how to organize a child's schedule, or the social skills needed to use community services. Also, the education and training of people with mental disabilities often relies heavily on behavioristic techniques and external rewards. This learning history may reduce the motivation to engage in an activity such as parenting that has few

This parent's disability does not interfere with her
enjoyment of shared activities with her children.
(Michael Weisbrot/Stock, Boston)

tangible rewards. A history of academic and social failures may lead to low
self-esteem in mentally retarded adults, and this makes it difficult for them to
praise their children (Espe-Sherwindt and Kerlin, 1990). "Developmental jealousy" is another emotional issue common among parents with mental disabilities. When children acquire intellectual skills and become more capable
than the parent, a sadness about limitations may surface (Greenspan & Budd,
1986).

Researchers have been able to identify the circumstances under which parents who are mentally retarded are more likely to succeed—when parents are
only mildly retarded, in a stable marriage, and have only one child (Greenspan
& Budd, 1986). The same stresses and supports that predict positive parenting for
nonimpaired parents are important for those with limited intellectual abilities,
including physical health, financial well-being, and formal or informal support
networks. When extended family members and professionals have confidence in

parents with mental disabilities and they provide opportunities for competence to emerge, both child and parent thrive (Tymchuk, Andron, & Unger, 1987). For example, it is often the grandparents who offer guidance, model child-rearing strategies and provide appropriate toys for their grandchildren.

How do lower levels of intelligence affect a parent's ability to socialize a child? There are three areas that researchers cite as potential pitfalls. First, when parents do not understand basic concepts, they may be less able to teach their children about the world. Children are then developmentally at risk for delayed language and cognitive skills (Feldman, Case, Towns, & Betel, 1985). Second, mental retardation may also be associated with a lack of practical intelligence that jeopardizes the quality of care the child receives. Parents may be underprotective and make judgment errors that endanger the child. For example, they may not provide appropriate nutrition or medical care. Similarly, because they may overestimate the child's capabilities and cannot foresee negative consequences, they may allow the child to be unsupervised in a dangerous place. Finally, impaired intelligence may be a problem in terms of discipline. If the parent has limited abilities in perspective-taking, he or she may have difficulties understanding the child's behavior and providing appropriate guidance (Greenspan & Budd, 1986).

Physical and Sensory Disabilities

The physical demands of giving birth and caring for a child may put parents with physical or sensory disabilities at risk. Although adults with disabilities are accustomed to confronting physical and psychological barriers in the world around them, the parenting role requires new adaptations and introduces new prejudices into their daily routines. When the general public mistakenly equates disability with general incompetence, parents who are hearing impaired or blind, or have motor problems face unique challenges.

The developmental history of a parent with a physical or sensory disability may include some of the difficulties outlined in Chapter 11. If they were overprotected as children, they may be unprepared for independent living or for intimate relationships. If a disability has interfered with labor force participation, the parent may be economically disadvantaged. When a physical or sensory disability occurs after marriage and childbearing, it stresses the family relationships in which parenting is embedded. For some people, disability leads to social isolation and the parent will lack the social support networks that buffer stressful child rearing years. However, many people with disabilities have learned, prior to parenthood, that they must rely on others to help them negotiate daily life (Baskin & Riggs, 1988).

Women who view their bodies as imperfect because of a disability may be particularly proud when they are successful in bearing a child. Pregnancy and childbirth connect them with other women and validate their status as adults. Physical and sensory disabilities may require caregiving adaptations. For example, parents with hearing impairments may need to rely on monitors that use lights or vibrations as signals to alert them when an infant is crying. A blind mother might decide to attach a bell to her crawling infant or wandering toddler. Practical problems such as these are most frequent during the child's early years.

Friends and relatives may need to provide children with experiences that the parent cannot. For example, only a sighted person can teach colors; only a hearing person can answer children's questions about sounds. If parents are unable to drive and public transportation is inadequate, parents with certain disabilities may have to rely on other people to transport their children. However, when a parent's access to places or activities is blocked, the children's experience may be compromised since they cannot share the activity as other families do. This can happen when a nursery school or dance studio does not have ramps or elevators that offer access for wheelchairs (Baskin & Riggs, 1988).

Children make adaptations to parents' disabilities. Infants learn that in order to attract the attention of a hearing-impaired parent they must use touch and visual cues, not sound. Other babies accommodate to a parent's visual impairment when they move toward a spoon to get food, rather than waiting for the parent to find the child's mouth. Parents who move slowly because of mobility problems may find their preschool children adjusting their own pace during outings or relying on visual contact to ensure safety.

There is no empirical evidence suggesting that a parent's physical or sensory disability leads to child maladjustment (Baskin & Riggs, 1988); however, when children take on responsibilities that parents who are not disabled manage in other households, they may feel angry. There is a danger that what begins as "helping" the parent can lead to a dependency relationship in which the child is being asked to assume an adult-like role. Another important issue, especially for school-age children and adolescents, is how the parent's disability is perceived by peers. Although early exposure to disability may have a positive effect on children's acceptance of individual differences, there is a danger that they will be teased by others and feel embarrassed.

Intervention

Because of their high-risk status, many parents with disabilities are closely scrutinized by child protective agencies. In custody cases, courts may highlight the disability and fail to consider whether it interferes with the parent's ability to care for the child. Rather than focusing on terminating parental rights, some experts believe that agencies should be protecting parental rights, trying to help these parents do a better job, and educating the public about the strengths and capabilities of parents with disabilities.

Social workers must be educated to realize that although parents with mental disabilities are at risk, they may be able to improve their parenting skills (Greenspan & Budd, 1986). Inappropriate parenting behaviors must not be misinterpreted as hostility toward the child or disinterest in the parenting role. For example, parents with mental disabilities can be taught decision making and can learn to engage in responsive, child-centered interaction (Espe-Sherwindt and Kerlin, 1990). Sometimes creative interventions are needed. Day care centers, a temporary live-in therapist, or a group living situation may assist the parent in nurturing and educating the child (Greenspan et al., 1986).

Parents with physical or sensory disabilities must have support systems adapted to their needs. One frustration expressed by this population is that access to parent education is often denied. When doctors do not take time to communicate with pregnant and parenting women who are hearing impaired, important information may not be communicated. Unless parenting books are available in braille, many parents cannot use them. Advocacy groups can support child rearing by sharing information about adaptive equipment and services that enable parents with disabilities to enjoy normal activities. Supportive public policies, such as legislation requiring buildings to be accessible, can enable this high-risk population to parent more effectively.

CHILD MALTREATMENT

The previous sections highlight some of the adverse child outcomes that are associated with parenting under high-risk conditions. One of the most devastating and difficult to understand is child maltreatment by parents. Although it may seem unconscionable for a parent to harm a defenseless child, a closer look at the dynamics of child abuse and neglect offers some logical, although heartbreaking, explanations. With this theoretical understanding comes hope for prevention and treatment.

According to the Children's Defense Fund (Figure 12-2), 2.9 million cases of child maltreatment are reported each year (Children's Defense Fund, 1994). However, this figure may underestimate the problem because it is difficult to secure accurate data on the incidence of child maltreatment. Despite increased public and professional concern for this issue, underreporting

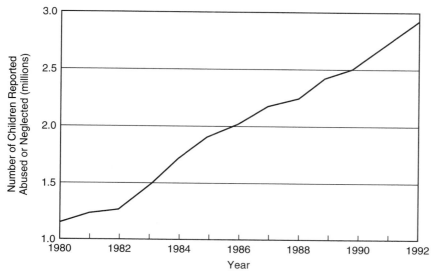

FIGURE 12-2. Abuse and neglect.
Reprinted with permission from The State of America's Children Yearbook: 1994. *Washington DC: Children's Defense Fund.*

occurs. One problem is that the definition of abuse and neglect may be culturally determined. What many Americans perceive as cruel treatment may be part of cultural tradition elsewhere. Also, the taboo against child maltreatment and the belief that family matters are private contribute to unreported cases.

Types of Maltreatment

Categories of child maltreatment are defined legally and psychologically. *Physical abuse* is the most often reported type of child maltreatment. The abusing parent may harm the child by shaking, shoving, beating, or burning her or him. Although this type of maltreatment accounts for only 10 percent of the total cases of abuse, it is the most likely type to be lethal to the child. Physically abused children may be overly aggressive or abnormally withdrawn. They are likely to exhibit discipline problems in school and to be wary of adults (Eckenrode, Laird & Doris, 1993).

The most prevalent type of maltreatment is *neglect*. Failing to provide the child with proper food, clothing, medical care, or education constitutes neglect. Neglected children often appear unkempt, ill, withdrawn, and inappropriate in social situations.

There has been an increasing concern about *sexual abuse,* which involves fondling, intercourse, or exposing genitals to the child. A child who is being abused in this way may exhibit symptoms ranging from fear, depression, and anger to sexually inappropriate behavior. Long-term effects also include feelings of stigma, poor self-esteem, problems trusting others and sexual maladjustment (Browne & Finkelhor, 1986).

Emotional maltreatment includes actively ridiculing the child or passively ignoring the child's needs for emotional support. When a child repeatedly hears "You can't do anything right" or "Shut up, stupid," self-esteem may be permanently damaged. Children who have been neglected emotionally by an unresponsive caregiver are often developmentally delayed. In infants, one of the most serious symptoms of emotional neglect is nonorganic failure to thrive, a growth disorder caused by lack of affection and stimulation.

Table 12-1 summarizes the physical and behavioral indicators associated with different types of child maltreatment.

Causes of Maltreatment

In the same way that our perspective on the parenting process includes the influence of many factors, our explanations for child maltreatment must be complex. Child maltreatment by parents is determined by characteristics of the individual parent, the family situation, the social context, and cultural values. The number and intensity of risk factors that come together determine the likelihood of abuse and neglect (Belsky, 1980).

When child abuse first became a subject of study in the early 1960s, it was assumed that *parent psychopathology* was the cause. Abusing parents were seen as evil people and attempts were made to uncover the mental disorder that caused this behavior. Studies failed to identify the "abusing personality" but

TABLE 12-1. Physical and Behavioral Indicators of Child Abuse and Neglect

Type of CA/N	Physical Indicators	Behavioral Indicators

Physical abuse	Unexplained Bruises and Welts:
	  on face, lips, mouth
	  on torso, back, buttocks, thighs
	  in various stages of healing
	  clustered, forming regular patterns
	  reflecting shape of article used to inflict
	    (electric cord, belt buckle)
	  on several different surface areas
	  regularly appear after absence, weekend,
	    or vacation
	
	Unexplained Burns:
	  cigar, cigarette burns, especially on soles,
	    palms, back, or buttocks
	  immersion burns (sock-like, glove-like
	    doughnut shaped on buttocks or genitalia)
	  patterned like electric burner, iron, etc.
	  rope burns on arms, legs, neck, or torso
	
	Unexplained Fractures:
	  to skull, nose, facial structure
	  in various stages of healing
	  multiple or spiral fractures
	
	Unexplained Lacerations or Abrasions:
	  to mouth, lips, gums, eyes
	  to external genitalia
		Wary of Adult Contacts
		
		Apprehensive When Other
		  Children Cry
		
		Behavioral Extremes:
		  aggressiveness
		  withdrawal
		
		Frightened of Parents
		
		Afraid to Go Home
		
		Reports Injury by Parents

did find that abusive parents often lack experience caring for children, do not understand child development, and consequently have unrealistic expectations about parenting (Check, 1989). Abusive behavior is more likely in adults who have poor impulse control and low self-esteem. Sometimes substance abuse weakens natural inhibitions that might prevent harming another person. Physical abuse is an inappropriate emotional outlet for those who are angry and frustrated; sexual abuse is an inappropriate means of sexual gratification.

Because abusers often have a history of maltreatment, some researchers have focused on the intergenerational transmission of abuse. Congruent with social learning theory, a direct modeling effect has been supported by empirical data; that is, parents who have been exposed repeatedly to harsh parenting tend to reflexively use these techniques with their own children. With only negative models of child rearing, they lack information about how to parent effectively (Simons et al., 1991). To break the cycle of abuse, it may be necessary for adults to consciously reject the attitudes and behaviors of their own parents (Trickett & Susman, 1988).

Intergenerational transmission of maltreatment may also be explained in terms of attachment theory. Abused children may never learn how to form and nurture positive relationships. This legacy from the past is carried into future

301

TABLE 12-1. Physical and Behavioral Indicators of Child Abuse and Neglect *(continued)*

Type of CA/N	Physical Indicators	Behavioral Indicators
Physical neglect	Consistent Hunger, Poor Hygiene, Inappropriate Dress Consistent Lack of Supervision, Especially in Dangerous Activities or Long Periods Constant Fatigue or Listlessness Unattended Physical Problems or Medical Needs Abandonment	Begging, Stealing Food Extended Stays at School (early arrival and late departure) Constantly Falling Asleep in Class Alcohol or Drug Abuse Delinquency (e.g., thefts) States There Is No Caretaker
Sexual abuse	Difficulty in Walking or Sitting Torn, Stained, or Bloody Underclothing Pain or Itching in Genital Area Bruises or Bleeding in External Genitalia, Vaginal or Anal Areas Venereal Disease, Especially in Preteens Pregnancy	Unwilling to Change for Gym or Participate in PE Withdrawal, Fantasy, or Infantile Behavior Bizarre, Sophisticated, or Unusual Sexual Behavior or Knowledge Poor Peer Relationships Delinquent or Runaway Reports Sexual Assault by Caretaker

Emotional maltreatment	Habit Disorders (sucking, biting, rocking, etc.)
	Conduct Disorders (antisocial, destructive, etc.)
	Neurotic Traits (sleep disorders, speech disorders, inhibition of play)
	Psychoneurotic Reactions (hysteria, obsession, compulsion, phobias, hypochondria)
		Behavior Extremes:
		  compliant, passive
		  aggressive, demanding
		Overly Adaptive Behavior:
		  inappropriately adult
		  inappropriately infant
		Developmental Lags (physical, mental, emotional)
		Attempted Suicide

parent-child relationships. The same personal history that interfered with attachment relationships may also prevent adults from developing a social support network that could enhance parenting. However, only 30 percent of abused children repeat the cycle with their own children (Kaufman & Zigler, 1987). Those who can overcome their personal histories and create positive relationships with their children generally have experienced nurturance from a significant other at some point in their development (Egeland, Jacobvitz, & Sroufe, 1988).

Our description of the parenting process in Chapter 1 highlighted the importance of parent cognitions or beliefs. Researchers have found that parent perceptions of child behavior and child-rearing practices differ in abusive and nonabusive families. For example, a study that surveyed parents of children four to eleven years found that abusive parents were less satisfied with their child's characteristics and perceived child rearing as more difficult and less enjoyable (Trickett & Susman, 1988). In another study, a sense of parental powerlessness was more likely to be found in families referred for physical abuse. When parents believe that they cannot influence their children's behavior, they are more likely to become tense and annoyed by a "difficult" child (Bugental, Mantyla, & Lewis, 1989). Not understanding children's motivations, abusers sometimes become very angry because they believe that their children are intentionally trying to irritate them (Emery, 1989).

The child-rearing styles used by maltreating parents have been examined. Using the theoretical model outlined in Chapter 2, abusive parents are expected to be low on responsiveness. Neglecting parents are likely to be unresponsive and undemanding (Baumrind, 1994). Abusive parents report using more severe forms of physical punishment (e.g., striking the face, hitting with an object, pulling hair) rather than reasoning. They tend to discourage independence and autonomy in their children (Trickett & Susman, 1988).

Most abusers do not intend to hurt their children and many are shocked and frightened when they discover what they have done. Researchers have found that abusive parents are more prone to angry responses because they do not know how to manage their anger. Box 12-3 describes one program that is designed to teach parents how to express anger constructively.

Social scientists now believe that, although parents who abuse their children do share some common personal characteristics, it is these traits in combination with other circumstances that predict abuse. For example, there are *child characteristics* that may contribute to an abusive situation. The age of the child is a factor to consider, since most abuse occurs in children under the age of three. Caring for infants and toddlers can be exhausting, and these children lack the independence needed to escape parental anger. Infants may be particularly vulnerable to "shaken baby syndrome," brain injury caused when a baby is shaken in anger. With the exception of sexual abuse, boys are more likely than girls to be victims. Boys may be more vulnerable because of their higher activity levels and higher likelihood of having developmental problems (Belsky, 1980).

An aversive cry, a lack of social responsiveness, or negative behavior may trigger abuse. Some studies have found that babies born prematurely or children who are ill are at higher risk for abuse, because the stress of caring for them can turn a vulnerable parent into an abuser. As highlighted in the previous section, this scenario often occurs when substance-abusing parents attempt to care for the difficult child who has been affected prenatally by drugs. On the other hand, a passive child who does not make demands on the parent may be neglected (Belsky, 1980).

Some scholars have taken the position that the causes of child abuse and neglect are primarily social-structural, rather than psychological (Baumrind, 1994). An ecological perspective requires an examination of the family in the social context to identify potential threats to adaptive parenting. For example, *stressful situations* contribute to maltreatment. Although abusive parents are represented in all social classes, a higher percentage live in poverty, have large families, manage single-parent households, and lack social support (Emery, 1989). There is an increased likelihood of maltreatment among those who have unplanned or unwanted pregnancies (Altemeier, O'Connor, Sherrod, & Vietze, 1984), which makes the potential for abuse higher in teen parenting situations. Also, unemployment of the father has been found to be a common precipitating factor in child abuse (Steinberg, Catalano, & Dooley, 1981). All families are called upon to cope with a certain amount of stress, but when tolerable levels of stress are exceeded, abuse is more likely.

The immediate environment, both physical and social, may play a role in triggering abusive behavior in the high-risk parent. For example, sexual abuse by fathers is more likely to occur when the mother is absent, sick, or powerless (Check, 1989). Studies of low socioeconomic neighborhoods reveal higher levels of maltreatment when neighbors are transient, child care is unavailable, and there are few opportunities for family recreation (Coulton, Korbin, Su, & Chow, 1995; Garbarino & Sherman, 1980). Maltreating parents tend to be socially isolated. When they are confronted by stressful parenting situations, they lack connections to others that might buffer the stress. Social isolation may also explain intergenerational aspects of abuse, because isolated

---

Box 12-3 Teaching Parents How to Express Anger

The physical and emotional abuse of children is sometimes linked to uncontrollable parental anger. Child abusers are usually angrier than other parents and are less capable of managing their anger, but all parents can benefit from learning anger management techniques. To this end, the Institute for Mental Health Initiatives has created a program that clinicians can use to help parents deal with their anger. The program is built on the acronym **RETHINK.** Each of the seven letters represents an important part of anger management. A clinician can help parents by teaching them to:

Recognize when they are angry, when their children are angry, or when anger is covering other feelings, such as shame, fear, stress, or fatigue.

Empathize with the person who is making them angry. What is he or she feeling or thinking?

Think about the same situation in a different way. Often, anger comes from the way we look at things. Parents should try to find humor in the situation. What can parents tell themselves to change the way they feel?

Hear what the other person is saying—feelings as well as the words themselves. Parents should repeat what they hear to make sure they understand correctly.

Integrate love and respect with an honest expression of their anger. Children can learn that a parent's angry feelings will not break the bonds of love.

Notice what their bodies feel like when they get angry. This may include increased heart rate, breathing changes, headache, upset stomach, muscle tension.

Keep attention on the present problem. Don't bring up old grudges.

Practice is important if anger-management skills are to become part of a parent's behavioral repertoire. Clinicians can suggest ways to learn and apply **RETHINK** skills by selecting a skill to work on each week or by having the parent keep an "anger" journal.

Originally published as Clinicians can help parents RETHINK their anger in *Child and Adolescent Behavior Letter,* 9(5), 1–3, 1993.

parents may not be exposed to new child-rearing beliefs (Trickett & Susman, 1988).

Finally, the *cultural context* plays a role in child maltreatment. Two characteristics of the United States make at-risk parents vulnerable. First, the acceptance of violence and physical punishment differentiates us from other countries. For example, it is illegal to spank a child in Sweden, but physical punishment is considered acceptable in the United States (Steinberg & Belsky, 1991). Second, the U.S. legal system regards children as parental property. The government regards family matters as private and is reluctant to intervene.

It should be evident that the causes of child maltreatment are interrelated. Interviews with abusive parents illustrate ways in which multiple risk factors combine to increase vulnerability. One example is the child who had an undiagnosed milk allergy who vomited and had diarrhea for the first six months of life. He was inconsolable, yet the pediatrician told the mother that nothing was wrong. She was repulsed by the child and felt like a "bad mother." This particular parent had been abused as a child and her husband had left her a single parent. This scenario includes all the ingredients for maltreatment—a parent who is vulnerable because of her developmental history, child characteristics that create stress, and a lack of social support.

Effects on Children

The way in which children react to child abuse can be discussed in terms of immediate reactions and long-term effects. Children may become fearful of the parent and adept at figuring out how to avoid the parent's wrath. They tend to be lonely and hungry for affection. They may have difficulties forming intimate relationships because they are accustomed to rejection and ambivalence. It is not unusual to find older children who are victims of abuse exhibiting aggressive behavior and failing academically (Check, 1989; Emery, 1989).

One of the most lasting effects on some abused children is the increased tendency to abuse their own children when they become parents. However, this cycle can be broken by the protective factors of social support. Children who are able to break the cycle of abuse are those who are nurtured by a nonabusive adult during childhood, later participate in therapy, and have more stable relationships with a mate (Egeland et al., 1988). Long-term outcomes for children are more positive when they understand that the abuse was not their fault and when they find other important adult role models (Check, 1989).

Intervention

Social policy regarding child maltreatment has changed in recent history; parental treatment of children is no longer considered a private family matter.

From an early age, children learn "protective behaviors" and are advised of their privacy and safety rights. All fifty states have child protection laws that require professionals to report suspected child abuse and neglect. Physicians and other service providers are trained to recognize signs of maltreatment and the high-risk situations that make families more vulnerable.

If parents at risk for maltreatment are identified, intervention can provide the educational and emotional support needed to cope with raising a child in stressful situations. Parents who might not tell someone that they are at risk for maltreating their children may present other signs. For example, a father who repeatedly brings a healthy child to the emergency room and insists that something is wrong with the child may be asking for help in an indirect manner. When the potential for maltreatment is high, prevention might include parent education about child development, teaching alternative child-rearing strategies, strengthening social support networks, and improving the economic conditions that create unmet physical needs.

One approach to prevention has been the use of home visitor programs with high-risk mothers (Olds & Henderson, 1989). First-time parents who are single, low-income, or young demonstrate lower incidences of abuse and neglect when they receive education, support, and linkages to other services from a nurse visitor. This intervention begins during pregnancy and may continue for a period of one to two years after the child is born. Program researchers are continuing to investigate how long such programs should continue in order to accrue benefits in the most cost-effective manner.

One of the most well-known organizations devoted to this problem is Parents Anonymous. This nationwide organization provides support groups and a 24-hour phone hotline that parents can call when they are stressed or fear hurting their children. Another approach is to provide child care so that parents can get respite from child-related stress. Therapeutic day care offers a setting in which the child and parent can interact with supervision during the day (Check, 1989).

What can be done to intervene when maltreatment is detected? Children usually need therapy to help them understand what has happened and to repair their battered self-esteem. Parents may need individual counseling and group support in order to redirect their impulses and change their behavior. The trend is to treat parents and their children in the home, rather than removing the children to foster care. Home-based treatment enables parents and children to cope with the situation as it exists, or to identify ways to reduce the stressful nature of the context. Even when they have a history of abusive interaction patterns, parents and children are usually attached to one another and want to be together. Separating children from their parents is considered a drastic step; however, when the child is in danger, removal from the home may be necessary. See Box 12-4 for a description of foster parenting.

SUMMARY

- Certain people are considered at risk for parenting because of their developmental history, personal characteristics, and stressful situations. Our review of the literature on teen parenting, substance-abusing parents, and

Box 12-4 Foster Parenting

Foster homes provide a temporary alternative when children's well-being is jeopardized in their own homes. If parents have been unable to provide adequate care and children have been neglected or abused, social service agencies will seek a substitute caregiver through a foster placement. Most of these placements are involuntary, but some parents look to the foster care system as a "last resort" attempt to meet the child's needs until family conditions improve.

Foster parents are primarily women who have had experience raising their own children (Dando & Minty, 1987). Most foster parents receive little training for this role, despite the fact that the children they are choosing to nurture on a temporary basis may come to the foster home with many problems. They are motivated by a desire to help others and view themselves as providing an important service; however, the foster parent role is perceived ambiguously by foster children, biological parents, and society at large. A small number of foster parents may choose to adopt a child for whom they have cared if the biological parents terminate their rights. A larger number continue contact with foster children after they are returned to their families of origin or are adopted by a new family.

When a *biological parent* surrenders a child to foster care, he or she may feel loss, failure, or anger (Dando & Minty, 1987). Although contact between children and their parents is recom-

mended, the role is not clearly defined. Unless a relative is providing the foster care, parents generally are not involved in selecting their child's placement. Mixed emotions regarding the foster parent may include jealousy and gratitude. If foster care is to be temporary, parents must be given the assistance they need to improve their situation by reducing the risk factors that resulted in the removal of the child from the home.

Foster children experience a loss when they are removed from their parents (Dando & Minty, 1987). When children in foster care are subjected to several placements or are separated from siblings, they face multiple losses. The conflict or adverse environmental conditions that created the need for foster care may put the child at risk for emotional problems. Young children may be confused; older children may feel a mixture of anger, relief, and guilt.

Legislation encourages agencies to reduce the number and duration of foster placements. Aggressive efforts to reunite families can result in premature discharge from foster homes and later reentry into the foster care system. The reluctance to terminate parental rights leads to children remaining in foster care for many years, unable to return to their families of origin or to be permanently adopted. If the foster care system is to function effectively as a temporary support for parents in high-risk situations, the rights of children, biological parents, and foster parents must be balanced.

parents with disabilities reveals common themes across these diverse groups.

- Although they may be more prone to fail because of stressful situations and fewer social supports, parents at risk should not be treated as homogeneous groups. A respect for individual differences within groups enables us to recognize the ways in which parents and children can overcome the high-risk conditions.
- Child maltreatment may occur in high-risk parenting situations, but there are ways to reduce the likelihood that this will happen. Most notably, social networks and supportive public policies may create protective factors for many vulnerable parents. Improving the context of poor parent-child relationships is often the key to prevention and remediation.

CHAPTER 13

Working Parents and Child Care

When parents work outside the home, the parenting process is affected. In Chapter 1 we introduced Bronfenbrenner's (1979) term *exosystem* to describe a social setting that affects, but does not include, the child. The parental work setting is an example of this phenomenon (Crouter & McHale, 1993). The dual role of parent and worker presents individuals and families with challenges and opportunities.

As we examine the lives of working parents and their children, two overlapping issues must be considered. First, we want to know how parental employment itself affects parenting and child development. This chapter considers the way in which employment influences a family's social class, the amount of time they have to spend together, and their beliefs and attitudes about the world. Second, the impact of nonparental care on children and their parents is an area of concern. In exploring this topic, we will discuss various types of child care and attempt to define "quality care" for different-aged children. Since it is impossible to separate any of these issues from the wider social context, this chapter also examines public policy as it relates to working parents and child care.

WORK AND FAMILIES

Children of working parents are indirectly influenced by their parents' occupational status. Income level, quality and quantity of parent-child interaction, role modeling, and degree of involvement with other caregivers and peers are affected by mothers' and fathers' work responsibilities. How does parental employment or nonemployment influence parents and children?

Social Class

The occupational status of parents determines a family's social class. Recall that in our overview of the parenting process in Chapter 1, social class was introduced as an important factor influencing parent-child relations. Family size and stability, access to education and health care, and physical and social environments are associated with social class. Throughout this text the relationship between social class and parenting strategies, goals, and stresses has been elaborated. One of the explanations of why lower-class, middle-class, and upper-class children experience different child-rearing environments is the variation in income, status, and work demands associated with their parents' jobs (Hoffman, 1984).

As noted in Chapter 2, several studies have suggested a link between social class and different child-rearing styles (Kohn, 1963; Hoffman, 1984). For example, lower-class parents tend to use more power-assertive techniques in guiding their children's behavior, while middle- and upper-class parents are more likely to use reasoning techniques. These different styles of parent-child interaction may reflect parents' experience in the work place. While the lower-class worker is dominated by a supervisor and unable to affect the rules that govern her or his work environment, the middle- or upper-class employee enjoys a certain amount of autonomy and the ability to influence work routines and procedures. When parents' jobs require reasoning, persuading, and explaining, they may be more likely to use firm but flexible parenting styles (Greenberger, O'Neil, & Nagel, 1994). It is also important to note that lower-class families tend to have larger families, higher stress, and fewer resources. Under these conditions, the use of power-assertive techniques to manage daily routines is probably more adaptive.

As parents assume responsibility for socializing the child, they consciously or unconsciously prepare the child for the world the parent knows through work. The lower-class parent may value obedience and conformity because these traits serve the adult well in the factory. Conversely, the white-collar worker may value the self-direction, independence, and interpersonal skills that are needed in the office or boardroom. There are exceptions to this pattern. Some parents actively teach their children to follow in their own footsteps, while others may encourage behaviors that will enable a child to be upwardly mobile and more able to adapt to a changing future.

The Dual Role: Worker and Parent

When a person simultaneously assumes the role responsibilities of both worker and parent, the child-rearing process may be either helped or hindered. If the mother or father gains personal satisfaction and raises the family's standard of living through work, employment may serve as a morale booster, enhancing self-esteem and facilitating positive parent-child interactions. Parents with challenging and stimulating jobs are more likely to engage in developmentally sound parenting, suggesting positive links between parental employment and child rearing (Greenberger et al., 1994). However, if job demands serve as stressors in the family system by adversely affecting the parent's mood and energy level, employment may interfere with parenting. Although this issue is usually raised in discussions of maternal employment (Hoffman, 1989), the same processes may be relevant for fathers.

Working parents often experience *role overload*; they take on the responsibilities of many different roles and, as a result, experience increased stress. For the working parent, there is seldom enough time in the week to accomplish all the tasks required of various roles; trying to be a competent worker, responsive parent, loving spouse, and efficient household manager is exhausting. Both mothers and fathers report "spillover" between the worlds of work and home (Galinsky & David, 1988). A bad day at the office can translate into an irritable parent sharing dinner with a child. A sleepless night comforting a toddler with an ear infection may result in mistakes on the assembly line or in the office the next morning.

When job demands interfere with child-rearing demands, the parent experiences *role conflict*. If a child's school concert is scheduled at the same time as the parent's meeting with the boss, it is clear that work and family are interfering with each other. In general, parents working fewer hours and having more control over their work schedules are less likely to be caught in conflict on a regular basis (Galinsky, 1988). There is also evidence that supportive work places, including flexible supervisors, are associated with lower levels of work-family role strain for mothers (Warren & Johnson, 1995). Family expectations may determine how conflicted a father feels. If neither the father nor the child expects a high level of paternal involvement in school activities, the scenario described would not increase stress, but different expectations could result in a guilt-ridden father or a dissatisfied child.

Recent research has explored the ways in which *psychological investment* in both work and parenting influences child-rearing practices and perceptions of children's behavior (Greenberger & Goldberg, 1989). One study measured commitment to the parental role, parental beliefs regarding their unique significance in the lives of their children, time spent working, and the importance of work in parents' life. Employed men and women with high levels of commitment to parenting expected mature behavior from their children, but they also tended to describe their children favorably. This study found that in two-parent, middle-class families, investment in work did not occur at the expense of children. Some people remain passionate about both work and family without feeling overloaded by the demands of these multiple roles. Perhaps parents who are least stressed by dual roles truly enjoy the time they spend with their children, are energized by their work, have good time-management skills and an optimistic outlook on life.

Working Fathers

Because fathers are expected to be employed outside the home, the effects of their work on fathering, on mothering, and on children's developmental outcomes are often overlooked, yet a father's job, income, and attitude toward work will influence his involvement with his children and the way in which he coparents with the child's mother.

Since the beginning of the industrial revolution in the mid-nineteenth century, fathers have been assigned the "breadwinner" role in most families. Even when both parents work outside the home, the father is usually the primary wage earner determining the child's economic well-being. In fact, breadwinning is the criterion by which some people judge how well men fulfill their fathering responsibilities. However, by identifying fatherhood with breadwinning, society may have unintentionally limited male involvement in other aspects of child care (Lamb, 1986). The desire of contemporary fathers to nurture and care for their children may be hindered by a dated image of parenting roles that does not accurately reflect today's world.

CATHY 1995 Cathy Guisewite. Reprinted with permission of UNIVERSAL PRESS SYNDICATE. All rights reserved.

Various jobs place different demands on workers. The amounts of stress and satisfaction associated with a father's occupation will influence his paternal role. The children of a corporate executive may enjoy the economic benefits of father's employment, but find that his lengthy work hours preclude extensive father-child activities. Frequent travel or late meetings at the office may reduce the amount of time available for parenting. Even when father is home, he may be "psychologically absent" if he is thinking about work. On the other hand, if a father enjoys his work, his self-esteem may be enhanced and this bodes well for effective parenting.

For some men, a job is merely a way to earn money. Fathers in lower status jobs may not look to their work as a source of emotional fulfillment and, therefore, they may have more time and energy to invest in their children. However, fathers in blue-collar jobs are also more likely to hold more than one job, thus reducing their availability at home.

The work patterns of fathers may indirectly influence mother-child interaction. A study conducted in Australia showed that when working-class fathers in rural communities were away from home during most of their children's waking hours, mothers were less effective parents. These mothers had smaller social networks and were less likely to participate in community activities. In short, fathers' absence from family life because of work made the family a less stimulating setting for both mothers and children (Cotterell, 1986). It would be interesting to find out if the same dynamic occurs in other cultures, such as rural American communities.

The work setting extends the boundaries of the family. Children get a glimpse of the world beyond the home as they learn about father's work place and they are presented with male role models for the future. The work place is also a social setting in which fathers may exchange information about child rearing with other parents. For example, a father attempting to teach his daughter to ride a bicycle may seek suggestions from coworkers. As fathers listen to others discuss parenting issues, ranging from vacation plans to coping with curfews, they may bring some of these ideas home to discuss with mothers or to implement themselves.

A father's *unemployment* can adversely affect parenting by reducing financial resources and threatening paternal self-esteem. Researchers have found that an unemployed father may find it difficult to be at home with his children (Elder, Van Nguyen, & Caspi, 1985). When a father is feeling negative and pessimistic, he may be more punitive and less nurturant with the children. The father's irritability and inconsistent discipline can lead to a deterioration of the father-child relationship, and has been linked to depression and delinquency in adolescents (McLoyd, 1989; Lempers, Clark-Lempers, & Simons, 1989). A longitudinal study of families who suffered economic loss during the Great Depression found that unemployed fathers became more rejecting and nonsupportive of their children. However, the consequences for children could be buffered by a warm and affectionate mother. That is, even in the presence of a harsh father, some children did not suffer long-term consequences because their mothers were so supportive.

Fathers' employment has both positive and negative effects on the parenting process. As breadwinners, role models, and individuals who attach different meanings to employment, working fathers indirectly influence their children and their parenting partners. The work setting can be problematic if it exhausts time and energy that a father might devote to parenting, but it is also a potential source of social support for fathers dealing with parenting tasks.

Working Mothers

Historically, mothers contributed to the economic strength of the family by engaging in productive labor based in the home. However, when the industrial revolution of the late nineteenth century led fathers out of the home and into the work place, women were left behind to assume exclusive responsibility for household tasks and child rearing. At the same time, the growth in the U.S. economy provided some women "the luxury of motherhood as a profession" (McCartney & Phillips, 1988).

Although the nurturing, at-home mother and the breadwinning, at-work father may have been common during the first half of the twentieth century, the past four decades have witnessed dramatic increases in the number of mothers working outside the home. In 1960 only 28 percent of mothers with minor children were employed, but today that figure has risen to 67 percent. Most notably, there has been an increase in the number of employed mothers of infants and preschoolers; most mothers are participating in the work force before their children reach school age (U.S. Bureau of Census, 1992). This phenomenon can be attributed to the increase in single-parent families, a changing economy that necessitates two incomes in intact families, and more emphasis on the career goals of women.

As women entered the work force in record numbers, concerns about the impact of this trend on children and families have been investigated. The effects of maternal work vary widely according to many contributing factors, including a mother's attitudes about working outside the home, her feelings about separating from her child, the number of hours she works, and the child's sex and age.

Early studies of maternal employment recognized that *mothers' attitudes* about work influence family relationships. Mothers work for different reasons. It appears that employment preference, rather than employment status alone, affects the parenting process (Hoffman, 1984, 1989). For example, employed mothers who feel committed to the dual role, in contrast with those who are ambivalent, are more likely to use authoritative parenting styles and, thus, facilitate positive child outcomes (Goldberg & Easterbrooks, 1988). When economic pressures force a mother to seek outside employment despite her desire to stay at home, the resulting anxiety may stress the mother-child relationship. The same outcome might occur for the mother who wants to work, but is at home because her spouse is unsupportive or she cannot find a job. In fact, studies have found higher levels of depression in mothers of infants who prefer employment but remain at home (Hock & DeMeis, 1990).

There are individual differences in mothers that affect the relationship between parenting and employment. *Maternal separation anxiety* is a term used to describe a mother's negative feelings about leaving her child. Women appear to have different definitions of motherhood. One group holds a traditional view of mothering as central, excluding other roles, but there are also women who believe that motherhood and other roles can be pursued simultaneously. Although these differences are evident when the child is born and remain relatively stable during the infancy period, cultural values and social support influence maternal separation anxiety (Hock, DeMeis, & McBride, 1988). For example, three weeks after giving birth, a friend was asked by her mother, "Are you going to return to work *or* be a mother." If family and friends express strong beliefs about exclusive mothering, anxiety may increase.

Maternal employment has been linked to independence training of the child. Working mothers are more likely than nonworking mothers to encourage child autonomy. While the employed mother welcomes the child's independence because it reduces potential role overload, the full-time homemaker may see this development as a threat to her role status in the family (Hoffman, 1989).

The *number of hours* a mother works will influence the amount of time she spends with her children and her availability to fulfill other family responsibilities. Several studies have cited advantages associated with part-time employment (Hoffman, 1989). When mothers work more than twenty hours per week, they are more likely to be stressed and dissatisfied. Studies comparing stay-at-home mothers with those who work either full-time or part-time find that mothers working part-time provide more educational stimulation for their children, impose less rule control (Gottfried & Gottfried, 1988), and have the most positive attitudes toward their children (Bronfenbrenner & Crouter, 1982). For those who argue that "quality" time is more important than "quantity" of time, Hoffman (1984) notes that employed mothers consciously set aside time to be with their children and interact more intensely with them during these periods.

There are also *sex differences* that must be considered when discussing the effects of maternal employment on children. In general, outcomes are more favorable for girls than for boys. For example, daughters of working mothers score higher than daughters of nonworking mothers on measures of school performance and social adjustment. They also have higher educational and career aspirations, indicating that working mothers may be important role models for their daughters. (Hoffman, 1989). Educated mothers who work full-time view their preschool daughters in a positive light, but are much more negative in describing their sons (Bronfenbrenner, Alvarez, & Henderson, 1984). For these mothers, working may enhance self-esteem and they may translate these feelings into a positive outlook for their young daughters. It is possible that the higher activity level of boys frustrates mothers with less time and energy.

Finally, the *timing* of maternal employment influences parenting. T. Berry Brazelton (1987a, 1987b), a psychoanalytically oriented pediatrician, believes that the duration of the parent-child relationship is a critical variable. According to his model, during the first four months of life the infant and parent are learning to regulate their interactions with each other. He argues that maternal employment during this period can interfere with the learning process and threaten the parent-child relationship. While there are no data supporting this idea, the theoretical argument is consistent with current views on socioemotional development.

The ways in which parental employment influence family life depend on attitudes about work, feelings about separation from children, spousal support, children's ages, work schedules, and the availability of quality child care.
(Spencer Grant/Photo Researchers)

Brazelton is a strong advocate for paid parental leaves for working parents, because he believes that both parent and child are at risk if they have not established a sense of competence and intimacy with each other before the mother returns to work. In 1993 the United States passed the Family and Medical Leave Act, giving parents the right to take up to twelve weeks of unpaid leave to care for their babies. This law protects job security; however, many parents cannot afford to take time off without pay. Most psychologists support the concept of parental leave, because it can facilitate breastfeeding and caretaker sensitivity (Stipek & McCroskey, 1989). There is no agreement, however, on Brazelton's four-month guideline. Individual differences in infants (e.g., temperament) and mothers (e.g., maternal separation anxiety) may result in an optimal leave period that is shorter or longer than four months for different mother-child dyads.

The question of timing can also be approached from a different vantage point. The literature on divorce suggests that a mother's entering the work force can be disruptive for children of any age if the family is undergoing stress at that time. It is common for newly divorced mothers to return to work while they are still adjusting to the single-parent role. Under these conditions, children are more vulnerable than if their mothers worked prior to the divorce (Hoffman, 1984).

While the original research on children of working mothers focused on school-age children, the recent trend has been to look more closely at younger age groups, to evaluate family processes that exist before maternal employment begins, and to follow children longitudinally (Belsky, 1990; Gottfried & Gottfried, 1988). These approaches will provide more information about the long-term consequences of maternal employment.

To summarize, the relationship between maternal employment and the parenting process has many facets, including a mother's attitudes about work, her feelings about being separated from her child, her work schedule, the child's sex, and available social support. In the best of all worlds, a mother's feelings about working outside the home will be consistent with her behavior; her desire to work, delay employment following childbirth, or remain at home full-time will be supported by family-oriented policies in society and in the work place.

DUAL-WORKER FAMILIES

In many cases, maternal employment is embedded within the dual-worker family. The complexity of the family system almost guarantees that there will be no simple interpretations of the data on the topic of parenting and work influences!

The time employed adults spend on domestic tasks has been referred to as "the second shift" (Hochschild, 1989). When both parents are employed, the division of labor in the home is affected. Employed mothers reduce their investment in household tasks and recreational activities in order to have time for child care and paid work. Although fathers tend to participate in household and child care tasks more if their wives are employed, their level of involvement remains low relative to that of their spouses (Hoffman, 1989; Crouter, Perry-Jenkins, Huston, & McHale, 1987). Fathers who are highly involved in domestic tasks tend to come from families in which mothers are employed full-time and have more than one child. While this phenomenon can reduce maternal stress, it has the potential of increasing paternal stress. It is possible that two "superparents" will emerge, only to be disappointed when they cannot be all things to all people (Galinsky & David, 1988; Scarr, 1985).

Even low levels of paternal participation can have both direct and indirect effects on the parenting process. First, there is evidence that children of working mothers are less stereotypic in their sex-role attitudes (Hoffman, 1989). There is a higher likelihood that both parents are modeling roles that are not bound by strict gender stereotypes. Second, when fathers are more involved in child care, their children are more academically and socially competent (Gottfried & Gottfried, 1988).

In some households, parents function as "sequential single parents," in an effort to accomplish all the work that must be done at home and at the office. This scenario may also exist when parents choose to work different shifts so that child care can be shared without relying on resources outside the family (Menaghan & Parcel, 1990). While this arrangement might reduce some aspects of role overload, it is a potentially stressful situation for the marital relationship. Recall that the theoretical model of parenting outlined in Chapter 1 discussed the quality of the marital relationship as an important influence on the parenting process and child outcomes.

EMPLOYED SINGLE PARENTS

With the increasing numbers of single parents in the work force, the impact of combining work and family responsibilities for this group must be studied. Employment is often crucial to the economic status of single mothers. More than 50 percent of unemployed single mothers live in poverty, compared with less than 10 percent of employed single mothers (Burden, 1986). A supportive work place can enable single mothers to reduce their reliance on public assistance and lead to economic self-sufficiency (Parker, 1994).

In a study of working parents, single female parents had the highest levels of stress in handling multiple responsibilities of job and home. They spent an average of seventy-five hours per week balancing job and family with little financial or emotional assistance. Despite this burden, their job performance and satisfaction were at high levels, but physical and emotional well-being was threatened (Burden, 1986).

Single male parents appear to be similar to nonparent employees, possibly because their children are less likely to live with them full-time. One study found that single fathers spent the greatest number of hours at work, had the highest salary levels, and did not appear stressed by multiple roles (Burden, 1986).

PUBLIC POLICY

As families try to integrate the worlds of work and family, public policy must keep pace with reality. Sandra Scarr (1985) argues that our current policies are based on an outdated image of the family and that nations must respond to the situation as it actually exists. In an effort to assist families juggling dual roles and maintain appropriate developmental contexts for generations of future workers, the business world has examined its policies. Box 13-1 summarizes various ways in which corporations have been responsive to the needs of working parents.

When both parents work outside the home, family dynamics shift. Most notably, fathers tend to be more involved in child rearing when both parents are employed. When single mothers are also wage earners, they are at risk for job-family role strain. Public policy and corporate support must keep pace with the

Box 13-1 Family-Friendly Policies: Corporations Respond to the Needs of Working Parents

As researchers are discovering that family-responsive programs increase worker productivity, corporations are taking a closer look at the needs of working parents. They have responded in a number of creative ways in an effort to reduce family stress and parent role strain.

1. *Flexible Work Schedules and Places*—It is estimated that as many as 33 percent of the companies nationally allow some workers to choose arrival and departure times within certain constraints. This option enables working parents to work around their children's school and after-school activities. Part-time work and job sharing are popular options for employed parents who need flexible schedules. Some employers offer the option of completing job responsibilities at home, possibly linked to work by computer, as a way of increasing flexibility.

2. *Benefit Programs*—One of the most crucial benefits is parental leave. Larger companies must comply with the federal law that mandates up to twelve weeks of unpaid leave for fathers and mothers who need time during childbirth or adoption, or while caring for a sick child. Although a few companies offer paid leaves as part of a benefit package, there is general resistance from the business community because of the costs.

   Some employers offer child care vouchers or subsidies as an option in their benefits packages. Flexible benefits allow employees to choose the benefits they need, rather than assuming that everyone's needs are the same. Under such a system, the dual-worker family can arrange their benefits so that one spouse chooses health insurance while the other spouse chooses child care assistance.

3. *Child Care Services*—Some companies directly subsidize community child care while others have built on-site child care centers. On-site child care is particularly likely to occur in female dominated professions, for example, hospitals employing large numbers of nurses, and in large companies that have the money to offer start-up assistance for a day care center. Parents enjoy the proximity to their children and feel reassured that they can more closely monitor the quality of care.

4. *Information and Referral Services*—Many corporations offer resource and referral services that help parents locate and choose appropriate child care programs. Employers may hire an in-house consultant to provide this information or, more commonly, they may contract with an existing community organization. This type of assistance for working parents is a relatively low-cost, low-risk undertaking for companies.

Adapted from Hughes, D., & Galinsky, E. (1988). Balancing work and family lives: Research and corporate applications. In A. E. Gottfried & A. W. Gottfried (Eds.), *Maternal employment and children's development*. New York: Plenum Press

needs of dual-worker families and single parents. Child care is one form of support for working parents that has received much attention in recent decades. In the next section, child care issues related to parenting are examined.

CHILD CARE

Although studies may find that parental employment is associated with individual differences in children and child-rearing practices, the child's experiences when parents are working are also important. With large numbers of mothers working outside the home, the demand for day care has increased.

Professionals and the public are eager to understand the impact of nonmaternal care on the parenting process.

Historically, parents have shared their child-rearing responsibilities with others, most often with relatives and friends. However, when twentieth century women began to define motherhood as a profession isolated in the home, shared child rearing began to be viewed suspiciously. Child care providers who could have been viewed as supportive partners were cast as competitors to parents (McCartney & Phillips, 1988). Given the current data regarding the number of mothers working outside the home, a more realistic approach may be to recognize the ways in which child care strengthens and supports families.

Types of Child Care

Employed parents rely on a variety of different child care arrangements. Children may be cared for in their own home (by a parent, a relative, or a non-relative), in another person's home, or at a day care center. Table 13-1 indicates that home-based care is the most common child care arrangement; however, center-based care is growing and this trend is expected to continue (Hofferth & Phillips, 1987). What are the advantages and disadvantages of various forms of care?

In-Home Care

Some working parents prefer to have children cared for in their own homes. Parents of infants are the most likely to choose this arrangement because they believe that very young children need individualized attention. Concern about the threat of infectious disease in group settings also motivates many parents to seek in-home providers. Another advantage is that the child does not have to leave familiar surroundings. Parents are relieved of the burden of transporting the child and the child's routines are not disrupted because of the parents' work schedules or the child's illness.

In-home care presents several disadvantages. First, although some families can arrange for a parent or relative to provide the necessary care, others do not have this option. It is difficult to find private caregivers who will commit

TABLE 13-1. Percentage of Children with Employed Mothers in Different Types of Child Care Arrangements

Age of Child	In-Home Care	Family Day Care	Child Care Centers	Parent Cares For Child While On the Job	Child "Self-Care"	Grade School
2 years and under	39.2	35.7	15.8	9.2	—	—
3–4 years	31.1	24.5	32.9	7.9	—	3.6
5–14 years	10.7	3.6	1.9	2.0	2.7	79.2

Source: U.S. Bureau of Census, 1991.

themselves to a family for an extended period of time. Second, this is generally the most expensive day care option, although it can be cost effective if there are several children to be cared for in the same family. Most important, the lack of supervision is troublesome. The infant who is preverbal cannot report on the caregiver's abilities. The parent must rely on the caregiver's report of the daily routine and try to ascertain if, in fact, the desired nurturance and stimulating one-to-one interaction are occurring.

Family Day Care

When parents desire a homelike environment and a small number of children with one caregiver, they use family day care. In this situation, the caregiver is often a mother with young children of her own at home. This arrangement offers the least expensive form of child care with the greatest opportunity for flexible hours. Again, parents of infants rely heavily on this type of care because it is a family-like environment with a seeming potential for intimate, nurturing interactions.

Family day care homes are largely unregulated. Although some states require licensing for homes that serve a certain number of children, most family day care providers are not registered with the appropriate agencies. The unlicensed home-based caregiver is unlikely to be trained in child development and often does not consider day care her "profession." These characteristics may lead to a sudden decision to stop providing child care, thus presenting a potentially unstable situation for the child.

Recognizing the interrelatedness of dual roles of worker and parent, some corporations have developed on-site child-care centers for their employees. (*Janice Fullman/The Picture Cube*)

In some communities, family day care providers have joined together to enhance professional development and strengthen the services they provide. Caregiver networks offer professional training, emotional support, toy-lending libraries, group insurance rates, bookkeeping assistance, and substitute caregivers. Parents sometimes prefer to enroll their children in a family day care home that is linked to a network because they feel the support for the provider will translate into higher quality care for their children. Caregivers who belong to networks may be more invested in the child care profession and less likely to leave the field.

Center-Based Care

Child care centers offer group care in a school-like setting. Centers may be community-based, nonprofit enterprises or they may be national franchises that operate for profit. In an effort to support families, churches have provided child care space and sponsorship over a longer period of time than any other single institution in the United States (Lindner, 1986).

Parents of preschool children will often choose child care centers because they perceive this age group as increasingly peer oriented and find the more explicit educational components appealing. Centers can offer a wider array of materials and play spaces then a home. Center-based care is licensed by the state; thus, parents know that the program must meet certain minimum standards. The stability of the child care center is comforting to most parents; they know that the program will exist in the months to come and that, if a teacher is absent, a substitute will be provided.

A potential disadvantage of center-based care is that many different caregivers will be interacting with the child, although some parents judge this to be an advantage because of its potentially enriching effect on the child. The low status and low wages of child care workers lead to staff turnover, an undesirable situation when children are attempting to form emotional attachments to significant adults. Also, centers must be run as businesses and may not have the flexibility to accommodate parents' work schedules. Finally, contagious diseases spread quickly in group settings and parents may rightfully fear an increase in illness if they enroll their infants in a child care center. Recent studies have shown that children under one year of age who are cared for in centers are more likely to contract respiratory tract and gastrointestinal infections. However, these same children will have fewer infections for the remainder of their preschool years because they have built up immunities early on. The increased incidence of ear infections in infants attending child care centers is also a concern, because repeated ear infections can impair hearing which, in turn, interferes with language development (Hayes, Palmer, & Zaslow, 1990).

Box 13-2 outlines some of the alternative child care arrangements on which parents rely when their children are ill and cannot attend a regular program.

What Is Quality Care?

The experience of children in nonparental care varies with setting and caregiver characteristics. What are indicators of quality? Caregiver training, a low

Box 13-2 Day Care for Sick Children

If you have chosen a child care arrangement outside your own home, your child will probably not be able to attend the program when sick. For many working parents, as they comfort an ill child in the middle of the night, they are also concerned over what to do about child care the next day. Parents complain that it is easier to miss work for car trouble than to say that your child is sick!

Most working parents and professionals know the necessity of having a good back-up system for regular child care arrangements, especially for sick children. Although many companies allow their employees to use their own sick time to care for sick children, this is often inadequate, especially when there is more than one child in the family. Also, there are times when it is very difficult to be absent from the work place.

Some options include:

1. In a dual-career family parents often alternate time off for children's illnesses, trying to weigh the relative importance of each spouse's commitments when the crisis occurs. Data suggest that the responsibility of caring for a sick child is shared more equally when both parents are professionals than when one has a job of lower status (Catalyst, 1988). Obviously, this plan is not feasible for single parents.
2. A friend, neighbor, or relative who does not work outside the home can be a good back-up child care provider in some situations; however, if this person has children at home, she

probably does not want to expose them to illness. One study found that African-American mothers are more likely than Anglo mothers to receive this type of support from their relatives (Benin & Keith, 1995).
3. Some day care centers offer isolation rooms, staffed by nurses, for children who are mildly ill. This practice is not widespread because few centers have the space or the personnel to commit to such a program.
4. Recognizing the needs of parents with sick children, one midwest manufacturing company offers its employees a twofold benefit. Parents are referred to health care workers who will care for the sick child at home and the company helps parents pay for this service (Catalyst, 1988).
5. Hospitals have responded to this special service need by creating day care programs for sick children. With catchy names like "Sunshine Suite" or "Ginger Ail," these programs are staffed by pediatric nurses. Parents who anticipate using the program register the child in advance of the sickness, filling out appropriate forms and touring the facility. When the morning arrives that the child is too ill to go to day care, the parent calls the hospital and transports the child to the hospital. Such programs are usually more expensive than regular child care, but for those workers who cannot be absent, the arrangement offers peace of mind.

adult-to-child ratio, and small group size have been identified as important characteristics of child care settings, because they tend to predict positive interaction in the setting and good developmental outcomes for children (NICHD Early Child Care Network, 1995; Phillips & Howes, 1987; Ruopp, Travers, Glantz, & Coelen, 1979). The optimal ratios for various age groups have been defined by early childhood professionals (see Table 13-2). Note that for infants and toddlers, it is recommended that fewer children be nurtured and educated by a single caregiver. This is consistent with information presented earlier in this book regarding the need for caregivers to be responsive to the subtle cues of infants and the fact that young children are often on very individualized schedules.

TABLE 13-2. Staff-Child Ratios Within Group Size

Age of Children*	6	8	10	12	14	16	18	20	22	24
					Group Size					
Infants (birth–12 mos.)	1:3	1:4								
Toddlers (12–24 mos.)	1:3	1:4	1:5	1:4						
Two-year-olds (24–36 mos)		1:4	1:5	1:6**						
Two- and three-year-olds			1:5	1:6	1:7**					
Three-year-olds					1:7	1:8	1:9	1:10**		
Four-year-olds						1:8	1:9	1:10**		
Four- and five-year-olds						1:8	1:9	1:10**		
Five-year-olds						1:8	1:9	1:10		
Six- to eight-year-olds (school age)								1:10	1:11	1:12

*Multi-age grouping is both permissible and desirable. When no infants are included, the staff-child ratio and group size requirements shall be based on the age of the majority of the children in the group. When infants are included, ratios and group size for infants must be maintained.

**Smaller group sizes and lower staff-child ratios are optimal. Larger group sizes and higher staff-child ratios are acceptable only in cases where staff are highly qualified (see Staff Qualifications, Component D).

Source: Reprinted with permission from the National Association for the Education of Young Children, 1509 16th Street, N.W., Washington, DC 20036.

The parent's choice of setting and caregiver will depend on many factors, including the child's age and temperament, the availability and cost of various child care options, and parental attitudes and values. In short, dreams and realities influence their decisions. One study found parents choosing centers instead of family day care homes because they desired more educational and social opportunities for their children, but their reasons for choosing a particular center were convenience, location, and cost (Atkinson, 1987). Another study found that parents with more stressed, complex lives and less effective parenting practices chose lower quality programs (Howes & Olenick, 1986). Cultural preferences also influence child care decisions (Fuller, Holloway, Râmbaud, & Eggers-Pierola, 1995). A recent survey found that Latino families are less likely than either black or white families to enroll their children in center-based care. According to this study, Latinos prefer home-based care in their neighborhood or provided by relatives (West, Hausken, & Collins, 1993).

Many parents are surprised to learn how expensive child care can be. Lower-class families spend as much as 27 percent of their income on day care, while the same cost may represent only 5 percent of the upper-class family's income. See Figure 13-1 (Casper, Hawkins & O'Connell, 1994). Although caregivers earn relatively low wages, the cost of quality care is high when staff-child ratios and group size recommendations are followed. Public programs to assist parents meet the expense of child care are limited.

Because nonparental child care influences child development, choosing a program is a very important parenting decision. How do parents approach the issue of finding quality care? The general pattern is for parents to begin their

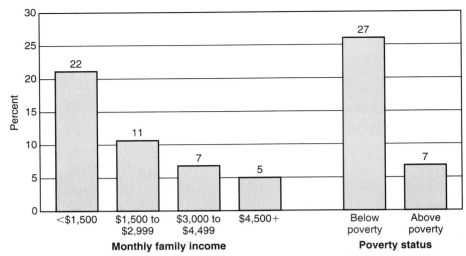

FIGURE 13-1. Percentage of monthly family income spent on child care: Fall 1991. *Source:* U.S. Bureau of Census (1992).

search by asking relatives and close friends for information. If this does not work, parents ask casual acquaintances for help or use formal mechanisms, such as newspaper ads, agencies, and telephone directories (Powell, 1989). Some parents engage in little information seeking and may not even visit the program prior to enrollment (Bradbard, Endsley, & Readdick, 1983). Although many educated parents understand the importance of structural characteristics associated with quality care (e.g., group size), they often decide about placement on the basis of "a general feeling" about the program (Bogat & Gensheimer, 1986). Child care professionals advise a visit to the program to observe the routine, meet the staff, and determine if aspects of quality are present. Box 13-3 lists some of the factors that parents will want to keep in mind when choosing a child care program.

Effects of Nonparental Care

Research findings on the effects of day care have been accumulating since the 1970s and early reviews of the phenomenon indicated little cause for concern (Belsky & Steinberg, 1978). These early studies compared home-reared children with children attending high-quality day care centers and uncovered few differences for most children. With respect to cognitive development, middle-class children neither suffered nor excelled as a result of child care. However, lower-class children in day care were more likely to be cognitively advanced than their home-reared peers. A recent wave of research has focused on child care quality. For example, in a longitudinal study Howes (1990a) found that children who enter low-quality care in infancy are more distractible and less task-oriented in kindergarten.

Box 13-3 Choosing Child Care

What should a parent look for when evaluating child care options? What is quality day care and how do you recognize it when you see it? Here is a brief list of important items to check when visiting a prospective center.

HEALTH AND SAFETY

- Adult supervision is constant; no children are left unattended.
- Setting is reasonably clean and the procedures for preparing food and diapering children are sanitary.
- Meals and snacks are nutritious and served at appropriate intervals.

PHYSICAL SPACE

- Children have enough space to be able to engage in a variety of activities without disturbing each other.
- Soft, cozy spaces are available.
- Child-sized furniture is used.
- The setting is attractive and takes into account the child's perspective.

MATERIALS, EQUIPMENT, AND ACTIVITIES

- Enough materials are available so that children do not have to compete for them, with enough variety so that children have many options for play (e.g., books, art supplies, manipulatives, riding toys, gross motor equipment).
- Equipment is in good repair and accessible to the children so that they can make choices and engage in play independently.
- Daily schedule allows for a balance of activities: large group, small group, individual, quiet, active, indoor, and outdoor.
- A program of age-appropriate activities is planned to stimulate physical, cognitive, social, and emotional development.

CAREGIVERS

- Teacher has training in child development.
- Children are treated with respect and affection.
- There are enough caregivers to meet the recommended ratios.
- Teacher is a model for language development.
- Conversations with children include eye contact and appropriate vocabulary.
- No physical punishment is used.

RELATIONS WITH PARENTS

- Staff communicates with parents about children's activities, development, and program policies.
- Parents may visit at any time.
- Staff will discuss and respond to parent concerns.

Two brochures on choosing care are available from the National Association for the Education of Young Children (NAEYC): *Finding the Best Care for Your Infant or Toddler* and *How to Choose a Good Early Childhood Program*.

A child's social development may also be affected by the child care setting. Children in centers with trained caregivers, small groups, and low adult-child ratios are more social with peers and adults. Their social competence and adjustment appears to depend on the quality of care (Phillips, McCartney & Scarr, 1987). Quality may also influence parent-child interactions. Peterson and Peterson (1986) found that children in poor-quality child care were less compliant with their mothers' requests in a laboratory situation. The verbal interaction between mother and child was more sustained and positive when the child had experienced high-quality care outside the home.

In recent years, child care researchers and policy makers have focused on the socioemotional domain. Recall from Chapter 5 that the establishment of an attachment relationship is one of the most important developmental tasks for infants during the first year of life, because it sets the stage for future social development. Knowing that parental sensitivity and responsivity are key factors in the development of a secure attachment, two questions have been raised with respect to children of working parents: Does attachment to a substitute caregiver replace attachment to parent? Does nonmaternal care threaten the parent-child bond?

Research indicates that children develop an "intermediate" attachment to the caregiver. However, this bond does not replace or interfere with attachment to parents (Ainslie & Anderson, 1984). Although some parents might be jealous of the relationship between the child and the caregiver, most recognize that it is in the child's best interest to be interacting with someone who can foster child development through nurturance and education.

A heated public debate about the way in which maternal employment and child care influence socioemotional development is currently taking place. The crux of the debate centers on the finding that an "insecure avoidant" attachment is more likely to be observed in one-year-olds if the mother has been employed more than half-time and the child has been attending a day care center. This finding has led Jay Belsky (1988) to conclude that infants of employed mothers are at risk for developing emotional insecurity and later social maladjustment. Several researchers have observed that boys are more vulnerable to this adverse effect than girls are (Belsky & Rovine, 1988; Gamble & Zigler, 1986).

K. Allison Clarke-Stewart (1989b, 1990) has reviewed the evidence and offers a different interpretation. She argues that the observed differences between the fully employed groups and others are small and that the laboratory procedure used to assess attachment may not be valid for infants who are accustomed to being separated routinely from mothers. Other investigators have cautioned that the published data on this topic may be biased, because studies are often not published unless they reveal significant differences between groups (Roggman, Langlois, Hubbs-Tait, & Rieser-Danner, 1994). Further research on this important issue is needed to fully understand the impact of nonparental care on socioemotional development. In the absence of conclusive data, efforts can be made to educate parents about indicators of quality and about infant cues that reflect the child's adaptation to nonparental care.

Cultural Context

The findings associated with early entry into child care and working parents are not universal; that is, in other countries the concerns that we have demonstrated are not always present. For example, a longitudinal study of Swedish school-age children found that those who had begun day care before the age of one year and those who were in center-based care scored higher on cognitive tests. Also, teachers found these early day care children to be more independent, persistent, and self-confident (Andersson, 1989). Why should children be so different in Sweden? The answer may lie in the cultural context and the question of quality. Sweden has national policies that are very family oriented. For example, parental leave policies enable either parent to stay home for up to one year without losing their seniority or jeopardizing family finances. When they decide to return to work, highly trained personnel offer quality care in the community. Parents in Sweden truly have choices that the employed parent in the United States may not have.

Unfortunately, the Swedish model cannot be transported to the United States; parental and national goals differ. Michael Lamb (1993) discusses the way in which child care systems reflect the larger social structure and economic needs of a nation. He notes that in countries where child care is viewed as a public responsibility, nonparental care is widely available and the facilities are of high quality. In contrast, countries that believe child care issues are a private concern, to be handled by individual families, have fewer services of poorer quality. This latter group includes the United States, the United Kingdom, and Canada. The lack of public support for child care in the United States is also based on unfounded fears that this institution will weaken the family's role and erode the mother-child bond (McCartney & Phillips, 1988). An alternative perspective might describe parental efforts to improve child care as a sign of their commitment to their child rearing (Lindner, 1986).

Continuity Between Home and Child Care

Children of working parents typically experience at least two different environments, one at home and another at the child care setting. The parenting process is influenced by the *mesosystem*, the connections among these settings (Bronfenbrenner, 1979). It is generally believed that child development is enhanced when the demands of the settings are compatible and the interactions between home and child care provider are frequent. Ideally, parents and provider share similar child-rearing values, goals, and adult-child interaction styles (Powell, 1989). Sometimes values conflicts are rooted in social class and cultural differences, such as when poor immigrant women become live-in child care providers for more affluent families. Language barriers and differing life experiences may create a gap between parental expectations and caregiving behaviors (Wrigley, 1995).

The impact of *discontinuity* on the child may depend on several factors, including the degree of dissimilarity between the settings, the relative amounts of time children are in different environments, at what point in the child's life these experiences occur, and how prepared the child is for the discrepancy (Peters & Kontos, 1987). If the differences are minor and brief, children usually do not suffer. However, for many children a day care system based on white, middle-class values may be vastly different from the home environment. Non-Anglo and lower-class children seem most vulnerable in this regard, especially if the child care setting undermines the family's role. Sara Lightfoot (1978) has described the home setting of black, Hispanic, and Native American children as "worlds apart" from the life they encounter at school. Parental involvement and staff members who reflect neighborhood values can minimize the potentially negative effects of these differences.

As previously discussed, individual differences in children may determine how adaptive they are in a new situation and how well they handle discontinuity. Some children require more support than others. Also, if a child is trying to cope with a sensitive developmental period (e.g., stranger anxiety), he or she is more likely to be stressed by discrepancies between home and day care setting. Child care specialists urge parents to prepare children by talking about and visiting the day care setting ahead of time. This provides a foundation for overlap between the two settings and minimizes discontinuity for the child.

It has been suggested that children might benefit from a manageable amount of discontinuity, because they must be prepared to adjust to different environments throughout life (Long & Garduque, 1987). As long as both settings make developmentally appropriate demands on the child, it may be beneficial for the child to learn to cope with the reality of discontinuity. Even very young children come to expect different responses from different adults. For example, they know that mother, father, and teacher may each react in a slightly different manner when children are aggressive and they realize that naptime routines at home and at the center may be different. Perhaps the level of consistency within each setting is more important than the discontinuity between the two settings; that is, if family life and routines are predictable and day care life is not plagued by staff turnover and inconsistent rules, the child's development may not be jeopardized, even if the settings make different demands on the child (Powell, 1989).

As children simultaneously experience the home and child care settings, they may be subject to two positive environments, two negative environments, or a positive and a negative environment. There are cumulative risks for the child when a poor home environment is coupled with a poor day care environment. For example, if authoritarian parents are working in stressful jobs and they send their child to a day care center that has large groups of children left with untrained caregivers, child development is compromised because the child goes from one bad environment to another. On the other hand, high-quality child care might compensate for the poor environment experienced in a stress-ridden home. In this situation, discontinuity between home and school may be desirable because the bad effects of one setting are offset by the good effects of another. Similarly, a child whose home life is positive may not be as vulnerable to the potentially negative effects of low-quality day care (Belsky, 1990).

Because parents and caregivers engage in a collaborative child-rearing process, their relationship can indirectly influence child development. Although the day care provider is a potential source of social support for the parent, researchers have found that caregivers often have negative attitudes toward parents with poor parenting skills. These same parents are less likely to use the day care staff for family support and their children tend to have lower levels of cognitive, language, and social development (Kontos & Wells, 1986; Kontos & Dunn, 1989). Thus, the lack of communication between home and day care is most likely to exist in at-risk families, where positive linkages could support parenting and facilitate child development.

Parents often assume that child care problems are over when formal schooling begins. However, in most cases the school day ends before the working day does, and holiday schedules do not coincide. After-school day care programs for elementary school children have been developed to meet this need. These programs offer supervised care at the school or at a community location for children whose parents cannot be at home after school or during vacations. When group care is unavailable or undesirable, the parent might arrange for an at-home babysitter or a neighbor to watch the child. Less frequently, children are transported to family day care homes. During the summer, camps and teenage babysitters often provide the necessary supervision.

Many parents allow their children to take care of themselves. Formerly referred to as *latchkey children,* they are now called *self-care children.* As noted in Table 13-1, almost 3 percent of the children in kindergarten and beyond are in self-care. What are the advantages and disadvantages of this arrangement and how does it affect child development?

Feelings of independence and competence can emerge from the increased responsibility of self-care. Children may not want the regimentation of a group program after a day of school, and they may use the time alone to complete homework and household tasks. However, self-care children may also feel lonely and isolated from peers. No matter how well prepared children are, parents worry when children are left alone. Safety is an issue; will the child respond appropriately in an emergency situation? Parental anxiety can detract from work performance.

In an attempt to determine the developmental impact of the self-care experience, a recent study surveyed 5,000 eighth-grade students and their parents in southern California (Dwyer & Richardson, 1990). The investigators found

FIGURE 13-2. Reported percentage of kids in self-care by age: Fall 1991.
Source: U.S. Bureau of Census (1994).

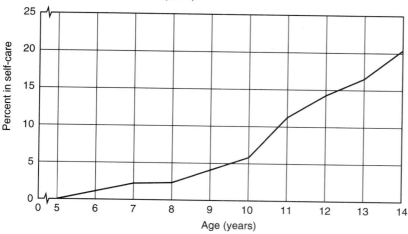

significant differences between children who engaged in self-care and those who did not. Eighth-graders who cared for themselves were at a significantly higher risk of using alcohol, cigarettes, and marijuana. More important, the number of hours in self-care predicted substance abuse, with those who were alone more than eleven hours a week being at a higher risk level.

Parents often wonder if there is an appropriate age at which to allow self-care. As indicated in Figure 13-2, children are more likely to be left alone as they get older. In the California study mentioned above, the age at which self-care began did prove to be an important variable. Those children who began self-care in elementary school were more likely to engage in risk-taking behaviors when they were in eighth grade. Those who did not become self-care children until junior high were less influenced by their peers.

While the age of the child and amount of unsupervised time may be important variables, these aspects alone do not explain why some children in self-care do not succumb to peer pressures and antisocial behavior. Laurence Steinberg (1986) noted that not all self-care children were at risk, because the quality of the experience itself varies. From a large-scale study in the Midwest, he determined that those who were monitored by parents from a distance were less susceptible to peer pressure. In Steinberg's study, it was the children who did not go home but "hung out" at a friend's house or a public place who got into trouble. Self-care children did better if parents phoned them after school and provided a structured after-school routine. Parents who engaged in authoritative child rearing had self-care children who were more able to resist the undesirable influence of antisocial peer activities. Again, good parent-child relations seem to influence the child's behavior in a variety of settings.

Recent studies have compared children with different types of after-school experiences and have found that social class and program quality are important variables. In middle-class communities, where concerns for personal safety are minimal, children attending poor-quality after-school programs are more likely to have social, emotional, and academic problems than their peers who go home to parental care or self-care (Vandell & Corasaniti, 1988). In contrast, low-income children who attend formal programs that provide academic activities and enrichment lessons have better grades, behavior, and peer relations than their peers who are at home alone or under adult supervision (Posner & Vandell, 1994).

To summarize, working parents of school-age children may choose among various child care programs or allow children to care for themselves. Parents must carefully consider the age at which self-care will begin, the amount of unsupervised time, and how the experience is structured. An authoritative parenting style, coupled with parental monitoring of the child's after-school activities, is associated with better child outcomes.

SUMMARY

- It is evident that parental employment and child care affect parenting and child development. Income and occupational status determine the financial well-being of the family, and the social structure of the work place is reflected in the child-rearing styles that various parents adopt. Employed parents are confronted with a challenging balancing act as they try to meet their role responsibilities at home and at the work place.

- The amounts of stress and satisfaction associated with work will affect parent-child interactions. The number of hours spent working, the personal meaning of work for individual parents, and feelings about being separated from the child will determine how the parenting process is affected by parental employment or unemployment. The historical context is also important; a father's identification as the family breadwinner is now juxtaposed with a trend toward increasing numbers of mothers entering the work force.
- Although it is difficult to separate the effects of parental employment from the effects of child care, recent investigations have found few developmental differences between children experiencing nonparental care and those who are exclusively home-reared. The reported higher incidence of insecure attachment among infants in full-time care outside the home deserves more attention to determine how it relates to child care conditions, parenting behaviors, or methodological issues.
- In the same way that nurturing home environments produce good child outcomes, quality programs designed to support working parents can also benefit children. All of these issues must be considered within the cultural context, with an understanding that the amount of public support that a nation gives to working parents will influence the parenting process and developmental outcomes for children.

Epilogue

As we conclude this volume and reflect back on our coverage of parenting, it is apparent that recurring themes have been interwoven in the text. The theories and findings from empirical studies are at best "works in progress." The underlying themes that guide our evolving knowledge and inform our perspective on the field can be summarized as follows.

1. Parenting is a *dynamic process*. Child rearing is no longer viewed from a mechanistic perspective that focuses only on child outcomes. Rather, a developmental systems approach is needed to capture the interdependent and ever-changing nature of parenting.
2. Parent-child relationships are *multiply determined*. Characteristics of the parent, child, and context contribute, both directly and indirectly, to the variation in relationships. The interaction among these factors produces many different parenting patterns.
3. The parenting context includes *multiple settings*. In the immediate environment, the influence of family structure, coparenting relationships, and social support networks must be considered. Historical, political, and cultural factors are also important contextual determinants.
4. Parenting influences *child development*. Children's personalities, competencies, and physical and emotional well-being are affected by child-rearing activities and beliefs.
5. Parenting influences *adult development*. Participation in child-rearing activities changes adults emotionally and intellectually. The parenting role introduces new challenges, presents opportunities for constructing self, and changes the expectations of others.
6. Parenting influences *society*. The behavior of parents and children as they participate in the child-rearing process contributes to cultural values and priorities. The way in which they are socialized through the parenting process affects their individual contributions to the society.
7. Parenting is a *life-span* phenomenon. Participation in this process begins during the prenatal period and continues until death. At any one time, individuals may be involved as parents, children, and members of society.
8. Parenting theory and research can influence *social policy*. Current knowledge related to parenting has the potential to optimize developmental outcomes for children, parents, and society. This includes applications in

areas such as parent education, laws, schools, community planning, and prevention programs.

9. The study of parenting is *multidisciplinary*. Although this text relies heavily on current research in developmental psychology, the fields of family sociology, medicine, history, education, and anthropology have also contributed to our understanding of child rearing.

10. Parenting research relies on a *variety of methods*. The research on some topics is well developed, but it is noticeably weak in other areas. Future research must reflect the complexity of the process, particularly with respect to diversity issues. It is hoped that new methodologies will be developed to supplement classic research designs.

11. There is *no one route* to "good" parenting. There are multiple pathways to healthy developmental outcomes for parents, children, and society.

References

AARONSON, L.S., & MACNEE, C.L. (1989). Tobacco, alcohol, and caffeine use during pregnancy. *Journal of Obstetrics, Gynecology, and Neonatal Nursing, 18,* 279–287.

AINSLIE, R.C., & ANDERSON, C.W. (1984). Day care children's relationships to their mothers and caregivers: An inquiry into the conditions for the development of attachment. In R.C. Ainslie (Ed.), *The child and the day care setting: Qualitative variations and development.* New York: Praeger.

AINSWORTH, M.D.S., BELL, S.M., & STAYTON, D. (1974). Infant-mother attachment and social development: "Socialization" as a product of reciprocal responsiveness to signals. In M.P.M. Richards (Ed.), *The integration of the child into a social world* (pp. 99–135). London: Cambridge University Press.

AINSWORTH, M.D.S., BLEHAR, M.C., WATERS, E., & WALL, S. (1978). *Patterns of attachment: A psychological study of the strange situation.* Hillsdale, NJ: Lawrence Erlbaum Associates.

ALDOUS, J. (1978). *Family careers: Developmental changes in families.* New York: Wiley.

ALDOUS, J. (1985). Parent-child relations as affected by the grandparent status. In V.L. Bengston & J.F. Robertson (Eds.), *Grandparenthood.* Beverly Hills, CA: Sage.

ALTEMEIER, W.A., O'CONNOR, S.M., SHERROD, K.B., & VIETZE, P.M. (1984). Prospective study of antecedents for nonorganic failure to thrive. *Journal of Pediatrics, 106,* 360–365.

ALTER, J., & WILSON, P. (1982). *Teaching parents to be the primary sexuality educators of their children, final report, vol. III: Curriculum guide to courses for parents* (Report No. SP-024-161). Atlanta, GA: Centers for Disease Control. (ERIC Document Reproduction Service No. ED 243816).

AMATO, P.R. (1994). Father-child relations, mother-child relations, and offspring psychological well-being in early adulthood. *Journal of Marriage and the Family, 56,* 1031–1042.

AMATO, P.R., & KEITH, B. (1991). Parental divorce and the well-being of children: A meta-analysis. *Psychological Bulletin, 110,* 26–46.

AMERICAN ACADEMY OF PEDIATRICS. (1995). *Caring for your school-age child: Ages 5 to 12.* New York: Bantam Books.

AMES, L.B., & ILG, F.L. (1976). *Your two year old: Terrible or tender.* New York: Dell Publishing Company.

ANDERSON, S.A. (1988). Parental stress and coping during the leaving home transition. *Family Relations, 37,* 160–165.

ANDERSSON, B. (1989). Effects of public day-care: A longitudinal study. *Child Development, 60,* 857–866.

APFEL, N.H., & SEITZ, V. (1991). Four models of adolescent mother-grandmother relationships in black inner-city families. *Family Relations, 40,* 421–429.

AQUILINO, W.S. (1990). The likelihood of parent-child coresidence: Effects of family structure and parental characteristics. *Journal of Marriage and the Family, 52,* 405–419.

AQUILINO, W.S. (1991). Family structure and home-leaving: A further specification of the relationship. *Journal of Marriage and the Family, 53,* 999–1010.

AQUILINO, W.S., & SUPPLE, K.R. (1991). Parent-child relations and parent's satisfaction with living arrangements when adult children live at home. *Journal of Marriage and Family Living, 53,* 13–57.

ARCHBOLD, P.G. (1983). The impact of parent-caring on women. *Family Relations, 32,* 39–45.

ARDITTI, J.A., & KELLEY, M. (1994). Fathers' perspectives of their co-parental relationships postdivorce. *Family Relations, 43,* 61–67.

ARDITTI, J.A., & MADDEN-DERDICH, D.A. (1993). Noncustodial mothers: Developing strategies of support. *Family Relations, 42,* 305–315.

ARIES, P. (1962). *Centuries of childhood: A social history of family life.* R. Baldick, translator. New York: Knopf.

ATKINSON, A.K., & RICKEL, A.U. (1984). Postpartum depression in primiparous parents. *Journal of Abnormal Psychology, 93,* 115–119.

ATKINSON, A.M. (1987). A comparison of mothers' and providers' preferences and evaluations of day care services. *Child and Youth Care Quarterly, 16,* 35–47.

ATTNEAVE, C. (1982). American Indians and Alaska Native families: Emigrants in their own homeland. In M. McGoldrick, J. Pearce, & J. Giordano (Eds.), *Ethnicity and family therapy* (pp. 55–83). New York: The Guilford Press.

AZRIN, N.H., & FOXX, R.M. (1974). *Toilet training in less than a day.* New York: Pocket Books.

BAILEY, J.M., BOBROW, D., WOLFE, M., & MIKACH, S. (1995). Sexual orientation of adult sons of gay fathers. *Developmental Psychology, 31,* 124–129.

BALLENSKI, C.B., & COOK, A.S. (1982). Mothers' perceptions of their competence in managing selected parenting tasks. *Family Relations, 31,* 489–494.

BANDURA, A. (1986). *Social foundations of thought and action: A social cognitive theory.* Englewood Cliffs, NJ: Prentice Hall.

BARBER, B.K. (1994). Cultural, family, and personal contexts of parent-adolescent conflict. *Journal of Marriage and the Family, 56,* 375–386.

BARBER, B.L. (1994). Support and advice from married and divorced fathers. *Family Relations, 43,* 433–438.

BARNETT, R.C., KIBRIA, N., BARUCH, G.K., & PLECK, J.H. (1991). Adult daughter-parent relationships and their associations with daughters' subjective well-being and psychological distress. *Journal of Marriage and the Family, 53,* 29–42.

BARRANTI, C.C.R. (1985). The grandparent/grandchild relationship: Family resource in an era of voluntary bonds. *Family Relations, 34,* 343–352.

BARRATT, M.S. (1991). School-age offspring of adolescent mothers: Environments and outcomes. *Family Relations, 40,* 442–447.

BARRY, D. (1984). *Babies and other hazards of sex.* Emmaus, PA: Rodale Press.

BASKIN, B.H., & RIGGS, E.P. (1988). Mothers who are disabled. In B. Birns & D.F. Hay (Eds.), *The different faces of motherhood,* New York: Plenum Press.

BATES, J.E., MARVINNEY, D., KELLY, T., DODGE, K.A., BENNETT, D.S., & PETIT, G.S. (1994). Child-care history and kindergarten adjustment. *Developmental Psychology, 30,* 690–700.

BATES, J.E., OLSON, S.L., PETTIT, G.S., & BAYLES, K. (1982). Dimensions of individuality in the mother-infant relationship at six months of age. *Child Development, 53,* 446–461.

BAUMRIND, D. (1967). Child care practices anteceding three patterns of preschool behavior. *Genetic Psychology Monographs, 75,* 43–88.

BAUMRIND, D. (1971). Current patterns of parental authority. *Developmental Psychology Monograph, 4.*

BAUMRIND, D. (1978). Parental disciplinary patterns and social competence in children. *Youth and Society, 9,* 239–276.

BAUMRIND, D. (1980). New directions in socialization research. *Psychological Bulletin, 35,* 639–652.

BAUMRIND, D. (1993). The average expectable environment is not good enough: A response to Scarr. *Child Development, 64,* 1299–1317.

BAUMRIND, D. (1994). The social context of child maltreatment. *Family Relations, 43,* 360–368.

BAUMRIND, D. & MOSELLE, K. (1985). A developmental perspective on adolescent drug abuse. *Advances in Alcohol and Substance Abuse, 4,* 41–67.

BECKMAN, P.J. (1984). A transactional view of stress in families of handicapped children. In M. Lewis (Ed.), *Beyond the Dyad* (pp. 281–298). New York: Plenum.

BECKMAN-BELL, P. (1981). Child-related stress in families of handicapped children. *Topics in Early Childhood Special Education, 1,* 45–53.

BECVAR, R.J., & BECVAR, D.S. (1982). *Systems theory and family therapy: A primer.* Lanham, MD: University Press of America.

BELL, R. (1977). History of the child's influence: Medieval to modern times. In R. Bell & L. Harper (Eds.), *Child effects on adults* (pp. 30–42). Hillsdale, NJ: Lawrence Erlbaum Associates.

BELL, S., & AINSWORTH, M.D.S. (1972). Infant crying and maternal responsiveness. *Child Development, 43,* 1171–1190.

BELLISTON, L., & BELLISTON, M. (1982). *How to raise a more creative child.* Allen, TX: Argus Communications.

BELSKY, J. (1980). Child maltreatment: An ecological integration. *American Psychologist, 35,* 320–335.

BELSKY, J. (1981). Early human experience: A family perspective. *Developmental Psychology, 17,* 3–23.

BELSKY, J. (1984). The determinants of parenting: A process model. *Child Development, 55,* 83–96.

BELSKY, J. (1988). The "effects" of infant day care reconsidered. *Early Childhood Research Quarterly, 3,* 225–272.

BELSKY, J. (1990). Parental and nonparental child care and children's socioemotional development: A decade review. *Journal of Marriage and the Family, 52,* 885–903.

BELSKY, J., LERNER, R.M., & SPANIER, G.B. (1984). *The child in the family.* Reading, MA: Addison-Wesley.

BELSKY, J., ROBINS, E., & GAMBLE, W. (1984). The determinants of parental competence: Toward a contextual theory. In M. Lewis (Ed.), *Beyond the dyad.* New York: Plenum Press.

BELSKY, J., & ROVINE, M. (1988). Nonmaternal care in the first year of life and infant-parent attachment security. *Child Development, 59,* 157–167.

BELSKY, J., & ROVINE, M. (1990). Patterns of marital change across the transition to parenthood: Pregnancy to three years postpartum. *Journal of Marriage and the Family, 52,* 5–19.

BELSKY, J., & STEINBERG, L. (1978). The effects of daycare: A critical review. *Child Development, 49,* 929–949.

BELSKY, J., & TOLAN, W.J. (1981). Infants as producers of their own development: An ecological analysis. In R.M. Lerner & N.A. Busch-Rossnagel (Eds.), *Individuals as producers of their development: A life-span perspective.* New York: Academic Press.

BENEDICT, H. (1979). Early lexical development: Comprehension and production. *Journal of Child Language, 6,* 183–200.

BENGTSON, V.L., & BLACK, K.D. (1973). Intergenerational relations and continuities in socialization. In P. Baltes & K.W. Schaie (Eds.), *Life-span developmental psychology: Personality and socialization.* New York: Academic Press.

BENIN, M., & KEITH, V.M. (1995). The social support of employed African American and Anglo mothers. *Journal of Family Issues, 16,* 275–297.

BERCHTOLD, N. (1989, August). Depression after delivery: Help from the childbirth educator. *International Journal of Childbirth Education,* 14–16.

BERG, B. (1991, November). Bedwetting cures. *Parents,* 101–107.

BERNAL, G. (1982). Cuban families. In M. McGoldrick, J. Pearce, J. Giordano (Eds.), *Ethnicity and Family Therapy* (pp. 187–207). New York: The Guilford Press.

BERNHEIMER, L.P., YOUNG, M.S., & WINTON, P.J. (1983). Stress over time: Parents with young handicapped children. *Developmental and Behavioral Pediatrics, 4,* 177–181.

BERNSTEIN, L. (1994, January). Thumbs away: Commonsense strategies for weaning your child from thumbs and pacifiers. *Parents,* 73–74.

BETTES, B.A., & WALKER, E. (1986). Symptoms associated with suicidal behavior in childhood and adolescence. *Journal of Abnormal Child Psychology, 14,* 591–604.

BIGNER, J.J. (1989). *Parent-child relations: An introduction to parenting.* New York: Macmillan Publishing Company.

BIGNER, J.J., & BOZETT, F.W. (1990). Parenting by gay fathers. In F. Bozett & M. Sussman (Eds.), *Homosexuality and family relations* (pp. 155–175). New York: The Haworth Press.

BIGNER, J.J., & JACOBSEN, R.B. (1989). Parenting behaviors of homosexual and heterosexual fathers. *Journal of Homosexuality, 18,* 173–186.

BILLER, H.B. (1970). Father absence and the personality development of the male child. *Developmental Psychology, 2,* 181–201.

BILLER, H.B. (1981). Father absence, divorce, and personality development. In M.E. Lamb (Ed.), *The role of the father in child development* (pp. 489–552). New York: John Wiley.

BLACHER, J., & BAKER, B.L. (1994). Out-of-home placement for children with retardation: Family decision making and satisfaction. *Family Relations, 43,* 10–15.

BLOCK, J.H., & BLOCK, J. (1980). The role of ego-control and ego-resiliency in the organization of behavior. In W.A. Collins (Ed.), *Minnesota Symposia on Child Psychology, 13,* Hillsdale, NJ: Erlbaum.

BLOCK, J.H., BLOCK, J., & GJERDE, P.F. (1986). The personality of children prior to divorce: A prospective study. *Child Development, 57,* 827–840.

BOGAT, G.A., & GENSHEIMER, L.K. (1986). Discrepancies between the attitudes and actions of parents choosing day care. *Child Care Quarterly, 15,* 159–169.

BOOTH, T. (1989, November). Teaching coping skills: Coercion or choice. *International Journal of Childbirth Education,* 25–26.

BORNSTEIN, M.H., & LAMB, M.E. (1992). *Development in infancy: An introduction.* New York: McGraw-Hill, Inc.

BOWLBY, J. (1969). *Attachment and loss. vol. I: Attachment.* New York: Basic Books.

BOWLBY, J. (1979). *The making and breaking of affectional bonds.* New York: Tavistock.

BOUVARD, M. (1988). *The path through grief: A practical guide.* Portland, OR: Breitenbush Books, Inc.

BOWMAN, M., & AHRONS, C. (1985). Impact of legal custody status on fathers' parenting post-divorce. *Journal of Marriage and the Family, 47,* 481–488.

BOWMAN, P.J. (1993). The impact of economic marginality among African American husbands and fathers. *Family ethnicity: Strength in diversity* (pp. 120–137). Newbury Park, CA: Sage Publications.

BOYKIN, A.W., & TOMS, F.D. (1985). Black child socialization: A conceptual framework. In H.P. McAdoo & J. McAdoo (Eds.), *Black children: Social, educational, and parental environments* (pp. 33–52). Beverly Hills: Sage.

BOZETT, F.W. (1989). Gay fathers: A review of the literature. In F. Bozett (Ed.), *Homosexuality and the family* (pp. 137–162). New York: The Haworth Press.

BRACKBILL, Y. (1979). Obstetrical medication and infant behavior. In J.D. Osofsky (Ed.), *Handbook of infant development.* New York: Wiley.

BRADBARD, M.R., ENDSLEY, R.C., & READDICK, C.A. (1983). How and why parents select profit-making day care programs: A study of two southeastern college communities. *Child Care Quarterly, 12,* 160–169.

BRADLEY, E.J., & PETER, R.D. (1991). Physically abusive and nonabusive mothers' perceptions of parenting and child behavior. *American Journal of Orthopsychiatry, 61,* 455–460.

BRADLEY, R.H. (1995). Environment and parenting. In M.H. Bornstein (Ed.), *Handbook of parenting: vol. 2. Biology and ecology of parenting.* Mahwah, NJ: Lawrence Erlbaum Associates.

BRAZELTON, T.B. (1987a). Issues for working parents. *American Journal of Orthopsychiatry, 56,* 14–25.

BRAZELTON, T.B. (1987b). *Working and caring.* Reading, MA: Addison-Wesley.

BRAZELTON, T.B. (1990). Saving the bathwater. *Child Development, 61,* 1661–1671.

BRENNER, B. (1990). *The preschool handbook: Making the most of your child's education.* New York: Pantheon Books.

BRISTOL, M.M., & GALLAGHER, J.J. (1986). Research on fathers of young handicapped children: Evolution, review, and some future directions. In J.J. Gallagher & P.M. Vietze (Eds.), *Families of handicapped persons: Research, programs, and policy issues.* Baltimore, MD: Paul H. Brookes Publishing Company.

BRODY, G.H., MOORE, K., & GLEI, D. (1994). Family processes during adolescence as predictors of parent-young adult attitude similarity: A six year longitudinal analysis. *Family Relations, 43,* 369–373.

BRODZINSKY, D.M., & HUFFMAN, L. (1988). Transition to adoptive parenthood. *Marriage and Family Review, 12,* 267–286.

BRONFENBRENNER, U. (1979). *The ecology of human development: Experiments by nature and design.* Cambridge, MA: Harvard University Press.

BRONFENBRENNER, U. (1989). Ecological systems theory. In R. Vasta (Eds.), *Annals of child development,* vol. 6 (pp. 187–251). Greenwich, CT: JAI Press.

BRONFENBRENNER, U., ALVAREZ, W.F., & HENDERSON, C.R. (1984). Working and watching: Maternal employment status and parents' perceptions of their three-year-old children. *Child Development, 55,* 1362–1378.

BRONFENBRENNER, U., & CROUTER, A. (1982). Work and family through time and space. In S. Kammerman & C. Hayes (Eds.), *Families that work: Children in a changing world* (pp. 39–83). Washington, DC: National Academy Press.

BRONSTEIN, P., STOLL, M.F., CLAUSON, J., ABRAMS, C.L., & BRIONES, M. (1994). Fathering after separation or divorce: Factors predicting children's adjustment. *Family Relations, 43,* 469–479.

BROWN, B. (1990). Peer groups. In S.S. Feldman & G.L. Elliot (Eds.), *At the threshold: The developing adolescent.* Cambridge, MA: Harvard University Press.

BROWN, B.B., MOUNTS, N., LAMBORN, S.D., & STEINBERG, L. (1993). Parenting practices and peer group affiliation in adolescence. *Child Development, 64,* 467–482.

BROWN, M.H., CROMER, P.S., & WEINBERG, S.H. (1986). Shared book experiences in kindergarten: Helping children come to literacy. *Early Childhood Research Quarterly, 1,* 397–405.

BROWNE, A., & FINKELHOR, D. (1986). Impact of child sexual abuse: A review of the research. *Psychological Bulletin, 99,* 100–117.

BRUBAKER, T.H. (1983). Introduction. In T.H. Brubaker (Ed.), *Family relationships in later life.* Beverly Hills, CA: Sage.

BRUBAKER, T.H. (1990a). An overview of family relationships in later life. In T.H. Brubaker (Ed.), *Family relationships in later life.* Newbury Park, CA: Sage.

BRUBAKER, T.H. (1990b). Family in later life: A burgeoning research area. *Journal of Marriage and the Family, 52,* 959–981.

BRUNER, J. (1983). *Child's talk: Learning to use language.* New York: Norton.

BRUNER, J. (1985). Vygotsky: A historical and conceptual perspective. In J.V. Wertsch (Ed.), *Culture, communication, and cognition: Vygotskian perspectives.* New York: Cambridge University Press.

BUCHANAN, C.M., MACCOBY, E.E., & DORNBUSCH, S.M. (1991). Caught between parents: Adolescents' experience in divorced homes. *Child Development, 62,* 1008–1029.

BUCHANAN, C.M., ECCLES, J.S., & BECKER, J.B. (1992). Are adolescents the victims of raging hormones: Evidence for activational effects of hormones on moods and behavior at adolescence. *Psychological Bulletin, 111,* 62–107.

BUCK, N., & SCOTT, J. (1993). She's leaving home: But why? An analysis of young people leaving the parental home. *Journal of Marriage and the Family, 55,* 863–874.

BUGENTAL, D.B., MANTYLA, S.M., & LEWIS, J. (1989). Parental attributions as moderators of affective communication to children at risk for physical abuse. In D. Cicchetti & V. Carlson (Eds.), *Child maltreatment: Theory and research on the causes and consequences of child abuse and neglect* (pp. 254–279), New York: Cambridge University Press.

BURDEN, D.S. (1986). Single parents and the work setting: The impact of multiple job and homelife responsibilities. *Family Relations, 36,* 37–43.

BUSS, A.H., & PLOMIN, R. (1984). *Temperament: Early developing personality traits.* Hillsdale, NJ: Erlbaum.

CALDERONE, M.S., & RAMEY, J.W. (1982). *Talking with your child about sex: Questions and answers for children from birth to puberty.* New York: Ballantine Books.

CALLAHAN, C.M. (1980). The gifted girl: An anomaly? *Roeper Review, 2,* 16–20.

CALLAN, V.J. (1986). The impact of the first birth: Married and single women preferring childlessness, one child, or two children. *Journal of Marriage and Family, 48,* 261–269.

CALLANAN, M.A. (1985). How parents label objects for young children: The role of input in the acquisition of category hierarchies. *Child Development, 56,* 508–523.

CALVERT, S.L., & TAN, S. (1994). The impact of virtual reality on young adults' physiological arousal and aggressive thoughts: Interaction versus observation. *Journal of Applied and Developmental Psychology, 15,* 125–139.

CAMARA, K., & RESNICK, G. (1989). Styles of conflict resolution and cooperation between divorced parents: Effects on child behavior and adjustment. *American Journal of Orthopsychiatry, 59,* 560–576.

CAMPBELL, F.A., BREITMAYER, B., & RAMEY, C.T. (1986). Disadvantaged single teenage mothers and their children: Consequences of free educational day care. *Family Relations, 35,* 63–68.

CAMPBELL, F.L., TOWNES, B.D., & BEACH, L.P. (1982). Motivational bases of childbearing decisions. In F.L. Fox (Ed.), *The childbearing decision: Fertility attitudes and behavior.* Beverly Hills, CA: Sage.

CAMPEN, J. (1991, August). Statistics corner. *International Journal of Childbirth Education,* 13–16.

CAPALDI, D.M., & PATTERSON, G.R. (1991). Relation of parental transitions to boys' adjustment problems: I. A linear hypothesis. II. Mothers at risk for transitions and unskilled parenting. *Developmental Psychology, 27,* 489–504.

CAPLAN, P.J., & HALL-MCCORQUODALE, I. (1985). The scapegoating of mothers: A call for change. *American Journal of Orthopsychiatry, 55(4),* 610–613.

CAPLAN, T., & CAPLAN, F. (1983). *The early childhood years: The 2 to 6 year old.* New York: Bantam Books.

CAREY, S. (1978). The child as word learner. In M. Halle, J. Bresnan, & G. Miller (Eds.), *Linguistic theory and psychological reality.* Cambridge, MA: MIT Press.

CARLSON, V., CICCHETTI, D., BARNETT, D., & BRAUNWALD, K. (1989). Disorganized/disoriented attachment relationships in maltreated infants. *Developmental Psychology, 25,* 525–531.

CASPER, L.M., HAWKINS, M., O'CONNELL, M. (1994). *Who's minding the kids? Child care arrangements: Fall 1991.* US Bureau of Census, Current Population Reports, US Government Printing Office, Washington, DC.

CASPER, V., SCHULTZ, S., & WICKENS, E. (1992). Breaking the silences: Lesbian and gay parents and the schools. *Teachers College Record, 94(1),* 109–137.

CATALYST. (1988). Workplace policies: New options for fathers. In P. Bronstein & C.P. Cowan (Eds.), *Fatherhood today: Men's changing role in the family* (pp. 323–340). New York: Wiley.

CERNACK, J.M., & PORTER, R.H. (1985). Recognition of maternal axillary odors by infants. *Child Development, 56,* 1593–1598.

CESAREAN FACT SHEET. (1991, November). *International Journal of Childbirth Education,* 16–17.

CHAMBERLAIN, P., & PATTERSON, G.R. (1995). Discipline and child compliance in parenting. In M.H. Bornstein (Ed.), *Handbook of parenting: vol. 4. Applied and practical parenting.* Mahwah, NJ: Erlbaum.

CHAN, S. (1992). Families with Asian roots. In E.W. Lynch & M.J. Hanson (Eds.), *Developing cross-cultural competence* (pp. 181–257). Baltimore, MD: Paul H. Brookes Publishing Company.

CHAO, R.K. (1994). Beyond parental control and authoritarian parenting style: Understanding Chinese parenting through the cultural notion of training. *Child Development, 65,* 1111–1119.

CHASE-LANSDALE, P.M., BROOKS-GUNN, J., & PAIKOFF, R.L. (1991). Research and programs for adolescent mothers: Missing links and future promises. *Family Relations, 40,* 396–403.

CHASE-LANSDALE, P.M., BROOKS-GUNN, J., & ZAMSKY, E.S. (1994). Young African-American multigenerational families in poverty: Quality of mothering and grandmothering. *Child Development, 65,* 373–393.

CHASNOFF, I.J., GRIFFITH, D.R., FREIER, C., & MURRAY, J. (1992). Cocaine/polydrug use in pregnancy: Two-year follow-up. *Pediatrics, 89,* 666–669.

CHEAL, D.J. (1983). Intergenerational family transfers. *Journal of Marriage and the Family, 45,* 805–813.

CHECK, W.A. (1989). *Child abuse.* New York: Chelsea House Publishers.

CHEN, C., & STEVENSON, H.W. (1989). Homework: A cross-cultural examination. *Child Development, 60,* 551–561.

CHERLIN, A., & FURSTENBERG, F.F. (1985). Styles and strategies of grandparenting. In V.L. Bengston & J.F. Robertson (Eds.), *Grandparenthood.* Beverly Hills, CA: Sage.

CHERLIN, A.J., & FURSTENBERG, F.F. (1986). *The new American grandparent: A place in the family, a life apart.* New York: Basic Books.

CHERLIN, A.J., FURSTENBERG, F.F. JR., CHASE-LANSDALE, P.L., KIERNAN, K.E., ROBINS, P.K., MORRISON, D.R., & TEITLER, J.O. (1991). Longitudinal studies of effects of divorce on children in Great Britain and the United States. *Science, 252,* 1386–1389.

CHILDREN'S DEFENSE FUND. (1994). *The state of America's children yearbook 1994*, Washington, DC: Children's Defense Fund.

CICIRELLI, V.G. (1983). Adult children and their elderly parents. In T.H. Brubaker (Ed.), *Family relationship in later life*. Beverly Hills, CA: Sage.

CICIRELLI, V.G. (1984). Marital disruption and adult children's perception of their siblings' help to elderly parents. *Family Relations, 33,* 613–621.

CICIRELLI, V.G. (1991). Attachment theory in old age: Protection of the attached figure. In K. Pillemer & K. McCartney (Eds.), *Parent-child relations throughout life*. Hillsdale, NJ: Erlbaum.

CILLESSEN, A.H.N., VAN IJZENDOORN, H.W., & VAN LIESHOUT, C.F.M., & HARTUP, W.W. (1992). Heterogeneity among peer-rejected boys: Subtypes and stabilities. *Child Development, 63,* 893–905.

CLARK, B. (1983). *Growing up gifted: Developing the potential of children at home and at school*. Columbus, OH: Charles E. Merrill Publishing Co.

CLARKE, J.I. (1993). *Help! For parents of school-age children and teenagers*. San Francisco, CA: Harper.

CLARKE-STEWART, K.A. (1978). Popular primers for parents. *American Psychologist, 33,* 359–369.

CLARKE-STEWART, K.A. (1989a). Single-parent families: How bad for the children? *NEA Today,* 60–64.

CLARKE-STEWART, K.A. (1989b). Infant day care: Maligned or malignant? *American Psychologist, 44,* 266–273.

CLARKE-STEWART, K.A. (1990). "The effects of infant day care reconsidered" reconsidered: Risks for parents, children, and researchers. In N. Fox & G. Fein (Eds.), *Infant day care: The current debate* (61–86). Norwood, NJ: Ablex.

CLARKE-STEWART, K.A., & GRUBER, C.P. (1984). Day care forms and features. In R.C. Ainslie (Ed.), *The child and the day care setting*. New York: Praeger.

CLEMENS, A.W., & AXELSON, L.J. (1985). The not-so-empty nest: The return of the fledgling adult. *Family Relations, 34,* 259–264.

CLEMES, H., & BEAN, R. (1990). *How to raise children's self-esteem*. Los Angeles, CA: Price Stern Sloan.

CLINGEMPEEL, W.G., & SEGAL, S. (1986). Stepparent-stepchild relationships and the psychological adjustment of children in stepmother and stepfather families. *Child Development, 57,* 474–484.

COCHRAN, M. (1990). Factors influencing personal social initiative. In M. Cochran, M. Larner, D. Riley, L. Gunnarson, & C. Henderson, Jr. (Eds.), *Extending families: The social networks of parents and their children* (pp. 297–306). London/New York: Cambridge University Press.

COCHRAN, M., & BRASSARD, J. (1979). Child development and personal social networks. *Child Development, 50,* 601–616.

COGLE, F.L., & TASKER, G.E. (1982). Children and housework. *Family Relations, 31,* 395–399.

COHEN, M. (1976). *Selecting educational equipment and materials*. Washington, DC: Association for Childhood Education International.

COHEN, P.M. (1983). A group approach for working with families of the elderly. *The Gerontologist, 23,* 248–250.

COHN, D.A. (1990). Child-mother attachment of six-year-olds and social competence at school. *Child Development, 61,* 152–162.

COIE, J.D., & DODGE, K. (1983). Continuities and changes in children's social status: A five year longitudinal study. *Merrill-Palmer Quarterly, 29,* 261–282.

COIE, J.D., DODGE, K.A., & COPPOTELLI, H. (1982). Dimensions of types of social status: A cross-age perspective. *Developmental Psychology, 18,* 557–560.

COLANGELO, N., & BROWER, P. (1987). Labeling gifted youngsters: Long-term impact on families. *Gifted Child Quarterly, 32(2)*, 75–78.

COLE, C., & RODMAN, H. (1987). When school-age children care for themselves: Issues for family life educators and parents. *Family Relations, 36*, 92–96.

COLEMAN, M. (1991). Planning for the changing nature of family life in schools for young children. *Young Children, 46*, 15–20.

COLLETTA, N.D. (1981). Social support and risk of maternal rejection by adolescent mothers. *The Journal of Psychology, 109*, 191–197.

COMER, J.P., & POUSSAINT, A.F. (1992). *Raising black children.* New York: Penguin Books.

COMPAS, B.E., BANEZ, G.A., MALCARNE, V., & WORSHAM, N. (1991). Perceived control and coping with stress: A developmental perspective. *Journal of Social Issues, 47*, 23–43.

CONNERS, L.J., & EPSTEIN, J.L. (1995). Parent and school partnerships. In M.H. Bornstein (Ed.), *Handbook of parenting: vol. 4. Applied and practical parenting.* Mahwah, NJ: Erlbaum.

COOKE, B. (1991). Thinking and knowledge underlying expertise in parenting: Comparisons between expert and novice mothers. *Family Relations, 40*, 3–13.

COONEY, T.M., PEDERSEN, F.A., INDELICATO, S., & PALKOVITZ, R. (1993). Timing of fatherhood: Is "on-time" optimal? *Journal of Marriage and the Family, 55*, 205–215.

COOPERSMITH, S. (1967). *The antecedents of self-esteem.* New York: W.H. Freeman.

CORNELL, D.G. (1983). Gifted children: The impact of positive labeling on the family system. *American Journal of Orthopsychiatry, 53(2)*, 322–335.

CORNELL, D.G., & GROSSBERG, I.W. (1987). Family environment and personality adjustment in gifted program children. *Gifted Child Quarterly, 31*, 59–64.

COTTERELL, J.L. (1986). Working and community influences on the quality of child rearing. *Child Development, 57*, 362–374.

COULTON, C.J., KORBIN, J.E., SU, M., & CHOW, J. (1995). Community level factors and child maltreatment rates. *Child Development, 66*, 1262–1267.

COWAN, C.P., & COWAN P.A. (1995). Interventions to ease the transition to parenthood: Why they are needed and what they can do. *Family Relations, 44*, 412–423.

COWAN, P.A. (1988). Becoming a father: A time of change, an opportunity for development. In P. Bronstein & C.P. Cowan (Eds.), *Fatherhood today: Men's changing role in the family.* New York: Wiley.

CRARY, E. (1993). *Without spanking or spoiling: A practical approach to toddler and preschool guidance.* Seattle, WA: Parenting Press.

CREASEY, G.L., & KOBLEWSKI, P.J. (1991). Adolescent grandchildren's relationships with maternal and paternal grandmothers and grandfathers. *Journal of Adolescence, 14*, 373–387.

CRNIC, K.A., & BOOTH, C.L. (1991). Mothers' and fathers' perceptions of daily hassles of parenting across early childhood. *Journal of Marriage and the Family, 53*, 1042–1050.

CRNIC, K.A., FRIEDRICH, W.N., & GREENBERG, M.T. (1983). Adaptation of families with mentally retarded children: A model of stress, coping, and family ecology. *American Journal of Mental Deficiency, 88*, 125–138.

CRNIC, K.A., & GREENBERG, M.T. (1990). Minor parenting stresses with young children. *Child Development, 61*, 1628–1637.

CRNIC, K.A., GREENBERG, M.T., RAGOZIN, A.S., ROBINSON, N.M., & BASHAM, R.B. (1983). Effects of stress and social support on mothers of premature and full-term infants. *Child Development, 54*, 209–217.

CROFT, D.J. (1979). *Parents and teachers: A resource book for home, school, and community relations.* Belmont, CA: Wadsworth Publishing Company, Inc.

CROOK, C.K. (1978). Taste perception in the newborn infant. *Infant Behavior and Development, 1,* 52–69.

CROSBIE-BURNETT, M., & GILES-SIMS, J. (1994). Adolescent adjustment and stepparenting styles. *Family Relations, 43,* 394–399.

CROSBIE-BURNETT, M., & HELMBRECHT, L. (1993). A descriptive study of gay male stepfamilies. *Family Relations, 42,* 256–263.

CROSS, W.E. (1990). Race and ethnicity: Effects on social networks. In M. Cochran, M. Larner, D. Riley, Gunnarson, L., & Henderson, C.R. (Eds.), *Extending families: The social networks of parents and their children.* New York: Cambridge University Press.

CROUTER, A.C., & MCHALE, S.M. (1993). The long arm of the job: Influences of parental work on childrearing. In T. Luster & L. Okagaki (Eds.), *Parenting: An ecological perspective* (pp. 179–202). Hillsdale, NJ: Erlbaum.

CROUTER, A.C., PERRY-JENKINS, M., HUSTON, T.L., & MCHALE, S.M. (1987). Processes underlying father-involvement in dual-earner and single-earner families. *Developmental Psychology, 23,* 431–440.

CURTNER-SMITH, M.E., & MACKINNON-LEWIS, C.E. (1994). Family process effects on adolescent males' susceptibility to antisocial peer pressure. *Family Relations, 43,* 462–468.

DANDO, I., & MINTY, B. (1987). What makes good foster parents? *British Journal of Social Work, 17(4),* 383–399.

DANIELS, P., & WEINGARTEN, K. (1988). The fatherhood click: The timing of parenthood in men's lives. In P. Bronstein & C.P. Cowan (Eds.), *Fatherhood today: Men's changing role in the family* (pp. 36–52). New York: Wiley.

DARLING, N., & STEINBERG, L. (1993). Parenting style as context: An integrative model. *Psychological Bulletin, 113,* 487–496.

DEAL, J.E., HALVERSON, C.F. JR., & WAMPLER, K.S. (1989). Parental agreement on childrearing orientations: Relations to marital, family, and child characteristics. *Child Development, 60,* 1025–1034.

DECASPER, A.J., & FIFER, W.P. (1980). Of human bonding: Newborns prefer their mothers' voices. *Science, 208,* 1174–1176.

DEFRAIN, J., FRICKE, J., & ELMEN, J. (1987). *On our own: A single parent's survival guide.* Lexington, MA: Lexington Press.

DEKOVIC, M., & GERRIS, J.R.M. (1994). Developmental analysis of social cognitive and behavioral differences between popular and rejected children. *Journal of Applied Developmental Psychology, 15,* 367–386.

DELISLE, J.R. (1990). The gifted adolescent at risk: Strategies and resources for suicide prevention among gifted youth. *Journal for the Education of the Gifted, 13,* 212–228.

DEMO, D., & ACOCK, A. (1988). The impact of divorce on children. *Journal of Marriage and the Family, 50,* 619–648.

DENHAM, T.E., & SMITH, C.W. (1989). The influence of grandparents on grandchildren: A review of the literature and resources. *Family Relations, 38,* 345–350.

DERDEYN, A.P., & SCOTT, E. (1984). Joint custody: A critical analysis and appraisal. *American Journal of Orthopsychiatry, 54,* 199–209.

DEREZOTES, D.S., & SNOWDEN, L.R. (1990). Cultural factors in the intervention of child maltreatment. *Child and Adolescent Social Work, 7,* 161–175.

DEVILLIERS, P.A., & DEVILLIERS, J.G. (1992). Language development. In M.H. Bornstein & M.E. Lamb (Eds.), *Developmental psychology: An advanced textbook.* Hillsdale, NJ: Erlbaum.

DEVRIES, R.G. (1988). Normal parents: Institutions and the transition to parenthood. *Marriage and Family Review, 12,* 287–312.

Diagnostic and statistical manual of mental disorders (DSM IV). (1994). Washington, DC: American Psychiatric Association.

DICHTELMILLER, M., MEISELS, S.J., PLUNKETT, J.W., BOZYNSKI, M., CLAFLIN, C., & MAN-
GELSDORF, S.C. (1992). The relationship of parental knowledge to the development of extremely low birth weight infants. *Journal of Early Intervention, 16*
210–220.

DIX, T. (1991). The affective organization of parenting: Adaptive and maladaptive
processes. *Psychological Bulletin, 110,* 3–25.

DIX, T.H., RUBLE, D.N., GRUSEC, J., & NIXON, S. (1986). Social cognition in parents:
Inferential and affective reactions to children of three age levels. *Child Development, 57,* 879–894.

DOESCHER, S.M., & SUGAWARA, A.I. (1992). Impact of prosocial home- and school-based
interventions on preschool children's cooperative behavior. *Family Relations, 41,*
200–204.

DONNELLY, B.W., & VOYDANOFF, P. (1991). Factors associated with releasing for adoption among adolescent mothers. *Family Relations, 40,* 404–410.

DORR, A., & RABIN, B.E. (1995). Parents, children, and television. In M.H. Bornstein
(Ed.), *Handbook of parenting: vol. 4. Applied and practical parenting.* Mahwah, NJ:
Erlbaum.

DOUGHERTY, D.M. (1993). Adolescent health: Reflections on a report to the U.S. Congress. *American Psychologist, 48,* 193–201.

DOUGLASS, R.L. (1983). Domestic neglect and abuse of the elderly: Implications for
research and service. *Family Relations, 32,* 395–402.

DREIKURS, R. (1964). *Children: The challenge.* New York: Hawthorn Books, Inc.

DREIKURS, R., & GREY, L. (1968). *A new approach to discipline: Logical consequences.* New
York: Hawthorn Books.

DUBOIS, D.L., EITEL, S.K., FELNER, R.D. (1994). Effects of family environment and parent-child relationships on school adjustment during the transition to early adolescence. *Journal of Marriage and the Family, 56,* 405–414.

DUDLEY, J.R. (1991). Increasing our understanding of divorced fathers who have infrequent contact with their children. *Family Relations, 40,* 279–285.

DUMAS, J.E., & LAFRENIERE, P.J. (1993). Mother-child relationships as sources of support
or stress: A comparison of competent, average, aggressive, and anxious dyads.
Child Development, 64, 1732–1754.

DUNKLE, R.E. (1985). Comparing the depression of elders in two types of caregiving
arrangements. *Family Relations, 34,* 235–240.

DUNN, J. (1985). *Sisters and brothers.* Cambridge, MA: Harvard University Press.

DUNN, J. (1995). *From one child to two: What to expect, how to cope, and how to enjoy your
growing family.* New York: Fawcett Columbine.

DUNPHY, D.C. (1963). The social structure of urban adolescent peer groups. *Sociometry,
26,* 230–246.

DWYER, K.M., & RICHARDSON, J.L. (1990). Characteristics of eighth-grade students who
initiate self-care in elementary and junior high school. *Pediatrics, 86,* 448–454.

DYER, E.D. (1963). Parenthood as crisis: A re-study. *Marriage and Family Living, 25,*
196–201.

Easing the transition from preschool to kindergarten: A guide for early childhood
teachers and administrators. Washington, DC: U.S. Department of Health and
Human Services.

ECKENRODE, J., LAIRD, M., & DORIS, J. (1993). School performance and disciplinary
problems among abused and neglected children. *Developmental Psychology, 29,*
53–62.

EDWARDS, C.A. (1994). Leadership in groups of school-age girls. *Developmental Psychology, 30,* 920–927.

EGELAND, B., & FARBER, E. (1984). Infant-mother attachment: Factors related to its
development and changes over time. *Child Development, 55,* 753–771.

EGELAND, B., JACOBVITZ, D., & SROUFE, A.L. (1988). Breaking the cycle of abuse: The mother-child intervention project. *Child Development, 59,* 1080–1088.

EIDEN, R.D., TETI, D.M., KORNS, K.M. (1995). Maternal working models of attachment, marital adjustment, and the parent-child relationship. *Child Development, 66,* 1504–1518.

EIGER, M.E., & OLDS, S.W. (1972). *The complete book of breastfeeding.* NY: Bantam Books.

EISENBERG, N., FABES, R.A., CARLO, G., TROYER, D., SPEER, A.L., KARBON, M., & SWITZER, G. (1992). The relations of maternal practices and characteristics to children's vicarious emotional responsiveness. *Child Development, 63,* 583–602.

EISENBERG, N., LENNON, R., & ROTH, K. (1983). Prosocial development: A longitudinal study. *Developmental Psychology, 19,* 846–855.

ELARDO, R., BRADLEY, R., & CALDWELL, B.M. (1975). The relation of infants' home environments to mental test performance from six to thirty-six months: A longitudinal analysis. *Child Development, 46,* 71–76.

ELDER, G.H., ECCLES, J.S., ARDELT, M., & LORD, S. (1995). Inner-city parents under economic pressure: Perspectives on the strategies of parenting. *Journal of Marriage and the Family, 57,* 771–784.

ELDER, G.H., JR., VAN NGUYEN, T., & CASPI, A. (1985). Linking family hardship to children's lives. *Child Development, 56,* 361–375.

ELKIND, D. (1967). Egocentrism in adolescence. *Child Development, 38,* 1025–1034.

ELKIND, D. (1987). *Miseducation: Preschoolers at risk.* New York: Alfred A. Knopf.

EMERY, R.E. (1982). Interparental conflict and the children of discord and divorce. *Psychological Bulletin, 92,* 310–330.

EMERY, R.E. (1988). Mediation and the settlement of divorce disputes. In E.M. Hetherington & J.D. Arasteh (Eds.), *Impact of divorce, single parenting, and stepparenting on children* (pp. 53–72). Hillsdale, NJ: Erlbaum.

EMERY, R.E. (1989). Family violence. *American Psychologist, 44,* 321–328.

EMERY, R.E., & TUER, M. (1993). Parenting and the marital relationship. In T. Luster & L. Okagaki (Eds.), *Parenting: An ecological perspective.* Hillsdale, NJ: Erlbaum.

EPSTEIN, L.H., WING, R.R. (1987). Behavioral treatment of childhood obesity. *Psychological Bulletin, 101,* 331–342.

ERIKSON, E.H. (1963). *Childhood and society* (2nd ed.). New York: Norton.

ESPE-SHERWINDT, M., & KERLIN, S.L. (1990). Early intervention with parents with mental retardation: Do we empower or impair? *Infants and Young Children, 2,* 21–28.

FABER, A., & MAZLISH, E. (1980). *How to talk so kids will listen and listen so kids will talk.* New York: Avon Books.

FARRAN, D.C., METZGER, J., & SPARLING, J. (1986). Immediate and continuing adaptations in parents of handicapped children. In J.J. Gallagher & P.M. Vietze (Eds.), *Families of handicapped persons: Research, programs, and policy issues.* Baltimore, MD: Paul H. Brookes Publishing.

FAWCETT, J.T. (1988). The value of children and the transition to parenthood. *Marriage and Family Review, 12,* 11–34.

FEATHER, N.T. (1991). Variables relating to the allocation of pocket money to children: Parental reasons and values. *British Journal of Social Psychology, 30,* 221–234.

FEATHERSTONE, H. (1980). *A difference in the family: Living with a disabled child.* New York: Penguin Books.

FEIN, E. (1991). Issues in foster care: Where do we stand? *American Journal of Orthopsychiatry, 61,* 578–583.

FEIN, R.A. (1976). Men's entrance to parenthood. *The Family Coordinator, 25,* 341–348.

FELDMAN, M.A., CASE, L., TOWNS, F., & BETEL, J. (1985). Parent education project I: Development and nurturance of children of mentally retarded parents. *American Journal of Mental Deficiency, 90,* 253–258.

FELDMAN, S.S., NASH, S.C., & ASCHENBRENNER, B.G. (1983). Antecedents of fathering. *Child Development, 54,* 1628–1636.

FELDMAN, W., FELDMAN, E., & GOODMAN, J.T. (1988). Culture versus biology: Children's attitudes towards thinness and fatness. *Pediatrics, 81,* 190–194.

FELL, L., DAHLSTROM, M., & WINTER, D. (1984). Personality traits of parents of gifted children. *Psychological Reports, 54,* 383–387.

FELSON, R.B., & ZIELINSKI, M.A. (1989). Children's self-esteem and parental support. *Journal of Marriage and the Family, 51,* 727–735.

FERGUSSON, D.M., HORWOOD, L.J., & SHANNON, F.T. (1986). Factors related to the age of attainment of nocturnal bladder control: An 8-year longitudinal study. *Pediatrics, 78,* 884–890.

FERNALD, A., TAESCHNER, T., DUNN, J., PAPOUSEK, M., BOYSSEN-BARDIES, B., & FUKUI, I. (1989). A cross-language study of prosodic modifications in mothers' and fathers' speech to preverbal infants. *Journal of Child Language, 16,* 477–502.

FIELD, T. (1990). *Infancy.* Cambridge, MA: Harvard University Press.

FIELD, T., DEMPSEY, J., HATCH, J., TING, G., & CLIFTON, R. (1979). Cardiac and behavioral responses to repeated tactile and auditory stimulation by preterm and term neonates. *Developmental Psychology, 15,* 406–416.

FINE, M.J., & HENRY, S.A. (1989). Professional issues in parent education. In M.J. Fine (Ed.), *The second handbook on parent education: Contemporary perspectives.* New York: Academic Press.

FISCHER, L.R. (1988). The influence of kin on the transition to parenthood. *Marriage and Family Review, 12,* 201–219.

FLAKS, D.K., FICHER, I., MASTERPASQUA, F., & JOSEPH, G. (1995). Lesbians choosing motherhood: A comparative study of lesbian and heterosexual parents and their children. *Developmental Psychology, 31,* 105–114.

FLOYD, F.J., & PHILLIPPEE, K.A. (1993). Parental interactions with children with and without mental retardation: Behavior management, coerciveness, and positive exchange. *American Journal on Mental Retardation, 97,* 673–684.

FOGEL, A. (1984). *Infancy: Infant, family, and society.* St. Paul, MN: West Publishing Co.

FOREHAND, R., NEIGHBORS, B., DEVINE, D., & ARMISTEAD, L. (1994). Interparental conflict and parental divorce. *Family Relations, 43,* 387–393.

FRAIBERG, S. (1975). The development of human attachments in infants blind from birth. *Merrill-Palmer Quarterly, 21,* 315–334.

FRANK, S.J., AVERY, C.B., & LAMAN, M.S. (1988). Young adults' perceptions of their relationships with their parents: Individual differences in connectedness, competence, and emotional autonomy. *Developmental Psychology, 24,* 729–737.

FRANKLIN, A.J., & BOYD-FRANKLIN, N. (1985). A psychoeducational perspective on black parenting. In H.P. McAdoo & J. McAdoo (Eds.), *Black children: Social, educational, and parental environments* (pp. 194–210). Beverly Hills, CA: Sage.

FRAZEN, L., & FELIZBERTO, P. (1982). Baby walker injuries. *Pediatrics, 70,* 106–109.

FRENCH, V. (1977). History of the child's influence: Ancient Mediterranean civilizations. In R. Bell & L. Harper (Eds.), *Child effects on adults* (pp. 3–29). Hillsdale, NJ: Erlbaum.

FRENCH, V. (1995). History of parenting. In M.H. Bornstein (Ed.), *Handbook of parenting,* vol. 2 (pp. 263–285), Mahwah, NJ: Erlbaum.

FREY, K.S., GREENBERG, M.T., & FEWELL, R.R. (1989). Stress and coping among parents of handicapped children: A multidimensional approach. *American Journal on Mental Retardation, 94,* 240–249.

FULLER, B., HOLLOWAY, S.D., RAMBAUD, M., & EGGERS-PIEROLA, C. (1995). How do mothers choose child care? Competing cultural models in poor neighborhoods. Paper presented at the Biennial Meeting of the Society for Research in Child Development, Indianapolis, IN.

FURMAN, W. (1995). Parenting siblings. In M.H. Bornstein (Ed.), *Handbook of parenting: vol. 1. Children and parenting.* Mahwah, NJ: Erlbaum.

FURSTENBERG, F.F., BROOKS-GUNN, J., & CHASE-LANSDALE, L. (1987). *Adolescent mothers in later life.* New York: Cambridge University Press.

FURSTENBERG, F.F., BROOKS-GUNN, J., & MORGAN, S.P. (1989). Teenaged pregnancy and childbearing. *American Psychologist, 44,* 313–320.

FURSTENBERG, F.F., JR., & NORD, C.W. (1985). Parenting apart: Patterns of childrearing after marital disruption. *Journal of Marriage and the Family, 47,* 893–905.

GABEL, H., MCDOWELL, J., & CERRETO, M. (1983). Family adaptation to the handicapped infant. In S.G. Garwood & R.R. Fewell (Eds.), *Educating handicapped infants* (pp. 455–493), Rockville, MD: Aspen.

GABLE, S., CRNIC, K., & BELSKY, J. (1994). Coparenting within the family system: Influences on children's development. *Family Relations, 43,* 380–386.

GAGE, M.G., & CHRISTENSEN, D.H. (1991). Parental role socialization and the transition to parenthood. *Family Relations, 40,* 332–337.

GALEN, H. (1991). Increasing parental involvement in elementary school: The nitty-gritty of one successful program. *Young Children, 46,* 18–22.

GALINSKY, E. (1987). *The six stages of parenthood.* Reading, MA: Addison-Wesley.

GALINSKY, E., & DAVID, J. (1988). *The preschool years: Family strategies that work from experts and parents.* New York: Ballantine Books.

GALLAGHER, J.J., BECKMAN, P., & CROSS, A.H. (1983). Families of handicapped children: Sources of stress and its amelioration. *Exceptional Children, 50,* 10–19.

GALLAGHER, J., & COCHE, J. (1987). Hothousing: The clinical and educational concerns over pressuring young children. *Early Childhood Research Quarterly, 2,* 203–210.

GAMBLE, T.J., & ZIGLER, E. (1986). Effects of infant day care: Another look at the evidence. *American Journal of Orthopsychiatry, 56,* 26–55.

GANONG, L.H., & COLEMAN, M. (1987). Do mutual children cement bonds in stepfamilies? *Journal of Marriage and the Family, 49,* 686–698.

GARBARINO, J., & SHERMAN, D. (1980). High-risk neighborhoods, and high-risk families. *Child Development, 51,* 188–198.

GARCIA COLL, C.T., MEYER, E.C., & BRILLON, L. (1995). Ethnic and minority parenting. In M.E. Bornstein (Ed.), *Handbook of parenting* (pp. 189–209), Hillsdale, NJ: Erlbaum.

GARCIA-PRETO, N. (1982). Puerto Rican families. In M. McGoldrick, J. Pearce, & J. Giordano (Eds.), *Ethnicity and family therapy* (pp. 164–186). New York: The Guilford Press.

GAZELLA, J.G. (1982, February). Choosing a pediatrician. *Baby Talk,* 21–22.

GEASLER, M., DANNISON, L., & EDLUND, C. (1993). *Sexuality education help for parents of preschool children.* Kalamazoo, MI: Western Michigan University.

GEASLER, M.J., DANNISON, L.L., & EDLUND, C.J. (1995). Sexuality education of young children: Parental concerns. *Family Relations, 44,* 184–188.

GEBOY, M.J. (1981). Who is listening to the "experts"? The use of child care materials by parents. *Family Relations, 30,* 205–210.

GEEN, R.G. (1994). Television and aggression: Recent developments in research and theory. In D. Zillman, J. Bryant, & A.C. Huston (Eds.), *Media, children, and the family: Social scientific, psychoanalytic, and clinical perspectives.* Hillsdale, NJ: Erlbaum.

GELLES, R.J. (1989). Child abuse and violence in single-parent families: Parent absence and economic deprivation. *American Journal of Orthopsychiatry, 59,* 492–501.

GIBSON, J.T. (1988, July). You can lead a kid to the potty, but . . . *Parents,* 150.

GIDDAN, N., & VALLONGO, S. (1988). *Parenting through the college years.* Charlotte, VT: Williamson Publishing.

GINSBURG, G.S., & BRONSTEIN, P. (1993). Family factors related to children's intrinsic/extrinsic motivational orientation and academic performance. *Child Development, 64,* 1461–1474.

GLADIEUX, J.D. (1978). Pregnancy—the transition to parenthood: Satisfaction with the pregnancy experience as a function of sex role conceptions, marital relationship, and social network. In W. Miller & L. Newman (Eds.), *The first child and family formation.* Chapel Hill, NC: Carolina Population Center.

GLEASON, J.B. (1988). Language and socialization. In F. Kessel (Ed.), *The development of language and language researchers.* Hillsdale, NJ: Erlbaum.

GLICK, P.C. (1977). Updating the life cycle of the family. *Journal of Marriage and the Family, 39,* 5–13.

GLICK, P.C., & LIN, S.L. (1986). More adults are living with their parents: Who are they? *Journal of Marriage and the Family, 48,* 107–112.

GOER, H. (1995). *Obstetric myths versus research realities: A guide to the medical literature.* Granby, MA: Bergin & Garvey.

GOLDBERG, W.A. (1988). Introduction: Perspectives on the transition to parenthood. In G.Y. Michaels & W.A. Goldberg (Eds.), *The transition to parenthood: Current theory and research.* New York: Cambridge University Press.

GOLDBERG, W.A., & EASTERBROOKS, M.A. (1988). Maternal employment when children are toddlers and kindergarteners. In A.E. Gottfried & A.W. Gottfried (Eds.), *Maternal employment and children's development* (pp. 121–154). New York: Plenum Press.

GOLDMAN, J.D.G., & GOLDMAN, R.J. (1983). Children's perceptions of parents and their roles: A cross-national study in Australia, England, North American, and Sweden. *Sex Roles, 9(7),* 791–812.

GOLDSCHEIDER, F.K., & GOLDSCHEIDER, C. (1989). Family structure and conflict: Nest-leaving expectations of young adults and their parents. *Journal of Marriage and the Family, 51,* 87–97.

GOLDSCHEIDER, F., & GOLDSCHEIDER, C. (1993). Whose nest? A two-generational view of leaving home during the 1980's. *Journal of Marriage and the Family, 55,* 851–862.

GOLDSCHEIDER, F.K., & WAITE, L.J. (1987). Nest-leaving patterns and the transition to marriage for young men and women. *Journal of Marriage and the Family, 49,* 507–516.

GOLOMBOK, S., & TASKER, F. (1996). Do parents influence the sexual orientations of their children? Findings from a longitudinal study of lesbian families. *Developmental Psychology, 32(1),* 3–11.

GONZALEZ-MENA, J., & EYER, D.W. (1980). *Infancy and caregiving.* Palo Alto, CA: Mayfield.

GOODNOW, J.J. (1988). Children's household work: Its nature and functions. *Psychological Bulletin, 103,* 5–26.

GOODNOW, J.J., & COLLINS, A. (1990). *Development according to parents: The nature, sources, and consequences of parents' ideas.* Hillsdale, NJ: Erlbaum.

GOPNIK, A. (1988). Three types of early words. *First Language, 8,* 49–70.

GORDON, T. (1970). *P.E.T. Parent effectiveness training: The tested new way to raise responsible children.* New York: Plume Books.

GORTMAKER, S.L., DIETZ, W.H., SOBOL, A.M., & WELHER, C.A. (1987). Increasing pediatric obesity in the United States. *American Journal of the Diseases of Childhood, 141,* 535–540.

GOTTFRIED, A.E., & GOTTFRIED, A.W. (1988). *Maternal employment and children's development: Longitudinal research.* New York: Plenum.

GOTTLIEB, B.H., & PANCER, S.M. (1988). Social networks and the transition to parenthood. In G.Y. Michaels & W.A. Goldberg (Eds.), *The transition to parenthood: Current theory and research.* New York: Cambridge University Press.

GOTTMAN, J.S. (1990). Children of gay and lesbian parents. In F. Bozett & M. Sussman (Eds.), *Homosexuality and family relations* (pp. 177–196). New York: The Haworth Press.

GREEN, R., MANDEL, J.B., HOTVEDT, M.E., GRAY, J., & SMITH, L. (1986). Lesbian mothers and their children: A comparison with solo parent heterosexual mothers and their children. *Archives of Sexual Behavior, 7,* 175–181.

GREENBERG, M., & MORRIS, N. (1974). Engrossment: The newborn's impact upon the father. *American Journal of Orthopsychiatry, 44,* 520–531.

GREENBERGER, E., & GOLDBERG, W.A. (1989). Work, parenting, and the socialization of children. *Developmental Psychology, 25,* 22–35.

GREENBERGER, E., O'NEIL, R., & NAGEL, S.K. (1994). Linking workplace and homeplace: Relations between the nature of adults' work and their parenting behaviors. *Developmental Psychology, 30,* 990–1002.

GREENBERGER, E., & STEINBERG, L. (1981). The workplace as a context for the socialization of youth. *Journal of Youth and Adolescence, 10,* 185–210.

GREENBERGER, E., & STEINBERG, L. (1986). *When teenagers work: The psychological and social costs of adolescent employment.* New York: Basic Books.

GREENE, B. (1990). Sturdy bridges: The role of African-American mothers in the socialization of African-American children. *Women and Therapy, 10,* 205–225.

GREENFIELD, P.M. (1994). Video games as cultural artifacts. *Journal of Applied Developmental Psychology, 15,* 3–12.

GREENFIELD, P.M., CAMAIONI, L., ERCOLANI, P., WEISS, L., LAUBER, B.A., & PERUCCHINI, P. (1994). Cognitive socialization by computer games in two cultures: Inductive discovery or mastery of an iconic code? *Journal of Applied Developmental Psychology, 15,* 59–85.

GREENFIELD, P.M., & COCKING, R.R. (1994). Effects of interactive entertainment technologies on development. *Journal of Applied Developmental Psychology, 15,* 1–2.

GREENSPAN, S., & BUDD, K.S. (1986). Research on mentally retarded parents. In J.J. Gallagher & P.M. Vietze (Eds.), *Families of handicapped persons: Research, programs, and policy issues.* Baltimore, MD: Paul H. Brookes Publishing Company.

GREIF, G.L. (1985). *Single fathers.* Lexington, MA: Heath.

GRIFFITHS, D.L., & UNGER, D.G. (1994). Views about planning for the future among parents and siblings of adults with mental retardation. *Family Relations, 43,* 221–227.

GROSSMAN, F.K., POLLACK, W.S., & GOLDING, E. (1988). Fathers and children: Predicting the quality and quantity of fathering. *Developmental Psychology, 24,* 82–91.

GROTEVANT, H., & COOPER, C. (1986). Individuation in family relationships: A perspective on individual differences in the development of identity and role-taking skill in adolescence. *Human Development, 29,* 82–100.

GROWING CHILD/GROWING PARENT. (1983). *Growing parent: A sourcebook for families.* Chicago, IL: Contemporary Books, Inc.

GRUSEC, J.E., & GOODNOW, J.J. (1994). Impact of parental discipline methods on the child's internalization of values: A reconceptualization of current points of view. *Developmental Psychology, 30,* 4–19.

GUIDUBALDI, J., CLEMINSHAW, H.K., PERRY, J.D., NASTASI, B.K., & LIGHTEL, J. (1986). The role of selected family environment factors in children's post-divorce adjustment. *Family Relations, 35,* 141–151.

GUSTAFSON, R. (1993). Conditioning treatment of children's bedwetting: A follow-up and predictive study. *Psychological Reports, 72,* 923–930.

GUTIERREZ, J., & SAMEROFF, A. (1990). Determinants of complexity in Mexican-American and Anglo-American Mothers' conceptions of child development. *Child Development, 61,* 384–394.

HAGESTAD, G.O. (1987). Parent-child relations in later life: Trends and gaps in past research. In J.B. Lancaster, J. Altmann, A.S. Rossi, & L.R. Sherrod (Eds.), *Parenting across the lifespan: Biosocial dimensions.* New York: Aldine DeGruyter.

HAGESTAD, G.O. (1988). Demographic change and the life course: Some emerging trends in the family realm. *Family Relations, 37,* 405–410.

HAIRE, D. (1991, August). Parent education in childbirth: A long way in forty years. *International Journal of Childbirth Education,* 7–10.

HALPERN, R. (1990). Poverty and early childhood parenting: Toward a framework for intervention. *American Journal of Orthopsychiatry, 60,* 6–18.

HAMBURG, D.A., & ADAMS, J.E. (1967). A perspective on coping behavior. *Archives of General Psychiatry, 17,* 277–284.

HAMBURG, D.A., & TAKANISHI, R. (1989). Preparing for life: The critical transition of adolescence. *American Psychologist, 44,* 825–827.

HAMNER, T.J., & TURNER, P.H. (1990). *Parenting in contemporary society.* Englewood Cliffs, NJ: Prentice Hall.

HANSON, M.J. (1992). Ethnic, cultural, and language diversity in intervention settings. In E.W. Lynch & M.J. Hanson (Eds.), *Developing cross-cultural competence* (pp. 3–18). Baltimore, MD: Paul H. Brookes Publishing Company.

HANSON, S.M.H., & SPORAKOWSKI, M.J. (1986). Single parent families. *Family Relations, 35,* 3–8.

HARE, J., & RICHARDS, L. (1993). Children raised by lesbian couples: Does the context of birth affect father and partner involvement? *Family Relations, 42,* 249–255.

HARJO, S.S. (1993). The American Indian experience. In H.P. McAdoo (Ed.), *Family ethnicity: Strength in diversity* (pp. 199–207). Newbury Park, CA: Sage.

HARKNESS, S., & SUPER, C. (1995). Culture and parenting. In M.H. Bornstein (Ed.), *Handbook of Parenting, vol. 2 Biology and Ecology of Parenting* (pp. 211–234). Mahwah, NJ: Erlbaum.

HARRIS, K.M., & MORGAN, S.P. (1991). Fathers, sons, and daughters: Differential paternal involvement in parenting. *Journal of Marriage and the Family, 53,* 531–544.

HARRIS, T. (1969). *I'm OK—you're OK.* New York: Harper & Row.

HARRISON, A.O., WILSON, M.N., PINE, C.J., CHAN, S.Q., & BURIEL, R. (1990). Family ecologies of ethnic minority children. *Child Development, 61,* 347–362.

HARRIST, A.W., PETTIT, G.S., DODGE, K.A., & BATES, J.E. (1994). Dyadic synchrony in mother-child interaction: Relation with children's subsequent kindergarten adjustment. *Family Relations, 43,* 417–424.

HARTUP, W.W., LAURSEN, B., STEWART, M.I., & EASTERSON, A. (1988). Conflict and the friendship relations of young children. *Child Development, 59,* 1590–1600.

HAUSER, S.T., & BOWLDS, M.K. (1990). Stress, coping, and adaptation. In S.S. Feldman & G.L. Elliot (Eds.), *At the threshold: The developing adolescent* (pp. 388–413). Cambridge, MA: Harvard University Press.

HAWKINS, A.J., & BELSKY, J. (1989). The role of father involvement in personality change in men across the transition to parenthood. *Family Relations, 38,* 378–384.

HAWLEY, T.L., & DISNEY, E.R. (Winter 1992). Crack's children: The consequences of maternal cocaine abuse. *Social Policy Report, 6(4),* Society for Research in Child Development.

HAYES, C. (1987). *Risking the future: Adolescent sexuality, pregnancy, and childbearing* (vol. 1). Washington, DC: National Academy Press.

HAYES, C.D., PALMER, J.L., & ZASLOW, M.J. (1990). *Who cares for America's children?: Child care policy for the 1990s.* Washington, DC: National Academy Press.

HEERMANN, J.A., JONES, L.C., & WIKOFF, R.L. (1994). Measurement of parent behavior during interactions with their infants. *Infant Behavior and Development, 17,* 311–321.

HELLIGMAN, D. (1992, November). How to handle nightmares and night terrors. *Parents, 162–166*.

HERNANDEZ, D.J. (1988). Demographic trends and the living arrangements of children. In E.M. Hetherington & J.D. Arasteh (Eds.), *Impact of divorce, single parenting, and stepparenting on children* (pp. 3–22). Hillsdale, NJ: Erlbaum.

HERNANDEZ, D.J. (1993). *America's children*. New York: Russell Sage.

HERRERA, J.F., & WOODEN, S.L. (1988). Some thoughts about effective parent-school communication. *Young Children, 43*, 78–80.

HERZOG, D.B., KELLER, M.B., & LAVORI, P.W. (1988). Outcome in anorexia nervosa and bulimia. *Journal of Nervous and Mental Diseases, 176*, 131–143.

HESS, R.D. (1980). Experts and amateurs: Some unintended consequences of parent education. In M.D. Fantini & R. Cardenas (Eds.), *Parenting in a multicultural society*, New York: Longman.

HETHERINGTON, E.M. (1988). Parents, children, and siblings: Six years after divorce. In R.A. Hinde & J. Stevenson-Hinde (Eds.), *Relationships within families: Mutual influences* (pp. 311–331). New York: Oxford University Press.

HETHERINGTON, E.M. (1989). Coping with family transitions: Winners, losers, and survivors. *Child Development, 60*, 1–14.

HETHERINGTON, E.M., & CAMARA, K.A. (1984). Families in transition: The process of dissolution and reconstruction. In R.D. Parke (Ed.), *A review of child development research*, vol. 7 (pp. 398–439), Chicago: University of Chicago Press.

HETHERINGTON, E.M., STANLEY-HAGAN, M., & ANDERSON, E.R. (1989). Marital transitions: A child's perspectives. *American Psychologist, 44*, 303–312.

HEUVEL, A.V. (1988). The timing of parenthood and intergenerational relationships. *Journal of Marriage and the Family, 50*, 483–491.

HIGGINS, B.S. (1990). Couple infertility: From the perspective of the close-relationship model. *Family Relations, 39*, 81–86.

HIMELSTEIN, S., GRAHAM, S., & WEINER, B. (1991). An attributional analysis of maternal beliefs about the importance of child-rearing practices. *Child Development, 62*, 301–310.

HIRSCHFIELD, I.S., & DENNIS, H. (1979). Perspectives. In P.K. Ragan (Ed.), *Aging parents*. California: Ethel Percy Andrus Gerontology Center and USC Press.

HOBBS, D.F., & WUMBUSH, J.M. (1977). Transition to parenthood by black couples. *Journal of Marriage and the Family, 39*, 677–689.

HOCHSCHILD, A. (1989). *The second shift: Working parents and the revolution at home*. New York: Viking.

HOCK, E., DeMEIS, D.K., & McBRIDE, S. (1988). Maternal separation anxiety: Its role in the balance of employment and motherhood in mothers of infants. In A.E. Gottfried & A.W. Gottfried (Eds.), *Maternal employment and children's development* (pp. 191–229). New York: Plenum Press.

HOCK, E., & DeMEIS, D.K. (1990). Depression in mothers of infants: The role of maternal employment. *Developmental Psychology, 26*, 285–291.

HOFFERTH, S.L. (July 1989). What is the demand for and supply of child care in the United States? *Young Children, 44*, 28–33.

HOFFERTH, S.L., & PHILLIPS, D. (1987). Child care in the United States, 1970–1995. *Journal of Marriage and the Family, 49*, 559–571.

HOFFMAN, L.W. (1984). Work, family, and the socialization of the child. In R.D. Parke (Ed.), *The family: Review of child development research* (vol. 7, pp. 223–282). Chicago: University of Chicago Press.

HOFFMAN, L.W. (1988). Cross-cultural differences in childrearing goals. In R.A. LeVine, P.M. Miller, & M.M. West (Eds.), *Parental behavior in diverse societies* (pp. 99–122). San Francisco: Jossey-Bass.

HOFFMAN, L.W. (1989). Effects of maternal employment in the two-parent family. *American Psychologist, 44,* 283–292.

HOFFMAN, S.R., & LEVANT, R.F. (1985). A comparison of childfree and child-anticipated married couples. *Family Relations, 34,* 197–203.

HOLAHAN, C.J., VALENTINER, D.P., & MOOS, R.H. (1994). Parental support and psychological adjustment during the transition to young adulthood in a college sample. *Journal of Family Psychology, 8,* 215–223.

HOLINGER, P., & OFFER, D. (1982). Prediction of adolescent suicide: A population model. *American Journal of Psychiatry, 139,* 302–307.

HOLLENBECK, A.R., GEWIRTZ, J.L., SEBRIS, S.L., & SCANLON, J.W. (1984). Labor and delivery medication influences parent-infant interaction in the first post partum month. *Infant Behavior and Development, 7,* 201–209.

HOLMBECK, G.N., PAIKOFF, R.L., & BROOKS-GUNN, J. (1995). Parenting adolescents. In M.H. Bornstein (Ed.), *Handbook of parenting: vol. 1. Children and parenting.* Mahwah, NJ: Erlbaum.

HONZIK, M.P. (1967). Environmental correlates of mental growth: Prediction from the family setting at 21 months. *Child Development, 38,* 337–364.

HOOPES, J.L. (1982). *Prediction in child development: A longitudinal study of adoptive and nonadoptive families.* NY: Child Welfare League of America.

HOOYMAN, N.R., & LUSTBADER, W. (1986). *Taking care: Supporting older people and their families.* New York: The Free Press.

HOPKINS, J., MARCUS, M., & CAMPBELL, S.B. (1984). Postpartum depression: A critical review. *Psychological Bulletin, 95,* 498–515.

HOREJSI, C., CRAIG, B.H.R., PABLO, J. (1992). Reactions by Native American parents to child protection agencies: Cultural and community factors. *Child Welfare, 71,* 329–341.

HORTON, H.D., THOMAS, M.E., & HERRING, C. (1995). Rural-urban differences in Black family structure. *Journal of Family Issues, 16,* 298–313.

HOSSAIN, Z., & ROOPNARINE, J.L. (1994). African-American fathers' involvement with infants: Relationship to their functioning style, support, education, and income. *Infant Behavior and Development, 17,* 175–184.

HOWES, C. (1990a). Can the age of entry into child care and the quality of child care predict adjustment in kindergarten? *Developmental Psychology, 26,* 292–303.

HOWES, C. (1990b). Social status and friendship from kindergarten to third grade. *Journal of Applied Developmental Psychology, 11,* 321–330.

HOWES, C., & OLENICK, M. (1986). Family and child care influences on toddler's compliance. *Child Development, 57,* 202–216.

HOWES, P.W., & MARKMAN, H.J. (1989). Marital quality and child functioning: A longitudinal investigation. *Child Development, 60,* 1044–1051.

HUGGINS, S.L. (1989). A comparative study of self-esteem of adolescent children of divorced lesbian mothers and divorced heterosexual mothers. In F.W. Bozett (Ed.), *Homosexuality and the family* (pp. 123–135). New York: Harrington Park Press.

HUGHES, D., & GALINSKY, E. (1988). Balancing work and family lives: Research and corporate applications. In A.E. Gottfried & A.W. Gottfried (Eds.), *Maternal employment and children's development* (pp. 233–268). New York: Plenum Press.

HUMPHREY, J.H. (1988). *Children and stress: Theoretical perspectives and recent research.* New York: AMS Press, Inc.

HUMPHREY, M. (1975). The effect of children upon the marriage relationship. *British Journal of Medical Psychology, 48,* 273–279.

HUSTON, A.C., MCLOYD, V.C., & GARCIA COLL, C.T. (1994). Children and poverty: Issues in contemporary research. *Child Development, 65,* 275–282.

HYDE, J.S. (1990). *Understanding human sexuality.* New York: McGraw-Hill.

HYMEL, S., RUBIN, K.H., ROWDEN, L., & LeMARE, L. (1990). Children's peer relationships: Longitudinal predictions of internalizing and externalizing problems from middle to late childhood. *Child Development, 61,* 2004–2021.

HYSON, M.C., HIRSH-PASEK, K., RESCORLA, L., CONE, J., & MARTELL-BOINSKE, L. (1991). Ingredients of parental "pressure" in early childhood. *Journal of Applied Developmental Psychology, 12,* 347–365.

JACOBSON, J.L., & WILLE, D.E. (1986). The influence of attachment pattern on developmental changes in peer interaction from the toddler to the preschool period. *Child Development, 57,* 338–347.

JAYARATNE, T.E. (1993). Neighborhood quality and parental socialization among single, African American mothers: Child gender differences. Paper presented at the Biennial Meeting of the Society for Research on Child Development, New Orleans, LA.

JOE, J.R., & MALACH, R.S. (1992). Families with Native American Roots. In E.W. Lynch & Hanson, M.J. (Eds.), *Developing cross-cultural competence* (pp. 89–119). Baltimore, MD: Paul H. Brookes Publishing Company.

JOHNSON, B.H. (1986). Single mothers following separation and divorce: Making it on your own. *Family Relations, 35,* 189–197.

JOHNSTON, J.R., KLINE, M., & TSCHANN, J.M. (1989). Ongoing postdivorce conflict: Effects on children of joint custody and frequent access. *American Journal of Orthopsychiatry, 59,* 576–592.

JONES, E.F., FORREST, J.D., GOLDMAN, N., HENSHAW, S., LINCOLN, R., ROSOFF, J.I., WESTOFF, C.F., & WULF, D. (1986). *Teenage pregnancy in industrialized countries.* New Haven, CT: Yale University Press.

JONES, L.C. (1990, November). Postpartum emotional disorders. *International Journal of Childbirth Education,* 21–28.

JONES-MOLFESE, V.J. (1977). Responses of neonates to colored stimuli. *Child Development, 48,* 1092–1095.

JULIAN, T.W., McKENRY, P.C., & McKELVEY, M.W. (1994). Cultural variations in parenting: Perceptions of Caucasian, African-American, Hispanic, and Asian-American parents. *Family Relations, 43,* 30–37.

KACH, J.A., & McGHEE, P.E. (1982). Adjustment of early parenthood. *Journal of Family Issues, 3,* 375–388.

KALISH, R., & VISHER, E. (1982). Grandparents of divorce and remarriage. *Journal of Divorce, 5,* 127–140.

KALTER, N., KLONER, A., SCHREIER, S., & OKLA, K. (1989). Predictors of children's postdivorce adjustment. *American Journal of Orthopsychiatry, 59,* 605–618.

KALYANPUR, M., & RAO, S.S. (1991). Empowering low-income black families of handicapped children. *American Journal of Orthopsychiatry, 61,* 523–533.

KAPLAN, M.S. (1980). Evaluating parent education programs. In M.J. Fine (Ed.), *Handbook of parent education.* New York: Academic Press.

KARLSRUD, K. (1987, September). Colic: "Cause" and "cure." *Parents,* 198.

KARLSRUD, K. (1988, January). Choosing your baby's doctor. *Parents,* 137.

KATZ, L.G. (1986, February). Coping with separation anxiety. *Parents,* 150.

KAUFMAN, J., & ZIGLER, E. (1987). Do abused children become abusive parents? *American Journal of Orthopsychiatry, 56,* 142–145.

KAZAK, A.E. (1986). Families with physically handicapped children: Social ecology and family systems. *Family Process, 25,* 265–281.

KEIROUZ, K.S. (1990). Concerns of parents of gifted children: A research review. *Gifted Child Quarterly, 34,* 56–63.

KEITH, C. (1995). Family caregiving systems: Models, resources, and values. *Journal of Marriage and the Family, 57,* 179–189.

KEITH, V.M., & FINLEY, B. (1988). The impact of parental divorce on children's educational attainment, marital timing, and likelihood of divorce. *Journal of Marriage and the Family, 50,* 797–809.

KELLEY, M., POWER, T., & WIMBUSH, D. (1992). Determinants of disciplinary practices in low-income black mothers. *Child Development, 63,* 573–582.

KELLEY-BUCHANAN, C. (1988). *Peace of mind during pregnancy: An A-Z guide to the substances that could affect your unborn baby.* New York: Dell Publishing.

KENNEDY, G.E. (1991). Grandchildren's reasons for closeness with grandparents. *Journal of Social Behavior and Personality, 6,* 697–712.

KINARD, E., & REINHERZ, H. (1986). Effects of marital disruption on children's school aptitude and achievement. *Journal of Marriage and the Family, 48,* 285–293.

KING, V., & ELDER, G.H. (1995). American children view their grandparents: Linked lives across three rural generations. *Journal of Marriage and the Family, 57,* 165–172.

KITZINGER, S. (1985). *The complete book of pregnancy and childbirth.* New York: Afred A. Knopf.

KIVETT, V.R. (1993). Racial comparisons of the grandmother role: Implications for strengthening the family support system of older black women. *Family Relations, 42,* 165–172.

KIVNICK, H.Q. (1982). Grandparenthood: An overview of meaning and mental health. *Gerontologist, 22,* 59–66.

KIVNICK, H.Q. (1983). Dimensions of grandparenthood meaning: Deductive conceptualization and empirical derivation. *Journal of Personality and Social Psychology, 44,* 1056–1068.

KOBLINSKY, S.A., & TODD, C.M. (1989). Teaching self-care skills to latchkey children: A review of the research. *Family Relations, 38,* 431–435.

KOCHANSKA, G., & AKSAN, N. (1995). Mother-child mutually positive affect, the quality of child compliance to requests and prohibitions, and maternal control as correlates of early internalization. *Child Development, 66,* 236–254.

KOEPKE, J.E., & WILLIAMS, C. (1989). Child-rearing information: Resources parents use. *Family Relations, 38,* 462–465.

KOESTNER, R., RYAN, R.M., BERNIERI, F., & HOLT, K. (1984). Setting limits in children's behavior: The differential effects of controlling versus informational styles on intrinsic motivation and creativity. *Journal of Personality, 52,* 233–248.

KOHN, M.L. (1963). Social class and parent-child relationships: An interpretation. *American Journal of Sociology, 68,* 471–480.

KOLATA, G. (1986). Obese children: A growing problem. *Science, 232,* 20–21.

KONTOS, S., & DUNN, L. (1989). Attitudes of caregivers, maternal experiences with day care, and children's development. *Journal of Applied Developmental Psychology, 10,* 37–51.

KONTOS, S., & WELLS, W. (1986). Attitudes of caregivers and the day care experiences of families. *Early Childhood Research Quarterly, 1,* 47–67.

KORNHABER, A. (1985). Grandparenthood and the "new social contract." In V.L. Bengston & J.F. Robertson (Eds.), *Grandparenthood.* Beverly Hills, CA: Sage.

KORNHABER, A. (1986). *Between parents and grandparents.* New York: Berkley Books.

KRAMER, L., & BARON, L.A. (1995). Parental perceptions of children's sibling relationships. *Family Relations, 44,* 95–103.

KRUGER, A.C., & TOMASELLO, M. (1986). Transactive discussions with peers and adults. *Developmental Psychology, 22,* 681–685.

KRUMBOLTZ, J.D. & KRUMBOLTZ, H.B. (1972). *Changing children's behavior.* Englewood Cliffs, NJ: Prentice-Hall, Inc.

KUBLER-ROSS, E. (1969). *On death and dying.* New York: Macmillan Publishing Co., Inc.

KUCZYNSKI, L., KOCHANSKA, G., RADKE-YARROW, M., & GIRNIUS-BROWN, O. (1987). A developmental interpretation of young children's noncompliance. *Developmental Psychology, 23,* 799–806.

KUTNER, L. (1993, January). Why your child needs "blanky." *Parents,* 108.

KUTNER, L. (1993, September). Frights in the night. *Parents,* 88–90.

LADD, G.W. (1990). Having friends, keeping friends, making friends, and being liked by peers in the classroom: Predictors of children's early school adjustment? *Child Development, 61,* 1081–1100.

LADD, G.W., & PRICE, J.M. (1987). Predicting children's social and school adjustment following the transition from preschool to kindergarten. *Child Development, 58,* 1168–1189.

LADD, G.W., PROFILET, S.M., & HART, C.H. (1992). Parents' management of children's peer relations: Facilitating and supervising children's activities in the peer culture. In R.D. Parke & G.W. Ladd (Eds.), *Family relationships: Modes of linkage.* Hillsdale, NJ: Erlbaum.

LAIRD, R.D., PETTIT, G.W., MIZE, J., BROWN, E.G., & LINDSEY, E. (1994). Mother-child conversations about peers: Contributions to competence. *Family Relations, 43,* 425–432.

LAMB, M.E. (1977). Father-infant and mother-infant interaction in the first year of life. *Child Development, 48,* 167–181.

LAMB, M.E. (1986). The changing roles of fathers. In M.E. Lamb (Ed.), *The father's role: Applied perspectives,* New York: Wiley.

LAMB, M.E. (1993). Sociocultural perspectives on nonparental childcare. In M.E. Lamb, K.J. Sternberg, C.P. Hwang, & A.G. Broberg (Eds.), *Nonparental childcare: Cultural and historical perspectives.* Hillsdale, NJ: Erlbaum.

LAMB, M.E., KETTERLINUS, R.D., & FRACASSO, M.P. (1992). Parent-child relationships. In M.H. Bornstein & M.E. Lamb (Eds.), *Developmental psychology: An advanced textbook.* Hillsdale, NJ: Erlbaum.

LAMBORN, S.D., MOUNTS, N.S., STEINBERG, L., & DORNBUSCH, S.M. (1991). Patterns of competence and adjustment among adolescents from authoritative, authoritarian, indulgent, and neglectful families. *Child Development, 62,* 1049–1065.

LANCASTER, J.B., ALTMANN, J., ROSSI, A.S., SHERROD, L.R. (1987). Introduction. In J.B. Lancaster, J. Altmann, A.S. Rossi, & L.R. Sherrod (Eds.), *Parenting across the lifespan: Biosocial dimensions.* New York: Aldine De Gruyter.

LANG, A.M., & BRODY, E.M. (1983). Characteristics of middle-aged daughters and help to their mothers. *Journal of Marriage and the Family, 45,* 193–202.

LaROSSA, R. (1983). The transition to parenthood and the social reality of time. *Journal of Marriage and the Family, 45,* 579–589.

LAUER, R.H., & LAUER, J.C. (1991). The long-term relational consequences of problematic family backgrounds. *Family Relations, 40,* 286–290.

LAWTON, L., SILVERSTEIN, M., & BENGTSON, V. (1994). Affection, social contact, and geographic distance between adult children and their parents. *Journal of Marriage and the Family, 56,* 57–68.

LEADBEATER, B.J., & BISHOP, S.J. (1994). Predictors of behavior problems in preschool children of inner-city Afro-American and Puerto Rican adolescent mothers. *Child Development, 65,* 638–648.

LEE, V.E., BURKHAM, D.T., ZIMILIES, H., & LADEWSKI, C. (1994). Family structure and its effect on behavioral and emotional problems in young adolescents. *Journal of Research on Adolescence, 4,* 405–437.

LeMASTERS, E.E. (1957). Parenthood as crisis. *Marriage and Family Living, 19,* 352–355.

LEMPERS, J.D., CLARK-LEMPERS, D., & SIMONS, R.L. (1989). Economic hardship, parenting, and distress in adolescence. *Child Development, 60,* 25–69.

LEONARD, B.J., BRUST, J.D., & NELSON, R.P. (1993). Parental distress: Caring for medically fragile children at home. *Journal of Pediatric Nursing, 8,* 22–30.

LERNER, J.V. (1994). *Working women and their families.* Thousand Oaks, CA: Sage.

LESTER, B.M. (1985). Introduction: There's more to crying than meets the ear. In B.M. Lester & C.F.Z. Boukydis (Eds.), *Infant crying* (pp. 1–27). New York: Plenum Press.

LEVINE, R.A. (1988). Human parental care: Universal goals, cultural strategies, individual behavior. In R.A. LeVine, P.M. Miller, & M.M. West (Eds.), *Parental behavior in diverse societies* (pp. 3–12). San Francisco, CA: Jossey-Bass.

LEVY-SHIFF, R. (1994). Individual and contextual correlates of marital change across the transition to parenthood. *Developmental Psychology, 30,* 591–601.

LEVY-SHIFF, R., GOLDSHMIDT, I., & HAR-EVEN, D. (1991). Transition to parenthood in adoptive families. *Developmental Psychology, 27,* 131–140.

LEWIS, K.G. (1980). Children of lesbians: Their point of view. *Social Work, 25,* 198–203.

LEWIS, M., FEIRING, C., MCGUFFOG, C., & JASKIR, J. (1984). Predicting psychopathology in six-year-olds from early social relations. *Child Development, 55,* 123–136.

LEWIS, R.A. (1990). The adult child and older parents. In T.H. Brubaker (Ed.), *Family relationships in later life.* Newbury Park, CA: Sage.

LIEBERMAN, A.F., WESTON, D.R., & PAWL, J.H. (1991). Preventive intervention and outcome with anxiously attached dyads. *Child Development, 62,* 199–209.

LIESE, L.H., SNOWDEN, L.R., & FORD, L.K. (1989). Partner status, social support, and psychological adjustment during pregnancy. *Family Relations, 38,* 311–316.

LIGHTFOOT, S.L. (1978). *Worlds apart: Relationships between families and schools.* New York: Basic.

LIN, C.C., & FU, V.R. (1990). A comparison of child-rearing practices among Chinese, immigrant Chinese, and Caucasian-American parents. *Child Development, 61,* 429–433.

LINDNER, E.W. (1986). Danger: Our national policy of child carelessness. *Young Children, 2,* 3–9.

LIPSKY, D.K. (1985). A parental perspective on stress and coping. *American Journal of Orthopsychiatry, 55,* 614–617.

LITTWIN, S. (1986). *The postponed generation: Why America's grown-up kids are growing up later.* New York: William Morrow & Company.

LOCKE, J.L. (1994). Phases in the child's development of language. *American Scientist, 82,* 436–445.

LONG, F., & GARDUQUE, L. (1987). Continuity between home and family day care: Caregivers' and mothers' perceptions and children's social experiences. In D.L. Peters & S. Kontos (Eds.), *Continuity and discontinuity of experience in child care,* Norwood, NJ: Ablex.

LONG, T., & LONG, L. (1982). *Latchkey children: The child's view of self care.* (Report No. PS012604). Washington, DC: Catholic University of America. (ERIC Document Reproduction Service No. ED 211 229).

LOWENTHAL, M., & CHIRIBOGA, C. (1972). Transition to the empty nest: Crisis, challenge, or relief? *Archives of General Psychiatry, 26,* 8–14.

LUSTER, T., & RHOADES, K. (1989). The relation between child-rearing beliefs and the home environment in a sample of adolescent mothers. *Family Relations, 38,* 317–322.

LUSTER, T., & SMALL, S.A. (1994). Factors associated with sexual risk-taking behaviors among adolescents. *Journal of Marriage and the Family, 56,* 622–632.

LYNCH, E.W. (1992). Developing cross-cultural competence. In E.W. Lynch & M.J. Hanson (Eds.), *Developing cross-cultural competence* (pp. 35–62). Baltimore, MD: Paul H. Brookes Publishing.

MACCOBY, E. (1984). Middle childhood in the context of the family. In W.A. Collines (Ed.), *Development during middle childhood: The years from six to twelve.* Washington, DC: National Academy of Sciences Press.

MACCOBY, E.E. (1992). The role of parents in the socialization of children: An historical overview. *Developmental Psychology, 28,* 1006–1017.

MACCOBY, E.E., DEPNER, C.E., & MNOOKIN, R.H. (1988). Custody of children following divorce. In E.M. Hetherington & J.D. Arasteh (Eds.), *Impact of divorce, single parenting, and stepparenting on children* (pp. 91–116). Hillsdale, NJ: Erlbaum.

MACCOBY, E.E., & MARTIN, J.A. (1983). Socialization in the context of the family: Parent-child interaction. In E.M. Hetherington (Ed., P.H. Mussen, General Ed.), *Handbook of child psychology: vol. 4: Socialization, personality, and social development* (4th edition). New York: Wiley.

MACDERMID, S.M., HUSTON, T.L., & McHALE, S.M. (1990). Changes in marriage associated with the transition to parenthood: Individual differences as a function of sex-role attitudes and changes in the division of household labor. *Journal of Marriage and the Family, 52,* 475–486.

MACHIDA, S., & HOLLOWAY, S.D. (1991). The relationship between divorced mothers' perceived control over child rearing and children's post-divorce development. *Family Relations, 40,* 272–278.

MACPHEE, D., KREUTZER, J.C., & FRITZ, J.J. (1994). Infusing a diversity perspective into human development courses. *Child Development, 65,* 699–715.

MAHONEY, G. (1988). Enhancing the developmental competence of handicapped infants. In K. Marfo (Ed.), *Parent-child interaction and developmental disabilities* (pp. 203–219). New York: Praeger.

MAIN, M., & GOLDWYN, R. (1984). Predicting rejecting of her infant from mother's representation of her own experience: Implications for the abused-abusing intergenerational cycle. *Child Abuse and Neglect, 8,* 203–217.

MAIN, M., & SOLOMON, J. (1986). Discovery of a disorganized/disoriented attachment pattern. In T. Brazelton & M.W. Yogman (Eds.), *Affective development in infancy.* Norwood, NJ: Ablex.

MARCIA, J.E. (1980). Identity in adolescence. In J. Adelson (Ed.), *Handbook of adolescent psychology.* New York: Wiley.

MARCON, R.A. (1993, March). *Parental involvement and early school success: Following the "class of 2000" at year five.* Paper presented at the meeting of the Society for Research in Child Development, New Orleans, LA.

MARTIN, A. (1993). *The lesbian and gay parenting handbook.* New York: Harper Perennial.

MATHEWS, R., & MATHEWS, A.M. (1986). Infertility and involuntary childlessness: The transition to nonparenthood. *Journal of Marriage and the Family, 48,* 641–649.

MAY, K.A. (1982). Factors contributing to first-time fathers' readiness for fatherhood: An exploratory study. *Family Relations, 31,* 353–361.

MAYNARD, F. (1991, January). There's a thumbsucker born every minute. *Parents,* 74–79.

McADOO, J.L. (1981). Involvement of fathers in the socialization of black children. In H.P. McAdoo & J.L. McAdoo (Eds.), *Black families* (pp. 225–237). Beverly Hills, CA: Sage.

McBRIDE, B.A. (1990). The effects of a parent education/play group program on father involvement in child rearing. *Family Relations, 39,* 250–256.

McBRIDE, B.A., & MILLS, G. (1993). A comparison of mother and father involvement with their preschool age children. *Early Childhood Research Quarterly, 8,* 457–477.

McCARTNEY, K. & PHILLIPS, D. (1988). Motherhood and child care. In B. Birns & D.F. Hay (Eds.), *The different faces of motherhood* (pp. 157–184). New York: Plenum Press.

McClelland, J. (1995). Sending children to kindergarten: A phenomenological study of mothers' experiences. *Family Relations, 44,* 177–183.

McGillicuddy-DeLisi, A.V., & Sigel, I.E. (1995). Parental beliefs. In M.H. Bornstein (Ed.), *Handbook of parenting: vol. 3: Status and social conditions of parenting* (pp. 333–358), Mahwah, NJ: Erlbaum.

McGoldrick, M. (1982). Ethnicity and family therapy: An overview. In M. McGoldrick, J. Pearce, & J. Giordano (Eds.), *Ethnicity and family therapy* (pp. 3–30). New York: The Guilford Press.

McHale, S.M., Freitag, M.K., Crouter, A.C., & Bartko, W.T. (1991). Connections between dimensions of marital quality and school-age children's adjustment. *Journal of Applied Developmental Psychology, 12,* 1–17.

McHale, S.M., & Gamble, W.C. (1989). Sibling relationships of children with disabled and nondisabled brothers and sisters. *Developmental Psychology, 25,* 421–429.

McHale, S.M., & Huston, T.L. (1985). The effect of the transition to parenthood on the marriage relationship. *Journal of Family Issues, 6,* 409–433.

McKim, M.K. (1987). Transition to what: New parents' problems in the first year. *Family Relations, 36,* 22–25.

McLoyd, V.C. (1989). Socialization and development in a changing economy: The effects of paternal job and income loss on children. *American Psychologist, 44,* 293–303.

McLoyd, V.C. (1990). The impact of economic hardship on black families and children: Psychological distress, parenting, and socioemotional development. *Child Development, 61,* 311–346.

Mebert, C.J. (1991). Variability in the transition to parenthood experience. In K. Pillemer & K. McCartney (Eds.), *Parent-child relations throughout life.* Hillsdale, NJ: Erlbaum.

Medway, F.J. (1989). Measuring the effectiveness of parent education. In M.J. Fine (Ed.) *The second handbook on parent education: Contemporary perspectives* (pp. 237–255). San Diego: Academic Press.

Melby, J.N., Conger, R.D., Conger, K.J., & Lorenz, F.O. (1993). Effects of parental behavior on tobacco use by young male adolescents. *Journal of Marriage and the Family, 55,* 439–454.

Melina, L.R. (1986). *Raising adopted children.* New York: Harper & Row Publishers.

Menaghan, E.G., & Parcel, T. (1990). Parental employment and family life: Research in the 1980s. *Journal of Marriage and the Family, 52,* 1079–1098.

Mercer, R.T., Hackley, K.C., & Bostrom, A.G. (1983). Relationship of psychosocial and perinatal variables to perception of childbirth. *Nursing Research, 32,* 202–207.

Meyer, D.J. (1986). Fathers of children with mental handicaps. In M.L. Lamb (Ed.), *The father's role: Applied perspectives* (pp. 227–254). New York: Wiley.

Meyerowitz, J.H., & Feldman, H. (1966). Transition to parenthood. *Psychiatric Research Reports, 20,* 78–84.

Michaels, G.Y. (1988). Motivational factors in the decision and timing of pregnancy. In G.Y. Michaels & W.A. Goldberg (Eds.), *The transition to parenthood: Current theory and research.* New York: Cambridge University Press.

Miezio, P. (1983). *Parenting children with disabilities.* New York: Marcel Dekker.

Miller, B.C., & Sollie, D.L. (1980). Normal stresses during the transition to parenthood. *Family Relations, 29,* 459–465.

Miller, R.L., & Miller, B. (1990). Mothering the biracial child: Bridging the gaps between African-American and white parenting styles. *Women and Therapy, 10,* 169–179.

Mirande, A. (1988). Chicano fathers: Traditional perceptions and current realities. In P. Bronstein & C.P. Cowan (Eds.), *Fatherhood today: Men's changing role in the family* (pp. 93–106). New York: Wiley.

MITCHELL, B.A., WISTER, A.V., & BURCH, T.K. (1989). The family environment and leaving the parental home. *Journal of Marriage and the Family, 51,* 605–613.

MONTEMAYOR, R. (1986). Family variation in parent-adolescent storm and stress. *Journal of Adolescent Research, 1,* 15–31.

MONTGOMERY, R.J.V., GONYEA, J.G., & HOOYMAN, N.R. (1985). Caregiving and the experience of subjective and objective burden. *Family Relations, 34,* 19–26.

MORELLI, G.A., ROGOFF, B., OPPENHEIM, D., & GOLDSMITH, D. (1992). Cultural variation in infants' sleeping arrangements: Questions of independence. *Developmental Psychology, 28,* 604–613.

MORROW, R.D. (1989). Southeast Asian child rearing practices: Implications for child and youth care workers. *Child and Youth Care Quarterly, 18,* 273–287.

MOSCHELL, M. (1991, August). Wanted: Parent. *Family Times,* p. 3.

MOSIER, C.E., & ROGOFF, B. (1994). Infants' instrumental use of their mothers to achieve their goals. *Child Development, 65,* 70–79.

MURRAY, J.B. (1990). Psychophysiological aspects of nightmares, night terrors, and sleepwalking. *The Journal of General Psychology, 118,* 113–127.

MURRY, V.M. (1994). Black adolescent females: A comparison of early versus late coital initiators. *Family Relations, 43,* 342–348.

NATIONAL ACADEMY OF EARLY CHILDHOOD PROGRAMS. (1984). *Accreditation criteria and procedures.* Washington, DC: National Association for the Education of Young Children.

NATIONAL ASSOCIATION OF STATE BOARDS OF EDUCATION, TASK FORCE ON EARLY CHILDHOOD EDUCATION. (1988). *Right from the start.* Alexandria, VA: Author.

NELSON, K. (1985). *Making sense: The acquisition of shared meaning.* New York: Academic Press.

NELSON, M.K. (1983). Working-class women, middle-class women, and models of childbirth. *Social Problems, 30,* 284–297.

NELSON, W.P., & LEVANT, R.F. (1991). An evaluation of a skills training program for parents in stepfamilies. *Family Relations, 40,* 291–296.

NEUGARTEN B., & NEUGARTEN, D.A. (1987). The changing meanings of age. *Psychology Today, 21,* 29–33.

NEWBERGER, C.M., & WHITE, K.M. (1989). Cognitive foundations for parental care. In D. Cichetti & V. Carlson (Eds.), *Child maltreatment: Theory and research on the causes and consequences of child abuse and neglect* (pp. 302–313). New York: Cambridge University Press.

NEWCOMB, M., & BENTLER, P. (1989). Substance use and abuse among children and teenagers. *American Psychologist, 44,* 242–248.

NICHD EARLY CHILD CARE NETWORK. (1995). Child care in the 1990s: The NICHD study of early child care. Paper presented at Biennial Meeting of the Society for Research in Child Development, Indianapolis, IN.

NOVAK, J.S. (1990, May). Prenatal exercise guidelines. *International Journal of Childbirth Education,* 18–19.

NUGENT, J.K. (1991). Cultural and psychological influences on the father's role in infant development. *Journal of Marriage and the Family, 53,* 475–485.

NUGENT, J.K. (1994). Cross-cultural studies of child development: Implications for clinicians. *Zero to Three, 15(2),* 1, 3–8.

NUGENT, J.K., GREENE, S., WIECZORECK-DEERING, D., MAZOR, K., HENDLER, J., & BOMBARDIER, C. (1993). The cultural context of mother-infant play in the newborn period. In K. Macdonald (Ed.), *Parent child play.* Albany, New York: State University of New York Press.

O'BRIEN, M., PORTERFIELD, J., HERBERT-JACKSON, E., & RISLEY, T.R. (1979). *The toddler center.* Baltimore, MD: University Park Press.

OGBU, J. (1981). Origins of human competence: A cultural-ecological perspective. *Child Development, 52,* 413–429.

OKAGAKI, L., & FRENSCH, P.A. (1994). Effects of video game playing on measures of spatial performance: Gender effects in late adolescence. *Journal of Applied Developmental Psychology, 15,* 33–58.

OKAGAKI, L., & STERNBERG, R.J. (1993). Parental beliefs and children's school performance. *Child Development, 64,* 36–56.

OLDS, D.L., & HENDERSON, C.R. (1989). The prevention of maltreatment. In D. Cicchetti & Carlson, V. (Eds.), *Child maltreatment: Theory and research on the causes and consequences of child abuse and neglect.* New York: Cambridge University Press.

ON THEIR OWN: WHAT TO TELL YOUR LATCHKEY KIDS. (1989, August). *Ladies Home Journal,* 72.

OPPENHEIM, J. (1989). *The elementary school handbook: Making the most of your child's education.* New York: Pantheon Books.

OSOFSKY, J. (1990). Risk and protective factors for teenage mothers and their infants. *SRCD Newsletter,* Winter, 1–2.

OSOFSKY, J.D., & JACKSON, B.R. (December 1993/January 1994). Parenting in violent environments. *Zero to three, 14,* 8–12.

PALFREY, J.S., WALKER, D.K., BUTLER, J.A., & SINGER, J.D. (1989). Patterns of response in families of chronically disabled children: An assessment of five metropolitan school districts. *American Journal of Orthopsychiatry, 59(1),* 94–105.

PALM, G.F., & PALKOVITZ, R. (1988). The challenge of working with new fathers: Implications for support providers. In G.F. Palm & R.F. Palkovitz (Eds.), *Transitions to parenthood* (pp. 357–376). New York: Howarth Press.

PARK, K.A., & WATERS, E. (1989). Security of attachment and preschool friendships. *Child Development, 60,* 1076–1081.

PARKE, R.D. (1977). Some effects of punishment on children's behavior—Revisited. In P. Cantor (Ed.), *Understanding a child's world.* New York: McGraw-Hill.

PARKE, R.D. (1986). Fathers, families, and support systems: Their role in the development of at-risk and retarded infants and children. In J.J. Gallagher & P.M. Vietze (Eds.), *Families of handicapped persons: Research, programs, and policy issues* (pp. 101–113). Baltimore, MD: Paul H. Brookes Publishing.

PARKE, R.D., & BEITEL, A. (1986). Hospital-based intervention for fathers. In M.E. Lamb (Ed.), *The father's role: Applied perspectives.* New York: Wiley.

PARKER, J.G., & ASHER, S.R. (1987). Peer relations and later personal adjustment: Are low-accepted children at risk? *Psychological Bulletin, 102,* 357–389.

PARKER, L. (1994). The role of workplace support in facilitating self-sufficiency among single mothers on welfare. *Family Relations, 43,* 168–173.

PASSMAN, R.H. (1987). Attachments to inanimate objects: Are children who have security blankets insecure? *Journal of Consulting and Clinical Psychology, 55,* 825–830.

PASSMAN, R.H., & HALONEN, J.S. (1979). A developmental survey of young children's attachments to inanimate objects. *Journal of Genetic Psychology, 134,* 165–178.

PATTERSON, C.J. (1992). Children of lesbian and gay parents. *Child Development, 63,* 1025–1042.

PATTERSON, C.J. (1995). Families of the lesbian baby boom: Parents' division of labor and children's adjustment. *Developmental Psychology, 31,* 115–123.

PATTERSON, G.R. (1986). Performance models for antisocial boys. *American Psychologist, 41,* 432–444.

PATTERSON, G.R., & CAPALDI, D. (1991). Antisocial parents: Unskilled and vulnerable. In P.E. Cowan & M. Hetherington (Eds.), *Family transitions* (pp. 195–218). Hillsdale, NJ: Erlbaum.

PATTERSON, G.R., DeBARYSHE, B.D., & RAMSEY, E. (1989). A developmental perspective on antisocial behavior. *American Psychologist, 44,* 329–335.

PATTERSON, G.R., & DISHION, T.J. (1988). A mechanism for transmitting the antisocial trait across generations. In R. Hinde & J. Stevenson-Hinde (Eds.), *Relations between relationships within families.* Oxford: Oxford University Press.

PATTERSON, G.R., & STROUTHAMER-LOEBER, M. (1984). The correlation of family management practices and delinquency. *Child Development, 55,* 1299–1307.

PAYNE, A.C., WHITEHURST, G.J., & ANGELL, A.L. (1994). The role of home literacy environment in the development of language ability in preschool children from low-income families. *Early Childhood Research Quarterly, 9* 427–440.

PEARSON, J. (1990, November). Preconception planning. *International Journal of Childbirth Education,* 16–17.

PEARSON, J., & THOENNES, N. (1990). Custody after divorce: Demographic and attitudinal patterns. *American Journal of Orthopsychiatry, 60,* 233–296.

PEDERSON, D.R., BENTO, S., CHANCE, G.W., EVANS, B., & FOX, A.M. (1987). Maternal emotional responses to preterm birth. *American Journal of Orthopsychiatry, 57,* 15–21.

PEDRICK-CORNELL, C., & GELLES, R.J. (1982). Elder abuse: The status of current knowledge. *Family Relations, 31,* 457–465.

PELLEGRINI, A.D., PERLMUTTER, J.C., GALDA, L., & BRODY, G.H. (1990). Joint reading between black Head Start children and their mothers. *Child Development, 61,* 443–453.

PETERS, D.L., & KONTOS, S. (1987). Continuity and discontinuity of experience: An intervention perspective. In D.L. Peters & S. Kontos (Eds.), *Continuity and discontinuity of experience in child care* (pp. 1–16). Norwood, NJ: Ablex.

PETERS, M.F. (1985). Racial socialization of young black children. In H.P. McAdoo & J. McAdoo (Eds.), *Black children: Social, educational, and parental environments* (pp. 159–173). Beverly Hills, CA: Sage.

PETERSEN, A.C., COMPAS, B.E., BROOKS-GUNN, J., STEMMLER, M., EY, S., & GRANT, K.E. (1993). Depression in adolescence. *American Psychologist, 48,* 155–168.

PETERSON, C., & PETERSON, R. (1986). Parent-child interaction and daycare: Does quality of daycare matter? *Journal of Applied Developmental Psychology, 7,* 1–15.

PETERSON, F.L., & WALLS, D. (1991, November). Fatherhood preparation during childbirth education. *International Journal of Childbirth Education,* 38–39.

PETERSON, J., & ZILL, N. (1986). Marital disruption, parent-child relationships, and behavior problems in children. *Journal of Marriage and the Family, 48,* 295–307.

PETERSON, J.A. (1979). The relationships of middle-aged children and their parents. In P.K. Ragan (Ed.), *Aging parents.* California: Ethel Percy Andrus Gerontology Center and USC Press.

PHILLIPS, D., & HOWES, C. (1987). Indicators of quality child care: Review of research. In D.A. Phillips (Ed.), *Quality in child care: What does the research tell us?* Washington, DC: NAEYC.

PHILLIPS, D., McCARTNEY, K., & SCARR, S. (1987). The effect of quality of day care environment upon children's social and emotional development. *Developmental Psychology, 23,* 537–543.

PHINNEY, J. (1990). Ethnic identity in adolescents and adults: Review of research. *Psychological Bulletin, 108.* 499–514.

PIANTA, R.C., & BALL, R.M. (1993). Maternal social support as a predictor of child adjustment in kindergarten. *Journal of Applied Developmental Psychology, 14,* 107–120.

PILL, C.J. (1990). Stepfamilies: Redefining the family. *Family Relations, 39,* 186–193.

PILLEMER, K., & SUITOR, J.J. (1991a). Relationships with children and distress in the elderly. In K. Pillemer & K. McCartney (Eds.), *Parent-child relations throughout life.* Hillsdale, NJ: Erlbaum.

PILLEMER, K., & SUITOR, J.J. (1991b). "Will I ever escape my child's problems?" Effects of adult children's problems on elderly parents. *Journal of Marriage and the Family, 53,* 585–594.

PLOMIN, R., & DEFRIES, J.C. (1985). *The origins of individual differences in infancy: The Colorado Adoption Project.* New York: Academic Press.

POLLACK, S. (1990). Lesbian parents: Claiming our visibility. *Women and Therapy, 10,* 181–194.

POLLYCOVE, R., & CORRIGAN, T. (1991). *The birth book.* San Bruno, CA: Krames Communications.

PORTES, P.R., DUNHAM, R.M., & WILLIAMS, S. (1986). Assessing child-rearing style in ecological settings: Its relation to culture, social class, early age intervention and scholastic achievement. *Adolescence, 21,* 723–735.

POSNER, J.K., & VANDELL, D.L. (1994). Low-income children's after-school care: Are there beneficial effects of after-school programs? *Child Development, 65,* 440–456.

POULSEN, M.K. (1994). The development of policy recommendations to address individual and family needs of infants and young children affected by family substance abuse. *Topics in Early Childhood Special Education, 14,* 275–291.

POWELL, D.R. (1986). Research in review: Parent education and support programs. *Young Children, 41,* 47–53.

POWELL, D.R. (1988). Challenges in the design and evaluation of parent-child intervention programs. In D.R. Powell (Ed.), *Parent education as early childhood intervention: Emerging directions in theory, research and practice,* Norwood, NJ: Ablex.

POWELL, D.R. (1989). *Families and early childhood programs.* Washington, DC: NAEYC.

PRATT, C.C., WALKER, A.J., & WOOD, B.L. (1992). Bereavement among former caregivers to elderly mothers. *Family Relations, 41,* 278–283.

PRESSER, H.B. (1988). Shift-work and child care among young dual-earner American parents. *Journal of Marriage and the Family, 50,* 133–148.

PURNELL, M., BAGBY, B.H. (1993). Grandparents' rights: Implications for family specialists. *Family Relations, 42,* 173–178.

RADKE-YARROW, M., ZAHN-WAXLER, C., RICHARDSON, D.T., SUSMAN, A., & MARTINEZ, P. (1994). Caring behavior in children of clinically depressed and well mothers. *Child Development, 65,* 1405–1414.

RAFFAELLI, M. (1992). Sibling conflict in early adolescence. *Journal of Marriage and the Family, 54,* 652–663.

RAND, C., GRAHAM, D.L.R., & RAWLINGS, E.I. (1982). Psychological health and factors the court seeks to control in lesbian mother custody trials. *Journal of Homosexuality, 8,* 27–39.

RANDO, T.A. (1985). Bereaved parents: Particular difficulties, unique factors, and treatment issues. *Social Work, 30,* 19–23.

RATNER, N., & BRUNER, J.S. (1978). Games, social exchange, and the acquisition of language. *Journal of Child Language, 5,* 1–15.

RAUCH-ELNEKAVE, H. (1994). Teenage motherhood: Its relationship to undetected learning problems. *Adolescence, 29,* 91–104.

RAYMOND, C.L., & BENBOW, C.P. (1989). Educational encouragement by parents: Its relationship to precocity and gender. *Gifted Child Quarterly, 33,* 144–151.

RAYMOND, J. (1988, November). Healthy childbearing women in a high tech era. *International Journal of Childbirth Education,* 9–12.

RICHMAN, A.L., MILLER, P.M., & SOLOMON, M.J. (1988). The socialization of infants in suburban Boston. In R.A. LeVine, P.M. Miller, & M.M. West (Eds.), *Parental behavior in diverse societies. New directions for child development,* No. 40 (pp. 81–98). San Francisco, CA: Jossey-Bass.

RICKEL, A.U. (1989). *Teen pregnancy and parenting.* New York: Hemisphere Publishing Corporation.

RIESER, J., YONAS, A., & WIKNER, K. (1976). Radial localization of odours by human newborns. *Child Development, 47,* 856–859.

RILEY, D., & COCHRAN, M. (1985). Naturally occurring childrearing information for fathers: Utilization of the personal social network. *Journal of Marriage and the Family, 47,* 275–286.

RILEY, D., MEINHARDT, G., NELSON, C., SALISBURY, M.J., & WINNETT, T. (1991). How effective are age-paced newsletters for new parents? A replication and extension of earlier studies. *Family Relations, 40,* 247–253.

RINDFUS, R.R., & ST. JOHN, C. (1983). Social determinants of age at first birth. *Journal of Marriage and the Family, 45,* 553–565.

RISMAN, B.J. (1986). Can men "mother"? Life as a single father. *Family Relations, 35,* 95–102.

ROBERTO, K.A. (1990). Grandparent and grandchild relationships. In T.H. Brubaker (Ed.), *Family relationships in later life.* Newbury Park, CA: Sage Publications.

ROBERTS, F.B. (1983). Infant behavior and the transition to parenthood. *Nursing Research, 32,* 213–217.

ROBERTS, F.B., & MILLER, B.C. (1978, October). *Infant behavior effects on the transition to parenthood: A mini-theory.* Paper presented at the meeting of the National Council on Family Relations.

RODMAN, H., & PRATTO, D.J. (1980). *How children take care of themselves: A preliminary statement on magazine survey.* Unpublished report submitted to the Ford Foundation.

ROGGMAN, L.A., LANGLOIS, J.H., HUBBS-TAIT, L., & RIESER-DANNER, L.A. (1994). Infant day-care, attachment, and the "file drawer problem." *Child Development, 65,* 429–443.

ROOSA, M.W. (1988). The effect of age in the transition to parenthood: Are delayed childbearers a unique group? *Family Relations, 37,* 322–327.

ROOSA, M.W., TEIN, J, GROPPENBACHER, N., MICHAELS, M., & DUMKA, L. (1993). Mothers' parenting behavior and child mental health in families with a problem drinking parent. *Child Development, 55,* 107–118.

ROSENBERG, L. (1990, May). Bathroom reading. *Parents,* 225–231.

ROSENSTEIN, D., & OSTER, H. (1988). Differential facial responses to four basic tastes in newborns. *Child Development, 59,* 1555–1568.

ROSSI, A.S. (1968). Transition to parenthood. *Journal of Marriage and the Family, 30,* 26–39.

ROSSI, A.S., & ROSSI, P.H. (1991). Normative obligations and parent-child help exchange across the life course. In K. Pillemer & K. McCartney (Eds.), *Parent-child relations throughout life.* Hillsdale, NJ: Erlbaum.

ROTHBART, M.K., & DERRYBERRY, P. (1981). Development of individual differences in temperament. In M.E. Lamb & A. Brown (Eds.), *Advances in developmental psychology.* Hillsdale, NJ: Erlbaum.

ROTHENBERG, B.A., HITCHCOCK, S., HARRISON, M.L., & GRAHAM, M. (1995). *Parentmaking: A practical handbook for teaching parent classes about babies and toddlers.* Menlo Park, CA: The Banster Press.

ROTHENBERG, P.B., & VARGA, P.E. (1981). The relationship between age of mother and child health and development. *American Journal of Public Health, 71,* 810–817.

RUBIN, K., WATSON, K., & JAMBOR, T. (1978). Free-play behaviors in preschool and kindergarten children. *Child Development, 49,* 534–536.

RUBIN, K.H., LeMARE, L.J., & LOLLIS, S. (1990). Social withdrawal in childhood: Developmental pathways to peer rejection. In S.R. Asher & J.D. Coie (Eds.), *Peer rejection in childhood.* Cambridge, MA: Cambridge University Press.

RUETER, M.A., & CONGER, R.D. (1995). Antecedents of parent-adolescent agreements. *Journal of Marriage and the Family, 57,* 435–448.

RUOPP, R., TRAVERS, J., GLANTZ, F., & COELEN, C. (1979). *Children at the center: Final report of the National Day Care Study.* Cambridge, MA: Abt Associates.

RUSSELL, C.S. (1974). Transition to parenthood: Problems and gratifications. *Journal of Marriage and the Family, 36,* 294–301.

RUSSELL, G., & RADOJEVIC, M. (1992). The changing role of fathers: Current understandings and future directions for research and practice. *Infant Mental Health Journal, 13(4),* 296–311.

RUTTER, M. (1990). Psychosocial resilience and protective mechanisms. In J. Rolf, A.S. Masten, D. Cicchetti, K.H. Nuechterlein, & S. Weintraub (Eds.), *Risk and protective factors in the development of psychopathology.* New York: Cambridge University Press.

RYDER, R.G. (1973). Longitudinal data relating marriage satisfaction and having a child. *Journal of Marriage and the Family, 35,* 604–607.

SABATELLI, R.M., METH, R.L., GAVAZZI, S.M. (1988). Factors mediating the adjustment to involuntary childlessness. *Family Relations, 37,* 338–343.

SABATELLI, R.M., & WALDRON, R.J. (1995). Measurement issues in the assessment of the experiences of parenthood. *Journal of Marriage and the Family, 57,* 969–980.

SAMMONS, W.A.H., & LEWIS, J.M. (1985). *Premature babies: A different beginning.* Princeton, NJ: The C.V. Mosby Company.

SANDERS, G.F., & TRYGSTAD, D.W. (1989). Stepgrandparents and grandparents: The view from young adults. *Family Relations, 38,* 71–75.

SANIK, M.M., & MAULDIN, T. (1986). Single versus two parent families: A comparison of mothers' time. *Family Relations, 35,* 53–56.

SANTROCK, J.W., & WARSHAK, R.A. (1986). Development of father custody, relationships, and legal/clinical considerations in father-custody families. In M.E. Lamb (Ed.), *The father's role: Applied perspectives* (pp. 135–163). New York: Wiley.

SANTROCK, J.W., WARSHAK, R.A., & ELLIOT, G.L. (1982). Social development and parent-child interaction in father-custody and stepmother families. In M. Lamb (Ed.), *Nontraditional families* (pp. 289–314). Hillsdale, NJ: Erlbaum.

SARGENT, R.G., SCHULKEN, E.D., KEMPER, K.A., & HUSSEY, J.A. (1994). Black and white adolescent females' pre-pregnancy nutrition status. *Adolescence, 29,* 845–859.

SASSERATH, V.J. (1983). *Minimizing high-risk parenting.* Skillman, NJ: Johnson & Johnson Baby Products Company.

SATTER, E. (1983). *Child of mine: Feeding with love and good sense.* Palo Alto, CA: Bull Publishing Co.

SAUNDERS, J., & ESPELAND, P. (1986). *Bringing out the best: A resource guide for parents and gifted young children.* Minneapolis, MN: Free Spirit Publishing.

SAVIN-WILLIAMS, R.C., & BERNDT, T.J. (1990). Friendship and peer relations. In S.S. Feldman & G.L. Elliot (Eds.), *At the threshold: The developing adolescent* (pp. 277–307). Cambridge, MA: Harvard University Press.

SCANZONI, J. (1985). Black parental values and expectations of children's occupational and educational success: Theoretical implications. In H.P. McAdoo & J. McAdoo (Eds.), *Black children: Social, educational, and parental environments* (pp. 113–122). Beverly Hills, CA: Sage.

SCARR, S. (1985). *Mother care/other care.* New York: Basic Books.

SCHACTER, F.F., & STONE, R.K. (1987). *Practical concerns about siblings: Bridging the research-practice gap.* New York: Hayworth.

SCHAEFER, E.S. (1974). The ecology of child development: Implications for research and the professions. Presented at Annual Meeting of American Psychological Association.

SCHAPER, K.K. (1982). Towards a calm baby and relaxed parents. *Family Relations, 31,* 409–414.

SCHILLING, R.F., KIRKHAM, M.A., SNOW, W.H., & SCHINKE, S.P. (1986). Single mothers with handicapped children: Different from their married counterparts? *Family Relations, 35,* 69–77.

SCHILLING, R.F., SCHINKE, S.P., & KIRKHAM, M.A. (1985). Coping with a handicapped child: Differences between mothers and fathers. *Social Science and Medicine, 21,* 857–863.

SCHRAG, R.L. (1990). *Taming the wild tube: A family's guide to television and video.* Chapel Hill: University of North Carolina Press.

SEITZ, V., & APFEL, N. (1993). Long-term effects of a school for pregnant students: Repeated childbearing through six years postpartum. Paper presented at the Biennial Meeting of the Society for Research in Child Development, New Orleans.

SEITZ, V., ROSENBAUM, L., & APFEL, N. (1985). Effects of family support intervention: A ten-year follow-up. *Child Development, 56,* 376–391.

SELTZER, J.A., & BIANCHI, S.M. (1988). Children's contact with absent parents. *Journal of Marriage and the Family, 50,* 663–677.

SEX INFORMATION AND EDUCATION COUNCIL OF THE U.S. (SIECUS). (1989). *How to talk to your children about AIDS.* New York: SIECUS and NYU.

SHAFFER, D.R. (1994). *Social and personality development* (3rd ed.). Pacific Grove, CA: Brooks/Cole Publishing Company.

SHANAS, E. (1980). Older people and their families: The new pioneers. *Journal of Marriage and the Family, 42,* 9–15.

SHAPIRO, J. (1983). Family reactions and coping strategies in response to the physically ill or handicapped child: A review. *Social Science and Medicine, 17,* 913–931.

SHAPP, L.C., THURMAN, S.K., & DUCETTE, J.P. (1992). The relationship of attributions and personal well-being in parents of preschool children with disabilities. *Journal of Early Intervention, 16,* 295–303.

SHATZ, M., & GELMAN, R. (1973). The development of communication skills: Modifications in the speech of young children as a function of the listener. *Monographs of the Society for Research in Child Development, 38* (Serial No. 152).

SHERROD, K., VIETZE, P., & FRIEDMAN, S. (1978). *Infancy.* Monterey, CA: Brooks/Cole.

SHON, S.P., & JA, D.Y. (1982). Asian families. In M. McGoldrick, J. Pearce, & J. Giordano (Eds.), *Ethnicity and family therapy* (pp. 208–228). New York: The Guilford Press.

SIGEL, I. (1987). Does hothousing rob children of their childhood? *Early Childhood Research Quarterly, 2,* 211–235.

SILVER, M.H. (1993). Balancing "caring and being cared for" in old age: The development of mutual parenting. In J. Demick, K. Bursik, & R. DiBiase (Eds.), *Parental development.* Hillsdale, NJ: Erlbaum.

SILVERBERG, S.G. (in press). Parental well-being and their children's transition to adolescence. To appear in C. Ryoff & M. Seltzer (Eds.), *The parental experience in midlife.* Chicago: University of Chicago Press.

SILVERMAN, L., CHITWOOD, D., & WATERS, J. (1986). Young gifted children: Can parents identify giftedness? *Topics in Early Childhood Special Education, 6,* 23–33.

SILVERSTONE, B. (1979). Issues for the middle generation: Responsibility, adjustment, and growth. In P.K. Ragan (Ed.), *Aging parents.* California: Ethel Percey Andrus Gerontology Center and USC Press.

SIMKIN, P., WHALLEY, J., & KEPPLER, A. (1984). *Pregnancy, childbirth, and the newborn.* New York: Meadowlands.

SIMONS, R.L., BEAMAN, J., CONGER, R.D., & CHAO, W. (1993). Childhood experience, conceptions of parenting, and attitudes of spouse as determinants of parental behavior. *Journal of Marriage and the Family, 55,* 91–106.

SIMONS, R.L., WHITBECK, L.B., CONGER, R.D., & WU, C. (1991). Intergenerational transmission of harsh parenting. *Developmental Psychology, 27,* 159–171.

SINGER, J.L. (1973). *The child's world of make-believe.* New York: Academic Press.

SIRIGNANO, S.W., & LACHMAN, M.E. (1985). Personality change during the transition to parenthood: The role of perceived infant temperament. *Developmental Psychology, 21,* 558–567.

SISK, D. (1987). *Creative teaching of the gifted.* New York: McGraw-Hill.

SMALL, S.A., & EASTMAN, G. (1991). Rearing adolescents in contemporary society: A conceptual framework for understanding the responsibilities and needs of parents. *Family Relations, 40,* 455–462.

SMALL, S.A., & KERNS, D. (1993). Unwanted sexual activity among peers during early and middle adolescence: Incidence and risk factors. *Journal of Marriage and the Family, 55,* 941–952.

SMETANA, J.G. (1989). Adolescents' and parents' reasoning about actual family conflict. *Child Development, 60,* 1052–1067.

SMUTS, A.B. (1985). The National Research Council Committee on Child Development and the Founding of the Society for Research in Child Development, 1925–1933. In A.B Smuts & J.W. Hagen (Eds.), *History and research in child development. Monographs for the Society for Research in Child Development, 48,* (Serial No. 211).

SNAREY, J.R. (1993). *How fathers care for the next generation: A four-decade study.* Cambridge, MA: Harvard University Press.

SOLLIE, D.L., & MILLER, B.C. (1980). The transition to parenthood as critical time for building family strengths. In N. Stinnett, B. Chesser, J. DeFrain, & P. Knaub (Eds.), *Family strengths: Positive models for family life* (pp. 149–169). Lincoln, NE: University of Nebraska.

SOLOWAY, N.M., & SMITH, R.M. (1987). Antecedents of late birthtiming decisions of men and women in dual-career marriages. *Family Relations, 36,* 258–262.

SOMERS, M.D. (1993). A comparison of voluntarily childfree adults and parents. *Journal of Marriage and the Family, 55,* 643–650.

SPENCER, M.B. (1990). Development of minority children: An introduction. *Child Development, 61,* 267–269.

SPENCER, M.B., & DORNBUSCH, S.M. (1990). Challenges in studying minority children. In S.S. Feldman & G.L. Elliot (Eds.), *At the threshold: The developing adolescent* (pp. 123–146). Cambridge, MA: Harvard University Press.

SPITZE, G., & LOGAN, J. (1990). Sons, daughters, and intergenerational support. *Journal of Marriage and the Family, 52,* 420–430.

SROUFE, A. (1977). *Knowing and enjoying your baby.* Englewood Cliffs, NJ: Prentice-Hall, Inc.

SROUFE, A., FOX, N.E., & PANCAKE, V.R. (1983). Attachment and dependency in developmental perspective. *Child Development, 54,* 1615–1627.

STATHAM, J. (1986). *Non-sexist childrearing.* New York: Basil Blackwell.

STEINBERG, L. (1986). Latchkey children and susceptibility to peer pressure: An ecological analysis. *Developmental Psychology, 23,* 433–439.

STEINBERG, L. (1988). The ABC's of transformations in the family at adolescence: Changes in affect, behavior, and cognition. In E.M. Hetherington & R.D. Parke (Eds.), *Contemporary readings in child psychology* (3rd ed.). New York: McGraw-Hill.

STEINBERG, L. (1990). Interdependence in the family: Autonomy, conflict, and harmony in the parent-adolescent relationship. In S.S. Feldman & G. Elliot (Eds.), *At the threshold: The developing adolescent.* Cambridge, MA: Harvard University Press.

STEINBERG, L. (1993). *Adolescence* (3rd ed.). New York: McGraw-Hill.

STEINBERG, L., & BELSKY, J. (1991). *Infancy, childhood, and adolescence.* New York: McGraw-Hill.

STEINBERG, L.D., CATALANO, R., & DOOLEY, D. (1981). Economic antecedents of child abuse and neglect. *Child Development, 52,* 975–985.

STEINBERG, L., & DORNBUSCH, S. (1991). Negative correlates of part-time work in adolescence: Replication and elaboration. *Developmental Psychology, 27,* 304–313.

STEINBERG, L., ELMEN, J.D., & MOUNTS, N.S. (1989). Authoritative parenting, psychosocial maturity, and academic success among adolescents. *Child Development, 60,* 1424–1436.

STEMP, P.S., TURNER, R.J., & NOH, S. (1986). Psychological distress in the postpartum period: The significance of social support. *Journal of Marriage and the Family, 48,* 271–277.

STERN, M., & HILDEBRANDT, K.A. (1984). Prematurity stereotyping: Effects of labeling on adults' perceptions of infants. *Developmental Psychology, 20,* 360–362.

STERN, M., & HILDEBRANDT, K.A. (1986). Prematurity stereotyping: Effects on mother-infant interaction. *Child Development, 57,* 308–315.

STERNBERG, R.J., & WILLIAMS, M.W. (1995). Parenting toward cognitive competence. In M.H. Bornstein (Ed.), *Handbook of parenting: vol. 4. Applied and practical parenting* (pp. 259–275). Mahwah, NJ: Erlbaum.

STERNGLANZ, S.H., & NASH, A. (1988). Ethological contributions to the study of human development. In B. Birns & D.F. Hay (Eds.), *The different faces of motherhood* (pp. 15–46). New York: Plenum Press.

STEVENS, J. (1988). Social support, locus of control, and parenting in three low-income groups of mothers: Black teenagers, Black adults, and White adults. *Child Development, 59,* 635–642.

STEVENSON, D.L., & BAKER D.P. (1987). The family-school relation and the child's school performance. *Child Development, 58,* 1348–1357.

STEVENSON, H.W., & LEE, S. (1990). Contexts of achievement: A study of American, Chinese, and Japanese children. *Monographs of the Society for Research in Child Development, 55* (1–2, Serial No. 221).

STIGLITZ, E. (1990). Caught between two worlds: The impact of a child on the lesbian couple's relationship. *Women and Therapy, 10,* 99–116.

STIPEK, D., & MACIVER, D. (1989). Developmental change in children's assessment of intellectual competence. *Child Development, 60,* 521–538.

STIPEK, D., & MCCROSKEY, J. (1989). Investing in children: Government and workplace policies for parents. *American Psychologist, 44,* 416–423.

STIPEK, D.J., GRALINSKI, H., & KOPP, C.B. (1990). Self-concept development in the toddler years. *Developmental Psychology, 26,* 972–977.

STOLLER, E.P. (1983). Parental caregiving by adult children. *Journal of Marriage and the Family, 45,* 851–858.

STONEMAN, Z., BRODY, G.H., & ABBOT, D. (1983). In-home observations of young Down syndrome children with their mothers and fathers. *American Journal of Mental Deficiency, 87,* 591–600.

STRANIK, M.K., & HOGBERG, B.L.L. (1979). Transition into parenthood. *American Journal of Nursing, 79,* 90–93.

STULL, D.E., BOWMAN, K., & SMERGLIA, V. (1994). Women in the middle: A myth in the making? *Family Relations, 43,* 319–324.

SUBRAHMANYAM, K., & GREENFIELD, P.M. (1994). Effect of video game practice on spatial skills in girls and boys. *Journal of Applied Developmental Psychology, 15,* 13–32.

SUPER, C.M., & HARKNESS, S. (1981). Figure, ground, and gestalt: The cultural context of the active individual. In R.M. Lerner & N.A. Busch-Rossnagal (Eds.), *Individuals as producers of their development: A life-span perspective.* New York: Academic Press.

TAYLOR, B.J. (1985). *A child goes forth.* Minneapolis, MN: Burgess.

TAYLOR, R.J., CHATTERS, L.M., TUCKER, M.B., & LEWIS, E. (1990). Developments in research on black families: A decade review. *Journal of Marriage and the Family, 52,* 993–1014.

TEGLASI, H., & MACMAHON, B.H. (1990). Temperament and common problem behaviors of children. *Journal of Applied Developmental Psychology, 11,* 331–349.

TELTSCH, K. (1992, July 25). As more people need help, more men help out. *The Daily Tribune,* p. 8.

The dilemmas of childlessness. (1988, May 2). *Time,* 88,90.

THOMAN, E.B., & BROWDER, S. (1987). *Born dancing.* New York: Harper & Row.

THOMAS, A., & CHESS, S. (1977). *Temperament and development.* New York: Bruner/Mazel.

THOMAS, R.M. (1985). *Comparing theories of child development.* Belmont, CA: Wadsworth Publishing Co.

THOMPSON, R.A. (1991). Diversity. *SRCD Newsletter,* Chicago: University of Chicago Press.

THOMPSON, R.A. (1986). Fathers and the child's "best interests": Judicial decision-making in custody disputes. In M.E. Lamb (Ed.), *The father's role: Applied perspectives* (pp. 61–101). New York: Wiley.

THOMPSON, R.A., TINSLEY, B.R., SCALORA, M.J., & PARKE, R.D. (1989). Grandparents' visitation rights: Legalizing the ties that bind. *American Psychologist, 44,* 1217–1222.

THORNTON, M.C., CHATTERS, L.M., TAYLOR, R.J., & ALLEN, W.R. (1990). Sociodemographic and environmental correlates of racial socialization by black parents. *Child Development, 61,* 401–409.

THORTON, A., YOUNG-DeMARCO, L., & GOLDSCHEIDER, F. (1993). Leaving the parental nest: The experience of a young white cohort in the 1980's. *Journal of Marriage and the Family, 55,* 216–229.

TOMASELLO, M., & FARRAR, M. (1986). Joint attention and early language. *Child Development, 57,* 1454–1463.

TOMLINSON-KEASEY, C., & KEASEY, C.B. (1988). "Signatures" of suicide. In D. Capuzzi & L. Golden (Eds.), *Preventing adolescent suicide.* Muncie, IN: Accelerated Development, Inc.

TRICKETT, P.K., & SUSMAN, E.J. (1988). Parental perceptions of child-rearing practices in physically abusive and nonabusive families. *Developmental Psychology, 24,* 270–276.

TROLL, L.E. (1983). Grandparents: The family watchdogs. In T.H. Brubaker (Ed.), *Family relationships in later life.* Beverly Hills, CA: Sage.

TROLL, L.E. (1985). The contingencies of grandparenting. In V.L. Bengston & J.F. Robertson (Eds.), *Grandparenthood.* Beverly Hills, CA: Sage.

TRUTE, B. (1990). Child and parent predictors of family adjustment in households containing young developmentally disabled children. *Family Relations, 39,* 292–297.

TURNBULL, A.P., & BLACHER-DIXON, J. (1980). Preschool mainstreaming: Impact on parents. *New Directions for Exceptional Children, 1,* 25–46.

TURNBULL, A.P., & TURNBULL, H.R. (1982). Parental involvement in the education of handicapped children: A critique. *Mental Retardation, 3,* 115–122.

TYMCHUK, A.J., ANDRON, L., & UNGER, O. (1987). Parents with mental handicaps and adequate child care: A review. *Mental Handicaps, 15,* 49–54.

UNGER, D.G., & WANDERSMAN, L.P. (1988). The relations of family and partner support to the adjustment of adolescent mothers. *Child Development, 59,* 1056–1060.

U.S. BUREAU OF CENSUS. (1992a). *Statistical abstract of the United States* (112th ed.). Washington, DC: U.S. Government.

U.S. BUREAU OF CENSUS (1992b). Current population reports, Series P-20, No. 398, *Household and Family Characteristics, March 1991.* Printing Office, Washington, DC: U.S. Government.

U.S. BUREAU OF CENSUS (1993). Statistics on characteristics of single-parent households.

U.S. CONSUMER PRODUCT SAFETY COMMISSION. (1985). *Protect your child.* (U.S. Government Printing Office, No. 0-473-663). Washington, DC.

U.S. NATIONAL CENTER FOR HEALTH STATISTICS. (1985). Fecundity and infertility in the U.S. *Advancedata, 104* (Feb. 11). Hyattsville, MD: U.S. Department of Health and Human Services.

VADASY, P.F., FEWELL, R.R., GREENBERG, M.T., DERMOND, N.M., & MEYER, D.J. (1986). Follow-up evaluation of the effects of involvement in the fathers program. *Topics in Early Childhood Special Education, 6,* 16–31.

VANBREMEN, J.R., & CHASNOFF, I.J. (1994). Policy issues for integrating parenting interventions and addiction treatment for women. *Topics in Early Childhood Special Education, 14,* 254–274.

VANDELL, D.L., & CORASANITI, M.A. (1988). The relation between third graders' after school care and social, academic, and emotional functioning. *Child Development, 59,* 168–177.

VAN DEN BOOM, D.C. (1994). The influence of temperament and mothering on attachment and exploration: An experimental manipulation of sensitive responsiveness among lower-class mothers with irritable infants. *Child Development, 65,* 1457–1477.

VAN EVRA, J. (1990). *Television and child development.* Hillsdale, NJ: Erlbaum.

VEEVERS, J.E. (1980). *Childless by choice.* Toronto: Butterworth.

VEGA, W.A. (1990). Hispanic families in the 1980's: A decade of research. *Journal of Marriage and the Family, 52,* 1015–1024.

VENTURA, J.N. (1987). The stresses of parenthood reexamined. *Family Relations, 36,* 26–29.

VIDEKA-SHERMAN, L. (1982). Coping with the death of a child: A study over time. *American Journal of Orthopsychiatry, 52,* 688–698.

VISHER, E.B., & VISHER, J.S. (1989). Parenting coalitions after remarriage: Dynamics and therapeutic guidelines. *Family Relations, 38,* 65–70.

VOLLING, B.L., & BELSKY, J. (1991). Multiple determinants of father involvement during infancy in dual-earner and single-earner families. *Journal of Marriage and the Family, 53,* 461–474.

VORHEES, C.V., & MOLLNOW, E. (1987). Behavioral teratogenesis: Long-term influences on behavior from early exposure to environmental agents. In J.D. Osofsky (Ed.), *Handbook of infant development* (2nd edition, pp. 913–971). New York: Wiley.

VUCHINICH, S., VUCHINICH, R., & WOOD, B. (1993). The interparental relationship and family problem solving with preadolescent males. *Child Development, 64,* 1389–1400.

WAGGONER, K., & WILGOSH, L. (1990). Concerns of families of children with learning disabilities. *Journal of Learning Disabilities, 23,* 97–98, 113.

WAGNER, R.M. (1988a). Changes in extended family relationships for Mexican American and Anglo single mothers. *American Journal of Orthopsychiatry, 57,* 69–88.

WAGNER, R.M. (1988b). Changes in the friend network during the first year of single parenthood for Mexican American and Anglo women. *American Journal of Orthopsychiatry, 57,* 89–101.

WAISBREN, S.E. (1980). Parents' reactions after the birth of a developmentally disabled child. *American Journal of Mental Deficiency, 84,* 345–351.

WALDRON, H., & ROUTH, D.K. (1981). The effect of the first child on the marital relationship. *Journal of Marriage and the Family, 4,* 785–788.

WALKER, A.J., & PRATT, C.C. (1991). Daughters' help to mothers: Intergenerational aid versus caregiving. *Journal of Marriage and the Family, 53,* 3–12.

WALKER, A.J., PRATT, C.C., MARTELL, L.K., & MARTIN, S.S.K. (1991). Perceptions of aid and actual aid in intergenerational caregiving. *Family Relations, 40,* 318–323.

WALKER, A.J., PRATT, C.C., OPPY, N.C. (1992). Perceived reciprocity in family caregiving. *Family Relations, 41,* 82–85.

WALKER, L.J., & TAYLOR, J.H. (1991). Family interactions and the development of moral reasoning. *Child Development, 62,* 264–283.

WALLACE, P.M., & GOTLIB, I.H. (1990). Marital adjustment during the transition to parenthood: Stability and predictors of change. *Journal of Marriage and the Family, 52,* 21–29.

WALLERSTEIN, J., & BLAKESLEE, S. (1989). *Second Chances.* New York: Ticknor & Fields.

WALLERSTEIN, J., & CORBIN, S.B. (1989). Daughters of divorce: Report from a ten-year follow-up. *American Journal of Orthopsychiatry, 59,* 593–604.

WALLERSTEIN, J., & KELLY, J.B. (1980). *Surviving the break-up: How children and parents cope with divorce.* New York: Basic Books.

WANDERSMAN, L.P. (1980). The adjustment of fathers to their first baby: The roles of parenting groups and marital relationship. *Birth and the Family Journal, 7,* 155–161.

WANDERSMAN, L., WANDERSMAN, A., & KAHN, S. (1980). Social support in the transition to parenthood. *Journal of Community Psychology, 8,* 332–342.

WAPNER, S. (1993). Parental development: A holistic, developmental systems-oriented perspective. In J. Demick, K. Bursik, & R. DiBiase (Eds.), *Parental development.* Hillsdale, NJ: Erlbaum.

WARREN, J.A., & JOHNSON, P.J. (1995). The impact of workplace support on work-family role strain. *Family Relations, 44,* 163–169.

WASHINGTON, V. (1988). The black mother in the United States: History, theory, research, and issues. In B. Birns & D.F. Hay (Eds.), *The different faces of motherhood* (pp. 185–213). New York: Plenum Press.

WEBB, J.T., MECKSTROTH, E.A., & TOLAN, S.S. (1982). *Guiding the gifted child: A practical source for parents and teachers.* Columbus, OH: Ohio Psychology Publishing Company.

WEINER, L., & MORSE, B.A. (1992). Facilitating development for children with fetal alcohol syndrome. *The Brown University Child and Adolescent Behavior Letter,* Providence, RI: Manisses Communications Group, Inc.

WELLMAN, S., & PAULSON, J. (1984). Baby walker related injuries. *Clinical Pediatrics, 23,* 98–99.

WENTE, A., & CROCKENBERG, S. (1976). Transition to fatherhood: Lamaze preparation, adjustment difficulty, and the husband-wife relationship. *The Family Coordinator, 27,* 351–357.

WERTSCH, J.V. (1979). From social interaction to higher psychological processes: A clarification and application of Vygotsky's theory. *Human Development, 22,* 1–22.

WEST, J.E., HAUSKEN, G., & COLLINS, M. (1993). *Profile of preschool children's child care and education program experience.* Washington, DC: National Center for Educational Statistics.

WHITBECK, L.B., HOYT, D.R., & HUCK, S.M. (1993). Family relationship history, contemporary parent-grandparent relationship quality, and the grandparent-grandchild relationship. *Journal of Marriage and the Family, 55,* 1025–1035.

WHITE, B. (1975). *The first three years of life.* New York: Avon.

WHITE, L.K., & BOOTH, A. (1985). The quality and stability of remarriages: The role of stepchildren. *American Sociological Review, 50,* 689–698.

WHITE, L.K., & BRINKERHOFF, D.B. (1981). Children's work in the family: Its significance and meaning. *Journal of Marriage and the Family, 43,* 789–798.

WHITING, B.B., & WHITING, J.W.M. (1975). *Children of six cultures.* Cambridge, MA: Harvard University Press.

WIKLER, L. (1981). Chronic stresses of families of mentally retarded children. *Family Relations, 30,* 281–288.

WILKIE, C.F., & AMES, E.W. (1986). The relationship of infant crying to parental stress in the transition to parenthood. *Journal of Marriage and the Family, 48,* 545–550.

WILKIE, J.R. (1981). The trend toward delayed parenthood. *Journal of Marriage and the Family, 43,* 583–591.

WILLIAMS, E.R., & CALIENDO, M.A. (1984). *Nutrition: Principles, issues, and applications.* New York: McGraw-Hill.

WILLIS, W. (1992). Families with African American roots. In E.W. Lynch & M.J. Hanson (Eds.), *Developing cross-cultural competence* (pp. 121–150). Baltimore, MD: Paul H. Brookes Publishing Company.

WILSON, L. (1977). *Caregiver training for child care.* Columbus, OH: Merrill.

WILSON, M.N. (1989). Child development in the context of the black extended family. *American Psychologist, 44,* 380–385.

WINNICOTT, D.W. (1953). Transitional objects and transitional phenomena: A study of the first not-me possession. *International Journal of Psychoanalysis, 34,* 89–97.

WOITITZ, J.G. (1983). *Adult children of alcoholics.* New York: Health Communications Inc.

WOLFF, P. (1966). The causes, controls, and organization of behavior in the neonate. *Psychological Issues, 5* (Monograph No. 17).

WORTHINGTON, B.S. (1979). Nutrition in pregnancy: Some current concepts and questions. *Birth and the Family Journal, 6,* 181–192.

WRIGLEY, J.C. (1995). Value conflicts in the home: When parents and caregivers disagree. Paper presented at the Biennial Meeting of the Society for Research in Child Development, Indianapolis, IN.

YARROW, L. (1989, January). Pediatricians answer 20 nagging questions. *Parents,* 82–88.

YOUNG, K.T. (1990). American conceptions of infant development from 1955-1984: What the experts are telling parents. *Child Development, 61,* 17–28.

ZAHN-WAXLER, C., RADKE-YARROW, M., & KING, R.A. (1979). Childrearing and children's prosical initiations toward victims of distress. *Child Development, 50,* 319–330.

ZAHN-WAXLER, C., RADKE-YARROW, M., WAGNER, E., & CHAPMAN, M. (1992). Development of concern for others. *Developmental Psychology, 28,* 126–136.

ZARIT, S.H., & EGGEBEEN, D.J. (1995). Parent-child relationships in adulthood and old age. In M.H. Bornstein (Ed.), *Handbook of parenting: vol. 1. Children and parenting* (pp. 119–140). Mahwah, NJ: Erlbaum.

ZARLING, C.L., HIRSCH, B.J., & LANDRY, S. (1988). Maternal social networks and mother-infant interactions in full-term and very low birthweight, preterm infants. *Child Development, 59,* 178–185.

ZILL, N. (1988). Behavior, achievement, and health problems among children in stepfamilies: Findings from a national survey of child health. In E.M. Hetherington & J.D. Arasteh (Eds.), *Impact of divorce, single parenting, and stepparenting on children* (pp. 325–368). Hillsdale, NJ: Erlbaum.

ZUNIGA, M.E. (1992). Families with Latino roots. In E.W. Lynch & M.J. Hanson (Eds.), *Developing cross-cultural competence* (pp. 151–179). Baltimore, MD: Paul H. Brookes Publishing Company.

Author Index

Hernandez, D.J., 235
Herrera, J.F., 172
Herzog, D.B., 201
Hess, R.D., 24
Hetherington, E.M., 238, 240, 241, 243, 247–250, 253–255
Heuvel, A.V., 76
Higgins, B.S., 102
Hildebrandt, K.A., 271
Himelstein, S., 11
Hirsch, B.J., 271
Hirschfield, I.S., 220–224
Hirsh-Pasek, K., 153
Hitchcock, S.L., 124, 134, 135
Hobbs, D.F., 92
Hochschild, A., 316
Hock, E., 313, 314
Hofferth, S.L., 319
Hoffmann, L.W., 17, 309, 310, 313–316
Hoffman, S.R., 73
Hogberg, B.L.L., 99
Holinger, P., 196
Hollenbeck, A.R., 87
Holloway, S.D., 248, 323
Holmbeck, G.N., 188, 189, 193, 197
Holahan, C.J., 209
Holt, K., 175
Honzik, M.P., 137
Hoopes, J.L., 103
Hooyman, M.R., 221, 225, 226
Hopkins, J., 91, 92
Horwood, L.J., 159
Hossain, Z., 111
Hotvedt, M.E., 64
Howes, C., 169, 322–324
Howes, P. W., 44
Hoyt, D.R., 217
Hubbs-Tait, L., 326
Huck, S.M., 217
Huffman, L., 102, 103
Huggins, S.L., 65
Hughes, D., 318
Humphrey, J.H., 167
Humphrey, M., 103
Hussey, J.A., 287
Huston, A.C., 14, 284
Huston, T.L., 95, 316
Hyde, J.S., 80
Hymel, S., 168
Hyson, M.C., 153

Ilg, F.L., 124
Indelicato, S., 76

Ja, D.Y., 58
Jackson, B.R., 284

Jacobsen, R.B., 62, 64
Jacobson, J.L., 119
Jacobvitz, D., 302, 305
Jambor, T., 146
Jaskir, J., 119
Jayaratne, T.E., 54
Joe, J.R., 60–62
Johnson, P.J., 310
Johnston, J.R., 243, 247
Jones, E.F., 284, 291
Jones, L.C., 91, 111
Jones-Molfese, V.J., 113
Joseph, G., 64
Julian, T.W., 48, 49, 55

Kach, J.A., 76, 92, 93
Kahn, S., 100
Kalish, R., 218
Kalyanpur, M., 261, 269
Kalter, N., 247, 248
Kaplan, M.S., 24
Karbon, M., 145
Karlsrud, K., 116, 133
Katz, L.G., 120
Kaufman, J., 301
Kazak, A.E., 269
Keasey, C.B., 195
Keirouz, K.S., 277–280
Keith, B., 247
Keith, C., 226
Keith, V.M., 241, 249, 322
Keller, M.B., 20
Kelley, M., 55
Kelley-Buchanan, C., 79, 81, 82
Kelly, J.B., 242, 243, 245
Kemper, K.A., 287
Kennedy, G.E., 217, 219
Keppler, A., 79
Kerlin, S.L., 296, 298
Kerns, D., 89
Ketterlinus, R.D., 141, 142, 165, 189
Kibria, N., 214
Kiernan, K.E., 241, 247, 249
Kinard, E., 247
King, R.A., 145
King, V., 217
Kirkham, M.A., 266, 267
Kitzinger, S., 77, 78, 82, 84, 88
Kivett, V.R., 215
Kivnick, H.Q., 215–217
Kline, M., 242, 247
Kloner, A., 246, 248
Koblewski, P. J., 216
Koblinsky, S.A., 179
Kochanska, G., 142, 164
Koepke, J.E., 16, 41, 132
Koestner, R., 175

Subject Index